GOURMET COOKING
WITHOUT SALT

Gourmet Cooking Without Salt

Eleanor P. Brenner

ILLUSTRATED BY RICHARD ERDOES

Foreword by Stanley Mirsky, M.D.

DOUBLEDAY & COMPANY, INC.
Garden City, New York
1987

Library of Congress Cataloging in Publication Data
Brenner, Eleanor P
    Gourmet cooking without salt.
    Includes index.
    1. Salt-free diet—Recipes   I. Title.
RM237.8.B73   641.5'632

    ISBN: 0-385-24351-0 (pbk.)
Library of Congress Catalog Card Number 79-6856

With unbounding gratitude and love to Richard, the man who makes it all happen; to our children. Patty and Tony, and, of course, to Mother. I thank them, not only for being so understanding while suffering through those trial and error dinners, but for their continuing encouragement and constant love.

I would like to express my great appreciation and affection to Judy Block, who supported me at the most crucial time . . . to Janet Fisher, for those carloads of her superb home-grown vegetables and herbs, and the gallons of cream and crates of eggs . . . to Jemima Brown, my housekeeper and friend who has spent untold, uncomplaining hours in the kitchen with me during the testing and retesting of these recipes . . . to Anne De Rogatis, Barbara Brennan, Frances Mazola, Linda Scotto, and Suzie Adler for being such wonderful help during those sweltering bread-baking days . . . and to my dear friend Dorothy Friedman, without whose inspiration this book would have never been written; I will always remember her with joy, love, and laughter.

A special appreciation to my revered and beloved friend Dr. Walter Kempner, who has given sight to those who couldn't see . . . who has given hope to those who had none . . . and who has given life to those untold numbers of people for whom untimely death was the diagnosis.

Contents

Recipies indicated by an asterisk (*) may be located by consulting the Index.

Foreword

My introduction to the power of salt was at a clinic of Northwestern University Medical School, when a patient suffered heart failure from eating a salt-laden hot dog. Yet there is on nearly every dining table an innocuous salt shaker containing salt (sodium chloride), a crystalline compound that is essential for life but that for some people represents the old cross-and-bones label that appears on bottles of poison.

This book meets a real need, demonstrating that to be on a salt-restricted diet does not have to be a punishment. For all those of you on a salt-free diet, Eleanor Brenner presents exciting gourmet dishes that will titillate your taste buds without injuring your health.

Stanley Mirsky, M.D., F.A.C.P.
Diplomate, Internal Medicine
Assistant Clinical Professor
of Medicine, Mount Sinai
School of Medicine of the City
University of New York.
Attending Staff: Mount Sinai,
Lenox Hill, and Doctors Hospitals

Introduction

Fifteen years ago, my doctor imposed a sentence on me that made me feel I would be living in prison for the rest of my life. I was placed on a salt-free diet, and I confess to you now that my instant reaction was that I never would be able to do it. "How would I eat in restaurants? What about traveling? Would I ever be able to entertain again?" And then panic set in. "Why me? I'll be a freak for the rest of my life."

Fortunately, logic made an early and welcome appearance. I analyzed the problem and envisioned three options. I could reject the diet and take the consequences; I could spend the time feeling terribly sorry for myself; or I could adjust to what I considered the horrible fate and change my mode of eating. As to the first, I was smart enough to know that I was not going to reject what my doctors felt was necessary for my health, so that was out! The second I toyed with, but I realized very quickly what a dreary bore I could become. Did I want to be one of those people who constantly talk about their operations, illnesses, or problems? At first I would get empathy and understanding, then perhaps sympathy, but finally, nothing but yawns. So, I got over the anger; I got over feeling sorry for myself and I said, "Okay, this is it! What are you going to do about it?" I decided to change my way of eating, because I quickly realized that in no way was I prepared to change my style of living.

At that time, my children were quite young. Tony was eight and Patty was six. How was I to organize family meals for them, for my husband, hold down my designing job, and placate my housekeeper, whose responsibility it was to do the shopping and dinner preparation while I was at my office. How would I entertain? Would I cook one dish for my guests and family and another for me? At first that seemed to be my solution. My old, treasured recipes were used for the family and for our guests; and for myself unimaginative salt-free food, gleaned sometimes from recipes in two dull and dreary salt-free cookbooks that were on the market at the time. The complaints started. One of the children would tell me there was too much pepper in a dish, or my husband complained of not enough seasoning, and there I was, unable to even taste the food. Mealtime quickly degenerated from a pleasant occasion to a punishment. There was also the problem of the refrigerator. For instance, if there were leftovers, everything would have to be labeled. Any mistake could be disastrous for me. Should we get two refrigerators? The whole thing was developing into a circus. Frustration was building. I was envious of everything the family ate and more unhappy about what I was eating. One evening I didn't get home for dinner until ten o'clock and was greeted by a hysterical house-keeper who told me that there was nothing for me to eat because she thought she put salt into my food by mistake, but she wasn't sure, and conversely after dinner, my husband announced that he had just had the most tasteless dinner of his life. That was the point at which I decided I would stop living as a semi-invalid. I would change my household totally and try to bring back the fun, the joy, the pleasure of mealtime for all of us.

Then the slow, difficult process began. It was years of trial and error, and make no mistake, the percentage of failures on the first trials was very high. I found that evolving a method for low sodium cookery that incorporates taste with looks takes time and dedication, much more than in normal cooking. As you will see from my recipes, almost everything we use is fresh. It is also a fact that this type of cooking requires a great deal of preparation. Chopping and mincing, dicing and grating are common in my cooking, and I am forever grateful to the person who invented the Cuisinart, because it has taken so much of the time and trouble out of the preparation of gourmet dishes, and it has made complicated cooking a breeze. It occupies a place of prominence in our kitchen and is never out of sight.

In an active household such as ours, until the children went off to college, I never knew how many we would have for dinner when I left in the morning. Each child was a host or hostess to two or three friends, one or two nights a week. Add to that the fact that we have so many friends in politics, arts, fashion, business, both local and international, many of whom are last minute guests, and you can see that devising new recipes and menus could be an overwhelming prospect.

I first decided that I would try one menu and perfect that and go on from there. Unfortunately, that didn't last long because of the constant procession of guests. So I evolved my present solution of first trying out menus on the family, and I must say they good-naturedly put up with a lot. I am eternally grateful to them for their support and humor, criticism and praise.

Many of the recipes are adaptations of old recipes I couldn't part with. Some are friends' recipes made originally with salt and other denied ingredients and reworked to fit in with my needs, but most are recipes created in order to incorporate new flavor excitement and style into low sodium cooking.

One of my first big parties was a surprise birthday party for a dear friend. One of the guests was a very well-known heart specialist, and I must say it was with some trepidation that I approached the evening. After receiving compliments from my guests, none of whom had any idea they had eaten a meal totally devoid of salt, I made my announcement and was delighted to have the doctor say that never again would he believe his patients when they told him that low sodium cooking was so bland and awful. He himself couldn't tell the difference. Soon it became a game with me to mention casually to my guests, at the end of a sumptuous meal, that it was cooked entirely without salt. I loved the surprised looks on their faces.

It was also surprising to learn how many of my guests had been told by their doctors to cut down on salt, or to cut out salt entirely, and yet had no idea of how to go about getting some flavor into their diets, so they cheated. I was deluged with requests for recipes, requests I was delighted to accommodate, but I always gave out the recipes with an admonition to remember that I was not a doctor and that, if there were certain ingredients their doctors felt were not suitable for them, they should substitute. For example, low cholesterol patients should use salt-free margarine in place of salt-free butter, low sodium dry milk for cream, etc. I am permitted to use salt substitute, but *you* may not be. And I likewise admonish my readers: Check with your doctor if you feel there are any ingredients your particular diet does not allow. I make no claims that this is a fat-free, low cholesterol diet, simply that it is a flavorful and interesting, delicious and entertaining way of serving food that is cooked without salt. These recipes are not meant as cure-alls, but rather as exciting ways to titillate the palate, to satisfy the taste buds, and to bring flavor into your diet although the cooking is done without salt.

At the same time I was involved with my own personal cooking I recognized that other problems would have to be faced. In connection with my designing and also for personal pleasure, I have always done an enormous amount of traveling. My trips to Europe alone number two or three per year. Personal appearances at stores and charity functions throughout the country total perhaps three to four weeks a year, and family vacations, one at Christmas time and another in the summer, mean many meals away from home. How to cope?

I was amazed at how simply this problem resolved itself. Many years ago I purchased a stunning small brass basket in Portugal. This is my most constant companion while traveling in the United States. Into it I put my little bottle of salt substitute and a selection of spices and herbs such as dried chives, dried dill, dried oregano, dried basil, and garlic powder, each in an amusing bottle or container, and a miniature pewter pepper mill. I simply ask the waiter for broiled chicken or fish, to be prepared without salt or seasoning, a baked potato, and a plain salad of lettuce and tomatoes with oil and vinegar on the side. Then I perform a little table magic with my own assortment of herbs and spices. My basket is a conversation piece wherever I go; an honest-to-goodness boon to eating out.

European travel I thought would be more difficult, but there the results were even simpler and far more rewarding. Since I speak French, it was easy to say, *"S'il vous plaît, je désire la nouriture sans sel."* In Italian I quickly learned *"senza sale,"* in Portuguese, *"falto de sal,"* in Spanish *"sin sal,"* and discovered, to my joy, a sincere and touching desire to please on the part of almost every hotel and restaurant I visited. Add to that the fact that most European restaurants, small as they are, cook their dishes to order and, even more important, the food is grown so close to the market that freshness is assured. Unfortunately, except for the very biggest cities in the United States, the luxury of "to order" cooking does not generally exist, since a great deal of restaurant food is prepared or the chef is unable or unwilling to bother. For that reason my little brass box generally travels with me here, but not in Europe.

Now, let me tell you a little about our home and the ways we entertain. We have a rather large dining room, for which I have always been grateful, even in the years when dining rooms were not considered in vogue. The walls are now done in a huge black and white print which I find a fantastic foil for all kinds of paintings and accessories. Mirrors look beautiful against it, as do paintings of every size and description; and they are hung, seemingly at random throughout the room, but actually with a lot of thought. The room is dominated by a secondhand rectangular table with oversized Jacobean chairs that are covered in black patent leather, and a handsome sideboard on high legs. Apparently, no one wanted this white elephant in the days when dining rooms were at their low ebb of popularity, and the whole thing was a steal at a hundred seventy-five dollars nearly twenty-two years ago. A handsome nineteenth-century English oak mirror is hung over the sideboard and reflects the huge baker's rack on the opposite wall. This rack, when it was bought, was in a very sad and neglected condition, and when my husband first saw it at the ironworks, he begged me not to bring "that horror" into the house. But it happened to be very old and I thought it had great promise. When all the "nuts and bolts" were put into place and the brass was polished, it became one of his favorite pieces. It is laden with treasures and trash sitting side by side, candles by the dozen, pottery, china, some old, some new, a huge silver tureen filled with dried baby's breath, a small wine rack for our limited collection of rare wines, old boxes, an oil lamp brought into play at dinner, a ceramic mushroom sculpture, a silver wine cooler and water pitcher, and some shimmering crystal baskets. Any wonder it is a conversation piece? Seventeenth-century Venetian lanterns on seven-foot poles decorate the window wall and help to create a warm atmosphere in a most eclectic room, in addition to providing wonderful lamplight. Lighting, per se, is very important to me, for I feel it sets a mood, while the architecture and décor create the ambience. A nineteenth-century Dutch brass chandelier over the table is rarely used. Instead, we use masses of candles, clustered on the baker's rack, on the sideboard, on the dining-room table, and on a black slate table, the base of which was an old sewing machine and which does double duty as a dessert sideboard or salad server when we have a large crowd. (Candles, I must confess, became an economic necessity one year. Tony and Patty had gone into the candle-making business to help augment their allowances, and I was certainly their largest customer.) My grandmother's silver candelabras, three arms each, heavily chased and standing fifteen inches high, were found in my mother's storeroom many years ago, and because my mother doesn't really care for silver I confiscated them, and they are ever present on our table, lending an aura of elaborate elegance of times gone by.

My best company is my family, and no china or silver is reserved for special occasions or guests. What we have we enjoy together, and nothing pleases me more than to have the children, or their friends, tell me how beautiful they think dinner is at our house.

When I first married, I served as my mother served—the meat, on a well-and-tree platter, was passed first, then the vegetables were passed individually. This may have been fine in my mother's day, when finding servants was not a problem, but my husband complained that by the time the vegetables arrived the meat was cold and he disliked eating alone since I was always busy running into the kitchen for platters. So there evolved what I consider a simple, graceful, and elegant formula for our life-style today, and all of our serving is done in the same manner. We have collected all kinds of warmers, some lit by candles, some by denatured alcohol, and they are set up on a sideboard. (I might interject that there is another simple way to do this—by using electric warming trays, but I don't have any because I find them unattractive. I have tried to convey this to one of the hot tray manufacturers and, in fact, designed for one company something that I thought had the aesthetic beauty of a copper burner with the practicality of electric heat. Feeling it would not sell to the mass market, they rejected the design. I have not given up on this idea, as I feel it is a functional item for gracious entertaining.) The plates are heated on the back of the kitchen stove and brought to the sideboard. Food is brought in from the kitchen, and hot food is placed on the warmers and cold food set up next to it on the sideboard. For groups of six to eight, I stand in front of it and serve each guest individually, then they find their places at the table, marked for them by place cards, sometimes in clear lucite or porcelain or silver, or sometimes with a very simple card to which I have pinned a fresh daisy. For larger groups it seems to work better if the guests help themselves, and my husband and I guide them to their places at the table. My father, who was unacquainted with this type of serving, nicknamed our household "the best cafeteria on Park Avenue!"

Hot and cold hors d'oeuvres, or occasionally even a first course, are served with drinks in the living room. When soup or a first course is served in the dining room, it is always placed on the table before we go in to dinner. When we have finished it, the plates are cleared and I alone, or sometimes my cook and I, serve the family or guests the main course from the sideboard, permitting them to remain seated.

Salads are served from a skirted table that is pulled up next to the dining-room table, either as a first course or as one after the main course. Crisped and torn salad greens are placed in a large wooden or crystal bowl, and a silver tray holding a pepper mill, a small bowl with dry mustard and one or two other herbs or spices, a carafe of oil and one of vinegar, or another containing one of my own prepared salad dressings are placed next to the bowl. I quickly and lightly toss the salad at the last minute, for there is nothing more delicious than a perfectly tossed salad, and nothing worse than an overdressed limp salad that has rested in its bowl for even five minutes before serving.

Desserts are usually compotes of fruits of the season, fruits salads, or whole fresh fruits, sometimes served with low sodium cheese and homemade Melba Toast,* Cold Lemon Soufflé,* or Bittersweet Chocolate Mousse,* which I serve from my end of the table.

When we have a large group of thirty or more for dinner (I can set three tables of ten each in the dining room), the sideboard is cleared after the main course is served, and desserts are arranged on it, while coffee is set up on the black slate table. If the crowd is even larger (I have entertained up to 135 in our apartment), the children's rooms, each of which is set up as a sitting room, are pressed into service, and the foyer, which opens into a large gallery, is appropriated and the whole house becomes one big party where our guests move easily from one room to another. The bar is set up in Tony's room, hors d'oeuvres are passed throughout the house, and the main buffet is set up in the dining room. For this, of course, we have to bring in extra help. Fortunately, through the years, I have accumulated a list of delightful and wonderful people who help to make our parties successful and thus allow me to enjoy them with my guests.

Since I have collected at least eight different types and patterns of dinner and service plates and twelve to thirty plates in each pattern, these serve the multipurpose of being used for large parties to create an interesting effect and for dinners *en famille* when there might be a different pattern used every night of the week.

I am a firm believer that, although the food itself is very important, the setting and presentation not only help to make it taste more delicious but will turn every meal into a party. My dear readers, there are so many things I would like to tell you and share with you in menu planning, table settings, flower arrangements, party organizing, and food presentation, but they would require a book twice the size of this one. So I will have to content myself with helping you create exciting and wonderful dishes for your new low sodium life-style. Don't be afraid, but rather be grateful for it. Your new life-style will not only give you better health but will become an adventure in creative cookery that you might never have experienced.

I hope that this book will give you a glimpse into the exciting world of creating out of need and that it will obliterate the old belief that "diet means deprivation." May it start you on the road to new cooking pleasures and ideas so that you can add your own recipes in low sodium gourmet cooking to mine.

Prologue

Dear Reader:

PLEASE DO NOT LOOK AT EVEN ONE RECIPE WITHOUT FIRST READING THIS PROLOGUE!

A friend called me in panic. Her husband had been told by his doctor, No salt or else . . . he was hysterical . . . she was hysterical . . . he adored gourmet food . . . what should she do? She really didn't want to bother me, but she knew I was writing this book and would I please give her a few recipes in advance of publication?

Being a longtime member of the "no salt fraternity," I said, of course I would, and immediately had some recipes photocopied and mailed.

After ten days I phoned this lady to find out how her husband was adjusting to his new no-salt life-style and how she was managing with her new cuisine *sans sel.*

"Oh, this is impossible," she moaned. "There are so many ingredients in some of your recipes, Eleanor." To which I replied, "Yes, there are, but don't be intimidated by them. When you read a recipe you'll see that many ingredients need almost no preparation."

"Well, that's another thing," she said.

"What is?" I asked.

"They're so long."

"What's so long?" I queried, feeling that I was listening to an old Abbott and Costello routine.

"The recipes," she wailed. I then asked if she had read each one through. "Well, not exactly," she said, to which I took three deep breaths, counted to ten, and said, "If you read them through, you'd realize the step-by-step method is exactly that. It gives every detail to get rid of the guesswork. The preparation might be short even though the how, why, and where might not."

"But a long recipe scares me."

"Yes, I understand, but wouldn't you rather take the time to read each than not know what to do?"

"I guess I would," she concluded.

So I hope, dear reader, that you will too.

The following are random thoughts and facts that might become repetitious used in so many recipes and might well increase the length of the step-by-step recipes. But, for better or worse, here they are:

I. EGGS

They should always be at room temperature. When beating the egg yolks, always run your mixing bowl under very hot water for two to three minutes and then thoroughly dry it. This will warm your egg yolks (in the easiest manner possible) and thus help to increase their volume. Egg whites, conversely, should be beaten at room temperature, but no warmer, and also in a very well dried bowl.

II. WHIPPING HEAVY CREAM

Make sure that the cream is thoroughly chilled and the bowl and beaters have been placed in the freezer for at least five minutes before using. Obviously, you should never beat the cream in a warm place, for the colder the cream and the utensils, the more volume you will achieve.

III. LOW SODIUM DRY MILK

Follow the instructions on the bottle of the low sodium dry milk for the amount of water to be added when substituting it for regular milk. However, in a recipe where heavy cream is an ingredient and the words "or triple strength low sodium dry milk" follow, triple the amount of the dry milk powder to the water called for. This substitute, in all honesty, is not nearly as good as the regular milk or heavy cream because it is lacking in butter fat. But tripling the amount of the low sodium dry milk somehow does give it a semblance to the smooth thickness of heavy cream.

Yes, the triple strength low sodium dry milk will whip, but it will also collapse quickly because it is missing the butter fat. Therefore, you should not use this as a substitute for whipped heavy cream.

IV. BUTTER-MARGARINE

You will notice that in the recipes calling for butter I indicate "sweet butter." However, if you have a cholesterol problem and are trying to avoid that substance, use salt-free margarine instead.

V. SUGAR (OR SUBSTITUTE EQUIVALENT)

A substitute is intended for a person who is diabetic or is on a calorie-controlled "budget." You will note, however, that a substitute does not appear in certain recipes, such as Cold Lemon Soufflé* or Spongecake,* because I feel that it adversely affects the texture of the dessert.

VI. STERILIZING JARS

1. Use Ball, Mason, or any other canning jars.
2. Wash them in hot soapy water and rinse thoroughly in clean hot water.
3. Place the jars, lids, funnel, tongs, and any other utensils you might be using to transfer the food to the jars, in a huge deep pot. Cover completely with water.
4. Bring the water to a rolling boil over a high flame and boil the jars, lids, and utensils for 15 minutes.
5. Turn off the flame and let all of them remain in the hot water until you are ready to use them.

VII. THE FLAME-TAMER

A Flame-Tamer is a brand name for an aluminum disc that is designed for either electric or gas stoves. In some instances, when using a heavy saucepan placed on a Flame-Tamer over a low flame, it may substitute for a double boiler. At other times, if you wish to keep things hot, place the saucepan with the ingredients on the Flame-Tamer, over a low to low-medium flame. This will prevent the ingredients from scorching. I personally own six, one for each burner, and couldn't cook without them.

VIII. THE SOUFFLÉ COLLAR

The easiest way to build a collar for your soufflé dish is to use a length of extra-heavy aluminum foil that is 3 inches longer than the circumference of the dish. Measure the height of your soufflé dish plus 4 inches (or 5 or 6), and fold over the remainder of the foil. This is referred to in recipes as a "4-inch collar," etc. Place the unfolded edge of the foil against the outside of the soufflé dish and secure it to the dish with masking tape. Tightly press the rest of the foil around the dish and secure it with more masking tape. Spray the inside of the collar with a vegetable spray such as Mazola or Pam.

IX. BASIC INGREDIENTS: SPICES AND HERBS

To make life easy, I suggest that you always have the following ingredients on hand. They are so consistently used throughout that keeping a supply will aid in the preparation of many recipes.

HERBS		SPICES	DRY INGREDIENTS
Basil	(fresh or dried)	Black peppercorns	Low sodium
		White peppercorns	dry milk
Bay leaves	(dried)	Cayenne pepper	Unbleached
			flour
Chervil	(fresh or dried)	Chili powder — no salt	Salt
			substitute
Chives	(fresh or dried)	Cumin powder	Sugar
			substitute
Dill	(fresh or dried)	Curry powder — no salt	
		Mustard, dry	
Fennel	(fresh or dried)	Paprika	
Marjoram	(fresh or dried)		
Oregano	(fresh or dried)		
Parsley	(fresh only)		
Rosemary	(fresh or dried)		
Sage	(fresh or dried)		
Tarragon	(fresh or dried)		
Thyme	(fresh or dried)		

Garlic ⎤
Onions ⎬ the most used, the most often
Lemons ⎦

Thank you for your kind indulgence in reading this prologue. As I so want this book to bring pleasure and joy to your new no-salt life-style and as much ease as possible to your *cuisine sans sel,* I have tried to give you as much information as possible. I am sure there are some points that have been overlooked, but I sincerely hope not too many.

Wishing you good luck, good cooking, and good eating, I hopefully remain your constant cooking companion,

Eleanor P. Brenner

What is Salt? What is Sodium? What's the Problem?

As stated in Webster's Dictionary, salt is a white crystalline substance that consists of sodium and chlorine. Translating that to a chemical compound, salt contains approximately 40 percent sodium and 58 percent chlorine.

Actually all the foods we eat contain sodium. The big question is: What amount of sodium? For example a medium-size apple has three milligrams of sodium, a medium-size onion has ten milligrams of sodium, four ounces of beef have sixty-eight milligrams of sodium, and four ounces of halibut have sixty-one milligrams of sodium.

A dinner composed of recipes such as Onion Soup,* Chicken Supreme,* Saffron Rice Pilaf,* Mixed Green Salad,* with a Mustard Vinaigrette Dressing,* Summer Brandied Peaches,* accompanied by Lace Cookies,* contains under two hundred fifty milligrams of sodium.

When one realizes that an eight-ounce cup of commercial onion soup contains about 1,000 milligrams of sodium (over four times the sodium of this complete dinner) and that one teaspoon of salt contains 2,325 milligrams of sodium, over nine times the sodium content of this entire dinner, the general reaction is shock.

But then the question follows: Well, what's the problem with sodium? The answer obviously is the amount of sodium one consumes.

If you have hypertension, heart disease, kidney disease, migraine headaches, or suffer from water retention, then even moderate quantities of sodium are certainly a big problem. Today approximately 20 percent of Americans suffer from hypertension alone; and salt, or the sodium in salt, is a main cause of hypertension. In many cases, doctors treating patients suffering from hypertension have called salt a killer.

In recent studies of the Senate Select Committee on Nutrition and Human Needs, it was reported that Americans consume from six to eighteen grams of sodium per day (6,000 to 18,000 milligrams). As a result of these findings the United States Government has strongly suggested, in its official national nutritional goals for America, that this amount of salt (sodium) be drastically reduced in the daily diet for the general well-being of the population.

It is a mind-boggling fact to know that the average human being requires only two hundred and thirty milligrams of sodium per day and that the average American is consuming between twenty-five and seventy-five times the needed amount. Why, then, if large quantities of sodium may be harmful to your health, do people continue to use salt (sodium) in such excess?

We must realize that salt, which at one time was used as a curing and preserving agent when refrigeration was nonexistent, has unfortunately become the main seasoning ingredient employed by most cooks today; and that the abusive use of salt is not a need but rather a destructive habit. The wailing complaint that one hears most often is that food cooked without salt will not taste good . . . and this has been established as the excuse for not reducing the sodium one consumes in a daily diet. I hope that this book will not only help to change this attitude, but will also lead people into a new life-style filled with fascinating flavors, exciting new tastes, and a world of pleasure-filled eating.

What is Salt Substitute?

The main ingredient in all salt substitutes is potassium chloride, and under the provisions of the Code of Federal Regulations it is to be used as a nutrient and as a dietary supplement. That's the scientific jargon, but what does that mean when we add it to foods? If used along with herbs and spices, it does give a salt flavor and in many instances helps to heighten the seasoning. However, if used in excess it can leave a slightly bitter aftertaste.

What's the difference between salt substitute and seasoned salt substitute? While the main ingredient in both is potassium chloride, the seasoned salt substitute has spices as its secondmost important ingredient, which helps to give added flavor and eliminate some of the "bite" of the potassium chloride.

Are all brands the same? Can you use a salt substitute and a seasoned salt substitute interchangeably, or is each used for different foods? All brands use potassium chloride as the main ingredient, but the amount they incorporate with the other ingredients varies and can certainly alter its flavor. To date I prefer McCormick's Seasoned Salt Substitute. However, there are new low sodium seasoning mixes appearing on the market all the time, and there might be a better one next month or next year. As you read through the book you will notice there are some recipes calling for salt substitute, which obviously means the unseasoned kind. I have chosen to use this in those recipes because the seasoned salt substitute has a reddish color due to the paprika in it, and I didn't want it to alter the color of the food. At other times I chose the unseasoned salt substitute because I thought the spices from the seasoned salt substitute would interfere with the taste of the particular seasoning ingredients in those recipes. In the recipes calling for salt substitute seasoned or unseasoned, I have very carefully tried to avoid getting to the dangerous level of any possible aftertaste. However, if the level is too high or too low for your taste, change it accordingly.

What is the sodium content in salt substitutes? Can everyone use them? Almost all salt substitutes, seasoned or unseasoned, contain only one milligram of sodium per teaspoon. However, on very rare occasions, it is not permitted to certain people! Since the recipes calling for salt substitute may still be very successful without it, I have listed it as "salt substitute (optional)." In discussing this with a novice of *cuisine sans sel,* she asked, "Do you prefer it IN recipes?" To which I replied, "Yes, otherwise I wouldn't have listed it." On the other hand, you might prefer it OUT and that's what created the expression "It's a matter of personal taste."

The Sodium Content of Various Foods

As a complete listing of the sodium content of various foods requires a book of its own, I would like to suggest two such sources: "The Composition of Foods, Raw, Processed and Prepared," Handbook #8, United States Department of Agriculture, may be obtained by writing to the Department of Agriculture, Washington, D.C. However, if you do not want to wait for it, go to your local bookstore and buy *The Dictionary of Sodium, Fats and Cholesterol,"* by Barbara Kraus. These works are excellent and indispensable aids in calculating the amounts of sodium (as well as protein, fat, carbohydrates, calories, potassium, etc.) in the foods you eat.

In order to give you a general idea of the sodium content of some of the foods generally considered appropriate for low sodium diets, I have listed these foods under such headings as Fresh Fruits, Fresh Vegetables, Dairy Products, etc. Nevertheless, I still urge you to buy either or both of the books listed above.

Fresh Fruits

TYPE	QUANTITY	MILLIGRAMS OF SODIUM
Apple	1 medium	3.0
Apricot	1 medium	0.6
Avocado	1 medium	8.0
Banana	1 medium	1.8
Cantaloupe	½ of a medium	14.0
Coconut	1 cup grated	17.0
Cranberries	1 cup whole	1.0
Grapefruit	½ of a medium	1.3
Lemon (juice)	½ cup	2.0
Orange	1 medium	2.0
Peach	1 medium	3.0

TYPE	QUANTITY	MILLIGRAMS OF SODIUM
Pear	1 medium	3.0
Pineapple	½ cup	1.2
Strawberries	1 cup	1.0

Dairy Products

TYPE	QUANTITY	MILLIGRAMS OF SODIUM
Butter, sweet, unsalted	1 tablespoon	0.8
Buttermilk, non-fat, unsalted	½ cup	60.0†
Cheese, Cheddar, salt free or low sodium	1 ounce	1.0–40.0††
Cheese, cottage, no salt added	½ cup	10.0–60.0††
Cheese, Gouda, salt free or low sodium	1 ounce	1.0–40.0††
Cheese, Swiss, salt free or low sodium	1 ounce	1.0–40.0††
Cream, heavy (sweet)	½ cup	38.0†
Cream, sour, commercial, no salt added	½ cup	50.0†
Egg, whole	1 large	62.0†
Egg, white	(from) 1 large	53.0†
Egg, yolk	(from) 1 large	9.0
Milk, fresh whole	½ cup	61.0†
Milk, low sodium dry	½ cup	4.0
Yogurt, plain, commercial	½ cup	61.0†

NOTE 1: †A single dagger indicates that, although the item listed is a proper food for most low sodium diets, it is objected to by some physicians for particular patients. Therefore, check with your physician to find out:

> A. If you are allowed this food.
> B. How often?
> C. How much?

NOTE 2: ††This double dagger indicates a wide variance in the sodium count per product. Check the labels for the sodium content or ask the store proprietor, who may know or be able to find out the exact sodium content for you.

Fresh Vegetables

TYPE	QUANTITY	MILLIGRAMS OF SODIUM
Acorn squash	½ medium, cooked	1.6
Artichoke (globe)	1 medium, cooked	40.0†
Asparagus	1 6-ounce portion, cooked	1.5
Green beans (snap)	8 ounces, cooked	14.0
Broccoli	8 ounces, cooked	20.0
Cabbage	1 cup, shredded, raw	12.6
Carrot	1 large, raw	40.0†
Cauliflower	8 ounces, cooked	26.0
Corn	1 medium ear, cooked	3.2
Eggplant	8 ounces, cooked	2.0
Endive	6 large leaves, raw	7.0
Escarole	6 large leaves, raw	6.0
Mushrooms	10 large, cooked	13.0
Onion	1 medium, raw	10.0
Parsley	1 tablespoon, chopped, raw	2.0
Peas	1 cup, cooked	1.4
Peppers, green	1 medium, raw	8.0
Peppers, red	1 medium, raw	11.0
Potato, sweet	1 medium, cooked	14.6
Potato, white	1 medium, cooked	5.0
Radish	1 large, raw	3.4
Romaine	6 large leaves, raw	16.0
Tomato	1 medium, raw	4.0
Water chestnuts	8 ounces	45.0†
Watercress	1 cup, coarsely chopped, raw	23.0
Zucchini	1 cup sliced, cooked	2.0

NOTE 3: All foods indicated as cooked are done so without salt.

Poultry, Beef, Lamb, Veal

TYPE	QUANTITY	MILLIGRAMS OF SODIUM
Beef, brisket	4 ounces, cooked	68.0†
Beef, chuck	4 ounces, cooked	68.0†
Beef, sirloin	4 ounces, cooked	68.0†
Chicken, dark meat	4 ounces, cooked	100.0†
Chicken, dark meat with skin	4 ounces, cooked	100.0†
Chicken, white meat	4 ounces, cooked	77.0†
Chicken, white meat with skin	4 ounces, cooked	77.0†
Chicken livers	4 ounces, cooked	69.0†
Duck, dark meat only	4 ounces, raw	94.0†
Lamb, leg	4 ounces, cooked	79.0†
Lamb, rib chop meat	4 ounces, cooked	79.0†
Lamb, shoulder	4 ounces, cooked	79.0†
Veal, roast	4 ounces, cooked	91.0†
Veal, shank	4 ounces, cooked	91.0†
Turkey, dark meat only	4 ounces, cooked	112.0†
Turkey, white meat only	4 ounces, cooked	93.0†

NOTE: If the poultry, beef, lamb and veal are indicated as cooked, they are done so without salt.

Fish

TYPE	QUANTITY	MILLIGRAMS OF SODIUM
Bass	4 ounces, raw	80.0†
Bluefish	4 ounces, raw	76.0†
Cod	4 ounces, raw	80.0†
Flounder	4 ounces, raw	88.0†
Haddock	4 ounces, raw	69.0†
Halibut	4 ounces, raw	61.0†
Pike	4 ounces, raw	76.0†
Red snapper	4 ounces, raw	76.0†
Salmon	4 ounces, raw	110.0†
Salmon, canned, in water, no salt added	4 ounces	73.0†
Sardines, canned, in water, no salt added	4 ounces	92.0†
Shrimp, meat only	4 ounces, raw	152.0†

TYPE	QUANTITY	MILLIGRAMS OF SODIUM
Sole, gray	4 ounces, raw	88.0†
Sole, lemon	4 ounces, raw	88.0†
Tuna, canned, in water, no salt added	4 ounces	40.0†

Grains and Related Foods

TYPE	QUANTITY	MILLIGRAMS OF SODIUM
Barley	1 cup, raw	8.0
Bran	¼ cup	10.5
Bread, home-baked, no salt commercial, no salt	1 slice	7.0
Cornmeal	1 cup, raw	1.0
Cornstarch	1 tablespoon	trace
Flour, rice	1 cup	8.0
Flour, rye	1 cup	1.0
Flour, unbleached	1 cup	1.0
Flour, whole wheat	1 cup	4.0
Matzoh	1 slice	1.0
Matzoh meal	1 cup	2.0
Melba toast, home-baked commercial, no salt	1 slice	1.0
Rice, brown	1 cup, raw	18.0
Rice, white	1 cup, raw	1.0
Rice, wild	1 cup, raw	12.0
Spaghetti	1 cup, dry	1.0
Wheat (bulgur)	¼ cup	2.6
Yeast	1 package active dry	5.0

Herbs and Spices

TYPE	QUANTITY	MILLIGRAMS OF SODIUM
Basil, sweet dried	1 teaspoon	0.8
Bay leaf, dried	1 long	1.2
Cinnamon, powder	1 teaspoon	1.2
Chili powder (no salt added)	1 teaspoon	1.0
Cumin, dried	1 teaspoon	0.8
Curry powder (no salt added)	1 teaspoon	4.0
Dill weed, dried	1 teaspoon	0.8
Garlic, fresh, minced	1 ounce	1.0
Garlic powder	1 teaspoon	1.2
Ginger, ground, powder	1 teaspoon	1
Ginger root, fresh	1 inch	1.0
Horseradish root, fresh	1 inch	2
Mint, dry	1 teaspoon	1
Mint, fresh	1 tablespoon	0.9
Mustard, dry	1 teaspoon	0.8
Nutmeg, ground	1 teaspoon	1.8
Onion powder	1 teaspoon	5.6
Oregano, dried	1 teaspoon	2.0
Paprika, Hungarian	1 teaspoon	4.4
Paprika, Spanish	1 teaspoon	4.4
Pepper, black, ground	1 teaspoon	1.2
Pepper, red, ground (cayenne)	1 teaspoon	1.6
Pepper, white, ground	1 teaspoon	0.4
Rosemary, dried	1 teaspoon	2.8
Saffron, dried	1 teaspoon	1.6
Tarragon, dried	1 teaspoon	1.6
Thyme, dried	1 teaspoon	1.6

Miscellaneous

TYPE	QUANTITY	MILLIGRAMS OF SODIUM
Almonds, blanched	½ cup	3.0
Apricots, dried	½ cup, cooked	11.0
Black beans, dried	8 ounces	56.0†
Chestnuts, shelled	8 ounces	14.0
Chili sauce, unsalted	1 tablespoon	5.0
Chocolate, semi-sweet	1 ounce	1.0
Chocolate, unsweetened	1 ounce	1.0
Cream of tartar	1 teaspoon	8.0
Gelatin, unflavored	1 package	0.1
Honey	1 tablespoon	1.0
Ketchup, unsalted	1 tablespoon	5.0
Oil, corn	½ cup	
Oil, olive	½ cup	
Oil, peanut	½ cup	
Oil, sesame	½ cup	
Peanuts, unsalted	8 ounces	8.0
Prunes, dried	½ cup, cooked	5.0
Salt substitute	1 teaspoon	0.7
Sugar, brown	1 tablespoon	4.0
Sugar, white	1 tablespoon	0.7
Tomato paste, unsalted	1 tablespoon	7.0
Vinegar, apple cider	1 tablespoon	0.7
Vinegar, wine	1 tablespoon	0.7
Walnuts	½ cup	1.0

HORS D'OEUVRES

Great Beginnings

ERDOES

Hors d'Oeuvres

The guests have arrived . . . drinks are offered . . . and the anticipation of a wonderful evening fills the air. The "hors d'oeuvres—cocktail hour" in most cases sets the stage for the main performance yet to come.

There are many stage sets and props that will be used for different occasions, such as the large cocktail party by itself, the small informal dinner with close friends, the gang's over to see the Sunday football game on TV, the formal evening with visiting dignitaries, the ladies' luncheon, the Thanksgiving dinner, the surprise birthday party for Lorraine . . . and so on.

Many years ago there were standard rules for these occasions, the main one being a cocktail for each guest and canapés served on a silver tray by a uniformed maid. But how many of us have uniformed maids? And how many of us like the structured formality of times gone by? So, for those who prefer the excitement of today, let's get on with the show!

Presentation. This is listed first because it creates the setting for your hors d'oeuvres. Search the attic, the basement, the storage closet, and all the rooms in the house for those gifts and purchases that have long been collecting dust. Resurrect the crystal punch bowl. Fill it with crushed ice and a mélange of *crudités,* such as mounds of cherry tomatoes, radishes, cauliflower and broccoli flowerets, sticks of zucchini and carrots, and tiny bunches of watercress. Pull out the small basket that's in the back of the storage closet, line it with an unusual fabric or colorful napkin, and nest your cocktail forks in it. Take a few wine goblets and fill them with the flowers or small leaves of the season, tie ribbons around the bowls of the goblets with the streamers hanging down to the base of the stems and set them in the center of your hors d'oeuvres trays. The brass plant holder that sits forlornly on the table since the plant died . . . line it with colorful tissue paper or fabric and use it as a holder for your homemade Melba Toast,* take the glass apothecary jar, once filled with the homemade preserves that Aunt Kate gave you one Christmas, and use it as a container for Sauce Aïoli* or for Herb Mayonnaise.* The possibilities are limitless, and the fun and visual excitement that these objects create will provide a wonderful ambience for your party.

The Bar. This presents limitless possibilities. For a large party use a bridge table covered with either a thirty-nine inch round shape cut at a lumberyard, or a fold-up round top available at most department stores, covered with a pretty drop skirt. A big tin plant liner or a huge copper pot can become the ice bucket, or if you have a large pantry or kitchen that is accessible to your entertaining area, fill the sink with the ice and lay a huge plastic tray, a marble slab, or even a butcher's chopping board on the drainboard and set your glasses and liquor bottles on that. You can also take two snack tables, set three feet apart, upon which you can place a plank of wood that has had fabric stapled to it, and *voilà* . . . you have a bar! The board can be stored easily in the back of a closet and the fabric can be changed for each party to create a new theme, be it for Christmas, Thanksgiving, or Sunday brunch.

Flowers, Plants, and Leaves. They look sensational in huge copper pots, in baskets lined with glass or ceramic bowls, in the silver bowl your husband received when he won the tennis tournament, in cardboard milk containers with the tops cut off, or in coffee cans, each covered in different and unusual fabrics with ribbon trimmings, or in that soup tureen you bought at the bazaar . . . let your imagination run wild.

The Food. Consider the type of party you're giving. Is it a large cocktail party with waitresses and a bartender? If so, you have the luxury of being able to pass many trays with a wide variety of canapés and other finger foods, both hot and cold. If you have a large cocktail party in a servantless situation, set out various hors d'oeuvres in interesting containers and trays in many places so your guests may roam and mingle freely, finding another delicious hors d'oeuvre always at hand. For a dinner party, be it large or small, you will require fewer hors d'oeuvres. I find that most people don't want heavy hors d'oeuvres if a three- or four-course dinner is to follow. Therefore, I always do Crudités,* each time in a different container, depending upon the number of people, with one or two dips such as Mideastern Yogurt Sauce* or Curry Mayonnaise*; perhaps Endive Stuffed with Curried Chicken* or Herb Cheese in a Crock* accompanied by homemade Melba Toast.* On other occasions, when the hors d'oeuvres are also the first course, I might serve Shrimp and Egg Supreme* or an Onion and Cheese Quiche* or "Crêpes de Poisson.*

The hors d'oeuvres and cocktail hour is the time to welcome your friends, to unwind, and above all to enjoy each other's company in the warm hospitality of your home.

Crudites

Translated, these are simply raw
vegetables, generally served
with a choice of sauces
Serves a large crowd

The effect of this hors d'oeuvre is dramatic. The taste is delicious and
enormously appealing to both the weight-conscious and the low-sodium
guests. It is always served before dinner in our house, whether or not
other hors d'oeuvres are served.

1 small broccoli, separated into
 flowerets
1 small cauliflower, separated
 into flowerets
1 bunch of radishes, cut into
 flowers
6 carrots, peeled, cut in half,
 and cut into thin strips
4 zucchini, sliced in thin strips
3 fennels (white part only) sliced
 in eighths lengthwise

4 small cucumbers, scored and
 sliced into 1/4-inch-thick
 rounds or into thin strips
2 green peppers, seeded and cut
 into thin strips
2 red peppers, seeded and cut
 into thin strips
1 1/2 pints hard cherry tomatoes

1. In a huge crystal bowl or copper pot or deep ceramic container,
silver punch bowl, or whatever you have that will serve as an attractive
container for the vegetables, place crushed ice up to the top. Arrange the
vegetables, alternating the colors for an attractive appearance, such as
half the carrot sticks next to the cauliflower, next to the green peppers,
next to half of the cherry tomatoes, next to the cucumbers, next to the red
peppers, next to the broccoli, next to the remaining carrot sticks, next to
the fennel, next to the remaining cherry tomatoes, next to the zucchini,
which is next to the first carrots, and the radish flowers in the center.
Stand up all the sticks, pressing 1/3 of their length into the crushed ice,
such as the carrots, zucchini, and fennel, to form spears, and mound your
flowerets and cherry tomatoes.

Serving: Set the container with the *crudités* on your coffee table surrounded by individual bowls of sauces such as Sauce Aïoli,* Curry Mayonnaise,* and Yogurt Dill Sauce.*

Crudités Fondue

Serves a crowd

This is a wonderful hors d'oeuvre for a chilly evening in the late fall, or on a Sunday afternoon.

8 large carrots, peeled, cut into thin sticks

7 firm small zucchini, cut into long strips

1 head of cauliflower, separated into flowerets

1 head of broccoli, separated into flowerets

1 cup radishes, cut into petal-shaped flowers

14 green onions (scallions), trimmed

2 cups very firm cherry tomatoes

GARNISH: Cabbage leaves (preferably savoy)

SAUCE:

2 cups of olive oil

6 cloves of garlic, crushed

1 teaspoon freshly ground white pepper

$1/4$ teaspoon cayenne

1 teaspoon hot chili powder (salt free)

$1/2$ teaspoon Spanish paprika

$1/3$ cup cognac

1. In a wicker basket lined with the cabbage leaves, arrange the raw vegetables to create an attractive color pattern. Place a narrow glass (the same height as the basket) in the center of the *crudités* and place fondue forks in it.

2. Place all of the sauce ingredients in a fondue pot and heat until piping hot. You may heat this on the stove and then transfer the pot to a warmer such as brass, copper, iron, silver, or tin which contains Sterno or denatured alcohol, or to an electric warmer to keep hot, or you may heat the sauce from the beginning on the warmer.

Serving: Your guests will dip the carrot sticks, green onions, and zucchini into the hot sauce and munch away . . . or spear the broccoli and cauliflower flowerets, the cherry tomatoes, and radishes with the forks.

Italian Stuffed Mushrooms

Serves 12 as an hors d'oeuvre; 6 as a first course, or 9 to 12 as a vegetable accompanying a main course

36 small mushrooms (approximately 1½ pounds)
6 tablespoons freshly squeezed lemon juice (optional)
6 tablespoons sweet butter
½ cup finely minced onion
4 cloves garlic, finely minced
⅔ cup grated salt-free Swiss or Gouda cheese
2 eggs, lightly beaten

2½ tablespoons finely minced fresh parsley
1½ tablespoons seasoned salt substitute (optional)
⅛ teaspoon cayenne (optional)
¾ teaspoon freshly ground black pepper
½ cup matzoh meal (approximately)
Olive oil

1. Wash the mushrooms well in 1 quart of cold water. Drain the mushrooms, pat them dry with paper towels, and sprinkle with the lemon juice. Remove the stems from the caps and chop the stems finely.

2. In a medium-size skillet melt the butter over a medium flame and sauté the onion, garlic, and mushroom stems until the onions are translucent. Remove the skillet from the flame.

3. Add the cheese, eggs, parsley, salt substitute, cayenne, and pepper. Mix all the ingredients together and stir in enough matzoh meal to make a firm but not dry stuffing.

4. Preheat the oven to 350°.

5. Fill and mound the mushroom caps with the stuffing, place them in a well-oiled roasting pan. Drizzle a little olive oil on each.

6. Bake them for 20 minutes or until piping hot.

Serving: As an Hors d'Oeuvre: Place the stuffed mushrooms on a silver or ceramic tray and pass them at once.

As a First Course: Place 7 mushrooms on each plate, garnished with sprigs of parsley.

As an Accompaniment to the Main Course: Surround your main course with the mushrooms and garnish the platter with bunches of parsley.

NOTE: I generally prepare the stuffed mushrooms in the morning (through Step 5) but without preheating the oven (Step 4), and 45 minutes before I want the mushrooms ready, I let them stand at room temperature for 20 minutes, and oven bake them at 350° for 25 minutes or until they are piping hot.

Fish Beignets

Makes about 70 beignets

9 tablespoons unbleached flour
¼ tablespoon Spanish paprika
4½ tablespoons peanut oil
1½ cups milk (or low sodium dry milk)
2 teaspoons salt substitute (optional)
1 teaspoon freshly ground white pepper
⅓ teaspoon cayenne (or less to taste)

3 cups chopped cold Poached Sole,* flounder, or any flat white fish
1 tablespoon grated onion
5 cloves garlic, pressed
2 eggs
4 tablespoons ice water
Flour (unbleached)
White Bread Crumbs*
Peanut oil, enough for deep frying

1. Mix the flour and paprika and, stirring constantly, add the oil, a little at a time, until it is thoroughly absorbed.

2. Continue to stir, adding the milk a little at a time.

3. Heat the mixture in a heavy saucepan over a low flame, stirring constantly, until the mixture is thick and smooth.

4. Remove the saucepan from the flame and, stirring constantly, add the salt substitute, pepper, cayenne, fish, onion, and garlic until all the ingredients are completely blended.

5. Refrigerate until cold (approximately 3 hours).

6. Roll the fish mixture into 1-inch balls.

7. Beat the eggs with the ice water.

8. Roll the fish balls in the flour, then in the egg, and finally in the bread crumbs.

9. Preheat the oven to 180°.

10. Fry the fish balls in the hot oil in batches until browned, then place them in a roasting pan that has a triple thickness of paper toweling lining the bottom. Keep warm in the oven until all the beignets are fried and drained.

Serving: Arrange on a preheated serving platter accompanied by wooden skewers and Ginger Red Pepper Relish.*

Sardine Canapés

Makes 24 canapés

3 4½-ounce cans salt-free skinned and boned sardines, drained
1½ tablespoons freshly squeezed lemon juice
3 tablespoons finely minced fresh chives
2½ to 3 tablespoons Mayonnaise*
1 teaspoon dry mustard
¼ teaspoon cayenne
1 teaspoon salt substitute (optional)

½ teaspoon freshly ground white pepper
2 teaspoons dried dill
2 tablespoons sweet butter
6 slices of Russian Black Bread,* sliced very thin, toasted, and cut into quarters on the diagonal
Paprika

GARNISH: Sprigs of watercress and cherry tomatoes

1. In a large mixing bowl, mash the sardines and blend thoroughly with the lemon juice. Add the chives, mayonnaise, mustard, cayenne, salt substitute, white pepper, and dill. Mix until all the ingredients are thoroughly blended and smooth.
2. Preheat the oven to 350°.
3. Well butter the black bread toast points.
4. Spread the sardine mixture on the toast points and bake for approximately 10 minutes or until the mixture is piping hot.

Serving: Transfer the canapés to a preheated tray garnished with the watercress and cherry tomatoes.

Tuna Canapés Au Gratin

Makes 32 canapés

2 7-ounce cans tuna, packed in water with no salt added, mashed

4 hard-cooked eggs, mashed

1 medium Spanish onion, finely minced

3 cloves garlic, finely minced

1½ teaspoons dried dill

2 teaspoons salt substitute (optional)

⅔ teaspoon freshly ground white pepper

1½ tablespoons freshly squeezed lemon juice

1½ tablespoons dry vermouth

3½ to 4½ tablespoons Mayonnaise*

2 cups grated salt-free Gouda cheese

8 very thin slices Crusty Peasant Rye Bread,* cut into diagonal quarters

GARNISH: Sprigs of Parsley

1. Preheat the oven to 350°.

2. In a large mixing bowl combine and mix the tuna, eggs, onion, garlic, dill, salt substitute, pepper, lemon juice, vermouth, mayonnaise, and 1 cup of the cheese until thoroughly blended.

3. Toast the bread until it is a light golden brown.

4. Spread the mixture on the toast points and arrange them on an ungreased cookie sheet.

5. Sprinkle the remaining cheese on the canapés and bake for 10 minutes or until the cheese starts to melt.

6. Preheat the broiler to 550°.

7. Place the canapés 4 inches from the flame and broil for 2 to 3 minutes or until the cheese starts to bubble.

Serving: Transfer the canapés to a preheated silver, china, or ceramic tray garnished with the parsley.

Piquant Baked Tuna Balls

Makes about 40 balls

2 7-ounce cans tuna, packed in
   water with no salt added,
   and drained
2 teaspoons fresh lemon juice
2 teaspoons dry vermouth
1¼ cups soft fresh Bread
   Crumps*
3 tablespoons sweet butter,
   melted
3 tablespoons finely chopped
   fresh parsley
3 tablespoons finely chopped
   onion

2 tablespoons finely chopped
   fresh chives
3 cloves garlic, pressed
2 teaspoons salt substitute (optional)
¼ teaspoon cayenne
2 teaspoons dried dill
½ cup Sauce Aïoli*
½ cup finely grated salt-free
   Gouda Cheese
Cornflake crumbs, salt free

GARNISH: Watercress and
   cherry tomatoes

1. Preheat the oven to 350°.
2. Flake and mash the tuna and mix thoroughly with the lemon juice
and vermouth.
3. Mix the bread crumbs with the butter, add the parsley, onion,
chives, garlic, salt substitute, cayenne, dill, and the aïoli sauce and blend
thoroughly.
4. Add some of the tuna mixture, alternating with some of the cheese,
and mix thoroughly after each addition until both the tuna and cheese are
thoroughly blended with the bread crumb mixture.
5. Form the mixture into 1-inch balls, roll the balls in the cornflake
crumbs until they are completely covered.
6. Line 1 or 2 jelly-roll pans with foil and spray with vegetable shortening. Arrange the balls on the foil approximately 1 inch apart and bake for
10 to 15 minutes, or until they are piping hot and a light golden brown.

Serving: Arrange the balls on a preheated platter, garnish with watercress
and cherry tomatoes.

Sirloin Teriyaki

Makes 32 skewers. For lovers of beef in the Japanese style

2 pounds lean sirloin, cut into ½-inch cubes (approximately 64 pieces)

MARINADE:
4 cloves garlic, pressed
1 cup apricot preserves, puréed with ½ cup unsweetened pineapple juice
2 teaspoons dry mustard, dissolved in 3 tablespoons cold water

½ cup dry sherry
2 inches ginger root, grated
⅓ teaspoon cayenne
¼ cup freshly squeezed lemon juice
3 tablespoons brown sugar (or substitute equivalent)

2 16-ounce cans unsweetened pineapple chunks, drained

1. Place the steak cubes in a large plastic bag. In a blender process all the marinade ingredients together. Pour the marinade into the bag and seal it tightly. Refrigerate at least 3 hours, rotating the bag every half hour during the marinating process.

2. Drain the steak cubes but do not pat them dry. Save the marinade.

3. Preheat the broiler to 550°.

4. On wooden skewers about 5 to 6 inches long (allowing 2½ to 3½ inches of wood at one end), thread a pineapple chunk, a steak cube, a pineapple chunk, another steak cube, ending with a pineapple chunk.

5. Arrange the skewers on a broiler rack, brush well with the reserved marinade, and broil 4 to 5 inches from the flame for 1½ minutes.

6. Rotate the skewers one-quarter turn, brush again with the marinade, and broil 1½ minutes more.

7. Continue as with Steps 5 and 6 until all sides of the meat are broiled.

Serving: Put the copper saucepan filled with the Sauce Teriyaki* (recipe given below) or Apricot Mustard Sauce* in the center of a copper or brass tray and arrange the skewers of broiled sirloin around it. Set the tray on a brazier with a low warming flame and place it in the center of the coffee table.

Tell all your guests, "Help yourselves to skewers and dip to your delight."

NOTE: I sometimes double the marinade in order to make sauce teriyaki.

Sauce Teriyaki

2 cups marinade (from "Sirloin
    Teriyaki*)
2 tablespoons cornstarch mixed
    with ½ cup unsweetened
    pineapple juice

1. Blend the marinade with the cornstarch mixture.
2. Place the ingredients in a small copper saucepan, heat over a low-medium flame until the sauce is bubbling hot, thick, and smooth. Stir often.

Meat Balls Chinoise

Makes approximately 40 meat balls. A spicy and tangy constant crowd pleaser

2 eggs plus 1 egg yolk, lightly
    beaten together
1½ tablespoons instant coffee
    powder or crystals
¼ teaspoon cayenne (optional)
¾ teaspoon chili powder, salt
    free
½ teaspoon Spanish paprika
2 inches ginger root, freshly
    grated
5 cloves garlic, pressed
1 onion, finely chopped
5 tablespoons salt-free ketchup

2½ teaspoons seasoned salt sub-
    stitute (optional)
1 teaspoon freshly ground black
    pepper
2 tablespoons finely minced
    fresh chives
¾ cup medium finely chopped
    water chestnuts
½ cup medium finely chopped
    blanched almonds
    blanched almonds
2 pounds ground lean chuck
½ cup peanut oil (or more)

1. Combine all the ingredients except the oil. Blend thoroughly.
2. Form the mixture into 1-inch balls and place them on cookie sheets or jelly-roll pans. Cover and refrigerate at least 30 minutes.
3. When ready to cook, preheat the oven to 180°.
4. Heat the oil in a large, heavy skillet over a medium flame and brown the meat balls in batches, taking care that they do not touch each other. Remove them from the skillet and place on a baking or jelly-roll pan lined

with double thickness paper toweling. Place the meat balls in the oven to keep warm until all have been browned.

Serving: Arrange the meat balls on a preheated silver or copper tray. Spear each of them with a small wooden skewer and serve with a sauce such as Chili Garlic Almond,* Apricot Mustard,* Ginger Red Pepper Relish,* or any of your own salt-free piquant sauces in individual ceramic, crystal, or silver bowls.

Hawaiian Chicken

Makes about 3½ dozen appetizers

A great deal of preparation goes into these hors d'oeuvres, but the applause you receive makes the work worthwhile.

4 whole chicken breasts, split, boned, skinned, pounded into ½-inch thickness and cut into ½-inch squares

MARINADE:
¼ teaspoon cayenne
1 inch ginger root, freshly grated
1 to 2 teaspoons curry powder, salt free
4 cloves garlic, pressed
¼ cup freshly squeezed lemon juice
½ cup peanut oil

BATTER:
2 eggs, at room temperature, separated

1 tablespoon sweet butter, melted
½ cup heavy cream (or triple strength low sodium dry milk)
1 cup unbleached flour, sifted with 1 teaspoon salt-free baking powder, 2 tablespoons seasoned salt substitute (optional), and ¾ teaspoon finely ground white pepper
4 cups flaked unsweetened coconut
Peanut oil for frying

1. Place the chicken squares in a heavy plastic bag with the marinade and seal tightly. Refrigerate at least 3 hours, rotating the bag 3 to 4 times during the marinating period.

2. When you are ready to cook the chicken, drain it, discard the marinade, and pat the the chicken dry between double thickness of paper towels, refrigrate until the batter is ready.

3. Using an electric mixer on medium speed, beat the egg yolks for 5 minutes, then beat in the butter and the cream. Add the seasoned flour a little at a time, beating just until all the flour is absorbed and the batter is smooth.

4. Using the mixer on high speed, beat the egg whites until stiff peaks form. Fold them into the flour mixture and refrigerate for at least ½ hour.

5. Dip the chicken pieces into the batter, then roll them in the coconut.

6. Set the chicken pieces on a flat, dry surface.

7. Preheat the oven to 180°.

8. In a heavy skillet heat the oil over a medium-high flame. (There should be 1 inch of it in the skillet.)

9. Fry the chicken in small batches until golden brown, taking care that the pieces do not touch. Remove with a slotted spoon to a cookie sheet lined with paper towels, place in the oven to keep warm. Repeat until all the chicken is fried.

Serving: Place a bowl of Hawaiian Sauce* or Chutney* or Ginger Red Pepper Relish* in the center of a large silver or ceramic tray. Arrange the chicken pieces around the bowl and spear them with toothpicks.

Endives Stuffed with Curried Chicken

Serves a crowd

This hors d'oeuvre is a great boon to a busy hostess, as it can be prepared and arranged quite a few hours before the party.

½ cup Clarified Butter*
2 cups blanched, slivered almonds
3 cups coarsely diced Poached Chicken Breasts*
4 hard-cooked eggs, cut into quarters

3 tablespoons curry powder, salt free
¾ cup (or more) Sauce Aïoli*
6 firm endives, leaves separated

GARNISH: Sprigs of watercress or parsley

1. In a heavy skillet melt the clarified butter over a low-medium flame. Add the almonds and sauté until a light golden color, stirring often. Finely chop them by hand or in a food processor or grinder.

2. Combine the chicken and eggs and chop finely by hand or in a food processor or grinder.

3. Combine the melted butter, almonds, and chicken-egg mixture with

the curry and enough sauce aïoli to moisten well. Mix thoroughly and refrigerate at least 2 hours.

Serving: Stuff the individual endive leaves with the chicken mixture and arrange, in flower petal fashion, on large round silver or china platters. Serve immediately or cover tightly with plastic wrap and refrigerate until you are ready to serve. Garnish the center of the platter with sprigs of watercress or parsley.

Cheese Straws

Makes about 50 cheese straws

A perfect tidbit to accompany any kind of cocktail.

2 cups grated salt-free Gouda cheese
2 cups grated salt-free Swiss cheese
2 cups unbleached flour
¹/₂ teaspoon Spanish paprika
1 tablespoon seasoned salt substitute (optional)
¹/₂ teaspoon freshly ground white pepper
¹/₃ teaspoon cayenne (or more to taste)
2 teaspoons chili powder, salt free
1 cup sweet butter, melted

1. Thoroughly mix the cheeses, flour, paprika, salt substitute, pepper, cayenne, and chili.
2. Add the melted butter, a little at a time, mixing the ingredients thoroughly until the butter is absorbed.
3. Preheat the oven to 425°.
4. Roll the dough to ¹/₂-inch thickness, cut into strips ¹/₂ × 3 inches, and twist.
5. Bake the straws on ungreased cookie sheets for 8 minutes or until they are a light golden brown.
6. Cool them thoroughly on a wire rack and store in an airtight plastic container.

Serving: Mound the straws on a small silver tray or place some of them standing upright in a crystal wine goblet, or nest them in a small wicker or copper box that has been lined with Provence nappery.

Herb Cheese in a Crock

Serves a large crowd

This herb cheese is rather rich and will serve a large group adequately unless your guests are fanatic cheese lovers. Try this accompanied by a bowl of Minestrone* or Black Bean Soup* and hot Crusty Peasant Rye Bread* for an informal Sunday supper in the late autumn.

2 cups finely grated salt-free Gouda cheese

2 cups finely grated salt-free Cheddar cheese

2 cups finely grated salt-free Swiss cheese

2 tablespoons dried chives

1½ teaspoons ginger powder (optional)

1 tablespoon dried dill

1 teaspoon dried thyme

1½ teaspoons dried tarragon

1½ teaspoons hot chili powder, salt free

1 teaspoon dry mustard (or more to taste)

2 tablespoons salt substitute (optional)

1 teaspoon freshly ground white pepper

¼ teaspoon cayenne (or more to taste)

1 cup sweet butter, cut in small pieces

¼ cup heavy cream (or triple strength low sodium dry milk)

¼ cup brandy

Clarified Butter*

1. In a large, very heavy saucepan, placed on a Flame-Tamer over a low flame, heat all ingredients except the clarified butter, stirring constantly until all are blended and the sweet butter and cheese are thoroughly melted.

2. Spoon the mixture into a large crock or an assortment of small crocks. Cover tightly and chill.

3. Uncover and pour a thin layer of Clarified Butter* over the herb cheese and refrigerate for 12 to 24 hours.

Serving: Remove from refrigerator 1½ hours before serving.

NOTE: In all honesty, I would not make this recipe unless I had a food processor, which makes short shrift of the cheese grating ... an otherwise arduous task.

Brandade de Morue

Serves 12 as an hors d'oeuvre or
8 as a first course

You may know that this famous Mediterranean dish is traditionally made
with salt cod. Since that is obviously and absolutely a non sequitur in our
life-style, I have substituted fresh cod. The results are quite good, and this
recipe has been received with congratulations from a friend who adores
brandade de morue but is not allowed to eat salt.

2¹/₂ pounds cod fillet with the
   skin on
2 teaspoons salt substitute (optional)
¹/₂ cup freshly squeezed lemon
   juice
3 cups Court Bouillon*
³/₄ cup corn oil mixed with ³/₄
   cup olive oil
1¹/₂ cups heavy cream (or triple
   strength low sodium dry
   milk)

2 large Idaho potatoes, baked
   and hot
6 cloves garlic, finely minced
4 teaspoons onion powder
¹/₂ tablespoon salt substitute (optional)
¹/₈ teaspoon cayenne (optional)
1¹/₂ teaspoons freshly ground
   white pepper
Corn oil

1. Rub the fish with the salt substitute, place them in a plastic bag, and
add the lemon juice. Seal the bag tightly. Refrigerate at least 2 hours, rotating the bag 2 to 3 times during the marinating period.

2. Place the court bouillon in a fish poacher and bring it to a boil over a
high flame. Reduce the flame to low, add the cod fillets and the marinade
to the poacher. Cover and simmer for 8 to 10 minutes, or until the fish
flakes to the touch of a fork.

3. While the fish is poaching, heat the oils in a small saucepan over a
low-medium flame until very hot but not boiling.

4. In another saucepan, heat the cream in a small saucepan over a low-
medium flame until it is hot but definitely not boiling.

5. Remove the skin from the fish, flake it, and keep warm.

6. In the bowl of an electric mixer or food processor, add the flesh of
the baked potatoes (discarding the skin). Turn the beater to low-medium
speed (or use the plastic blade of a food processor, turning it on and off),
beat the potatoes until they are mashed.

7. Continuing to beat, gradually add the warm cod, hot oil, and cream.
Add the garlic, onoin powder, salt substitute, cayenne, and white pepper;
beat until the mixture is totally puréed.

8. Place it in a saucepan. Put the saucepan over a Flame-Tamer and stir the *brandade* constantly until it is piping hot. Slowly add more corn oil, if necessary, to keep the mixture moist.

Serving: For Hors d'Oeuvres: Place the *brandade* in the center of a preheated silver or ceramic tray. Arrange Thin Garlic Herb Toast* points around the *brandade*. Place the tray on a warmer containing denatured alcohol or Sterno or electric hot tray to keep warm and let your guests mound some of the *brandade* on the toast points. Just watch their expression when they taste your triumphant saltless *brandade de morue*.

For a First Course: Place it in individual preheated ramekins, then put them on attractive small plates. Either surround the ramekins with garlic toast points or pass them in a basket lined with a printed napkin.

NOTE: The *brandade* may also be served lukewarm, thus eliminating Step 8. Or it may be served cold. Eliminate Step 8, refrigerate it at least 4 hours, then place it on a chilled tray.

Puréed Eggplant

Serves 8 accompanied by hot
Pita Bread*

This is an extremely low sodium and highly flavorful appetizer.

2 large eggplants
6 tablespoons olive oil
1 large red onion, finely chopped
6 to 8 cloves garlic, minced
1 large green pepper, peeled, seeded, and finely diced
3 tablespoons freshly squeezed lemon juice (or more to taste)

2½ teaspoons seasoned salt substitute (optional)
⅛ teaspoon cayenne
½ teaspoon freshly ground black pepper

1. Preheat the oven to 425°.
2. Prick the eggplants with a fork in about 6 places and rub them with a little of the oil (about 1 tablespoon should do).
3. Bake for 50 minutes to 1 hour or until very tender.
4. In a heavy skillet, heat the reamining oil over a medium flame, sauté the onion and garlic until the onion is translucent. Add the pepper, stir well, and sauté until the onion is very tender and a pale golden color. Remove from the flame.

5. Scrape the eggplant pulp from the skin, add it to the onion mixture.

6. Purée the ingredients in a food processor (using the steel blade) or blender, a little at a time, until smooth.

7. Stir in the lemon juice, salt substitute, cayenne, and pepper, refrigerate at least 8 hours (preferably for at least a day). Before serving, taste and adjust seasoning.

Serving: Transfer the puréed eggplant into a crystal or china bowl, placing it on a tray and surrounding the bowl with warm pita bread cut into halves or quarters; or endive leaves; or hot Thin Garlic Herb Toast.* Let your guests spoon some of the mixture into the pockets of the pita bread or mound some of the mixture on the endive leaves or garlic toast.

Pâté Chaud (Hot Pâté)

Serves a crowd

This is one of the great favorites of our friends on those autumn Sundays while viewing a football game.

1½ pounds lean chuck, very
    finely ground
1½ pounds lean veal, very finely
    ground
8 cloves garlic, pressed
⅓ cup very finely minced onion
¼ teaspoon cayenne
2 teaspoons chili powder, salt
    free
1 teaspoon dried cumin
1 teaspoon dried sweet basil
¼ teaspoon dried marjoram
¼ teaspoon dried oregano
½ teaspoon dried thyme
½ teaspoon dried tarragon

1 teaspoon dried chervil
1 tablespoon seasoned salt sub-
    stitute (optional)
1½ teaspoons freshly ground
    black pepper
6 tablespoons Clarified Butter*
    at room temperature
1 cup strong Beef Stock*
3 tablespoons dry sherry
¼ cup brandy

GARNISH: ¼ cup finely chopped
    fresh parsley

1. Preheat the oven to 300°.

2. In a large mixing bowl place the ground chuck and veal, the garlic, onion, cayenne, chili, cumin, basil, marjoram, oregano, thyme, tarragon, chervil, salt substitute, pepper, and clarified butter. Mix thoroughly until all the ingredients are blended.

3. Add the beef stock, a little at a time, mixing constantly, until the mixture is blended. Stir in the sherry and brandy.

4. Spoon the mixture into a well-buttered 2-quart ovenproof crock and cover tightly.

5. Set the crock in a baking pan and pour enough boiling water to come up to two-thirds the height of the crock. Bake for 1½ hours, then increase the heat to 350°. Uncover and bake for 45 minutes or until the pâté is browned on top.

Serving: The pâté may be served from the crock or unmolded, sliced, and arranged on a preheated platter. Sprinkle it with the chopped parsley. Offer Crusty Peasant Rye Bread* or French Bread* and a crock of Garlic Herb Butter* along with the pâté.

Chicken Liver Pâté

Serves a crowd

A food processor makes quick work of the otherwise tiring process of chopping by hand.

⅔ cup sweet butter
¼ cup corn oil or peanut oil
5 cloves garlic, pressed
2 onions, finely sliced
2 pounds chicken livers
3 hard-cooked eggs, cut into
    chunks

2½ tablespoons cognac
½ teaspoon freshly ground
    white pepper
⅛ teaspoon cayenne
1½ tablespoons seasoned salt
    substitute (optional)

1. In a large, heavy skillet heat the butter and oil over a medium flame. Sauté the garlic and onions until the onions are translucent.

2. Push them aside, and sauté the chicken livers for about 5 minutes, or until the liver is a light golden color outside and pink on the inside.

3. Remove from the heat and add the eggs, cognac, pepper, cayenne, and salt substitute, mix well.

4. Add the mixture to a food processor and, using the steel blade with an on-off movement, purée just until smooth (or chop by hand until smooth).

5. Grease one or two crocks, depending on size, with the sweet butter and spoon in the liver mixture. Cover tightly and place a heavy weight on top of the mixture.

6. Refrigerate at least 12 hours (preferably overnight).

Serving: Serve this with toasted and lightly buttered Crusty Peasant Rye Bread.*

Chicken Crêpes

Serves 12, allowing 2 crêpes per person

Once you master crêpes, you will invent endless fillings of your own. This is one of our favorites.

6 tablespoons sweet butter
6 shallots, finely chopped
3 cloves garlic, pressed
1/2 medium green pepper, seeded and finely chopped
1/2 medium red pepper, seeded and finely chopped
1 large Spanish onion, finely minced
1 1/2 pounds very small mushrooms, sliced lengthwise
2 1/2 cups Poached Chicken Breasts* or Boiled Chicken,* skinned, boned, and diced

4 teaspoons salt substitute (optional)
1/2 to 3/4 teaspoon freshly ground white pepper
4 to 6 cups Sauce Velouté*
24 Basic Crêpes*
1/2 cup blanched, slivered almonds
8 ounces salt-free Gouda Cheese, grated (optional, see Note at end of recipe)

GARNISH: 1/2 cup finely chopped parsley

1. In a heavy skillet melt the butter over a medium-to-high flame. Add the shallots, garlic, green and red peppers.

2. Stir-fry until the vegetables are barely translucent. Transfer them with a slotted spoon to a large mixing bowl.

3. Turn the flame down to medium, sauté the onion and mushrooms until the onion is pale golden.

4. Transfer this mixture to the bowl containing the garlic-pepper mixture.

5. Add the chicken, salt substitute, and pepper, toss thoroughly.

6. Add one or more cups of the *sauce velouté* to the chicken mixture until all the ingredients are well sauced.

7. Preheat the oven to 325°.

8. Place the crêpes on a clean, dry flat surface, add 2 to 3 tablespoons of the chicken mixture to the center of each.

9. Fold one edge of each crêpe over the filling, then fold the opposite edge over this. Place them, seam side down, into one or two attractive ovenproof baking dishes, into which you have poured enough *sauce velouté* to well coat the bottom of each dish.

10. Pour the remainder of the sauce over the crêpes and sprinkle with the almonds.

11. Bake for 30 minutes or until piping hot.

Serving: Sprinkle with parsley and serve at once.

NOTE: If cheese is used, eliminate the almonds, and after 15 minutes of baking sprinkle the grated Gouda over the crêpes. Return to the oven for another 15 minutes, or until piping hot. Then place the crêpes under the broiler (550°) for 3 to 4 minutes (about 4 inches from flame) or until the cheese is bubbling. Sprinkle the parsley on top and serve at once.

Crêpes de Poisson

Makes 24 crêpes

An extremely elegant hors d'oeuvre or first course.

1½ pounds Cold Poached Sole,* flounder, or any other white fish fillet
2½ tablespoons freshly squeezed lemon juice
1½ tablespoons dry vermouth
⅔ cup finely grated salt-free Gouda cheese
3 tablespoons minced fresh chives
7½ tablespoons Sauce Aïoli*
3½ tablespoons Sour Cream* or Plain Yogurt*
1½ teaspoons dried dill (or more to taste)

2 cloves garlic, pressed
2½ teaspoons salt substitute (optional)
¼ teaspoon cayenne
½ teaspoon freshly ground white pepper
¼ cup coarsely ground blanched almonds
24 Basic Crêpes*
½ cup melted sweet butter, approximately

GARNISH: Lemon slices and freshly chopped parsley

1. Flake the fish and set aside.
2. Mix the lemon juice, vermouth, cheese, chives, sauce aïoli, the sour

6. Arrange them, seam side down, in a lightly buttered baking dish or cream or plain yogurt, the dill, garlic, salt substitute, cayenne, white pepper, and almonds.

3. Fold in the flaked fish.
4. Preheat the oven to 350°.
5. Place the crêpes on a clean, dry flat surface and add 2 to 3 table-

spoons of the fish mixture to the center of each crêpe. Fold one edge of the crêpe over the filling, then fold the opposite edge over this.

6. Arrange them, seam side down, in a lightly buttered baking dish or pan (or two if necessary), brush a little of the melted butter over each crêpe.

7. Bake them for 15 minutes.

8. Preheat the broiler to 550°.

9. Broil the crêpes 4 inches from the flame for 2 to 3 minutes or until very lightly browned.

Serving: If your baking pan is not attractive enough to serve from, transfer the crêpes (seam side down) to a preheated platter and garnish it with the lemon slices sprinkled with parsley.

NOTE: I generally have the basic crêpes in my freezer. I prepare the fish mixture in the morning, then I remove the crêpes from the freezer about 1 hour before I start to prepare this dish and let them defrost unwrapped on the kitchen counter.

Chopped Chicken Livers

Serves 6 to 8 as a first course or 12 as an hors d'oeuvre

A perennial favorite of our friends.

1/2 cup peanut oil
2 large onions, thinly sliced
2 cloves of garlic, very finely minced
1 pound chicken livers
12 hard-cooked eggs, very finely chopped

1/4 cup cognac (optional)
1/8 to 1/4 teaspoon cayenne
1 to 1 1/2 teaspoons freshly ground white pepper
1 1/2 tablespoons seasoned salt substitute (optional)
Peanut oil

1. In a large, heavy skillet heat the oil over a medium flame, sauté the onions and garlic until the onions are translucent.

2. Add the chicken livers, stir well, and sauté until they are tender and no longer bloody.

3. Chop them finely, either by hand or in a food processor, using the plastic blade. Take care that the livers are not puréed, but only finely chopped.

4. Combine the livers with the eggs and stir well to blend.

5. Stir in the cognac, cayenne, white pepper, salt substitute, and enough peanut oil to moisten well.

6. Spoon the mixture into a crock or a pretty serving dish, cover tightly, and refrigerate overnight.

Serving: Before serving, taste and correct the seasoning if necessary. Serve with rye Melba Toast.*

Shrimp and Egg Supreme

Serves 20 as an hors d'oeuvre or
12 as a first course

Everyone clamors for this recipe whether or not they are on a low sodium regimen. However, if shrimp is not on your list of allowed foods, bypass this recipe.

3 pounds Boiled Shrimp*
36 hard-cooked eggs
6 cups Sauce Aïoli*
2 6-ounce cans tomato paste,
**   salt free**
1 cup chili sauce, salt free
4 tablespoons finely minced
**   fresh chives**
4 tablespoons finely minced
**   fresh parsley**

3 tablespoons finely minced
**   fresh dill (optional)**
¼ to ⅓ teaspoon cayenne (or to
**   taste) (optional)**
2 teaspoons freshly ground white
**   pepper**
2 tablespoons seasoned salt sub-
**   stitute (optional)**

1. Cut the shrimp into thirds if large, in half if small.

2. Cut the eggs into eighths.

3. In an enormous ceramic or glass bowl, beat the aïoli with a wire whisk, blend in the tomato paste, chili sauce, chives, parsley, dill, cayenne, pepper, and salt substitute.

4. Add the shrimp and eggs. Stir thoroughly with a large wooden spoon. Cover tightly and refrigerate overnight.

Serving: I generally serve this as an hors d'oeuvre in a large green ceramic lettuce leaf bowl, accompanied by hot Rolled Cheese and Herb Bread* that has been sliced, buttered lightly, and toasted.

Fish Pâté

Serves 4 to 6 as a main course or
8 to 12 as a first course

Many years ago, before I started to eat low sodium foods, one of my favorite dishes was the fabulous fish pâté served at a three-star restaurant in Paris. This recipe, while not an exact duplicate or even a close adaptation, is however quite delicious and pleases Dick and myself just as much.

Butter
2½ pounds sole fillets, cut into small pieces
4 egg whites
1¾ cups heavy cream (or triple strength low sodium dry milk)
1½ tablespoons salt substitute (optional)
¾ teaspoon freshly ground white pepper
⅛ to ¼ teaspoon cayenne (optional or to taste)
3 tablespoons very finely chopped fresh dill
1½ pounds salmon steak (approximately) skinned, boned, and cut into 2-inch strips

1. Preheat the oven to 350°.
2. Heavily butter a 9 × 5 × 3-inch enamel or Pyrex loaf pan.
3. Place half of the sole and 2 egg whites in a food processor and, using the steel blade, blend until smooth. (Or grind the fish twice, place it in a mixing bowl with the egg whites, and beat until smooth, using the medium speed on your electric mixer.)
4. Spoon the mixture into a chilled large bowl, repeat the mixing process for the other half of the sole and egg whites, and spoon into the same bowl.
5. Gradually add 2 tablespoons of cream at a time to the fish mixture, either beating by hand with a wire whisk or using an electric mixer on medium speed, until the cream is thoroughly absorbed before adding the next 2 tablespoons, etc.
6. Then beat in the salt substitute, pepper, cayenne, and dill.
7. Pour half the fish mixture into the prepared loaf pan, arrange pieces of the salmon lengthwise over the fish mixture.
8. Pour in the remaining fish mixture, smooth it with a spatula or heavy wooden spoon, and cover it with heavily buttered wax paper.
9. Put the loaf pan in a roasting pan, pour enough boiling water into the latter to reach halfway up on the loaf pan.

10. Bake the pâté until set, about 45 minutes.

11. Cool it in the pan.

Serving: Turn the pâté out onto an oblong silver or china platter. If you wish to serve it lukewarm, place bunches of baby watercress around it and serve it with Sauce Nantua.* If you prefer it cold; refrigerate at least 6 hours (preferably overnight) and garnish with finely minced dill, scored and thinly sliced cucumbers, and cherry tomatoes. Serve it with Herb Mayonnaise.*

Garlic Cheese Mousse

Serves a crowd

For garlic lovers only.

2 to 3 teaspoons sweet butter
1 small onion, finely chopped
6 to 8 cloves garlic, pressed
1¼ cups milk (or low sodium dry milk)
4 eggs, separated
6 ounces salt-free Gouda cheese, grated
6 ounces salt-free Cheddar cheese, grated
¼ cup dry sherry
Juice of 1 lemon

Rind of ½ lemon, grated
1 tablespoon seasoned salt substitute (optional)
¼ teaspoon cayenne (or to taste)
¾ teaspoon freshly ground white pepper
⅛ teaspoon freshly grated nutmeg
¼ teaspoon Spanish paprika
2 envelopes unflavored gelatin
½ cup cold water
1 cup heavy cream, whipped

1. In a small skillet melt the butter over a medium flame, sauté the onion and garlic until the onion is translucent. Set aside.

2. In a small saucepan heat the milk over a low flame until it is lukewarm (110°).

3. Using an electric beater, beat the egg yolks for 2 minutes on low-medium speed. Still beating, add the milk, a little at a time, until thoroughly blended. Then add the cheeses, sherry, lemon juice, lemon rind, onion and garlic mixture, salt substitute, cayenne, pepper, nutmeg, and paprika.

4. In a small saucepan, sprinkle the gelatin on the cold water, heat it over a low flame, stirring constantly, until the gelatin is dissolved. Remove it from the flame. Stir the gelatin into the cheese mixture, refrigerate for 10 minutes or until the mixture is cool.

5. With an electric beater, beat the egg whites on high speed until peaks form and hold their shape but are not dry.

6. Stir one fourth of the egg whites into the cheese mixture. Fold the heavy cream into the cheese mixture. Fold the remaining egg whites into the mixture, spoon the mousse into a lightly greased 2-quart mold. Refrigerate it for at least 8 hours.

Serving: This may be served with Poppy or Sesame Seed Crackers* or any Melba Toast* given.

Onion and Cheese Quiche

Serves 16 to 20 as an hors d'oeuvre

There is always one of these in our freezer ready and waiting for unexpected company.

4 tablespoons sweet butter or Clarified Butter* (I prefer the latter)

1½ very large Spanish onions, sliced paper thin and separated into rings

5 cloves garlic, pressed

Pastry dough, see Pastry Crust — 2 9-inch Crusts*

¼ cup cognac

6 eggs, very lightly beaten

3 cups heavy cream (or triple strength low sodium dry milk)

½ teaspoon freshly grated nutmeg

⅛ to ¼ teaspoon cayenne

2 tablespoons seasoned salt substitute (optional)

¼ teaspoon freshly ground white pepper

1 cup grated salt-free Swiss cheese

1 cup grated salt-free Gouda cheese

1. In a medium-size skillet melt the butter over a low flame, sauté the onions and garlic until the onions are translucent.

2. Preheat the oven to 425°.

3. Line an 8½ × 13½ × 2-inch Pyrex baking pan (well buttered and lightly floured) with the pastry dough. Prick the dough with a fork in 3 or 4 places. Line with wax paper and sprinkle with 2 cups of dried beans or uncooked rice. Bake for 10 minutes. Remove the pan from the oven. Remove the wax paper with the beans or rice.

4. Mix the cognac, eggs, cream, nutmeg, cayenne, salt substitute, and pepper.

5. Mix the cheeses together.

6. Sprinkle half the cheese into the pie shell, spoon in the onions, then sprinkle on the remainder of the cheese.

7. Pour the cream mixture evenly over this, bake for 20 minutes. Reduce the heat to 325°, bake for 25 to 30 minutes more or until a toothpick inserted into the quiche about 2 inches from the edge comes out clean.

Serving: Let the quiche cool for at least 3 to 5 minutes before cutting into squares. It may be served from the baking pan, which I generally lay into a wicker basket, or the squares may be transferred to a preheated serving tray.

NOTE: This freezes very well if wrapped airtight. Defrost in the refrigerator for 12 hours, or leave it on the counter for 2 hours. Preheat the over to 325° and heat, uncovered, for approximately 30 to 35 minutes or until the quiche is piping hot.

Moroccan Quiche

Serves 8 for hors d'oeuvres or 4 to 6 for a first course

1 tablespoon corn oil
1 onion, finely chopped
4 cloves garlic, finely chopped
3/4 pound lean lamb, finely ground
1/8 teaspoon cayenne
1 1/2 inches ginger root, freshly grated
1/3 cup finely chopped Cooked Apricots*
1/4 cup finely chopped Cooked Prunes*
3 eggs, very lightly beaten
1 1/4 cups heavy cream (or triple strength low sodium dry milk)

1/8 cup apricot brandy
1/4 teaspoon freshly grated nutmeg
2 teaspoons seasoned salt substitute (optional)
1/2 teaspoon freshly ground white pepper
1 9-inch Pastry Crust,* baked
1/4 cup blanched slivered almonds
Cream or 1 egg white, lightly beaten (optional)

1. Preheat the oven to 425°.

2. In a large, heavy skillet, heat the oil over a medium flame, sauté the onion and garlic until the onion is translucent.

3. Add the lamb, cayenne, and ginger, stirring constantly until the meat is lightly browned. Add the apricots and prunes. Mix well and remove the mixture from the flame.

4. Mix the eggs, cream, brandy, nutmeg, salt substitute, and pepper.

5. Spoon the lamb and fruit mixture into the shell and evenly sprinkle with the almonds.

6. Pour the cream mixture over the almonds. Brush the rim of the crust with a little cream or egg white and bake the quiche for 15 minutes. Reduce the heat to 325°, bake for 12 to 15 minutes more or until a toothpick inserted about 2 inches from the edge comes out clean.

Serving: Put the pan on a heatproof platter or insert it into a silver holder if you have one. Join your guests, slice the quiche into pie-shaped wedges, and transfer them onto pretty plates.

NOTE: This freezes very well if wrapped airtight in aluminum foil and then sealed in double plastic bags. Defrost the quiche in the refrigerator for 6 hours or leave on the counter for 1 hour. Preheat the oven to 325°, heat the quiche uncovered for approximately 20 to 25 minutes or until it is piping hot.

Salmon Quiche

Serves 8 as an hors d'oeuvre or
4 to 6 as a first course

One of the most elegant quiches and unfortunately one of the most expensive.

1 cup flaked cold Poached
   Salmon Hot or Cold,* or
   salt-free canned salmon
   drained thoroughly and
   flaked
3 tablespoons fresh lemon juice
2 tablespoons sweet butter (or
   Clarified Butter,* which I
   prefer)

3 tablespoons finely chopped
   onion
2 tablespoons finely chopped
   fresh parsley
1 tablespoon finely chopped
   fresh chives
3 eggs, very lightly beaten
1/4 cup dry sherry

1¼ cups heavy cream (or triple strength low sodium dry milk)

¼ teaspoon freshly grated nutmeg

¼ teaspoon cayenne

2 teaspoons seasoned salt substitute (optional)

¼ teaspoon freshly ground white pepper

1½ tablespoons finely chopped fresh dill

1 9-inch Pastry Crust,* baked

Milk or 1 egg white, lightly beaten (optional)

1. Preheat the oven to 425°.

2. Mix the salmon with the lemon juice and refrigerate for 1 hour.

3. In a heavy skillet, melt the butter over a low-medium flame and sauté the onions, parsley, and chives until the onions are translucent. Remove from the heat.

4. Mix together the eggs, sherry, heavy cream or triple strength low sodium dry milk, nutmeg, cayenne, salt substitute, pepper, and dill.

5. Mix the salmon and the onion mixture together.

6. Pour the mixture into the pastry shell. Brush the rim with milk or egg white, and bake for 15 minutes. Reduce the heat to 325° and bake for 12 to 15 minutes more, or until a toothpick inserted into the quiche (about 2 inches from the edge) comes out clean.

Serving: Put the pan on a heatproof platter or insert it in a silver holder, if you have one. Join your guests and slice the quiche into pie-shaped wedges and transfer them onto pretty plates.

NOTE: This freezes very well if wrapped airtight in aluminum foil and sealed in double plastic bags. Defrost it in the refrigerator for 6 hours or leave it on the counter for 1 hour. Preheat the oven to 325° and heat the quiche uncovered for approximately 20 to 25 minutes or until it is piping hot.

Spicy Oriental Chicken Quiche

Serves 8 as an hors d'oeuvre or 4 as a luncheon or supper main course

1 cup diced cooked chicken
(Poached* or Boiled*)

MARINADE:
2 inches ginger root, freshly
grated
2 teaspoons hot curry powder,
salt free
1 tablespoon finely chopped
fresh parsley
1 tablespoon finely chopped
fresh chives
2 tablespoons honey
1/8 cup Cointreau
1/2 cup heavy cream (or triple
strength low sodium dry
milk)

1 tablespoon sweet butter or
Clarified Butter* (I prefer
the latter)

1 onion, finely chopped
2 cloves garlic, finely chopped
1 cup heavy cream (or triple
strength low sodium dry
milk)
3 eggs, very lightly beaten
2 teaspoons seasoned salt substitute (optional)
1/8 to 1/4 teaspoon cayenne
1/2 teaspoon freshly ground
white pepper
1/8 teaspoon freshly grated
nutmeg
Cream (or triple strength low
sodium dry milk) or 1 egg
white, lightly beaten (optional)
1 9-inch Pastry Crust,* baked

1. Preheat the oven to 425°.
2. In a large mixing bowl, mix together the chicken, ginger, curry, parsley, chives, honey, Cointreau, and cream (or triple strength low sodium dry milk). Cover tightly and refrigerate at least 3 hours, stirring the chicken 4 to 6 times during the marinating process.
3. In a heavy skillet over a low-medium flame, melt the butter and sauté the onion and garlic until the onion is translucent. Remove it from the flame.
4. Mix together the heavy cream (or triple strength low sodium dry milk), eggs, salt substitute, cayenne, pepper, and nutmeg.
5. Combine the chicken mixture, onion mixture, and cream mixture, mix thoroughly.
6. Pour into the baked shell. Brush the rim with cream (or triple strength low sodium dry milk) or egg white (optional) and bake for 15 minutes. Reduce the heat to 325° and bake for 12 to 15 minutes more or until

a toothpick inserted into the quiche (about 2 inches from the edge) comes out clean.

Serving: Put the pie plate on a heatproof platter or insert it into a silver holder if you have one. Join your guests and slice the quiche into pie-shaped wedges and transfer them onto pretty plates.

NOTE: This freezes very well if wrapped airtight in aluminum foil and sealed in double plastic bags. Defrost the quiche in the refrigerator for 6 hours or leave it on the counter for 1 hour. Preheat the oven to 325° and heat the quiche uncovered for approximately 20 to 25 minutes or until it is piping hot.

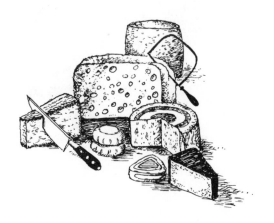

SOUPS
Delicate or Robust and Hearty

POTAGE

Soups

Stop! Don't open that can, especially if you are on a low sodium diet. It is true that there are salt-free soups on the market, but I have never found one that could reasonably compare with a good homemade one. It is also true that soup making does take a little time, but once you get it all together, slow cooking takes care of the rest and you can go about your business. Soups are dependent, to a large measure, on stocks, and at our house we try to keep Chicken Stock,* Vegetable Stock,* and Fish Stock,* as well as Beef Stock* and Veal Stock,* ready to use. You can do a lot of stock cooking in one day, buying vegetables when they are at the height of the season ... charming your butcher out of some knuckle-bones, or your fish dealer out of fish heads. At that point, you have half the battle won. I have given basic recipes for these stocks, and it is up to your imagination to develop new and exciting recipes.

One little secret I have discovered in my search for flavorful low sodium cooking is that wine, either dry red or dry white, when added to stock, intensifies the flavor. White wines spark up veal, chicken, and fish; the red does the same for beef stock.

It goes without saying that if a soup is hot it should be served piping hot; if cold, ice cold. I like to serve my hot soups from tureens of tin-lined copper pots (which I have collected from all over Europe) into heated soup bowls, and my cold soups in chilled bowls, sometimes as a vichyssoise surrounded by ice. How refreshing on a summer day!

From the beginning of our marriage, I remember soup as a pleasant Sunday-night supper in our house. It was satisfying by itself, if we had eaten heavily during the day, or accompanied by salads and crusty breads, or by cold leftovers attractively arranged on platters. I have continued the tradition. Very often these suppers never see the inside of the dining room, but are set up on a huge provincial desk in the living room with the soup in a tureen warmed by either a candle or an alcohol burner.

Summers are eagerly awaited as the time for making refreshing, cold vegetable soups, such as broccoli, asparagus, or gazpacho. Winters call for steaming Onion Soup,* Beef, Mushroom, Barley Soup,* and cream soups.

Our soup bowls range from clay onion soup crocks to wide-lipped colorful hand-painted soup dishes and bowls. We even use mugs for the heavier soups, and I eschew the theory that dishes have to match, feeling instead that they should complement each other.

There's a soup for all seasons, and a season for all soups, so let's get those stock pots brewing!

Jellied Madrilène

Serves 6

An elegant and non-fattening soup.

3 envelopes unflavored gelatin
3 cups salt-free tomato juice
5 cups Beef Stock,* simmered and boiled down to 3½ cups, clarified
¾ cup dry sherry
¾ to 1 teaspoon finely ground white pepper
⅛ teaspoon cayenne

⅓ cup freshly squeezed lemon juice
4½ teaspoons seasoned salt substitute (optional)

GARNISH:
¼ cup freshly minced chives
6 lemon wedges

1. Soften the gelatin in 2 cups of the tomato juice.
2. Place the hot beef stock in a heavy saucepan. Add the gelatin mixture and stir constantly over a low-medium flame until the gelatin is totally dissolved and absorbed (about 3 to 5 minutes). Remove from the heat.
3. Stir in the remaining tomato juice, sherry, pepper, cayenne, lemon juice, and salt substitute.
4. Pour the soup into a glass bowl. Cover and chill until partially set, about 1 hour, then stir the soup briskly with a fork a few times.
5. Chill at least 6 additional hours before serving.

Serving: When ready to serve, whip the madrilène with a fork and spoon it into chilled individual bowls. Garnish it with the chives and wedges of lemon.

NOTE: It is quite superb when ¾ cup of Sour Cream* mixed with the chives is generously spooned on top of the madrilène. However, though still very elegant, it is sadly no longer non-fattening.

Gazpacho

Serves 10 to 12

This delicious "stoveless" easy soup will be a welcome treat during the hot summer months.

3 16-ounce cans salt-free tomatoes

3 16-ounce cans salt-free tomato juice

2 large Spanish onions, cut into small chunks

1 large green pepper, seeded and cut into small pieces

1 large cucumber, peeled and sliced

$1/2$ to $2/3$ cup peanut oil

Juice of 3 lemons, freshly squeezed

$1/4$ cup cider vinegar

6 cloves garlic, pressed

$1/8$ to $1/4$ teaspoon cayenne (optional)

$1^1/2$ teaspoons freshly ground pepper

2 to 3 teaspoons sugar (or substitute equivalent)

$4^1/2$ teaspoons seasoned salt substitute (optional)

2 tablespoons chopped fresh dill

2 tablespoons chopped fresh chives

1. Place all the ingredients in a large bowl and stir thoroughly.
2. Purée the mixture in 3 or 4 batches in a blender or food processor.
3. Pour the purée into a large glass bowl, cover tightly, and refrigerate at least 8 hours (it is better chilled for a day).

Serving: Stir well and spoon the gazpacho into a chilled soup tureen or individual bowls. In separate small bowls, arranged on a tray, offer:
Fresh tomatoes, skinned, seeded, and chopped
Spanish onions, finely chopped
Cucumbers, skinned, seeded, and finely chopped
Green peppers, seeded and finely chopped
Red peppers, seeded and finely chopped

Vichyssoise

Serves 6

It is equally good served piping hot in the winter, when it is called cream of leek and potato soup, as when it is served ice cold in the summer, when it is universally known as vichyssoise.

5 tablespoons sweet butter
6 medium leeks, white part only, well washed and finely chopped
1 large Bermuda onion, finely chopped
5 medium potatoes, peeled and thinly sliced
5 cups strong Chicken Stock*
1 teaspoon freshly ground white pepper

2 teaspoons salt substitute (optional)
$1/8$ teaspoon cayenne (optional)
1 cup heavy cream (or triple strength low sodium dry milk) mixed with $1^1/_2$ cups milk (or low sodium dry milk)

GARNISH: $1/3$ cup chopped fresh chives

1. In a heavy saucepan, melt the butter on a medium flame and sauté the leeks and onion until the onion is translucent.

2. Add the potatoes, chicken stock, pepper, salt substitute, and cayenne. Simmer over a low-medium flame 40 minutes.

3. Purée the potato mixture thoroughly in a blender or food processor in 2 or 3 batches, pour into a large glass or ceramic bowl.

4. Then, stirring the purée constantly, slowly pour in the cream and milk mixture until it has been absorbed.

5. Chill in the refrigerator for a minimum of 12 hours.

Serving: An hour before serving, place the soup bowls in the refrigerator to thoroughly chill. When ready to serve, spoon the vichyssoise into the bowls and garnish with the chives.

NOTE: If you want to serve this soup hot, follow the recipe through Step 4, then transfer the soup to a heavy saucepan, place it on a Flame-Tamer, and heat over a low-medium flame for $1/2$ hour or until piping hot, stirring the soup often.

Serving: Transfer the soup to preheated cream soup bowls with their own covers, garnish with the chives, and cover. Put a bowl at each place setting, call your guests in, and thoroughly enjoy your cream of leek and potato soup.

Cold Cream of Broccoli Soup

Serves 8 to 10

If you own a blender or food processor, this recipe is a snap . . . and delicious to boot.

5 carrots, sliced
2 large onions, coarsely chopped
6 cloves garlic, minced
1/4 teaspoon cayenne (optional)
1 tablespoon seasoned salt substitute (optional)
1 teaspoon freshly ground white pepper
1/2 cup dry vermouth
1/2 cup water

1 1/2 cups Boiled Rice*
6 cups coarsely chopped cooked broccoli
4 cups strong Chicken Stock*
1 cup heavy cream (or triple strength low sodium dry milk)

GARNISH: 1/3 cup chopped fresh chives

1. Place the carrots, onions, garlic, cayenne, salt substitute, and pepper in a medium-size saucepan. Add the vermouth and water. Stir and turn the flame to medium. Cover the saucepan tightly and cook for 30 minutes.

2. Place one quarter of the cooked vegetable mixture, rice, and broccoli in a blender or food processor and purée it well. Then add in one quarter of the chicken stock and the cream and blend thoroughly. Pour the mixture into a large glass bowl. Repeat 3 more times until all the ingredients are puréed and blended.

3. Chill at least 8 hours.

Serving: Serve in chilled bowls garnished with chives.

Cream of Asparagus Soup

Serves 6 to 8

Whether served hot or cold this soup is a great favorite during May and June, when asparagus are at their peak.

½ stick sweet butter

3 large leeks, well washed and finely chopped

1 large Spanish onion, finely chopped

2½ pounds very thin asparagus, washed and cut into small pieces (break off and discard tough tips)

6 cups strong boiling Chicken Stock*

1 teaspoon freshly ground white pepper

2 teaspoons salt substitute

1 teaspoon dried dill

⅛ teaspoon cayenne

5 tablespoons sweet butter

5 tablespoons unbleached flour

1½ cups heavy cream (or triple strength low sodium dry milk)

GARNISH: 4 tablespoons finely minced fresh parsley

1. In a large, heavy saucepan melt the butter over a medium flame and sauté the leeks and onions until the leeks are wilted and the onions are translucent.

2. Add the asparagus, chicken stock, pepper, salt substitute, dill, and cayenne. Stir and cover. Turn the flame to low and simmer for 45 minutes.

3. In a small skillet, melt the butter over a low-medium flame and slowly add the flour, a little at a time, stirring constantly until the flour is thoroughly blended.

4. Continuing to stir, add the cream, a little at a time, until well blended. Cover and keep warm on top of a Flame-Tamer over a very low flame.

5. Purée the asparagus mixture in a blender or food processor (this will probably have to be done in 3 or 4 batches) and return the purée to the saucepan.

6. Turn the flame to low and slowly stir in the warm cream mixture. Cover and simmer for 20 minutes or until piping hot.

Serving: Pour the soup into heated bowls and garnish with the parsley.

NOTE: If you want to serve this soup cold, stir the cream mixture into the purée (Step 6) but do not simmer! Transfer the soup to a glass bowl, cover, and refrigerate overnight.

Serving: Stir the soup and pour it into thoroughly chilled individual bowls. Garnish with the parsley.

Sherry, Cheese, and Cauliflower Creamed Soup

Serves 8

5 tablespoons sweet butter
4 large leeks, well washed and finely chopped
1 Spanish onion, finely chopped
5 tablespoons unbleached flour
5 cups strong Chicken Stock*
½ cup dry sherry
1 very large cauliflower (discard the tough ends and cut the remainder into small pieces)
2 teaspoons salt substitute
1 teaspoon freshly ground white pepper

⅛ to ¼ teaspoon cayenne
6 egg yolks
2 cups heavy cream (or triple strength low sodium dry milk)
¾ cup grated salt-free Gouda cheese

GARNISH: Hungarian paprika

1. In a large, heavy saucepan, melt the butter over a low-medium flame and sauté the leeks and onions only until the onions are translucent.

2. Stirring constantly, slowly add the flour until it is thoroughly mixed and blended.

3. Slowly stir in the chicken stock and the sherry.

4. Add the cauliflower, salt substitute, pepper, and cayenne. Stir and cover. Cook for 40 minutes.

5. Purée the vegetable mixture in blender or food processor (this will probably have to be done in 2 or 3 batches). Return the purée to the saucepan and heat over a very low flame until piping hot but not boiling.

6. In the meantime, using a wire whisk, beat the egg yolks, cream, and cheese until thoroughly blended.

7. Stirring the egg mixture briskly with the whisk, slowly add 1 cup of the hot puréed soup, a little at a time, and then slowly stir this mixture into the hot puréed soup on the stove.

8. Cover and simmer for 5 minutes but do not allow the soup to boil or it will curdle.

Serving: Pour the soup into a heated tureen and garnish with Hungarian paprika; or pour it into heated individual cream soup bowls, preferably with their own covers. Garnish each portion with the paprika, cover the bowls and put one at each place setting.

Curried Cream of Pea Soup Without the Cream

Serves 10 to 12

Thick and rich without the calories of creamed soups.

5 tablespoons Garlic Herb
  Butter*
1 large onion, minced
4 carrots, sliced thinly
4 cups shelled fresh peas
¹/₄ teaspoon cayenne
2 teaspoons salt substitute

¹/₂ teaspoon freshly ground
  white pepper
4 teaspoons curry powder
1 teaspoon dried cumin
8 cups strong Chicken Stock*
¹/₂ cup dry sherry
2 cups Boiled Rice*

1. In a large, heavy pot melt the garlic herb butter over a medium flame and sauté the onion until it is a golden color.

2. Add the carrots, peas, cayenne, salt substitute, pepper, curry, cumin, chicken stock, and sherry. Bring to a low boil over a high flame. Reduce the flame to low. Cover and simmer for 25 minutes.

3. Thoroughly purée half the mixture with half the rice in a blender or food processor and pour into a large bowl. Purée the remaining mixture with the rice and add it to the bowl.

4. Refrigerate at least 8 hours.

Serving: Transfer the soup to a very cold oversized brandy snifter, place it on the sideboard, and ladle the soup from it into chilled bowls. If you are serving the soup outdoors, ladle it into chilled large mugs. A marvelous accompaniment to this puréed soup is Cheese Straws.*

Cream of Tomato Soup, Hot or Cold

Serves 8

A favorite both winter and summer.

5 tablespoons sweet butter
1 medium-size Bermuda onion,
  finely chopped
4 tablespoons unbleached flour

3 16-ounce cans salt-free tomatoes, coarsely chopped (include liquid)

4 teaspoons seasoned salt substi-
    tute (optional)
1 teaspoon freshly ground white
    pepper
1/4 teaspoon cayenne
1/4 cup dry sherry
2 cups heavy cream (or triple
    strength low sodium dry
    milk)

1 cup milk (or low sodium dry
    milk)

GARNISH: Fresh parsley or
    chives, finely chopped

1. In a large, heavy saucepan melt the butter over a medium flame, sauté the onion until translucent.

2. Add the flour, a little at a time, stirring constantly, until the flour is absorbed and thoroughly mixed with the onion.

3. Add the tomatoes, salt substitute, pepper, cayenne, and sherry. Mix well, cover, and simmer for 20 minutes.

4. Purée this mixture in a blender or food processor and pour the mixture into either the top of a double boiler or into a saucepan on a Flame-Tamer.

5. In a small saucepan heat the cream and milk over a low flame, taking care not to boil. Slowly pour this mixture into the tomato purée, stirring constantly. Cover and heat over a very low flame for 10 to 15 minutes or until soup is piping hot.

Serving: If serving the soup hot, transfer it to a heated tureen or individual heated bowls and garnish with the parsley or chives.

NOTE: If you prefer cold cream of tomato soup, transfer the soup to an attractive ceramic serving bowl after the cream has been added to the purée (Step 5). Cover and refrigerate at least 8 hours.

Serving: Garnish with the parsley or chives and bring the soup to the table. Ladle it into chilled individual soup bowls.

If you own individual crystal shrimp servers that nestle into larger footed crystal bowls containing crushed ice, by all means use them; they look pretty and keep your soup icy cold. Garnish each portion with the parsley or chives. Place the shrimp servers on crystal plates and put one at each place at the table before calling your guests in to dinner.

Creamed Corn and Tomato Soup

Serves 6

3 tablespoons sweet butter
4 cloves garlic, pressed
2 large onions, coarsely chopped
2 8-ounce cans salt-free corn, drained
1 16-ounce can salt-free tomatoes, drained and coarsely chopped
4 cups Chicken Stock*
1 tablespoon seasoned salt substitute (optional)

1 teaspoon freshly ground black pepper
2 tablespoons salt-free curry powder
1 cup heavy cream (or triple strength low sodium dry milk)

GARNISH: 3 tablespoons finely minced fresh dill

1. In a small, heavy skillet melt the butter over a low-medium flame and sauté the garlic and onion just until the onion is translucent.

2. In a blender or food processor purée the onion mixture, corn, tomatoes, and 1 cup of the chicken stock. Remove the purée to a heavy saucepan, add the remaining broth, salt substitute, pepper, and curry, stir thoroughly, and cover. Heat over a medium-high flame, then turn the flame to low and simmer for 6 minutes.

3. Uncover and, stirring constantly, slowly pour the cream into the soup. Cover and let it simmer for 3 to 4 minutes or until the soup is piping hot.

Serving: Transfer the soup to a heated tureen or individual soup bowls and garnish it with dill. Serve at once.

Tomato Soup with Fresh Dill

Serves 6 to 8

This very low sodium soup is especially good when tomatoes are in their home-grown season.

4 tablespoons sweet butter
1 large onion, finely chopped
6 cloves garlic, finely chopped
6 large tomatoes, peeled, seeded,
    and chopped
1/4 cup freshly squeezed lemon
    juice
2 tablespoons brown sugar (or
    substitute equivalent)
2 tablespoons finely minced
    fresh dill

1 teaspoon freshly ground white
    pepper
2 teaspoons seasoned salt substi-
    tute (optional)
3 cups strong Chicken Stock*
1 cup dry white wine
1 cup Boiled Rice*

GARNISH: 1/4 to 1/2 cup finely
    minced fresh dill

1. In a medium-size heavy saucepan, heat the butter over a medium flame and sauté the onion and garlic until the onion is translucent.

2. Add the tomatoes, lemon juice, brown sugar, dill, pepper, salt substitute, chicken stock, and wine. Stir well, turn the flame to high, and bring to a low boil. Reduce the flame to low, cover the pot, and simmer for 15 minutes.

3. Purée the mixture with the boiled rice in a blender or food processor. You will probably have to do this in 2 batches.

4. Pour the soup into a glass bowl and refrigerate at least 8 hours.

Serving: Cold: Spoon the soup into a chilled tureen or individual bowls and garnish with dill.

Hot: After Step 3 heat the soup in a saucepan over a low flame for 20 minutes or until piping hot. Pour it into a heated tureen or individual bowls and sprinkle with dill.

Mushroom Bisque

Serves 10 to 12

1 stick sweet butter
1 large onion, finely chopped
2 pounds mushrooms, finely
    chopped
Juice of 1 lemon
1/3 cup brandy
1/2 cup unbleached flour
2 quarts Chicken Stock*
1/8 teaspoon cayenne
2 tablespoons seasoned salt sub-
    stitute (optional)
3/4 teaspoon freshly ground
    black pepper

2 1/2 cups heavy cream (or triple
    strength low sodium dry
    milk)
1 cup milk (or low sodium dry
    milk)
1 cup dry sherry

GARNISH: 1/3 cup finely chopped
    fresh chives

1. In a large skillet melt the butter over a medium-high flame and sauté the onion, stirring constantly, for 2 minutes. Add the mushrooms and sauté with the onions for 4 minutes, stirring often.

2. Reduce the flame to medium low and add the lemon juice and brandy. Stir well. Cover and simmer for 2 minutes.

3. Uncover and slowly add the flour, stirring until it is completely blended. Still stirring, slowly add the chicken stock, cayenne, salt substitute, and pepper. Cover and simmer for 20 minutes.

4. Remove from the flame and purée in a food processor or a blender.

5. In a large saucepan, on a low-medium flame, slowly heat the cream and milk. Do not boil. Stirring constantly, slowly add the puréed mushroom mixture.

6. When the mixture is thoroughly blended, turn the flame to low and add the sherry, stirring constantly. Cover and simmer for 3 to 4 minutes.

Serving: Pour the bisque into a heated tureen or in individual bowls and garnish with the chives.

Salmon Bisque

Serves 10 to 14

3 tablespoons sweet butter
1 medium onion, finely minced
1/4 cup finely chopped fresh
   parsley
3 8-ounce cans salt-free salmon,
   flaked (include liquid)
1 16-ounce can salt-free tomatoes, coarsely chopped (include liquid)
1³/4 cups dry white wine
1/4 cup brandy
2/3 cup water
1 cup salt-free tomato juice
Juice of 2 lemons
2 tablespoons seasoned salt substitute (optional)
1¹/2 teaspoons freshly ground
   white pepper

1/8 to 1/4 teaspoon cayenne (optional)
2 teaspoons dried tarragon
1 stick sweet butter
1/2 cup unbleached flour
2¹/2 cups heavy cream (or triple
   strength low sodium dry
   milk)
3 cups milk (or low sodium dry
   milk)
1/3 cup sherry

GARNISH: 1/3 cup finely minced
   fresh parsley

1. In a large, heavy saucepan, melt the butter over a medium flame and sauté the onion until translucent.

2. Add the parsley and stir well. Cook for another 2 minutes.

3. Add the salmon, tomatoes, wine, brandy, water, tomato juice, lemon juice, salt substitute, pepper, cayenne, and tarragon.

4. Turn the flame to low-medium, cover the saucepan, and simmer for 1/2 hour.

5. Purée the salmon mixture in a food processor or blender. Mix until it is creamy and smooth. Return the purée to the saucepan and heat over low-medium flame.

6. Melt the butter in a small skillet over a medium flame, stirring constantly. Slowly add the flour and stir until thoroughly blended. Continuing to stir, slowly add the cream and milk and heat thoroughly, taking care not to boil.

7. Set the saucepan on a low-medium flame and heat. Stirring the purée mixture constantly, slowly add the heated cream mixture. When completely blended, turn the flame to low and stir in the sherry.

8. Simmer for 5 to 10 minutes or until piping hot.

Serving: Pour the soup into a heated tureen or individual soup bowls, garnish with the parsley, and serve at once.

Crème de Poisson

Serves 8 to 12

Elegant and moderately expensive if you don't live near the sea, but a wonderful treat for special luncheons and dinners.

3 tablespoons sweet butter
3 large onions, chopped
6 cloves garlic, pressed
2 carrots, grated
5 cups Court Bouillon*
4 large potatoes, peeled and cut
into large chunks
1 bay leaf
1/2 teaspoon dried thyme
2 1/2 teaspoons dried dill weed
1 teaspoon dried tarragon
1 teaspoon dry mustard
1/8 teaspoon cayenne
2 teaspoons salt substitute (optional)
1/2 teaspoon freshly ground white pepper

2 1/2 cups dry white wine
1/2 cup dry sherry
2 1/2 pounds of a mixture of fish pieces: salmon, pike, cod, halibut, haddock, flounder, sole, etc.
4 egg yolks
1 cup heavy cream (or triple strength low sodium dry milk)

GARNISH: 1/4 cup finely chopped fresh parsley

1. In a heavy saucepan melt the butter over a medium flame and sauté the onions and garlic until the onions are translucent. Add the carrots, stir well, and sauté for 5 minutes more.

2. In another saucepan, bring the court bouillon to a rolling boil and add the onion mixture, potatoes, bay leaf, thyme, dill, tarragon, mustard, cayenne, salt substitute, pepper, white wine, and sherry. Stir well and simmer for 1 hour on a low flame.

3. Add the fish, mix well, cover, and cook for 10 more minutes or until the fish is tender and flakes to the touch of a fork.

4. Remove the bay leaf and purée half the soup at a time in a blender or food processor until the soup is thick and smooth.

5. Return the soup to the saucepan, cover, and bring to a boil over a medium-high flame. Remove it from the flame.

6. Lightly beat the egg yolks with a wire whisk and thoroughly mix them with the cream (or triple strength low sodium dry milk). Continuing to beat, very slowly add 3/4 cup of the hot soup to the cream mixture (this will prevent the eggs from curdling). Then add this mixture, very slowly, to the soup, while constantly beating the soup with a wire whisk.

Serving: Transfer it to a heated tureen or individual bowls, garnish with the parsley, and serve at once. A delicious and pretty accompaniment to the soup is Cheese Soufflé Bread*

NOTE: This soup may be made in advance, but add the cream and egg yolk mixture just before serving.

Harwich Port Fish Chowder

Serves 8 as a first course or 4 as a main course

3 tablespoons sweet butter
2 large onions, finely minced
4 cloves garlic, finely minced
3 leeks (very well washed), finely chopped
4 large potatoes, peeled and cut into eighths
1/2 cup finely minced fresh parsley
3 cups Fish Stock*
1 cup dry white wine
1 tablespoon salt substitute (optional)

1 1/2 teaspoons freshly ground white pepper
1/8 teaspoon cayenne (optional)
1 pound cod fillets, cut into strips 1 by 2 inches
1 pound haddock fillets, cut into strips 1 by 2 inches
1 1/2 cups heavy cream (or triple strength low sodium dry milk)

GARNISH: 2 tablespoons finely minced fresh chives

1. In a large, heavy pot, melt the butter over a medium flame and sauté the onions, garlic, and leeks, stirring constantly, until the onions are translucent.
2. Add the potatoes and sprinkle in the parsley.
3. Pour in the fish stock and wine. Sprinkle the salt substitute, pepper, and cayenne over all and stir well.
4. Raise the flame to high, cover, and bring to a boil.
5. Reduce the flame to low-medium and cook for 10 minutes.
6. Add the cod, haddock, and cream (or triple strength low sodium dry milk), stir well, and cover (make sure the cream does not boil). Cook for 7 to 10 minutes or until all the ingredients are piping hot and the fish flakes easily to the touch of a fork.

Serving: Transfer the chowder to a preheated soup tureen and garnish with the chives. Ladle the chowder into preheated soup bowls and offer hot Garlic Toast* with it.

Fish Chowder Bon Marché

Serves 8 to 10

This inexpensive dish was created when we spent some time on Cape Cod. The local fish store had loads of what they called "fish bits," which basically was the fall-off of small pieces of fish after filleting. It was only eighty-five cents a pound, and with a little ingenuity this recipe was born. Hope you enjoy it as much as we have.

4 tablespoons peanut oil
2 large onions, finely minced
8 cloves of garlic, minced
3 tablespoons finely minced
   fresh dill
3 tablespoons finely minced
   fresh parsley
2 large green peppers, seeded
   and chopped
4 cups water
3 cups dry white wine
½ to ¾ cup brandy
2 tablespoons seasoned salt substitute (optional)
¾ teaspoon freshly ground
   white pepper
⅛ to ¼ teaspoon cayenne

2 to 3 teaspoons salt-free curry
   powder (or more to taste)
5 carrots, diced
6 ripe tomatoes, peeled, seeded,
   and chopped
4 large potatoes, peeled and
   diced
3 pounds fish bits (cod, scrod,
   halibut, sole, flounder, etc.)
   soaked in ½ cup fresh
   lemon juice for at least 1
   hour
3 cups fresh corn sliced off
   the cob and kernels separated

GARNISH: Chives, finely minced

1. In a large, heavy pot, heat the oil over a medium flame and sauté the onions and garlic until the onions are a pale golden color.

2. Add the dill, parsley, and green peppers, cook for 3 minutes, stirring very often.

3. Pour in the water, wine, and brandy, add the salt substitute, pepper, cayenne, curry powder, carrots, tomatoes, and potatoes. Stir well and cover. Cook for 20 minutes.

4. Drain the fish bits and add to the broth. Add the corn. Stir well, cover, and cook for an additional 6 to 8 minutes or until the fish flakes to to the touch of a fork.

Serving: Pour into a heated large tureen and garnish with the chives.

A wonderful accompaniment to this chowder is hot crusty French Bread* sliced and spread with Garlic Herb Butter,* wrapped in foil, and heated in a 350° oven for 15 minutes, then unwrapped and placed under the broiler about 4 inches from the flame for 3 to 4 minutes or until the bread is lightly toasted and the garlic herb butter is bubbling.

Another of our favorites is to offer sliced toasted French Bread* and individual tiny bowls filled with Sauce Aïoli.* Each person spreads the toast with the sauce; some eat it as is, while others dunk it into the fish chowder. Either way it is delicious.

Black Bean Soup

Serves 10

Somehow, we always think of this soup when the weather is very cold.

2 cups dry black beans, soaked
    in water overnight
4 quarts Beef Stock*
$1/2$ cup corn oil
3 medium onions, finely chopped
4 cloves garlic, finely chopped
$1/8$ teaspoon cayenne
3 large ripe tomatoes, peeled,
    seeded, and chopped, or 1
    16-ounce can of salt-free to-
    matoes

3 carrots, diced
1 tablespoon seasoned salt sub-
    stitute (optional)
$1/2$ teaspoon freshly ground
    black pepper
2 to 3 teaspoons salt-free chili
    powder
$3/4$ cup dry sherry

1. Remove any of the beans that are floating on top of the water and wash the rest thoroughly in a colander.

2. Place them in a heavy pot, add the beef stock, and bring to a boil over a high flame. Cover, reduce the flame to low-medium, and cook for 3 hours.

3. While they are cooking, heat the oil in a heavy skillet and sauté the onions and garlic until the onions are translucent. Add the cayenne, tomatoes, carrots, salt substitute, pepper, and chili powder and stir. Cover and simmer for 5 minutes.

4. Add the tomato-onion mixture to the beans, stir well, and cook until the beans are very tender (about 1 to $1/2$ hours more).

5. Purée the mixture in a blender or food processor, and return the purée to the pot or a flameproof tureen. Add the sherry. Cover and heat over a low flame until the soup is very hot.

Serving: Serve the soup from the flameproof tureen or transfer it to a heated tureen or individual soup bowls and serve at once.

Chicken Curry Soup

Serves 8

A treat for curry lovers . . . and suprisingly a favorite of non-curry lovers as well.

5 tablespoons sweet butter
4 cloves garlic, pressed
1 large Bermuda onion, finely
   chopped
4 tablespoons unbleached flour
2½ cups diced Boiled Chicken*
1 cup dry white wine
4 cups Chicken Stock*
1½ tablespoons salt-free curry
   powder
⅛ to ¼ teaspoon cayenne
½ teaspoon cumin

2 teaspoons salt substitute (optional)
½ teaspoon freshly ground
   white pepper
2 cups milk (or low sodium dry
   milk)
½ cup dry sherry

GARNISH:
⅓ cup drained crushed pineapple, heated
⅓ cup toasted, slivered,
   blanched almonds

1. In a large, heavy saucepan, melt the butter over a low-medium flame and sauté the garlic and onion until the onion is a very pale golden color.

2. Stirring constantly, slowly add the flour, a little at a time, until all the flour is well mixed and absorbed with the onion and garlic.

3. Add the chicken and blend thoroughly.

4. Stirring constantly, slowly add the wine, chicken stock, curry, cayenne, cumin, salt substitute, and pepper. Cover. Turn the flame to low and simmer for 15 minutes.

5. Using a food processor, or a blender purée the chicken mixture and return it to the saucepan.

6. Turn the flame to very low and, stirring constantly, slowly add the milk. Cover and heat for 10 minutes or until the soup is piping hot. Add the sherry and simmer for 5 minutes more.

Serving: Transfer the soup to a heated tureen or heated individual soup bowls. Garnish with the pineapple and almonds. Serve at once.

Sweet and Sour Cabbage Soup

Serves 10 to 14

A marvelous blend of texture and flavor.

4 tablespoons oil
4 large onions, minced
8 cloves garlic, minced
2 large heads green cabbage, shredded
8 large ripe tomatoes, peeled, seeded, and chopped
1 cup dried apricots, cut into quarters
¾ cup pitted prunes, cut into quarters
2 cups grated carrots
4½ tablespoons brown sugar (or substitute equivalent)

½ cup lemon juice, freshly squeezed
½ tablespoon dried dill
1 tablespoon seasoned salt substitute (optional)
1½ to 2 teaspoons freshly ground black pepper
¼ to ½ teaspoon cayenne (optional)
2 cups dry white wine
4 cups salt-free tomato juice
4 cups water

1. Heat the oil in a very large pot over a medium flame and sauté the onions and garlic until the onions are a pale golden color, stirring often.

2. Add the cabbage, tomatoes, apricots, prunes, and carrots. Sprinkle in the sugar, lemon juice, dill, salt substitute, pepper, and cayenne. Add the wine, tomato juice, and water. Cover tightly and heat over a high flame for 10 minutes.

3. Lower the flame to low-medium and simmer for 1 to 1½ hours or until ingredients are tender and well blended. Stir 1 or 2 times during the simmering period.

Serving: Transfer the soup to a heated tureen, carry it to the dining table or sideboard, and proudly serve your family and guests. We all love to have Russian Black Bread* accompanied by a crock of sweet butter served with this hearty soup.

Onion Soup (Soupe À L'Oignon)

Serves 6 to 8

One winter, many years ago in Paris when the markets of Les Halles were open, Dick and I used to wander over there at two-thirty in the morning. It was freezing cold and on occasion snowing lightly, and as we barged through the door of our favorite and rather raunchy bistro, the aroma of that divine soup assailed our nostrils. In no way, dear reader, do I claim that this onion soup is as special or divine as that one was. After many years of trial and error, and trial and error, this is a pretty good imitation of that *soupe à l'oignon.*

6 tablespoons sweet butter
5 very large Spanish onions,
sliced paper thin
2¹/₂ tablespoons rice flour (or
unbleached flour)
¹/₂ to 1 teaspoon sugar (or sub-
stitute equivalent)
1 tablespoon seasoned salt sub-
stitute (optional)
1 teaspoon freshly ground white
pepper
6 cups strong Beef Stock* or
strong Chicken Stock* (see
Note 1)

1¹/₂ cups dry red wine (or dry
white wine if using chicken
stock)
¹/₃ cup cognac
8 to 16 ounces salt-free Swiss or
Gouda cheese, grated
French Bread,* sliced 1 inch
thick and toasted golden
brown
1¹/₂ tablespoons butter, cut into
tiny pieces

1. In a large, heavy saucepan, melt the butter over a medium flame. Add the onions, turn the flame down to very low, and sauté until deep golden brown, stirring them often with a wooden spoon.

2. Slowly stir in the flour until it is well blended, then sprinkle in the sugar (or substitute equivalent), salt substitute, and pepper. Stir to combine thoroughly.

3. Slowly add the beef or chicken stock, stirring constantly.

4. Add the wine and cognac, stir very well.

5. Turn the flame to high, cover the soup, and bring it to a boil. Turn the flame down to low and simmer the soup, covered, for 35 minutes.

Serving: Preheat the broiler to 550°.

Into preheated individual ovenproof brown pottery onion soup bowls, sprinkle in 2 heaping tablespoons of the cheese. Pour the piping hot soup over the cheese until the bowl is two thirds full. Place 1 slice of the

French bread toast on top of the soup in each bowl. Sprinkle 2 to 4 table-spoons of the grated cheese over the toast (the cheese should be level with the rim of the bowl). Sprinkle the bits of butter over the cheese.

Place the bowls (6 or 8) in a shallow baking pan. Place the pan on the broiler rack 5 inches from the flame. "Broil" the soup for 3 to 5 minutes or until the cheese is bubbling and has just begun to brown.

Put each bowl on a heavy heatproof pottery or ceramic plate and bring it to the table. Place the plate with the soup bowl on top of a pewter or copper service plate: "Soup's on . . ."

NOTE 1: Having had a friend who was a vegetarian and who adored onion soup, I devised a vegetarian soup recipe. She loved it, and I hope other vegetarians will too.

Substitute strong Vegetable Stock* for the beef or chicken stock.

Add 1½ tablespoons of salt substitute (optional) and ½ teaspoon cayenne.

Use white wine.

NOTE 2: More often than not, I make a triple recipe of the onion soup and prepare it through Step 5, then I pour it into 1-quart containers and freeze it.

When we want onion soup, I pull out as many containers as I will need and let them defrost in the refrigerator overnight or for 2 hours on the counter.

I pour the soup into a heavy saucepan and over a low flame heat it to piping hot.

It is then just a matter of following the serving instructions. When this soup is made and frozen, I use 1- or 2-day-old beef or chicken stock that has never been frozen. There is something about freezing, defrosting, and refreezing that has never appealed to me.

Minestrone

Serves 12 to 16

In the fall or winter, when we want a meatless dinner or supper, this soup is served as the main course, accompanied by one or two hot home-baked breads with sweet butter or Garlic Herb Butter.*

1 pound dried white beans,
    soaked overnight in water
    to cover
6 quarts water
5 tablespoons (or more) olive oil
8 cloves garlic, finely minced
3 large onions, coarsely chopped
1½ pounds mushrooms, sliced
    thinly lengthwise
4 leeks, well washed and thinly
    sliced
3 tablespoons chopped fresh
    parsley
3 tablespoons chopped fresh
    basil
3 tablespoons salt-free tomato
    paste
4 cups finely shredded green
    cabbage
6 zucchini, thinly sliced
5 large ripe tomatoes, peeled,
    seeded, and chopped

6 carrots, diced
3 large green peppers, seeded
    and diced
3 large red peppers, seeded and
    diced
2 teaspoons sugar (or substitute
    equivalent)
1½ tablespoons seasoned salt
    substitute (optional)
2 teaspoons freshly ground black
    pepper
¼ to ½ teaspoon cayenne
2½ quarts boiling water
1 quart dry white wine
2½ cups uncooked spaghetti
    shells or elbow macaroni or
    bow ties

GARNISH: 1 cup grated salt-free
Gouda cheese

1. Drain the beans and place them in a large, heavy pot. Add the 6 quarts of water, cover, and bring to a boil over a high flame. Reduce the flame to medium and cook for 1½ hours or until tender.

2. While they are cooking, heat the oil in a large, heavy pot over a medium flame. Sauté the garlic, onions, mushrooms, leeks, parsley, and basil until the onions are a pale golden color, stirring often.

3. Add the tomato paste, cabbage, zucchini, tomatoes, carrots, green peppers, red peppers, sugar, salt substitute, pepper, cayenne, water, and wine. Stir all the ingredients thoroughly. Cover, turn the flame to low, and cook for 1¼ hours or until all the vegetables are tender but not mushy. Add the beans and the pasta. Stir all the ingredients thoroughly and cook for 10 to 12 minutes or until the pasta is *al dente*.

Serving: Transfer to a heated tureen and serve at once. Offer grated cheese in a separate crock or bowl.

Beef, Mushroom, Barley Soup

Serves 8 to 10 as a first course or
4 to 6 as a main course

This wonderful main course has an earthy feeling, and we generally have it during the bitter winter months accompanied by a robust burgundy wine, followed by a tossed green salad Vinaigrette.* The dinner is completed with a platter of salt-free cheese, such as Gouda or Swiss, warm home-baked Crusty Peasant Rye Bread,* sweet butter, a bowl of tart apples, and cinnamon coffee.

6 tablespoons corn oil
2 pounds lean chuck, cut into 2-inch cubes
2 large onions, finely chopped
6 cloves garlic, pressed
12 beef bones
20 dried mushrooms, soaked, drained, and coarsely chopped
1½ tablespoons seasoned salt substitute (optional)
1½ teaspoons freshly ground black pepper
⅛ to ¼ teaspoon cayenne
12 tablespoons barley, well washed
5 cups boiling water
6 carrots, cut into tiny cubes
4 cups strong Beef Stock* or Chicken Stock*
1½ cups dry red wine
¼ cup finely minced fresh parsley

1. In a large, very heavy pot, heat the oil over a medium flame and brown the meat on all sides. Remove it with a slotted spoon.

2. Brown the onions and garlic until the onions are a deep golden color.

3. Return the beef to the pot. Add the beef bones, mushrooms, salt substitute, pepper, cayenne, and barley. Add the boiling water, making sure that it covers the ingredients. Cover the pot and reduce the flame to low-medium. Cook for 1½ hours. Add the carrots, beef or chicken stock, wine, and parsley. Stir and cook for 45 minutes more.

Serving: If you have heated the soup in a flameproof tureen or a copper pot, serve it directly from this and ladle it out into heated individual bowls. If you have heated the soup in a regular pot, transfer it either to a heated tureen or individual bowls.

NOTE: It is better to prepare this the day before and refrigerate it overnight. The next day, skim off all the fat and reheat over a very low flame for 40 minutes or until piping hot.

I prefer soups the second and third day, as the flavors seem to blend and settle in after a resting period; not to mention the great boon of a totally defatted soup.

Super Low Calorie Vegetable Soup

Yields approximately 7 quarts

Due to the lack of calories, to the large amount of nutrients, and the delicious taste, this soup is made quite often in our home. It is eaten for snacks, first courses, and makes a wonderful Sunday night supper accompanied by Russian Black Bread* heated with Garlic Herb Butter.*

3 tablespoons olive oil
8 large onions, coarsely chopped
8 cloves garlic, pressed
1½ pounds small mushrooms, thinly sliced lengthwise
3 large green peppers, cut into ½ by 2 inches strips
3 large red peppers, cut into ½ by 2 inches strips
3 16-ounce cans salt-free tomato juice
6 16-ounce cans salt-free tomatoes, cut into quarters
8 carrots, cut into ½-inch slices
1 small green cabbage, shredded
2½ tablespoons seasoned salt substitute (optional)
2½ teaspoons freshly ground black pepper

¾ teaspoon dried thyme
½ teaspoon dried oregano
1 teaspoon dried sweet basil
2 to 3 teaspoons brown sugar (or substitute equivalent)
Juice of 2 to 3 lemons
4 teaspoons salt substitute (optional)
2 bay leaves
⅛ to ¼ teaspoon cayenne (optional)
2 teaspoons salt-free chili powder (optional)
1 teaspoon dried cumin
1½ teaspoons dried dill weed
½ to 1 cup dry sherry (optional)

1. In a very large, heavy skillet, heat the oil over a low-medium flame and sauté the onions, garlic, and mushrooms until the onions are a golden brown.

2. Add the remaining ingredients to a very large, heavy enamel or stainless steel pot. Mix well. Turn the flame to high and bring to a boil. Reduce the flame to low, add the onion mixture, stir well, and cover. Simmer for 1 hour or until all the vegetables are tender but not mushy.

Serving: Transfer the soup to a heated tureen or individual bowls. Offer a warm Crusty Peasant Rye Bread* or a Russian Black Bread* accompanied by sweet butter. This is a filling and satisfying meatless supper.

NOTE 1: Always stir with a wooden or plastic spoon any recipe containing tomatoes. A metal spoon increases the acidity of the tomatoes and often gives a slightly bitter taste.

NOTE 2: The soup will keep in the refrigerator for at least 5 days. It may also be frozen in plastic containers and reheated.

Court Bouillon

Yields approximately 2 quarts

8 large carrots, thinly sliced
2 large onions, thinly sliced
1/2 bunch fresh parsley
3 sprigs fresh thyme or 1/2 teaspoon dried
2 bay leaves
6 peppercorns, slightly crushed
2 whole cloves

2 teaspoons salt substitute (optional)
1 1/2 teaspoons coarsely ground white pepper
Juice of 2 large lemons (optional)
1 quart water
1 quart dry white wine

1. Place all the ingredients in a large, heavy pot. Cover and bring to a boil over a high flame. Reduce the flame to low and simmer for 40 minutes.

2. Strain the bouillon through a fine sieve, cool it, and pour it into half-pint, pint, or quart containers. Place them in your freezer.

Fish Stock

Yields approximately 2½ quarts

6 tablespoons butter
6 carrots, peeled and coarsely
    chopped
4 large onions, coarsely chopped
4½ cups cold water
5 cups dry white wine
½ cup cider vinegar
½ cup lemon juice, freshly
    squeezed
8 peppercorns
1 tablespoon sugar (or substitute
    equivalent)

2 lemons, thinly sliced
1 bunch fresh parsley, coarsely
    chopped
3 tablespoons coarsely chopped
    fresh dill
8 pounds fish heads and bones
2 teaspoons salt substitute (op-
    tional)
1½ teaspoons freshly ground
    white pepper
3 cloves

1. In a very large, heavy saucepan or a fish poacher, melt the butter over a low-medium flame and sauté the carrots and onions for 6 to 7 minutes or until the onions are translucent.

2. Add the water, wine, vinegar, lemon juice, peppercorns, sugar, lemons, parsley, dill, fish heads and bones, salt substitute, pepper, and cloves. Cover.

3. Bring the flame to medium-high for 10 minutes or just until the stock is boiling. Reduce the flame to low and simmer for ½ hour.

4. Strain the stock through cheesecloth or a very fine mesh sieve. Cool and refrigerate or freeze in half-pint, pint, or quart plastic containers.

Veal Stock

Yields approximately 6 quarts

6 tablespoons corn oil
2¹/₂ pounds of the least expen-
    sive but good quality cuts of
    veal you can find, cut into
    small pieces
One large veal knuckle (or 6
    pounds of assorted veal
    bones)
4 large onions, coarsely chopped
6 cloves garlic, peeled and split
8 carrots, coarsely chopped
¹/₂ bunch fresh parsley, coarsely
    chopped

8 leeks, well washed and
    coarsely chopped
2¹/₂ teaspoons freshly ground
    white pepper
¹/₄ teaspoon cayenne (optional)
2 tablespoons salt substitute (op-
    tional)
4 quarts cold water
2¹/₂ cups dry white wine or very
    dry sherry

1. In a large, heavy skillet heat the oil over a medium-high flame and brown the veal and the veal knuckle (or bones). Remove them with a slotted spoon to a heavy 12-quart pot.

2. Sauté the onions, garlic, carrots, parsley, and leeks in the oil until the onions are translucent, stirring very often. Remove with a slotted spoon and add to the veal and bones in the pot.

3. Add the pepper, cayenne, salt substitute, and the water to the pot. Stir thoroughly. Cover, turn the flame to medium-high, and let the stock come to a boil. Reduce the flame to very low, stir in the wine, and cover. Simmer for 4 hours, stirring every hour or so.

4. Strain the stock through a fine sieve into a large glass bowl. Allow it to cool, then cover tightly and refrigerate overnight.

5. Remove the fat that has accumulated on top, and divide the stock into half-pint, pint, or quart plastic containers and freeze.

NOTE: If you want a stronger, more concentrated stock, return the strained, defatted stock to the pot and cook it uncovered over a low flame for 2 hours or until the strong stock is two thirds the volume of the original stock.

Beef Stock

Yields approximately 6 quarts

6 tablespoons corn oil
3½ pounds lean chuck, cut into
   1-inch cubes
4 large onions, coarsely chopped
10 cloves garlic, peeled and split
6 carrots, coarsely chopped
3 green peppers, seeded and
   coarsely chopped (optional)
3 red peppers, seeded and
   coarsely chopped (optional)
1 bunch fresh parsley, coarsely
   chopped

6 leeks, well washed and
   coarsely chopped
6 pounds beef bones
2½ teaspoons freshly ground
   black pepper
¼ to ⅓ teaspoon cayenne
2 tablespoons seasoned salt substitute (optional)
4 large tomatoes, peeled and
   coarsely chopped
4 quarts cold water
1 quart dry red wine

1. In a large, heavy skillet heat the oil over a medium-high flame and brown the meat. Remove the meat to a heavy 12-quart pot.

2. In the same skillet, sauté the onions, garlic, carrots, peppers (green and red), parsley, and leeks in the oil until the onions are translucent, stirring very often. Remove all the vegetables with a slotted spoon to the pot with the beef.

3. Add the beef bones, pepper, cayenne, salt substitute, tomatoes, and water. Stir thoroughly, cover, turn the flame to medium-high, and let the stock come to a boil. Reduce the flame to very low, stir in the wine, and cover. Simmer for 4 hours, stirring every hour or so.

4. Strain the stock through a fine sieve into a large glass bowl. Let it cool. Then cover tightly and refrigerate overnight.

5. The next day, remove the fat that has accumulated on the top and place the stock in half-pint, pint, or quart plastic freezer containers and freeze.

NOTE: If you want a stronger, more concentrated stock, return the strained defatted stock to the pot and cook it uncovered over a low flame for 2 hours or until the strong stock is two thirds the volume of the original stock.

Chicken Stock

Yields approximately 8 quarts of
stock and 2 cooked chickens

If I had to choose the most important stock to always have in the freezer, chicken stock would win hands down. In addition, the chicken from this recipe can be used for any other recipes calling for cooked (or boiled) chicken.

2 chickens, 4 to 4½ pounds,
    with all giblets except the
    liver (which makes the
    stock slightly bitter)
8 chicken necks, skinned
8 chicken wings (optional)
15 carrots, scraped and cut into
    2-inch pieces
4 large Bermuda onions, peeled
    and cut into eighths
1 small bunch fresh parsley
12 leeks, cut into 3-inch slices

4 to 6 cloves garlic, split
3 large red sweet peppers,
    seeded and quartered (op-
    tional)
3 sprigs fresh dill
⅛ teaspoon cayenne (optional)
2½ teaspoons freshly ground
    white pepper
2½ tablespoons seasoned salt
    substitute (optional)
8 quarts water

1. Put all the ingredients in a large, heavy stock pot, cover and bring to a boil over a medium flame.

2. Turn it to low and simmer for 2 to 2½ hours or until the chicken and vegetables are tender.

3. Remove the chicken and reserve (see Note 2).

4. Strain the stock through a fine sieve and discard the vegetables.

5. Refrigerate the stock overnight and the next day skim off all the fat.

6. The stock may then be poured into half-pint, pint, or quart plastic freezer containers and frozen.

NOTE 1: If you want a stronger, more concentrated stock, return the strained, defatted stock to the pot and cook uncovered over a low flame for 2 hours or until the strong stock is two thirds the volume of the original stock.

NOTE 2: As stated in the beginning of the recipe, the chicken may be used for any recipe calling for cooked or boiled chicken. The chicken may also be served hot with Fresh Horseradish* as an accompaniment or cold with a choice of sauces such as Cranberry Orange Relish,* Curry Mayonnaise,* or Chili Garlic Almond Sauce.*

Vegetable Stock

Yields approximately 2 quarts

4 tablespoons sweet butter
4 large onions, sliced paper thin
8 leeks, cut into 1-inch pieces
8 cloves garlic, finely chopped
2 large green peppers, seeded and cut into chunks
2 large red peppers, seeded and cut into chunks
8 carrots, cut into 1-inch pieces
1 pound mushrooms, thinly sliced lengthwise
3 large ripe tomatoes, peeled, seeded, and coarsely chopped
1 large sweet potato, peeled and cut into eighths

1 bunch fresh parsley
3 sprigs fresh dill
3 tablespoons chopped fresh chives
1½ tablespoons seasoned salt substitute (optional)
⅛ to ¼ teaspoon cayenne (optional)
1½ teaspoons freshly ground black pepper
1 quart water
1 quart dry white wine
¼ cup brandy

1. In a very large, heavy pot, melt the butter over a medium flame. Add the onions, leeks, and garlic, sauté, stirring often, until the onions are a light golden color.

2. Add all the other ingredients to the pot, turn the flame to high, and bring the liquids to a boil. Turn the flame to low, cover, and simmer for 3½ hours.

3. Strain the stock through a very fine sieve into a large bowl.

4. Cool the stock (I do not remove the minuscule layer of fat). Ladle it into plastic half-pint, pint, or quart freezer containers. Cover tightly and refrigerate for 3 to 4 hours, then transfer the containers to the freezer.

NOTE: If you want a stronger, more concentrated stock, return the strained stock to the pot and cook it uncovered over a low flame for 2 hours, or until the strong stock is two thirds the volume of the original stock.

A METHOD TO CLARIFY STOCK

The reason this is entitled "A" method rather than "The" method is that there must be as many methods for clarifying stock as there are cooks. Though I prefer this one, it is still just "A" method to clarify stock.

1. The cold stock must have been strained and all the fat removed.

2. Use 2 egg whites and 2 eggshells (crushed) for every 5 to 6 cups of stock you want to clarify.

3. Bring the cold stock to a boil in a heavy saucepan over a medium flame.

4. Using an electric mixer on high speed, or a wire whisk, beat the egg whites until they are frothy but not stiff.

5. Stirring the boiling stock constantly, add the egg whites and crushed shells. Continue stirring until the stock comes to a rolling boil. Remove the saucepan from the flame.

6. Line a fine sieve with triple layers of cheesecloth and pour the stock through that into a bowl.

7. Your stock is now clarified, no longer cloudy, and completely clear. Redundant? Ah yes . . . but true!

SALADS
One of the Chorus or the Star

ERDOES

Salads

For versatility, excitement, and in many cases economy, salads are the answer. Leftovers become enticing new dishes in such salads as Chicken Salad Chinoise* and Molded Avocado and Chicken Salad.* Both would make marvelous luncheon dishes, Sunday brunches, or suppers during the long, hot summer.

The array of colors and textures that one can achieve in creating salads can result in the most artistic visual part of the meal. As this chapter will illustrate, do not limit yourself to the thought that salad is the ubiquitous piece of wilted iceberg lettuce and a slice of soggy tomato that often accompany a meal simply because it is expected. Rather, think of salads as sparking up the meal and becoming one of the highlights. For example, if you're having a simple dinner in which the main course is broiled chicken, think of what the texture, color, and taste of Mideastern Orange and Banana Fruit Salad* or a Pineapple Cranberry Mold* would achieve as an accompaniment. For the main course at a luncheon, create a Tuna and Vegetable Aspic* or a Molded Egg Salad with Tomatoes and Avocados.* How about a Tomato and Mozzarella Salad* for dinner during August, when home-grown tomatoes are at their peak, as is the temperature? Another of our favorite summer suppers is a Salade Niçoise Deluxe.* If you like tuna and a cool kitchen, why not try it, preceded perhaps by a bowl of Gazpacho* or Vichyssoise* and followed by Bittersweet Chocolate Mousse* and fresh strawberries. Have you ever been in the mood for a cold vegetarian dinner? Try the French Vegetable Salad in Tomato Flowers* or the Bulgur Wheat Salad* served with the marinated Green Bean and Onion Salad.*

Are you giving an informal brunch or supper? Try the "make-it-yourself salad bar," accompanied by a marvelous hot or cold soup served in oversized mugs, and a selection of warm home-baked breads, with crocks of sweet butter or Garlic Herb Butter.* For instance, surround a huge bowl of crisp mixed greens such as watercress, Boston lettuce, Bibb lettuce, romaine lettuce, endive, arugula, and curly red lettuce with different and interesting containers filled with slivered Poached Chicken Breasts,* flaked salt-free tuna, thin strips or cubes of salt-free cheeses, Garlic Croutons,* green onions (scallions) sliced into paper-thin rings, tiny mushrooms, fresh orange sections, an assortment of salt-free walnuts, pecans, or almonds, grated carrots, shredded green and red cabbage,

Steamed Green Beans,* Asparagus al Dente,* sliced avocado, finely minced hard-cooked eggs, and cooked, cubed cold potatoes. Offer such salad dressings as Mustard Vinaigrette,* Mideastern Yogurt Dill Sauce,* and Russian Dressing* in low vases, wide-lipped decanters, or bowls. Your salad bar party is moderately inexpensive, superb for a servantless home, delicious to the taste buds, exciting to the eye, and super for a large crowd, when cold brunches and suppers are the easiest and coolest way to entertain.

I hope this chapter will give you new ideas for exotic and unusual salads to add to your own list and to start you on the road to creating many others.

The Mixed Green Salad

The "mixed green salad" is the most misused and abused expression in food terminology. In many homes and restaurants it generally means iceberg lettuce that is either slightly rusted or wilted, with perhaps the addition of a soft slice of tasteless cucumber. On occasion you are served the above, but with the glorious addition of a pale pink tomato wedge (with the taste of a semi-raw potato) and perhaps even an onion ring. Of course, you are offered a variety of gelatinous-looking dressings, which we wouldn't eat even if we could. So here and now we denounce this shame, and in our glorious reformation we present the concept for a proper and superb "mixed green salad."

1. *What to buy:*

Boston lettuce	Watercress
Bibb lettuce	Escarole
Romaine lettuce	Chicory
Curly red lettuce	

2. *How to wash, dry, and store:*

Many cooks will say, "Absolutely do not wash your salad greens until you are ready to use them." That's a wonderful idea if you have a salad chef in your home. But I find it impractical and even nerve-racking. Can you imagine cooking dinner for six and then washing, thoroughly drying, and tearing your greens at the last moment? What a relaxed evening that would be! Since I assume that you do not have a staff in your kitchen, this is the next best way to prepare your greens.

Washing: Fill your kitchen sink halfway with very cold water. Separate the lettuce leaves completely from the core and place them in the water. Let them soak for 5 minutes, then run cold water over each leaf.

Drying: Place the leaves on a rack (or in a huge colander) to drain. Place a double thickness of paper towels on a clean flat surface. Place as many lettuce leaves on the towels as they will hold (but no more than 2 layers) and tightly roll them up (jelly-roll fashion). The lettuce will still be slightly damp.

Storing: Transfer the leaves to a single-ply paper towel and roll it up. The leaves should be completely covered. Place them in a plastic bag, seal it, and put it in the vegetable crisper in your refrigerator. The leaves will stay wonderfully crisp and delicious for 2 days.

Serving: Tear the leaves into bite-size pieces (I generally remove most of the stems from the watercress). Place them in a bowl of glass, crystal, ceramic, pottery, or china large enough to hold the salad comfortably with plenty of room to allow tossing. The moment you want to eat your salad is the moment you add your dressing. One word of caution, do not drown it! Use Basic Vinaigrette,* Mustard Vinaigrette,* or Herb Vinaigrette* Dressing. Toss very well and proudly serve one of the best mixed green salads your guests will ever eat.

Beefsteak Tomato and Onion Salad

Serves 6

This is divine all year, but especially in the summer when home-grown garden tomatoes are at the peak. Luckily, we have very good friends who share their crop with us.

**2 large bunches watercress,
   stems removed
6 large beefsteak tomatoes,
   cored and sliced ¼ inch
   thick**

**2 red onions, sliced paper thin
½ to ¾ cups Herb Vinaigrette
   Dressing***

1. Place the watercress on a large round crystal or china platter and arrange the tomatoes and onions in a pinwheel fashion on top of the watercress.

Serving: When you are ready to eat the salad, spoon the dressing over it. Serve each portion on a crystal, china, or ceramic plate.

Watercress and Endive Salad

Serves 12

You've heard the expression "worth its weight in gold"? Well, "they" must have coined that phrase when "they" priced Belgian endives.

6 Belgian endives, large and firm

4 large bunches watercress, stems removed

1¹/₄ cups Basic Vinaigrette Dressing* or Mustard Vinaigrette*

1. Cut the stems off the endives, then cut them in half width-wise and separate the leaves.
2. Arrange them in a large salad bowl and add the watercress.

Serving: The moment you want to eat your salad is the moment you add enough dressing to moisten the salad well but not drown it. Toss thoroughly and serve on crystal or china plates large enough to hold the salad comfortably.

NOTE: This salad is also superb when arugula is substituted for the watercress. In fact, many of our friends prefer it that way.

Watercress and Orange Salad

Serves 8

4 large bunches watercress, stems removed

3 very small red onions, sliced into paper thin rounds separated into rings

5 navel oranges, skinned and sectioned (see Note)

³/₄ cup Mustard Vinaigrette Dressing*

3 tablespoons orange juice, freshly squeezed (optional)

1. Place the watercress, onion rings, and orange sections in a large glass or ceramic bowl.

Serving: When you are ready to eat the salad, mix the dressing with the orange juice and pour the dressing over the salad. Toss thoroughly and serve at once on crystal, china, or pottery plates.

NOTE: *To section oranges:*
    1. Over a bowl (in order to catch the juices) peel the oranges, including the white membrane, with a very sharp small paring knife.
    2. Cut down along the membranes toward the center of the orange and gently lift out the sections.

Raw Mushroom Salad

Serves 4 as a first course or 6 as a salad accompanying a main course

1½ pounds very small mushrooms (tips of stems removed), sliced very thinly lengthwise
½ cup Basic Vinaigrette* or Mustard Vinaigrette*
4 Boston lettuce leaves (or 6 if serving 6)

4 tablespoons finely chopped fresh chives

GARNISH: 2 tablespoons finely chopped fresh parsley

    1. Place the mushrooms in a plastic bag. Pour the dressing over them. Seal the bag tightly and refrigerate for at least 1 hour, rotating the bag 2 or 3 times during the marinating.

Serving: Place the leaves of Boston lettuce in a white ceramic basket. Transfer the mushrooms and marinade to a large crystal bowl, sprinkle with the chives, and toss well. Garnish the mushrooms with the parsley. At the table, using silver or wooden tongs, place a large leaf of Boston lettuce on each salad plate and spoon some of the marinated mushroom salad into it. Serve this delicious and charmingly displayed salad to each of your guests.

Marinated Cabbage and Carrot Salad

Serves 6 to 8

The dressing is included with this recipe, as it breaks all the expected rules on the ratio of vinegar to oil. In all honesty, I have used it only for this salad.

DRESSING:
1/2 cup peanut oil
1/4 cup fresh lemon juice
1/2 cup apple cider vinegar
4 tablespoons fresh orange juice
3 cloves garlic, pressed (optional)
3 1/2 tablespoons sugar (or substitute equivalent)
2/3 teaspoon freshly ground black pepper
2 teaspoons seasoned salt substitute (optional)

2 teaspoons onion powder (optional)
1 large head red cabbage, finely shredded
8 carrots, finely grated
2 very small red onions, sliced into paper thin rounds separated into rings (optional)
1/2 cup coarsely chopped walnuts (optional)

1. Place all the dressing ingredients in a large glass jar. Cover tightly and shake vigorously so that the ingredients blend thoroughly.

2. Put the cabbage, carrots and onions in a large plastic bag. Pour the dressing into it. Seal it tightly. Refrigerate for at least 3 hours, rotating the bag 3 or 4 times during the marinating.

Serving: Transfer the salad and dressing to a large crystal or ceramic bowl. Add the walnuts. It looks especially pretty when placed in a green cabbage leaf ceramic bowl and served on matching plates.

Tomato Aspic

Serves 12

8 cups salt-free tomato juice
1¼ cups finely minced Spanish
  onion
6 cloves garlic, pressed
¼ cup sugar (or substitute
  equivalent)
¾ cup fresh lemon juice
¼ teaspoon cayenne
¾ to 1¼ teaspoons white pepper, freshly ground
1½ tablespoons seasoned salt
  substitute (optional)

½ to ⅔ cup dry vermouth (optional)
1 cup salt-free tomato juice
5 packages unflavored gelatin
¼ cup finely minced fresh
  chives
¼ cup finely minced fresh
  parsley

GARNISH: Sprigs of fresh
parsley

1. Pour the tomato juice into a heavy saucepan. Stir in the onion, garlic, sugar, lemon juice, cayenne, pepper, salt substitute, and vermouth. Turn the flame to low-medium and cook uncovered for 20 minutes, stirring often with a wooden spoon.

2. While this mixture is cooking, pour the 1 cup of tomato juice into a small bowl and sprinkle on the gelatin. Let it stand at room temperature for 10 minutes.

3. Stir the chives, parsley, and gelatin mixture into the tomato juice mixture. Turn the flame to low and simmer for 10 minutes (see Note 1).

4. Remove the mixture from the flame and cool it for 15 minutes.

5. Pour the mixture into a lightly oiled 3-quart mold. Refrigerate for at least 8 hours.

Serving: Run a sharp knife around the inside edges of the ring mold. Put it in 1½ inches of warm water in the kitchen sink for 20 seconds, jiggling the mold while it is in the water. Place an inverted silver, crystal, or china platter on top of the mold and quickly invert both mold and platter. Garnish with sprigs of parsley and offer Herb Mayonnaise* or Yogurt Dill Sauce.*

NOTE 1: If you want a clear aspic, strain the mixture through a fine sieve (pressing all of the liquid out) after completing Step 3.

NOTE 2: If you like a very spicy aspic, to Step 1 add 1 tablespoon hot salt-free chili powder and 1 teaspoon Spanish paprika, increase the cayenne to ⅓ teaspoon.

Tuna and Vegetable Aspic

Serves 6 to 8

Refreshing for luncheon or as a Sunday night supper during the hot summer.

3 7-ounce cans salt-free solid
    white meat tuna (packed in
    water), flaked
4 carrots, finely grated
1 onion, finely minced
3 green onions (scallions), sliced
    into paper-thin rings
2 tablespoons finely minced
    fresh dill
1 medium green pepper, seeded
    and finely chopped
1 medium red pepper, seeded
    and finely chopped
2 cups finely shredded red cabbage

3/4 cup fresh lemon juice
3 1/4 cups Court Bouillon,* Clarified*
4 packages unflavored gelatin
1 tablespoon seasoned salt substitute (optional)
2/3 teaspoon freshly ground white pepper
1/4 teaspoon cayenne

GARNISH:
2 bunches watercress, stems removed
6 hard-cooked eggs, cut into fourths

1. Place the tuna, carrots, onion, green onions, dill, green and red peppers and red cabbage in a mixing bowl and toss lightly, taking care not to mash the tuna. Refrigerate.

2. Place the lemon juice and clarified court bouillon in a heavy saucepan. Sprinkle the gelatin on top and let it stand at room temperature for 10 minutes. Place the saucepan over a low flame and heat the mixture until the gelatin is thoroughly dissolved (approximately 7 minutes). Remove it from the flame and let it cool for 10 minutes.

3. Stir in the salt substitute, pepper, and cayenne, mix well. Pour the gelatin into a large mixing bowl and refrigerate for 15 minutes or until it begins to thicken.

4. When it is slightly thickened, add the fish mixture and gently blend all the ingredients together.

5. Rinse out a 3-quart ring mold in ice water, wipe dry, and lightly grease with corn oil.

6. Spoon the mixture into the mold and refrigerate for at least 8 hours.

Serving: Run a sharp knife around the inside edges of the ring mold. Put it into 1 1/2 inches of warm water in the kitchen sink for 20 seconds, jiggling the mold while it is in the water. Place an inverted large round silver or ceramic tray on top of the mold and quickly invert both mold and platter.

Place the watercress around the aspic, with the quartered eggs arranged on top of it. Mix 1½ cups of Mayonnaise* with ¼ cup of finely minced fresh chives, and spoon it into a bowl small enough to fit into the center of the aspic.

Raw Vegetables in Aspic

Serves 8 to 12 for a luncheon

4 cups Chicken Stock,* Clarified*

4 packages unflavored gelatin

5 tablespoons sugar (or substitute equivalent)

4 tablespoons tarragon vinegar

2 tablespoons dry vermouth

2 tablespoons fresh lemon juice

1½ tablespoons seasoned salt substitute (optional)

1 teaspoon freshly ground black pepper

¼ teaspoon cayenne

1½ cups finely shredded red cabbage

1½ cups finely shredded green cabbage

4 green onions (scallions), cut into paper-thin rings

¼ cup finely minced fresh chives

¼ cup finely minced fresh parsley

1 cup finely chopped red pepper

1 cup finely chopped green pepper

2 cups grated carrots

GARNISH:

1 large bunch watercress, stems removed

12 cherry tomatoes, cut in half

1. Place the clarified chicken stock in a small saucepan. Sprinkle the gelatin and sugar on top of it. Let it stand at room temperature for 10 minutes.

2. Put the saucepan over a low flame and heat the mixture until the gelatin is completely dissolved (approximately 7 minutes). Remove it from the flame and stir in the vinegar, vermouth, lemon juice, salt substitute, pepper, and cayenne. Pour the mixture into a large glass bowl and refrigerate for about 15 minutes or until the gelatin mixture starts to thicken slightly.

3. Remove it from the refrigerator and add the red and green cabbage, green onions, chives, parsley, red and green peppers, and carrots. Stir thoroughly.

4. Spoon the mixture into a lightly oiled very cold 3-quart mold. Refrigerate for at least 8 hours.

Serving: Run a sharp knife around the inside edges of the ring mold. Put it into 1½ inches of warm water in the kitchen sink for 20 seconds, jiggling the mold while it is in the water. Place an inverted large ceramic, crystal, or silver platter on top of the mold and quickly invert both mold and platter. Garnish with the watercress and nestle the cherry tomatoes on top of the watercress. Offer Curry Mayonnaise* or Mideastern Yogurt Sauce* with this.

Molded Egg Salad with Tomatoes and Avocados

Serves 8 to 10 as a luncheon salad

2 cups cold Chicken Stock,* Clarified*

3 packages unflavored gelatin

16 hard-cooked eggs, finely minced

3 green onions (scallions), cut into paper-thin rings

1 large red pepper, finely chopped (optional)

⅓ cup finely minced fresh chives

1 cup Mayonnaise*

4 cloves garlic, pressed (optional)

1½ tablespoons salt substitute (optional)

1 teaspoon freshly ground white pepper

GARNISH:

1½ cups coarsely chopped watercress, stems removed

4 large tomatoes, cut into ¼-inch slices

2 avocados, cut lengthwise into thin slices and sprinkled with ¼ cup fresh lemon juice

½ cup Basic Vinaigrette Dressing* mixed with 4 tablespoons olive oil

¼ cup finely minced fresh chives

1. Place the clarified chicken stock in a heavy saucepan and sprinkle the gelatin on top. Let it stand at room temperature for 10 minutes. Place the saucepan over a very low flame and cook for 7 minutes or until the gelatin is completely dissolved. Remove it from the flame, transfer it to a bowl, and refrigerate for at least 15 minutes or until it begins to thicken slightly.

2. In a large bowl, mix the eggs, green onions, red pepper, chives, mayonnaise, garlic, salt substitute, and white pepper.

3. Add the gelatin to this mixture and thoroughly blend all the ingredients.

4. Lightly oil a very cold 3-quart mold and spoon the mixture into it. Refrigerate for at least 8 hours.

Serving: Run a sharp knife around the inside edges of the ring mold. Put it into 1½ inches of warm water in the kitchen sink for 20 seconds, jiggling the mold while it is in the water. Place an inverted large ceramic, crystal, or silver platter on top of the mold and quickly invert both mold and platter. Place the watercress around the molded salad, place the tomatoes and avocados in a pinwheel fashion on top of the watercress. Spoon the dressing mixed with the olive oil over the tomatoes and avocados. Garnish with the chives.

Pineapple Cranberry Mold

Serves 12 to 16

Thanksgiving wouldn't be Thanksgiving without this molded salad.

1 cup water
½ cup dry red wine
3 tablespoons lemon juice
1 cup orange juice
1 cup unsweetened pineapple
   juice
¾ cup sugar (or equivalent)
4 cups raw cranberries, well
   washed and picked over

Juice from 2 16-ounce cans unsweetened crushed pineapple
4 envelopes unflavored gelatin
Drained unsweetened crushed pineapple (from the 2 16-ounce cans)

GARNISH: Sprigs of watercress

1. In a large, heavy saucepan, bring the water, wine, lemon juice, orange juice, pineapple juice, and sugar to a boil over a medium flame.
2. Add the cranberries and stir well. Cook until the cranberry skins pop. Stir often.
3. Cover the cranberry mixture, reduce the flame to low, and simmer for 10 minutes.
4. In the meantime, place the pineapple juice in the top of a double boiler, add the gelatin, and heat over a low flame until the gelatin is completely dissolved. Stir often.
5. Add this mixture to the cranberry mixture and stir thoroughly.
6. Remove from the flame.
7. Add the crushed pineapple and stir thoroughly.
8. Pour the mixture into a lightly oiled 3-quart mold.
9. Refrigerate for at least 10 hours.

Serving: Run a sharp knife around the inside edge of the ring mold. Put it into 1½ inches of hot water in the kitchen sink for eight seconds, jiggling the mold while it is in the water. Place an inverted large silver, glass, or ceramic tray on top of the mold and quickly invert both the mold and platter. Garnish with watercress.

Molded Avocado and Chicken Salad

Serves 8 to 12 for a luncheon

1½ cups Chicken Stock,* Clarified*

3 envelopes unflavored gelatin

1½ tablespoons sugar (or substitute equivalent)

1 tablespoon salt substitute (optional)

¼ teaspoon cayenne

1 teaspoon freshly ground white pepper

2 large ripe avocados, cut into eighths and soaked in ½ cup fresh lemon juice

4 green onions (scallions), cut into paper-thin rings

¾ teaspoon finely grated lemon rind

⅔ cup coarsely chopped pecans

1½ cups Mayonnaise*

4 cups diced Boiled Chicken*

2½ tablespoons hot curry powder

⅛ cup fresh lemon juice

¾ cup Plain Yogurt*

4 cloves garlic, pressed

⅛ cup minced fresh dill

⅛ cup minced fresh parsley

¼ cup minced fresh chives

⅛ to ¼ teaspoon cayenne

1¼ cups heavy cream

GARNISH:
1 large bunch watercress, coarsely chopped, stems removed

Fresh pineapple, sliced

1. Pour the clarified chicken stock into a small, heavy saucepan and sprinkle on the gelatin. Let it stand for 10 minutes at room temperature. Place the saucepan over a low flame and cook for approximately 7 minutes or until the gelatin is thoroughly dissolved.

2. Add the sugar, salt substitute, cayenne, and white pepper. Thoroughly blend all the ingredients and remove from the flame. Cool for 5 minutes.

3. Purée the avocados and lemon juice in a food processor. Place the purée in a large glass mixing bowl.

4. Add the green onions, lemon rind, and cooled gelatin mixture, blend all the ingredients thoroughly.

5. Refrigerate the mixture just until the mixture begins to jell. Stir every 8 minutes or so while it is in the refrigerator.

6. Fold the pecans into the slightly jelled mixture, then fold in the mayonnaise and diced chicken.

7. In a medium-size glass bowl, add the curry powder to the lemon juice. Mix thoroughly, then add the yogurt, garlic, dill, parsley, chives, and cayenne. Blend thoroughly.

8. Fold this mixture into the avocado mixture.

9. Using an electric mixer on high speed, whip the heavy cream until it forms soft peaks and fold it into the avocado-chicken mixture.

10. Spoon this into a lightly oiled 3½-quart mold and refrigerate for at least 8 hours or until the mixture is very cold and firm.

Serving: Run a sharp knife around the inside edges of the ring mold. Put it into 1½ inches of warm water in the kitchen sink for 20 seconds, jiggling the mold while it is in the water. Place an inverted large silver, crystal, or ceramic tray on top of the mold and quickly invert both mold and platter. Place the watercress around the molded salad. Lay the sliced pineapple on top of the watercress.

Cold Cooked Broccoli Salad

Serves 8 to 12

I learned how to make this recipe from Renato, the proprietor of one of Capri's better restaurants.

8 cups cold Steamed Broccoli Flowerets*	⅛ teaspoon cayenne
1 cup olive oil	¾ teaspoon freshly ground black pepper
¼ cup fresh lemon juice	1 tablespoon seasoned salt substitute (optional)
4 cloves garlic, pressed	

1. Place the broccoli in a large bowl.

2. Combine the remaining ingredients in a large cruet, put the stopper in tightly, and shake vigorously. Pour this dressing over the broccoli and toss thoroughly.

Serving: Transfer the salad to individual crystal, china, or pottery plates and serve; offering an added twist or two from a pepper mill.

Potato Salad

Serves 10 to 16

One of our all-time favorites, which we always serve as part of our Labor Day picnic.

10 large potatoes, boiled, cooled, and diced

4 hard-cooked eggs, very finely chopped

3 green onions (scallions), cut into paper-thin rings

2 green peppers, chopped medium fine (optional)

6 cloves garlic, pressed

1/4 teaspoon cayenne

1 1/2 tablespoons salt substitute (optional)

3/4 teaspoon freshly ground white pepper

1/3 cup finely minced fresh chives

2 to 2 1/2 cups Mayonnaise*

GARNISH:

2 teaspoons Spanish paprika

1/3 cup finely minced parsley

1. Place the potatoes in a large glass bowl and toss well with the eggs, green onions, green peppers, and garlic.

2. In a small bowl, mix the cayenne, salt substitute, pepper, chives, and mayonnaise.

3. Fold this mixture into the potato mixture. Cover tightly and refrigerate for at least 8 hours.

Serving: Toss the salad well and spoon it into a serving dish. Sprinkle the center with paprika. Sprinkle the parsley around the edge of the salad.

Bulgur Wheat Salad
(Tabbouleh)

Serves 12

Mideastern in origin, this is a marvelous accompaniment to a summer buffet table when fresh mint is in season. It is an interesting variation on the salad theme.

3 cups bulgur wheat (soaked for 4 hours in 3 quarts water)

1 bunch watercress, finely chopped, stems removed

1 bunch fresh parsley, finely chopped

2 large green peppers, seeded and coarsely chopped

2 large red peppers, seeded and coarsely chopped

10 green onions (scallions), sliced into paper-thin rings

5 cloves garlic, crushed

½ cup finely chopped fresh mint

Juice of 4 lemons

Juice of 4 limes

½ cup olive oil

½ cup corn oil

2 tablespoons seasoned salt substitute (optional)

¼ teaspoon cayenne

2 teaspoons freshly ground black pepper

GARNISH: 2 large, firm, ripe tomatoes, cored and coarsely chopped

1. Drain the wheat in a strainer. Then place it between two thicknesses of cheesecloth and tightly twist until all the water is squeezed out.

2. Place the wheat in a large bowl, add the balance of ingredients, and mix thoroughly. Refrigerate for at least 8 hours to allow the flavors to blend, tossing the salad 3 to 4 times during the day.

Serving: Transfer the salad into a brightly colored ceramic bowl and either toss it lightly with the tomatoes or use them as garnish.

NOTE: The bulgur wheat is also known as burghul wheat and on occasion it is called cracked wheat. *Tabbouleh* is the Lebanese name for this salad.

Marinated Green Bean and Onion Salad

Serves 8 to 12

A very simple salad, and one of our favorites.

3 pounds Steamed Green Beans*
3 red onions, sliced paper thin
    and separated into rings
1 cup olive oil
$\frac{1}{8}$ cup fresh lemon juice
$\frac{1}{8}$ cup wine vinegar
6 cloves garlic, pressed
$1\frac{1}{2}$ teaspoons dry mustard (optional)
$\frac{1}{8}$ teaspoon cayenne
2 teaspoons seasoned salt substitute (optional)

1 teaspoon freshly ground black pepper
2 tablespoons finely chopped fresh dill (optional)
2 tablespoons finely chopped fresh parsley

GARNISH: $\frac{1}{4}$ cup finely chopped fresh mint (optional)

1. Place the beans and onions in a plastic bag.
2. Thoroughly blend the oil, lemon juice, vinegar, garlic, mustard, cayenne, salt substitute, pepper, dill, and parsley, pour into the bag with the beans and onions. Seal tightly.
3. Rotate the bag 1 or 2 times and place it in the refrigerator.
4. Refrigerate for at least 4 hours, rotating the bag 4 or 5 times during the marinating period.

Serving: Place the beans, onions, and marinade in a chilled glass bowl. Garnish with the fresh mint.

NOTE: Sometimes I add 3 large potatoes, boiled, cooled, and cubed, to the salad and increase the marinade by half.

Vegetable Salad with a Cottage Cheese Sauce

Serves 6 for a luncheon or 8 as a first course

6 beefsteak tomatoes, cut into ¼-inch wedges

2 large green peppers, seeded and cut into ¼-inch strips

4 kirby cucumbers, scrubbed and cut into ¼-inch rounds

2 small red onions, cut into paper-thin rings

1½ cups salt-free cottage cheese

8 tablespoons olive oil

3½ tablespoons fresh lemon juice

4 cloves garlic, pressed

⅛ to ¼ teaspoon cayenne

4 teaspoons finely chopped fresh dill (optional)

3 tablespoons finely chopped fresh chives

2 teaspoons finely chopped fresh basil

1 tablespoon seasoned salt substitute (optional)

¾ teaspoon freshly ground white pepper

GARNISH: ½ cup finely minced parsley

1. Place the tomatoes, green peppers, cucumbers, and onions in a large bowl.

2. Using a wire whisk, beat together the cottage cheese, olive oil, lemon juice, garlic, cayenne, dill, chives, basil, salt substitute, and pepper until thoroughly mixed but the cheese is still slightly lumpy.

3. Pour over the vegetables, toss well, and cover tightly. Refrigerate for at least 1 hour.

Serving: Toss the salad again and transfer it to a crystal or pottery bowl. Garnish with the parsley.

Tomato and Mozzarella Salad

Serves 10 as a salad and 4 as a
main course in the hot summer

From Naples, with love.

6 ripe but firm large beefsteak
  tomatoes
1½ pounds fresh salt-free mozzarella
⅔ cup olive oil
2 teaspoons seasoned salt substitute (optional)

⅔ teaspoon freshly ground
  black pepper
4 tablespoons finely minced
  fresh chives
3 tablespoons finely minced
  fresh basil

1. Slice the tomatoes into ½-inch rounds and arrange in one layer on a
large serving dish.

2. Slice the mozzarella thinly and arrange it over the tomatoes.

3. Spoon the oil over the cheese and sprinkle with the salt substitute
and pepper.

4. Mix the chives and basil and sprinkle over the salad.

5. Let the salad stand for 20 to 30 minutes at room temperature before
serving.

Serving: This is one of our favorite first courses. In the summer and on
some Sunday evenings I have offered it with warm Russian Black Bread*
or Crusty Peasant Rye Bread* accompanied by a crock of sweet butter as
a light supper. We especially enjoy this in August, when home-grown
tomatoes are at their peak in both flavor and abundance.

French Vegetable Salad in Tomato Flowers

Serves 8

Pretty, delicious, and caloric — naturally.

4 8-ounce cans salt-free carrots
   and peas, drained
3 green onions (scallions), cut
   into paper-thin rings (optional)
6 cloves garlic, pressed
¼ cup finely minced fresh
   parsley
¼ cup finely minced fresh
   chives
6 large potatoes, boiled, cooled,
   and cubed

⅛ to ¼ teaspoon cayenne
½ teaspoon freshly ground
   white pepper
1 tablespoon seasoned salt substitute (optional)
2 cups Mayonnaise*
8 firm, ripe large tomatoes

GARNISH:
2 tablespoons finely minced
   fresh dill (optional)
8 large leaves of Boston lettuce

1. Toss the carrots, peas, green onions, garlic, parsley, chives, and potatoes in a large glass bowl.

2. Mix the cayenne, pepper, and salt substitute with the Mayonnaise.*

3. Fold this mixture into the vegetables, cover tightly, and refrigerate
for at least 3 hours.

4. Cut the core out of each tomato. Starting at the top, (where the core
was) cut the tomato into 8 wedges, stopping ½ inch from the bottom.
Gently press the wedges outward to form the petals of an open flower.

5. Fill and mound the opening with the vegetable mixture and sprinkle
with the dill.

Serving: Arrange large leaves of a Boston lettuce on 8 faience salad plates
and place the stuffed tomato flowers on top of them.

Salade Niçoise Deluxe

Serves 8 to 10 for a deluxe cold
supper

This salad needs preparation in advance; but once you master it, it is easy
to prepare, quite grand in presentation, and equally grand in taste. Our
friends think it is well worth the effort. I hope yours will too.

1½ to 2 pounds Steamed Green
　　Beans,* chilled
1 large red onion, sliced into
　　paper-thin rings
3 green onions (scallions), sliced
　　into paper-thin rings
6 medium potatoes, boiled,
　　cooled, and cubed
6 carrots, grated
2 cups coarsely chopped red
　　cabbage (optional)
⅓ cup apple cider vinegar
1¼ cups olive oil
2 tablespoons dry vermouth
4 tablespoons chopped fresh
　　chives
3 tablespoons chopped fresh
　　parsley
1 teaspoon dried dill, or 1¼ ta-
　　blespoons finely minced
　　fresh dill
½ teaspoon dried tarragon
⅛ teaspoon cayenne
1 teaspoon dry mustard
1 tablespoon seasoned salt sub-
　　stitute (optional)
½ teaspoon freshly ground
　　black pepper

6 7-ounce cans salt-free tuna,
　　packed in water, drained
　　and very coarsely flaked
Juice of 2 large lemons
¾ to 1 cup olive oil
½ teaspoon freshly ground
　　white pepper
2 teaspoons salt substitute (op-
　　tional)
⅔ teaspoon dried dill, or 1 ta-
　　blespoon finely minced fresh
　　dill
2 tablespoons dry vermouth (op-
　　tional)
1 head romaine lettuce (sepa-
　　rated into leaves)
1 large bunch watercress, finely
　　chopped (stems removed)
5 large tomatoes, cored and cut
　　into eighths in wedges
8 hard-cooked eggs, cooled and
　　cut into quarters
1 jar pimientos, cut into thin
　　strips
¼ cup finely chopped fresh
　　parsley
¼ cup finely chopped fresh
　　chives

1. In a very large glass or ceramic bowl, lightly toss the string beans, red onion, green onions, potatoes, carrots, and cabbage.

2. Using a food processor with the plastic blade, or a blender, pour in the vinegar, olive oil, vermouth, chives, parsley, dill, tarragon, cayenne, dry mustard, salt substitute, and black pepper. Blend thoroughly.

3. Toss the vegetables lightly with the dressing. Tightly cover with plastic wrap and refrigerate for at least 3 hours.

4. Put the tuna in a medium-size glass bowl.

5. Using a food processor with the plastic blade, or a blender, pour in the lemon juice, olive oil, white pepper, salt substitute, dill, and vermouth. Blend thoroughly.

6. Lightly toss the tuna with the dressing, taking care not to mash the tuna. Tightly cover with plastic wrap and refrigerate for at least 1 hour.

Serving: Line a very large bowl with the romaine lettuce leaves. Add the watercress to the potato-green bean mixture and toss well. Arrange this on the leaves. Lightly toss the tuna and spoon this on top of the potato-bean mixture. Alternate the tomato wedges and egg quarters around the outer edge of the salad. Cut the pimientos into strips and arrange in a lattice over the tuna. Sprinkle the tomatoes and eggs with the parsley and chives.

Shrimp and Fish Salad Extraordinaire

Serves 6 to 8 for dinner or 12
ladies for lunch

If serving for dinner, offer Mushroom Bisque* to begin. Accompany the
salad with Thin Garlic Herb Toast* and complete your dinner with a
Cold Lemon Soufflé.*

2 cups coarsely chopped Boiled
　　Fresh Shrimp* or Boiled
　　Flash-Frozen Shrimp*
3 cups cold Poached Salmon,
　　Hot or Cold*, very coarsely
　　flaked (or poached halibut,
　　cod, or bass — the best is a
　　combination of all of them)
1/4 cup minced fresh parsley
1/3 cup minced fresh chives
1 small sweet red pepper, finely
　　chopped
1 small green pepper, finely
　　chopped
8 hard-cooked eggs, finely sieved
4 cups boiled, cooled, diced pota-
　　toes
3 green onions (scallions), cut
　　into paper-thin rings

4 cloves garlic, pressed
2 tablespoons minced fresh dill
1 tablespoon salt substitute (op-
　　tional)
1/4 teaspoon cayenne
2 1/2 teaspoons hot salt-free chili
　　powder
1/2 teaspoon freshly ground
　　white pepper
Juice of 1 lemon
1 teaspoon dry mustard
3 to 4 cups Mayonnaise*

GARNISH:
romaine lettuce
4 beefsteak tomatoes, cut in 1/4-
　　inch slices
2 tablespoons chopped fresh
　　chives

1. Lightly toss the shrimp, fish, parsley, chives, red and green peppers,
eggs, potatoes, green onions, garlic, dill, salt substitute, cayenne, chili
powder, and pepper until thoroughly mixed.

2. Mix the lemon juice with the dry mustard until smooth, stir into the
mayonnaise.

3. Add 1 cup of this mixture at a time and toss it lightly into the salad
until all of the mayonnaise is used (see Note). Refrigerate for at least 4
hours.

Serving: Arrange the romaine lettuce leaves on individual plates or on a
large platter. Spoon the salad onto the center of the plate or platter and

mound it. Place the tomatoes around the salad and sprinkle the chives over them.

NOTE: I stress tossing in order not to mash the fish, which mixing in a circular motion tends to do.

Chef's Salad

Serves 4 to 8 for lunch

1 large head romaine lettuce, shredded
1 bunch watercress, broken into small pieces (with stems off)
4 green onions (scallions), sliced into paper-thin rings
1 green pepper, finely diced
1 red pepper, finely diced
2 tablespoons finely chopped fresh parsley
1 clove garlic, split
1¼ pounds salt-free Swiss cheese, cut into strips ¼ inch by 1½ inches

4 large beefsteak tomatoes cut into eighths
4 cups cold Poached Chicken Breasts* cut into ¼ inch by 1½ inches
8 large hard-cooked eggs, cut into quarters
2 tablespoons chopped fresh chives
Paprika

1. Toss the lettuce, watercress, green onions, green and red peppers, and parsley, place in a large bowl.

2. On top of the greens arrange, in pinwheel shape, half of the cheese next to half of the tomatoes, next to half of the chicken, next to half of the eggs, next to the remainder of the cheese, tomatoes, chicken, and eggs.

3. Sprinkle the chicken with the chives and sprinkle the eggs with a touch of paprika.

Serving: Toss this salad at the table with Mustard Vinaigrette Dressing* or, if it is a buffet, let your guests help themselves to the dry salad and their own choice of dressing, such as Basic Vinaigrette,* Mustard Vinaigrette,* Herb Vinaigrette,* Russian,* or Yogurt Dill.*

Rice Salad

Serves a very large crowd at a buffet

1 stick sweet butter
2 cups blanched, sliced or sliv-
    ered almonds
1/2 cup peanut oil (approxi-
    mately)
2 very large Spanish onions,
    minced (about 2 pounds)
10 cloves garlic, minced
2 pounds mushrooms, sliced
    paper-thin lengthwise
10 carrots, grated
1/2 cup finely minced fresh
    parsley
1/2 cup finely minced fresh
    chives
3/4 cup green onions (scallions),
    sliced into paper-thin rings
    (white part only)
6 cups diced Poached Chicken
    Breasts*
1 1/2 cups shelled green peas,
    steamed (optional)
12 hard-cooked eggs, very finely
    minced

2 tablespoons seasoned salt sub-
    stitute (optional)
1/4 to 1/2 teaspoon cayenne
1 teaspoon freshly ground white
    pepper
1 cup peanut oil
3/4 cup corn oil
1/4 cup fresh lemon juice
1/4 cup apple cider vinegar
1 teaspoon freshly ground white
    pepper
2 tablespoons salt substitute (op-
    tional)
10 cups Boiled Rice*

GARNISH:
5 hard-cooked eggs (yolks and
    whites separated and finely
    minced)
1 cup coarsely chopped walnuts
1 cup finely minced fresh
    parsley
20 firm cherry tomatoes, cut in
    half

1. Using a small, heavy skillet, melt the butter over a low flame and lightly brown the almonds. Remove from the flame and set aside.

2. Using a large, heavy skillet, heat the peanut oil over a medium flame and sauté the onions and garlic until the onions are translucent.

3. Add the mushrooms, stir well, and sauté until they are tender and browned. Remove from the flame and set aside.

4. In an enormous bowl or pot, add the carrots, parsley, chives, green onions, chicken, peas, eggs, salt substitute, cayenne, and pepper. Blend thoroughly. Add the almonds and the onion and mushroom mixture and blend thoroughly.

5. In a large bowl, using a wire whisk, blend the peanut oil, corn oil, lemon juice, vinegar, pepper, and salt substitute.

6. Add one third of the rice and one third of the dressing at a time to the mixture and toss until all of the ingredients are thoroughly blended.

7. Cover tightly with plastic wrap and refrigerate overnight.

Serving: Toss the salad very well and spoon it into a very large round glass bowl. Arrange the egg yolks in a small circle in the center of the salad. Around this, form a ring with the egg whites. The next ring is the chopped walnuts, and after that, form a ring of parsley. The final ring will be the cherry tomatoes.

Chicken Salad

Serves 8 as a main course

A super and delicious way to put to good use the boiled chicken that is left over after making Chicken Stock.*

8 cups cubed Boiled Chicken*
1 green pepper, finely diced
3 green onions (scallions), sliced into paper-thin rings (white part only)
3 medium carrots, finely grated
1 cup of blanched, slivered almonds
8 hard-cooked eggs, finely chopped
2½ cups Sauce Aïoli* (approximately)

4 beefsteak tomatoes, cored and cut into thin wedges (or 32 cherry tomatoes cut in half)
2 heads romaine lettuce
4 kirby cucumbers, peeled and cut into rounds with a garnisher or a rippled knife or rippled blade
3 hard-cooked egg yolks, finely sieved
4 tablespoons finely minced fresh parsley

1. Combine all of the ingredients except the *aïoli* in a very large bowl. Add the *aïoli*, ¾ cup at a time, and toss the salad well after each addition. Use more or less sauce depending on whether you like a lightly or heavily dressed salad.

Serving: On 8 plates, arrange the leaves of a romaine to form the petals of a flower. Mound the chicken salad in the center of them and alternately arrange the tomatoes with the cucumber slices around the salad. Sprinkle a little of the egg yolk on top of each mound of chicken salad, and a little of the parsley over the tomatoes and cucumbers.

Gingered Chicken and Fruit Salad

Serves 6 for lunch

If you like ginger, you'll surely enjoy this.

1³/₄ cups Mayonnaise*
2 inches fresh ginger root,
    finely grated
3 cloves garlic, pressed
2 teaspoons salt substitute (op-
    tional)
¹/₂ cup finely minced fresh
    chives
Juice of 1 lemon
³/₄ teaspoon freshly ground
    white pepper
¹/₈ teaspoon cayenne
1¹/₂ tablespoons sugar (or substi-
    tute equivalent)
6 cups cubed Poached Chicken
    Breasts*

2 cups canned unsweetened
    pineapple chunks
1 cup Cooked Apricots,* cut
    into thin strips
³/₄ cup blanched, slivered al-
    monds
1 cup tart green apples, skinned,
    cored, cut into small cubes,
    and sprinkled with ¹/₄ cup
    fresh lemon juice

GARNISH:
1 large bunch watercress, stems
    removed
1 cantaloupe, peeled and cubed
¹/₂ cup blanched, slivered al-
    monds, lightly browned

1. Mix the mayonnaise with the ginger, garlic, salt substitute, chives, lemon juice, white pepper, cayenne, and sugar.

2. Add the chicken, pineapple, apricots, almonds, and apples, toss thoroughly.

Serving: Arrange the salad in the center of a round platter. Place the watercress around the salad and nestle the cantaloupe cubes on top of this. Sprinkle the almonds over all.

Chicken Salad Chinoise

Serves 8 to 10 for lunch or 4 to 6
as a main course at dinner

8 cups cubed Boiled Chicken*
1½ cups water chestnuts
(packed in salt-free water),
cut into ¼-inch slices
1 cup bamboo shoots (packed in
salt-free water), cut into
slivers
½ cup minced fresh chives
½ cup green onions (scallions),
cut into ¼-inch rings
2½ inches fresh ginger root,
finely grated
1 teaspoon freshly ground white
pepper
¼ teaspoon cayenne
1½ tablespoons salt substitute
(optional)

4 cloves garlic, pressed
2 teaspoons hot salt-free chili
powder
2 to 3 teaspoons sugar (or substitute equivalent)
¼ cup dry sherry
¼ cup fresh lemon juice
1½ cups corn oil (or peanut oil)
1½ cups fresh bean sprouts
1½ pounds fresh snow peas (see
Note), tips and string removed
1 cup blanched whole almonds
(optional)

1. Mix all the ingredients except the bean sprouts, snow peas, and almonds. Refrigerate for at least 1 hour.

2. When ready to serve, toss the salad, add the bean sprouts, half the
snow peas, and half the almonds.

Serving: Mound the salad on a chilled large platter surrounded by the
remaining snow peas, and sprinkle the remaining almonds on top of the
salad.

NOTE: We like the crispness of the raw snow peas, but if you prefer them
less crisp, parboil them for 30 seconds in boiling water, drain, cool,
and chill them in the refrigerator for at least 30 minutes.

Artichokes Stuffed with Chicken Salad

Serves 8 generously for a luncheon dish or a cold supper

If we are having this for a Sunday supper in the summer, I serve cold
Gazpacho* first, then the stuffed artichokes for a main course, accompanied by Thin Garlic Herb Toast* and, for dessert, raspberries or strawberries with Crème Fraîche.*

**8 large Cooked Artichokes* with
the leaves pressed widely
open
4 cups cubed Boiled Chicken*
1/4 cup finely diced green pepper
1/4 cup finely diced red pepper
4 hard-cooked eggs, finely
minced
1/4 cup finely minced fresh
chives
1/4 cup finely minced fresh
parsley
2 green onions (scallions), cut
into paper-thin rings**

**1 cup finely grated carrots
4 cloves garlic, pressed
3/4 teaspoon hot salt-free chili
powder
1 teaspoon freshly ground white
pepper
2 1/2 teaspoons salt substitute (optional)
2 cups Mayonnaise*
12 tablespoons Mayonnaise*
mixed with 1 tablespoon
salt-free curry powder and
1/4 teaspoon cayenne**

1. After preparing the artichokes, mix the chicken with the green and
red peppers.
2. Toss in the eggs, chives, parsley, green onions, carrots, garlic, chili
powder, pepper and salt substitute. Gently fold in the 2 cups of mayonnaise.

Serving: On individual large china plates place the artichokes and fill them
with the chicken salad, mounding it slightly. (It is important to spread the
leaves of the artichokes open while they are still warm and pliable, thus
giving them enough room to hold the mounded salad.) Spoon a generous
1 1/2 tablespoons of the mayonnaise-curry mixture on top of each salad.
This will become the sauce for the artichoke leaves.

Mideastern Orange and Banana Fruit Salad

Yields approximately 12 cups

I have used this salad as an accompaniment to Roast Duck,* Chicken Concubine,* Roast Stuffed Capon,* and Lamb Curry,* and also as one of many dishes at a buffet, as well as a dessert.

12 tablespoons honey	1 cup coarsely chopped walnuts
1/3 cup fresh lemon juice	1/2 cup fresh orange juice
2 tablespoons Grand Marnier	8 large firm bananas
5 large navel oranges	1/3 cup fresh lemon juice
1 cup coarsely chopped dried dates	1/4 cup grated orange rind

1. Combine the honey and lemon juice in a heavy saucepan and cook over a low flame, stirring constantly until the honey is dissolved. Stir in the Grand Marnier and simmer for 2 minutes. Remove from the flame.

2. After grating the 1/4 cup of orange rind, reserve it.

3. Peel the oranges, remove all the membrane, and cut out the segments. Place them in a bowl.

4. Mix the dates and walnuts with the orange juice and set aside.

Serving: Slice the bananas in 1/4-inch rounds and place them in a large serving dish. Toss them well with the lemon juice. Spoon the honey mixture over them, then spoon the date mixture over this. Arrange the orange segments over and around the fruit salad and sprinkle on the orange rind. Serve at once or cover tightly with plastic wrap and refrigerate for 2 hours or until thoroughly chilled.

FISH

Pièce de Résistance

Fish

Fish, to my everlasting joy, has finally acquired the place of prominence in the American cuisine it so richly deserves. Unfortunately, as its popularity has grown, so has its price. Therefore, it is vital that the fish, which now costs more than sirloin steak, is the freshest and of the finest quality available. If at all possible, fish should be purchased fresh in the morning and prepared that evening. Gourmet cooks don't have to be reminded that when buying whole fish one looks for bright, bulging eyes (a friend used to tell me, "Make sure they look back at you"), firm flesh, sweet odor, gills colored pink to red, and one shouldn't be afraid to sniff and closely examine the fish, even pressing with the fingers to make sure the flesh springs back.

Unfortunately, many of us live far inland or in large cities without direct access to harbors, and we have to rely on frozen fish or fillets resting limply in white enamel pans in the local supermarket. On the subject of frozen fish: please try to buy at a fish store rather than a supermarket, but, lacking a fish store, never buy frozen fish that has been thawed and refrozen. One telltale sign is the shifting of the fish to one side of the package. If you detect this, put it back. When using frozen or doubtfully fresh fish I have found that soaking the fish in lemon juice enhances its flavor and more than compensates for the expense. Therefore, many of my recipes recommend this.

As much as it is important for fish to be fresh, it is imperative that shellfish be *absolutely* fresh, since it deteriorates even more quickly than fish. Since it is almost impossible, in most places, to buy fresh shrimp, I recommend a fine quality raw flash-frozen deveined shrimp, which can be bought in reputable fish markets as well as in a few very fine supermarkets. Shrimp should move easily in the bag and not stick together, and they are bought according to their size. Most of my recipes call for the size that gives 10 to 12 to the pound, which admittedly is very expensive but can be substituted with 16 to 20 or even 20 to 24 to the pound with similar results (except for a broiled scampi recipe where it is important to use a large shrimp). A word of caution: The sodium content of shrimp is definitely higher than that of its finny friends. As you will see, a great deal of lemon juice is used in these recipes, as it helps to draw out some of the natural sodium. However, I must stress that the recipes calling for shrimp should be prepared only by those who have received their doctor's permission for shrimp to become an occasional part of their regimen.

Fish responds very well to herbs, and you will notice in my fish recipes that I use what may seem to be an excess of herbs and spices. This is one of the little tricks I have learned to cover the absence of salt in cooking and something that my personal taste buds find very satisfying. It may seem to be an inordinate amount of work to use 15 shallots in a recipe, but to me it is well worth the money and effort in the results. Cooking, after all, should be as much a joy to do as it is to eat the results. Here again, use your own judgment—cut down on shallots or parsley or tarragon, etc., to satisfy your own taste buds.

Many of my recipes call for dry white wine in much of the fish cookery. In our house we use the same wines in cooking as we use on the table, an imported yet inexpensive Muscadet, a French Pinot Chardonnay, a Soave, a Verdicchio—all are good wines to use and lend a sophisticated flavor to fish, as do their California equivalents. However, at no time should you use cooking wine or cooking sherry of the type sold in supermarkets, as these are loaded with salt.

The most important advice one can give about fish, aside from buying it fresh is, DO NOT OVERCOOK. Fish is done when it flakes easily to the touch of a fork. Don't forget that cooking continues after the fish has been removed from the flame, so here it is even more important not to overcook.

The cautions, instructions, and admonitions are over. The fun of cooking fish is just about to begin . . . and the joy of eating it thrillingly awaits you.

Gefüllte Fish

Serves 6 as a main course or 12
as a first course

It is definitely one of the most underrated gourmet dishes in the world.

3½ pounds white fish fillets, cut
    into small pieces
1½ pounds yellow pike fillets,
    cut into small pieces
2 medium onions, cut into small
    pieces

1½ teaspoons freshly ground
    white pepper
2 tablespoons salt substitute (optional)
2 teaspoons sugar (or substitute
    equivalent)

5 eggs, very, very well beaten
1/2 cup ice water
2 tablespoons matzoh meal (approximately)
6 large Spanish onions, very thinly sliced
8 carrots, sliced on the diagonal about 1/4 inch thick

6 pounds fishbones and heads divided into 3 parts (each wrapped and tied in double cheesecloth)
Cold water
1 teaspoon freshly ground white pepper
2 tablespoons salt substitute (optional)

1. Chop together the first 3 ingredients with the pepper, salt substitute, and sugar in a food processor using the steel blade (this will probably have to be done in 3 to 4 batches). Transfer the mixture to a very large wooden chopping bowl.

2. Constantly chopping the fish (with a steel blade chopper) by hand slowly add the beaten eggs, then the ice water, and finally the matzoh meal. Chop for another 3 to 5 minutes and set aside.

3. In each of 3 separate pots (approximately 8 quarts each and preferably of enamel) layer in one third of the onions and carrots. Place one of the cheesecloth packages of bones on top of the onions and carrots in each pot.

4. Add enough water to barely cover the fishbones. Sprinkle in the pepper and the salt substitute, cover.

5. Turn the flame to medium, bring the water to a low boil, and simmer until the onions are soft and mushy (approximately 15 minutes).

6. While the broth is cooking, make the fish balls.
   (a) Dip your hands into ice water and make a ball of the fish mixture about the size of a tennis ball, then shape into an oval and smooth it out.
   (b) Lay the fish ball on waxed paper and repeat until all the fish mixture has been used.

7. Remove the fishbones from the pot and make sure that the water is at a low boil.

8. With a large slotted spoon, place each fish ball into a pot in a single layer and not overlapping. Cover the pots and simmer for 45 minutes. Turn off the flame, uncover, and let the fish cool for 15 to 20 minutes.

9. With a slotted spoon place the gefüllte fish (single layer) in a large Pyrex or china dish.

10. Strain the broth, discard the onions, and pour the broth over the fish. Garnish each piece of fish with 2 or 3 carrot slices.

11. Cover and refrigerate overnight.

Serving: Place a lettuce leaf on each china plate and place a piece of the gefüllte fish on top of the lettuce. Offer homemade Horseradish,* which is traditionally served with this dish.

Yellow Pike Cantonese Style

Serves 4

2¹/₂ pounds yellow pike fillets, cut into 1-inch squares

1 teaspoon freshly ground white pepper

¹/₂ cup lemon juice, freshly squeezed

6 tablespoons unbleached flour

2 teaspoons dry sherry

2 egg whites

3 cloves garlic, finely minced

1 teaspoon salt substitute (optional)

¹/₈ teaspoon cayenne

1¹/₂ inches ginger root, finely minced

¹/₂ pound Chinese cabbage, thinly sliced

¹/₂ cup thinly sliced bamboo shoots

1 cup thinly sliced water chestnuts

2 teaspoons cornstarch

6 tablespoons water

1 teaspoon brown sugar (or substitute equivalent)

1¹/₂ inches ginger root, finely minced

2 cups peanut oil

4 tablespoons peanut oil

¹/₂ cup water

¹/₂ cup dry sherry

1. Rub the fish with the pepper and place it in a plastic bag. Pour the lemon juice over the fish. Seal the bag tightly and refrigerate. Marinate for at least 2 hours, turning the bag over 3 to 4 times during the marinating period.

2. Mix the flour, sherry, and egg whites together and beat with a wire whisk (or use low speed on an electric mixer) until thoroughly blended. Set aside.

3. Mix the garlic, salt substitute, cayenne, and ginger together and set aside.

4. Mix the cabbage, bamboo shoots, and water chestnuts together and set aside.

5. Mix the cornstarch, water, sugar, and ginger together. Stir until thoroughly blended. Set aside.

6. Drain the fish and pat dry between double thicknesses of paper towels. Dip the fish into the flour mixture and set on a plate.

7. In a large, deep, heavy skillet or wok, heat the 2 cups of peanut oil over a high flame until it starts to smoke. Deep-fry the fish until light golden brown. Remove with a slotted spoon to a double thickness of paper towels to drain.

8. In a large, heavy skillet or wok, place the 4 tablespoons of peanut oil and heat over a high flame until the oil starts to smoke. Add the garlic,

cayenne, and ginger mixture and stir well until the garlic starts to brown (about 10 to 15 seconds).

9. Add the cabbage mixture and stir-fry for 1 minute.

10. Add the water and sherry and stir well. Cover and cook for 2½ minutes.

11. Add the fish, stir well to mix all the ingredients. Then slowly add the cornstarch mixture, stirring constantly.

12. Stir-fry until the sauce thickens and all the ingredients are well coated.

Serving: Transfer to a heated platter and serve at once. Offer Boiled Rice* garnished with finely minced green onions.

A METHOD FOR BROILING FISH STEAKS AND FILLETS

1. Preheat the broiler to 550° for 15 minutes.

2. Cut the steaks 1 inch to 1½ inches thick (such as salmon, halibut, haddock, tile fish, striped bass, or swordfish).

3. Cut the fillets ⅜ inch to ½ inch thick (such as gray sole, lemon sole, flounder, yellowtail, or red snapper).

4. Wash them well and pat dry.

5. Dip the fish in melted Clarified Butter* or Lemon Butter Sauce* and lightly coat them with salt-free cornflake crumbs.

6. Place them on a hot well-oiled or buttered broiler tray.

7. Broil the 1½-inch steaks 4 inches from the flame, the 1-inch steaks 3 inches from the flame and the fillets 2 inches from the flame.

8. Broil the 1½-inch steaks for 6 minutes on one side, the 1-inch steaks for 4½ minutes on one side, and the fillets for 3 minutes on one side, making sure that you have basted the fish well with melted clarified butter or lemon butter sauce.

9. Using a large spatula so that the fish will not break, turn the steaks or the fillets.

10. Baste the fish thoroughly and often.

11. Broil until the steaks or the fillets are slightly crusty and flake easily to the touch of a fork. (The 1½-inch steaks will require approximately 8 to 10 minutes; the 1-inch steaks approximately 5 to 7 minutes; the fillets approximately 2 to 4 minutes.)

Serving: Using a large spatula, transfer the fish to a heated serving tray. Spoon a little of the clarified butter or lemon butter sauce over it. Garnish with freshly minced parsley and lemon wedges. You may serve the clarified butter or lemon butter sauce or other sauces such as Hollandaise,* Mustard Cream Sauce,* Mushroom Almond Sauce,* or Almond Tarragon Sauce.*

Halibut with a Mediterranean Sauce

Serves 6

The sauce is vastly improved if it is made the day before.

SAUCE:
2 large eggplants
1 cup pineapple juice
6 cloves garlic, pressed
2 large green peppers, seeded and coarsely chopped
2 large red peppers, seeded and coarsely chopped
2 large Bermuda onions, chopped
$^1/_2$ cup olive oil
2 1-pound cans salt-free tomatoes (with juice), coarsely chopped (Italian plum tomatoes preferably)
3 tablespoons salt-free tomato paste
2 teaspoons sugar (or substitute equivalent)

$^1/_2$ cup dry vermouth
$^1/_2$ cup dry white wine
1 bay leaf
$^2/_3$ teaspoon dried thyme
$^2/_3$ teaspoon dried sweet basil
2 teaspoons seasoned salt substitute (optional)
$^1/_2$ teaspoon freshly ground black pepper
$^1/_8$ teaspoon cayenne
6 halibut fillets cut $^3/_4$ inch thick, (each weighing approximately 8 ounces)
1 teaspoon freshly ground white pepper
$^1/_2$ cup fresh lemon juice
Flour for dredging
$^1/_2$ cup corn oil (approximately)

1. Peel the eggplants and cut them into cubes 1 inch to 1$^1/_2$ inches. Soak them in the pineapple juice for $^1/_2$ to 1 hour (this will help to remove any bitterness).

2. Mix the garlic, green and red peppers, and onions.

3. In a heavy, deep skillet, heat the oil over a medium flame and spoon in the onion-pepper mixture. Sauté until the onions are translucent and the vegetables are tender but not browned.

4. Drain the eggplant in a strainer and dry between double thicknesses of paper towels.

5. Remove the onion mixture with a slotted spoon to a bowl. Turn the flame under the skillet up to medium-high and add the eggplant (the bottom of the pan should be well coated with about $^1/_8$ inch of oil (if necessary add more). Lightly brown the eggplant, tossing it frequently.

6. When it is lightly browned, add the onion mixture, tomatoes, tomato paste, sugar, vermouth, white wine, bay leaf, thyme, basil, salt substitute, pepper, and cayenne. Stir all the ingredients very thoroughly. Turn the flame up to high and bring the sauce to a boil. Then lower the flame to medium and simmer for 20 minutes.

7. Cool and pour the sauce into a bowl or large jar; tightly cover and refrigerate for 1 day.

TWO HOURS BEFORE SERVING:

8. Sprinkle the fish with the white pepper and place it on a large glass dish. Pour the lemon juice over it, cover tightly, and refrigerate for 1 hour and 45 minutes.

9. About 30 minutes before serving, remove the sauce from the refrigerator, take out the bay leaf, and pour the sauce into a heavy saucepan. Place it on a Flame-Tamer and bring the sauce to a low boil over a medium-high flame, then reduce it to low and simmer for 20 minutes.

10. Remove the fish from the refrigerator. Dry it between double thicknesses of paper towels. Dredge in the flour.

11. In a large, heavy skillet, heat the oil over a medium-high flame, then brown the fish on each side until golden in color (about 5 minutes on each side). It should flake to the touch of a fork; if not, cook it a little longer over a low-medium flame.

Serving: Arrange the fish on a preheated large platter. Spoon the sauce over it and serve at once.

Steamed Bluefish

Serves 4

This simple dish is transformed into an exotic taste delight when sauced in the Cantonese manner.

1 2-pound bluefish, cleaned, with center bone removed
1/2 teaspoon freshly ground white pepper
2 teaspoons salt substitute (optional)
4 cloves of garlic, pressed
1/2 cup lemon juice, freshly squeezed

1/4 cup dry sherry
2 tablespoons peanut oil
1 cup hot Cantonese Sauce*

GARNISH: 2 green onions (scallions), sliced into thin rounds

1. Rub the fish with pepper, salt substitute, and garlic on all sides and in the cavity.

2. Place it in a plastic bag, add the lemon juice and sherry, and seal tightly. Refrigerate, marinate for at least 3 hours, turning the bag 3 or 4 times during the marinating.

3. Remove the fish and place it in a dish. Pour the marinade into a fish poacher and add enough water to bring liquid up to the rack.

4. On a high flame, bring the liquid to a boil, reduce the flame to medium, and lay the fish on the rack.

5. Cover and steam for 15 minutes, or until the fish flakes to the touch of a fork. Transfer to a heated platter.

6. In a small skillet, heat the peanut oil over a high flame until it starts to smoke, pour it over the fish. Spoon the cantonese sauce over it.

Serving: Garnish with the green onions and serve at once.

Stuffed Striped Bass

Serves 6

This dish, though quite easy to prepare, is not only delicious but most impressive in its presentation.

1 whole striped bass, about 5
    pounds, boned and cleaned
    (head and tail on or off, as
    you prefer)
Mushroom Herb Stuffing au
    Poisson*
6 tablespoons sweet butter,
    melted

½ cup dry white wine
Juice of 1 lemon
½ teaspoon freshly ground
    white pepper
Lemon Butter Sauce*

1. Preheat the oven to 350°.

2. Stuff the bass loosely with the mushroom stuffing and close the cavity with skewers.

3. Pour 2 tablespoons of butter in a baking pan large enough to hold the bass, and rotate the pan so that the bottom is lightly greased. Add the white wine, lemon juice, and pepper. Place the bass in the pan and brush or pour the remaining butter over it.

4. Bake for 45 minutes or until the fish flakes to the touch of a fork.

Serving: Remove the skewers, place the fish on a preheated platter, and serve at once. Offer the lemon butter sauce on the side.

Oriental Bluefish and Vegetables

Serves 4

2 pounds bluefish fillets, cut into
  strips ³/₄ inch by 2 inches
1 teaspoon freshly ground white
  pepper
¹/₂ cup dry sherry
¹/₃ cup peanut oil
6 green onions (scallions), cut
  into paper-thin rounds
1¹/₂ pounds baby lima beans
2¹/₂ pounds thin asparagus (use
  spears and only 1¹/₂ inches
  of each stalk)
1¹/₂ inches ginger root, finely
  minced

2 teaspoons salt substitute (optional)
¹/₄ cup dry sherry
6 cups Chicken Stock*
¹/₈ teaspoon cayenne (optional)
6 tablespoons cornstarch, mixed
  with 1 cup water

GARNISH: 2 green onions, sliced
  into paper-thin rounds

1. Rub the bluefish with the pepper. Place it in a plastic bag with the sherry. Seal tightly and refrigerate. Marinate for at least 2 hours, turning the bag 3 or 4 times during the marinating.

2. Heat the oil in a very large, heavy, deep skillet or wok over a high flame.

3. While the oil is heating, drain the fish (do not pat dry).

4. Add the green onions to the oil and stir-fry for 30 seconds. Add the fish and stir-fry for 2¹/₂ minutes.

5. Add the lima beans, asparagus, and ginger root, stir-fry for ¹/₂ minute.

6. Stir in the salt substitute, sherry, chicken stock, and cayenne. Cook for 5 minutes and stir often.

7. Slowly add the cornstarch mixture, stirring constantly until the sauce is thick (approximately 3 minutes).

Serving: Transfer to a heated platter and sprinkle on the green onions. Serve at once. Offer Hot Mustard Sauce* on the side.

Bourride

Serves 6 to 8

This recipe calls for three-step cooking. Panic not, for it is not nearly as time-consuming or difficult as it sounds, and the end result is a delicious treat!

STEP 1: *THE BROTH*

4 tablespoons olive oil
1 very large onion, thinly sliced
2 large carrots, thinly sliced
2 large leeks, cut lengthwise into
    quarters
3 large fresh tomatoes, coarsely
    chopped, or 2 cups canned
    salt-free tomatoes, coarsely
    chopped (Italian plum to-
    matoes preferably)
2 teaspoons sugar (or substitute
    equivalent)
2¹/₂ cups dry white wine

Juice of 2 lemons
2 bay leaves
1 teaspoon dried thyme
1 teaspoon dried fennel
2 teaspoons dried dill
6 cloves of garlic, pressed
¹/₈ to ¹/₄ teaspoon cayenne
1 tablespoon seasoned salt sub-
    stitute (optional)
¹/₂ to 1 teaspoon freshly ground
    black pepper
¹/₄ teaspoon saffron

1. In a large skillet heat the oil on a very low flame and add the onion, carrots, and leeks. Cover and simmer for 10 to 15 minutes or until the vegetables are tender. Do not brown.

2. Add the remaining broth ingredients and mix thoroughly. Cover and simmer over a low flame for 25 to 30 minutes.

3. Pour the broth through a strainer into a bowl and press the vegetables with the underside of a mixing spoon to press out all the juices.

NOTE: I generally make this in advance, cover it tightly, and refrigerate until I am ready to cook dinner.

STEP 2: *SAUCE AÏOLI**
See the Index for this recipe. It, too, is made in advance.

STEP 3: *COOKING THE FISH*
All of the fish given below should be about 1¹/₂ to 2 inches thick and cut into 4-inch chunks.

About 5 cups of the broth
1¹/₄ pound striped bass

1¹/₄ pound halibut
1¹/₄ pound snapper

1¼ pound cod
Sauce Aioli* (place half in a
   serving bowl and refrigerate; place the other half in
   a mixing bowl)

1 loaf salt-free French Bread*
   sliced 1 inch to 1½ inches
   and toasted

1. In a large saucepan, bring the broth to a boil over a high flame, add the fish, and cover. The liquid should cover the fish, but if it does not, add a mixture of half dry vermouth and half water until it does.

2. Preheat the oven to 180°, or if you prefer bring a pan of water to a low boil over a low-medium flame.

3. Cook the fish for approximately 8 minutes or until the fish barely flakes to the touch of a fork. Do not overcook.

4. When it is cooked, place it on a heated serving platter, cover, and keep it warm over the pan of boiling water or in the oven. If you warm it in the oven, spoon 2 teaspoons of broth over each piece beforehand.

5. Beat the *sauce aïoli* in the mixing bowl with a wire whisk, slowly pour in 1½ cups of the broth, beating all the time. When thoroughly mixed, slowly pour the mixture back into the broth on the stove, stirring it constantly with the whisk. Make sure that the flame is low-medium only. Continue stirring until the mixture lightly coats the spoon—about 5 to 6 minutes.

Serving: Pour the aïoli-broth into a preheated tureen. Bring the tureen, the fish platter, the toast, and the bowl of sauce aïole to the table. Place 2 pieces of the toasted French bread in each preheated large soup plate. Arrange a few pieces of fish on top of the toast, then ladle the broth over all. Offer the serving bowl of *sauce aïoli* and let everyone spoon as much of it into their own soup plates as desired.

Bass and Shrimp Curry

Serves 8

For those who are not permitted to have shrimp, this recipe is just as good using only the bass.

1/2 cup peanut or corn oil
2 large onions, finely chopped
4 cloves garlic, finely minced
2 1/2 teaspoons freshly grated ginger root
Juice of 1 lime
Juice of 1 lemon
2 teaspoons sugar (or substitute equivalent)
1 teaspoon hot Spanish paprika
2 tablespoons seasoned salt substitute (optional)
3 1/2 teaspoons salt-free curry powder
1/2 teaspoon salt-free chili powder

1/2 teaspoon ground cumin
1/4 to 1/2 teaspoon cayenne
1 tablespoon finely minced fresh dill
1 teaspoon dry mustard
1/2 cup unsweetened pineapple juice
2 tablespoons salt-free tomato paste
3/4 cup dry white wine
2 pounds bass fillets, skinned and cut into strips 1 inch by 3 inches
1 pound Boiled Shrimp* (or 3 pounds bass fillets and no shrimp)

1. In a large skillet heat the oil over a medium high flame.
2. Add the onions, garlic, and ginger root, sauté until the onions are a pale golden color.
3. Add the lime juice, lemon juice, sugar, paprika, salt substitute, curry, chili, cumin, cayenne, dill, dry mustard, pineapple juice, tomato paste, and wine. Cook on a high flame, stirring constantly, for 2 minutes.
4. Turn the flame to low. Cover and cook for 30 minutes.
5. Uncover, add the fish, and simmer for 4 to 7 minutes or just until the fish flakes to the touch of a fork. Do not overcook.
6. Add the shrimp and continue to simmer for 3 minutes.

Serving: Transfer the curry to a *gratin* dish. Serve it over Saffron Rice.*

Baked Sicilian Bass

Serves 8

Whether you are or aren't Sicilian, it makes little difference, because everyone who loves bass is surely going to enjoy this recipe.

8 fillets of striped bass (about 8 to 10 ounces each)

$^1\!/_2$ cup olive oil

$^1\!/_2$ cup white wine

3 large tomatoes, coarsely chopped

$^2\!/_3$ cup chopped fresh parsley

3 tablespoons chopped fresh basil

5 large cloves garlic, crushed

$1^1\!/_2$ tablespoons seasoned salt substitute (optional)

$^1\!/_2$ teaspoon cayenne

1 teaspoon freshly ground white pepper

GARNISH: 8 paper-thin slices of lemon dipped in freshly chopped parsley

1. Preheat the oven to 450°.
2. Rinse the fish and pat dry with paper towels.
3. In an attractive ovenproof dish pour in $^1\!/_4$ cup olive oil, add the white wine and fillets, being careful not to overlap them.
4. Evenly divide the tomatoes and spoon over the fish, juice and all.
5. Thoroughly mix the parsley, basil, garlic, salt substitute, cayenne, and pepper, sprinkle over the fillets.
6. Spoon the remaining oil over them, bake uncovered for 20 minutes or until the fish flakes easily to the touch of a fork.

Serving: Remove the bass from the oven and garnish it with lemon-parsley slices. Serve at once. A marvelous accompaniment is Saffron Rice Pilaf.*

Szechuan Bass

Serves 4

For those of you who like your bass hot and spicy.

A 3½-pound striped bass, center bone removed

¾ teaspoon freshly ground black pepper

⅓ cup lemon juice, freshly squeezed

¼ cup dry sherry

2 teaspoons cornstarch mixed with 2 tablespoons water

1½ tablespoons cornstarch

2 cups peanut oil

2½ tablespoons peanut oil

3 tablespoons green onions (scallions), thinly sliced into rounds

2½ teaspoons finely minced fresh ginger

2½ tablespoons salt-free ketchup

1½ tablespoons salt-free tomato paste

2½ tablespoons brown sugar (or substitute equivalent)

2½ tablespoons rice vinegar

1½ tablespoons dry sherry

2 teaspoons seasoned salt substitute (optional)

⅛ to ¼ teaspoon cayenne

1. Rub the bass on both sides and inside the cavity with black pepper. Place it in a large plastic bag, pour in the lemon juice and sherry, and seal the bag tightly. Refrigerate. Marinate for at least 2 hours, turning the bag over 3 or 4 times during the marinating.

2. Drain the fish and pat dry between double thicknesses of paper towels.

3. Rub the bass with the cornstarch mixture, coat it with the cornstarch, and set aside.

4. Preheat the oven to 180°.

5. In a large, heavy deep skillet or wok heat the 2 cups of peanut oil over a high flame and deep-fry the bass until it is a deep golden brown (approximately 10 minutes). Turn the bass during the frying period.

6. Remove it to paper towels and drain for 1 minute. Place it on a heated platter and put it in the oven while you are preparing the sauce.

7. In a small, heavy skillet, or wok heat 2½ tablespoons of the peanut oil over a high flame until it smokes. Stir-fry the green onions and ginger for 20 to 30 seconds, then stir in the ketchup, tomato paste, sugar, rice vinegar, sherry, salt substitute, and cayenne. Make sure that the ingredients are thoroughly blended. Cover and cook for 1½ minutes.

Serving: Spoon the sauce over the fish or, if you prefer, put the sauce in a bowl and serve it separately.

Crispy Sweet and Sour Bass

Serves 4

A salt-free adaptation of one of our old favorites.

1½ teaspoons cornstarch
3 tablespoons water
2 teaspoons seasoned salt substitute (optional)
½ to ¾ teaspoon freshly ground black pepper
2 pounds bass fillets, cut into strips approximately 2 by 4 inches
2 tablespoons cornstarch (approximately)
2 tablespoons dry sherry
2 tablespoons salt-free ketchup

2 tablespoons salt-free tomato paste
1½ tablespoons sugar (or substitute equivalent)
2 tablespoons dark rice vinegar
½ tablespoon cornstarch
3 cups peanut oil
¾ tablespoon peanut oil
¾ to 1 cup shelled fresh peas

GARNISH: 1 tomato, peeled, seeded, and cut into tiny pieces (optional)

1. Mix the cornstarch and water together. Add the salt substitute and pepper. Beat with a wire whisk until thoroughly blended.
2. Rub the fillets with this mixture.
3. Roll them in the cornstarch (shake off the excess because you want only a thin coating) and let them stand at least 5 minutes.
4. Mix the sherry, ketchup, tomato paste, sugar, vinegar, and cornstarch, set aside.
5. Preheat the oven to 180°.
6. In a large, heavy, deep skillet or wok heat the oil over a medium-high flame until very hot, deep-fry the fillets until they are golden brown. Remove to an ovenproof platter and place in the oven to keep warm.
7. In a small, heavy skillet or wok heat the ¾ teaspoon of oil over a medium-high flame and stir-fry the peas (with chopsticks) for 1 minute.
8. Add the sherry mixture and stir-fry constantly until the sauce has thickened (approximately 3 minutes).

Serving: Spoon the sauce over the fillets, sprinkle the tomatoes on top, and serve at once. Boiled Rice* is traditionally served with this dish.

Szechuan Baked Flounder Fillets
(in a Sweet and Pungent Sauce)

Serves 8

4 pounds flounder fillets, cut into strips 2 by 4 inches
¼ cup lemon juice, freshly squeezed
¼ cup dry sherry
4 tablespoons Hot Pepper Oil*
6 cloves garlic, finely minced
1 large Bermuda onion, sliced paper thin
1½ inches ginger root, finely minced
1 16-ounce can unsweetened peaches, drained and puréed

1 cup Cooked Apricots,* puréed with juice
⅓ cup rice vinegar
⅓ cup dry sherry
½ cup brown sugar (or substitute equivalent)
¼ teaspoon cayenne (only if you like your food very hot)
1 tablespoon cornstarch

GARNISH: 3 green onions (scallions), sliced into paper-thin rings

1. Place the fillets in a plastic bag. Pour in the lemon juice and sherry, seal tightly, and refrigerate. Marinate for at least 2 hours, turning the bag once or twice during the marinating.

2. In a large, heavy skillet or wok heat the pepper oil over a high flame and stir-fry the garlic and onions until the onions are translucent.

3. Add the ginger and stir-fry for 1 minute.

4. Stir in the peaches, apricots, vinegar, sherry, sugar, and cayenne. Cook for 3 minutes.

5. Add the cornstarch and stir constantly until the sauce starts to thicken.

6. Reduce the flame to low, cover the skillet, and cook for 15 minutes.

7. Preheat the oven to 550°.

8. Drain the fillets and pat dry between double thicknesses of paper towels.

9. In a large ovenproof casserole, spoon in a fourth of the sauce, lay some of the fillets on top, then repeat until all the ingredients are used, ending with the sauce.

10. Bake for approximately 12 to 15 minutes or until the fish flakes easily to the touch of a fork.

Serving: Take a preheated large platter and form a ring of rice around the border. Spoon the fish and sauce into the center of the ring and garnish with the sliced green onions.

Shanghai Flounder and Vegetables

Serves 4

Prepare the vegetables in advance, then dinner can be ready to serve in a matter of minutes.

2 pounds flounder fillets, cut into strips 1 inch by 2 inches

$3/4$ teaspoon freshly ground white pepper

$1/4$ cup lemon juice, freshly squeezed

$1/4$ cup dry sherry

15 dried Chinese mushrooms

$2^1/2$ tablespoons cornstarch

$1/3$ cup peanut oil or vegetable oil

$1^1/2$ to 2 inches ginger root, finely minced

3 green onions (scallions), white part only, sliced into paper-thin rings

1 8-ounce can water chestnuts packed in water, thinly sliced

$1^1/2$ cups fresh snow peas

$1/3$ cup dry sherry

$1^1/2$ cups Chicken Stock*

$1/2$ teaspoon freshly ground white pepper

1 teaspoon salt substitute (optional)

2 tablespoons cornstarch mixed with 6 tablespoons water

1 tablespoon Spicy Sesame Oil*

GARNISH: 2 tablespoons finely minced fresh chives

1. Rub the fillets with pepper and place in a plastic bag. Pour in the lemon juice and sherry, seal tightly, and refrigerate. Marinate for at least 2 hours, turning the bag 2 or 3 times during the marinating.

2. Wash the mushrooms and place them in a glass bowl. Cover with warm water and let them soak for 20 minutes. Drain, cut them into quarters, and set aside.

3. Drain the fish well (do not pat dry). Coat the fish with the $2^1/2$ tablespoons of cornstarch and set aside.

4. In a large, heavy skillet or wok heat the peanut oil over a high flame. Add the ginger and green onions, and stir-fry for 10 seconds. Add the flounder and stir-fry for $1^1/2$ minutes.

5. Add the water chestnuts, mushrooms, and snow peas and stir-fry for $1/2$ minute.

6. Add the sherry, chicken stock, pepper, salt substitute, stir-fry for 2 minutes.

7. While continuing to stir-fry, slowly add the cornstarch mixture until thoroughly absorbed and the sauce is thickened (approximately 2 minutes).

8. Continue to stir-fry and sprinkle in the Spicy Sesame Oil* until thoroughly blended.

Serving: Transfer to a heated serving platter, garnished with the chives, and serve at once.

Luau Flounder

Serves 4

2 pounds flounder fillets
1/2 cup lemon juice, freshly squeezed
7 water chestnuts, finely chopped
2 eggs, lightly beaten
6 green onions (scallions), white part only, sliced into paper-thin rounds
1 inch ginger root, finely minced
1 1/2 teaspoons salt substitute (optional)

1 teaspoon freshly ground white pepper
3 tablespoons cornstarch
1 teaspoon lemon juice, freshly squeezed
1 teaspoon rice vinegar
4 1/2 quarts water

GARNISH: 3 tablespoons finely chopped fresh chives

1. Place the flounder and lemon juice in a plastic bag, seal tightly, and refrigerate. Marinate for at least 2 hours, turning the bag 3 or 4 times during the marinating.

2. Drain the fish well, finely chop, and place in a large bowl. Add the water chestnuts, eggs, green onions, ginger, salt substitute, pepper, cornstarch, lemon juice, and rice vinegar. Mix all the ingredients until they are thoroughly blended.

3. Make 1-inch balls from the mixture and refrigerate for at least 20 minutes.

4. In the meantime, in a large pot bring the 4 1/2 quarts of water to a rolling boil over a high flame. Drop the flounder balls, one at a time, into the boiling water. When they float to the surface, they are ready.

5. Remove them with a slotted spoon to a double thickness of paper towels to drain (about 2 minutes).

Serving: Place them on a preheated serving platter, garnish with the chives. Serve the Hawaiian Sauce* in a separate bowl.

Snapper Creole Style

Serves 6

This recipe, a favorite of ours, is an adaptation of a New Orleans classic.

6 tablespoons sweet butter

1 very large Bermuda onion, finely chopped

2 medium green peppers, finely chopped

3 cloves garlic, pressed

1 teaspoon dried thyme

1 teaspoon dried rosemary

4 tablespoons chopped fresh chives

2 1-pound cans salt-free tomatoes (preferably Italian plum tomatoes)

1 teaspoon coarsely ground black pepper

$1/4$ teaspoon cayenne (optional)

1 tablespoon seasoned salt substitute (optional)

Juice of 1 lemon

$1^1/2$ teaspoons sugar (or substitute equivalent)

6 red snapper fillets, about 8 to 10 ounces each

GARNISH: $1/3$ cup finely minced fresh chives

1. In a heavy skillet, melt the butter over a medium flame and sauté the onion and green peppers until both become slightly translucent. Add the garlic, thyme, rosemary, and chives, stir well, and continue to sauté for another 2 minutes. Add the tomatoes, pepper, cayenne, salt substitute, lemon juice, and sugar, stir well. Turn the flame to low and simmer uncovered for 30 minutes.

2. Preheat the oven to 450° while the sauce is simmering.

3. Pour a third of the sauce into an attractive large baking pan, arrange the fillets in a single layer, and pour the remaining sauce over them.

4. Turn the oven down to 350° and bake the fish uncovered for 20 minutes or until it flakes to the touch of a fork.

Serving: Sprinkle the chives on top and bring this New Orleans treat to the table. Rice is the traditionally favorite accompaniment.

NOTE: I have also served this cold the next day as part of an instant unexpected smorgasbord, cutting the fillets into thirds. It was unexpectedly superb.

Red Snapper En Papillote

Serves 4 generously

The entire main course is enveloped in paper until the final moment . . .
then slash and *voilà!* But do read on and you'll see . . .

1 whole large red snapper,
   about 4 pounds
1/4 cup olive oil (approximately)
1 1/2 teaspoons salt substitute
   (optional)
1/2 teaspoon freshly ground
   white pepper
1 medium lemon, sliced into 1/8-
   inch rounds
3 tablespoons freshly chopped
   dill
1 pound small mushrooms,
   stems chopped finely and
   caps whole

2 large tomatoes, cut into
   eighths
1 large red pepper, cut into 1/4-
   inch rings
1 large green pepper, cut into
   1/4-inch rings
1 large onion, cut into 1/8-inch
   slices
4 cloves garlic, pressed
2 tablespoons fresh lemon juice
1/4 cup olive oil
3 tablespoons finely chopped
   fresh parsley

1. Preheat the oven to 375°.
2. Wash the fish thoroughly in cold water and dry with paper towels.
3. Rub the cavity with some of the oil, salt substitute, and pepper, and
place the lemon slices in the cavity.
4. Brush a 30-inch piece of parchment with some of the oil and lay the
fish on it. Brush with the remaining oil and sprinkle with the remaining
pepper. Sprinkle with dill.
5. Arrange the chopped mushroom stems on top of the fish, then add
half the tomatoes, half the red pepper, half the green pepper, and half the
onion. Arrange the remaining tomatoes, peppers, and onions in layers on
either side of the fish, lengthwise, touching the fish. Place the mushroom
caps over the layered vegetables.
6. Mix the garlic, lemon juice, olive oil, and parsley together and spoon
over the fish and vegetables.
7. Tie the ends of the parchment with kitchen string, enclosing the fish
and vegetables envelope style, and place the package on a cookie sheet or
in a baking dish. Bake for 45 minutes.

Serving: Remove the parchment package to a preheated large serving
platter and bring it to the table. Slice the paper down the center with a
sharp knife, turn back the edges and . . . a most special dinner is ready to
serve.

NOTE: If you do not have parchment paper, aluminum foil is a good substitute, though not nearly as chic in presentation.

Broiled Oriental Red Snapper

Serves 6

A 5-pound red snapper, center bone out

2 teaspoons freshly ground white pepper

½ cup lemon juice, freshly squeezed

9 green onions (scallions), thinly sliced

5 tablespoons peanut oil

4 inches fresh ginger root, finely minced

4 cloves garlic, finely minced

3 tablespoons peanut oil

3 teaspoons brown sugar (or substitute equivalent)

2 teaspoons seasoned salt substitute (optional)

½ cup dry sherry

2 tablespoons cornstarch mixed with ½ cup water

GARNISH: 1 inch ginger root, freshly grated, mixed with 2 teaspoons finely minced fresh chives

1. Make diagonal slashes, 1 inch apart, in the skin of the snapper. Rub the cavity and skin with the pepper. Place the fish in a plastic bag. Pour in the lemon juice, seal tightly, and refrigerate. Marinate for at least 2 hours, turning the bag over 3 or 4 times during the marinating.

2. Preheat the broiler.

3. Drain the fish and dry between double thicknesses of paper towels.

4. Place aluminum foil on a flat broiler pan. Place the green onions on the foil and lay the fish on top of them. Brush with 2½ tablespoons of oil.

5. Broil the fish 5 inches from the flame for 10 minutes, basting very often, or until the fish has browned.

6. Turn it, brush with 2½ tablespoons of oil, and broil, basting often, for 12 to 15 minutes more or until it is a deep golden brown and flakes to the touch of a fork.

7. In the meantime, place the ginger, garlic, 3 tablespoons of peanut oil, salt substitute, sugar, and sherry in a saucepan, stir well.

8. Slowly stir the cornstarch mixture into the saucepan.

9. Heat over a low flame, stirring constantly until the sauce is bubbling hot.

Serving: Lift the fish onto a preheated platter and spoon the sauce over it. Garnish with the ginger and chive mixture.

Poached Salmon, Hot or Cold

Serves 8

This very easy but quite divine dish could not be more of a crowd pleaser. Its only drawback is the price of salmon today.

A 5½-pound salmon
4 quarts Court Bouillon* (ap-
      proximately)

GARNISH:
8 thin lemon rounds, dipped into
      2 finely minced tablespoons
      parsley
Small bunches of parsley

1. Wrap the salmon in a double thickness of cheesecloth, allowing a very long piece of cloth on either end of the fish.

2. Place it in a fish poacher with the ends of the cheesecloth hanging over the edges. Pour the court bouillon over the fish. (If there is not enough to cover the fish, add a mixture of ⅞ water and ⅛ apple cider vinegar.) Cover.

3. Turn the flame to medium and bring the liquid to a boil. *Immediately* turn the flame to low and simmer for 45 minutes (or until the fish feels firm when gently pushed with the index finger).

4. Taking hold of the ends of the cheesecloth, lift the salmon out of the poacher and place it on a rack to drain. Let it cool for at least 5 minutes.

5. Place it on a large platter and remove the cheesecloth. Skin the salmon, leaving the head and tail intact.

Serving: Salmon Hot: Transfer it to a preheated large rectangular silver tray or a china platter and garnish with the parsley-lemon rounds. Place small bunches of parsley at the ends of the tray. Offer Hollandaise Sauce* or Sauce Mousseline.*

Salmon Cold: When it has finished cooking, take hold of the ends of the cheesecloth and lift the salmon out of the poacher, placing it on a large platter. Cool at room temperature for 25 minutes, then refrigerate for 4 hours or until completely chilled. Remove the cheesecloth and skin the fish, leaving the head and tail intact. Transfer it to a large rectangular tray or a china platter and garnish as above. Serve with Herb Mayonnaise.*

NOTE: You can cook and serve a striped bass in exactly the same way.

Salmon à la Crème

Serves 3 to 4

This dish is especially appreciated at lunch, brunch, or late night supper, accompanied by a crisp and lightly dressed mixed green salad.

2 tablespoons sweet butter
1 large onion, finely minced
3 tablespoons sweet butter
3 tablespoons flour
1 cup light cream (or double strength low sodium dry milk)
2½ teaspoons seasoned salt substitute (optional)
1 teaspoon freshly ground white pepper
⅛ to ¼ teaspoon cayenne
3 tablespoons finely minced fresh chives
1½ teaspoons dry mustard (optional)
3 tablespoons dry sherry
2¼ cups flaked, cooked salmon (use either leftover Poached Salmon, Hot or Cold,* or 3 7-ounce cans of salt-free salmon, packed in water, drained)
2 tablespoons finely minced fresh dill

1. In a small, heavy skillet melt the 2 tablespoons of butter over a medium flame and sauté the onion until it is translucent. Set aside.

2. In a heavy saucepan melt the 3 tablespoons of butter over a low flame and, stirring constantly, slowly add the flour. Continuing to stir, cook for 6 to 7 minutes.

3. Stirring constantly, slowly add the cream (or double strength low sodium dry milk), salt substitute, pepper, cayenne, chives, mustard, and the sherry.

4. Raise the flame to low-medium and beat all the ingredients with a wire whisk until the sauce is thick, smooth, and comes to a low boil.

5. Stir in the onion mixture and the salmon, cook for 3 minutes.

Serving: Spoon the mixture into a preheated *au gratin* pan and garnish with the dill. Serve over White Bread* toasted triangles or (and this is especially good) Rolled Cheese and Herb Bread* sliced ½ inch thick and toasted.

Boiled Fresh Shrimp

Serves 8 as an hors d'oeuvre or
4 as a first course

In all honesty, the shrimp unfortunately are slightly overcooked, but the sodium content is also reduced, which makes it all worthwhile.

1 pound medium-size fresh shrimp (approximately 24 to the pound)	**1 cup fresh lemon juice**
	4½ quarts water
	4½ quarts water
1½ quarts ice water	**½ cup fresh lemon juice**

1. Shell and devein the shrimp.
2. Wash the shrimp in the 1½ quarts of ice water.
3. Place the shrimp in a large bowl, pour the 1 cup of lemon juice over the shrimp, cover tightly, and refrigerate for at least 1 hour. Stir the shrimp twice during refrigeration.
4. Drain the shrimp.
5. In a large pot, bring the first 4½ quarts of water to a rolling boil over a high flame.
6. Add the shrimp. When the water *just starts* to come back to a boil, immediately drain the shrimp in a colander and run under cold water for 3 minutes.
7. In the meantime, discard the water from the pot. Rinse the pot well, add the second 4½ quarts of water and the ½ cup of lemon juice to the pot.
8. Bring the water to a rolling boil over a high flame. Add the shrimp. When the water *barely* starts to return to a boil, drain the shrimp in the colander. Immediately run very cold water over the shrimp for 3 minutes.
9. Drain the shrimp well and pat dry with paper towels.
10. Place them in a glass bowl, cover, and refrigerate for at least 2 hours or until very cold.

Serving: The shrimp may be used as an hors d'oeuvre or first course with a choice of sauces such as Spicy Cocktail Sauce,* Sauce Aïoli,* Russian Dressing,* or Curry Mayonnaise.*

As an hors d'oeuvre: Place the shrimp attractively on a crystal, silver, or china round platter or in a silver or china shell filled with crushed ice. Pass the shrimp with a small holder containing toothpicks, a bowl for sauce, and garnish with sprigs of parsley or watercress.

As a first course: Place the shrimp around one edge of a shallow soup bowl containing crushed ice. Form an indentation in the center of the ice and fill it with a small bowl containing your sauce. Garnish the soup bowl with a lemon wedge and sprigs of parsley.

NOTE: This recipe can be used for any other recipe calling for cooked or boiled shrimp.

Boiled Flash-Frozen Shrimp

Serves 4 as a first course, or 8 as an hors d'oeuvre

Because flash-frozen shrimp are cooked only once, and fresh shrimp twice, the former are therefore higher in sodium.

1 pound flash-frozen shrimp (approximately 24 to the pound)
$^{1}/_{2}$ cup lemon juice, freshly squeezed, mixed with $1^{1}/_{2}$ cups ice water

$2^{1}/_{2}$ quarts water, mixed with 1 cup lemon juice, freshly squeezed

1. Take the shrimp from the freezer, remove their wrapping, and soak for 10 minutes in the lemon juice and ice water.
2. Place them in a colander and let very cold water run over them for 5 minutes.
3. In the meantime, bring the water-lemon juice mixture to a rolling boil over a high flame and place the shrimp in it.
4. Let the water come back to a boil and cook the shrimp for 30 seconds after the water has boiled.
5. Drain the shrimp into a colander and run under cold water for 5 minutes.
6. Let them thoroughly drain, place them in a glass bowl, then pat dry with paper towels.
7. Cover and refrigerate for at least 2 hours.

Serving: See the preparation for cooking Boiled Fresh Shrimp* (preceding recipe).

NOTE: As with boiled fresh shrimp this recipe can be used for any other recipe calling for cooked boiled shrimp.

Shrimp Newburg

Serves 6

This dish, though very tasty, should not be prepared for those who are not permitted to eat shrimp.

4 tablespoons sweet butter, at room temperature, cut into small cubes
2 tablespoons unbleached flour
$1/4$ teaspoon cayenne
$1/2$ teaspoon dried mustard
$1/4$ teaspoon freshly ground white pepper
1 cup heavy cream (or triple strength low sodium dry milk)
2 cups milk (or low sodium dry milk)

$1/4$ teaspoon paprika
$3^1/2$ teaspoons seasoned salt substitute (optional)
2 tablespoons sweet butter
$1/2$ pound fresh mushrooms, thinly sliced lengthwise
4 egg yolks
3 pounds Boiled Fresh Shrimp*
$1/4$ cup dry sherry
$1/4$ cup brandy

GARNISH: $1/4$ cup chopped fresh parsley

1. Place enough water in the bottom half of a double boiler to reach $1/2$ inch below the top section, and bring it to a scald (but not to a boil) over a high flame.

2. Reduce the flame to low-medium and melt the butter in the top section, stirring occasionally.

3. Gradually add the flour, stirring constantly. When blended, add the cayenne, mustard, and pepper, stir for 2 to 3 minutes.

4. Very slowly add the cream, milk, paprika, and salt substitute, stirring constantly until the sauce thickens. Remove the top of the double boiler from the heat and let the cream mixture cool for 5 minutes.

5. In a small skillet heat the 2 tablespoons of butter on medium heat and sauté the mushrooms until barely tender. Turn the flame to simmer and continue cooking.

6. While the mushrooms are cooking, beat the egg yolks with a wire whisk in a mixing bowl until frothy, slowly pour a little of the cream mixture into them, stirring constantly, until all is thoroughly blended.

7. Return the mixture to the top section of the double boiler, stirring constantly. Slowly add the mushrooms, then the boiled shrimp, and finally the sherry and brandy.

8. Place the top part of the double boiler back into the bottom part and, stirring constantly, heat the shrimp Newburg over a medium flame for approximately 3 minutes or until piping hot.

Serving: Spoon the mixture into a heated *au gratin* dish and sprinkle on the parsley. This may be served with rice or a buttered pasta such as thin green noodles, which are as pleasing to the eye as to the palate.

Shrimp Scampi

Serves 14 as a first course, or 6
as a main course

Superb and delicious but unfortunately allowed only to those whose doctors permit them to have shrimp.

42 raw jumbo shrimp, shelled, deveined, and butterflied
³/₄ cup fresh lemon juice mixed with enough ice water to cover the shrimp
¹/₂ cup sweet butter
¹/₄ cup olive oil and ¹/₄ to ¹/₂ cup corn oil or peanut oil
8 cloves garlic, pressed
12 shallots, finely chopped
1 large onion, very finely chopped

2¹/₂ tablespoons fresh lemon juice
¹/₂ teaspoon dry mustard
1 teaspoon freshly ground white pepper
¹/₈ teaspoon cayenne
2 tablespoons, or more, sweet butter

GARNISH: 2 tablespoons finely minced fresh parsley

1. Soak the shrimp for 1 hour in the lemon juice and ice water.
2. Preheat the oven to 400°.
3. Drain the shrimp and rinse in fresh ice water, pat dry with paper towels.
4. Melt the butter and oil in a small, heavy skillet over a medium flame. Add the garlic, shallots, and onion. Cook, stirring often, just until the onion is a pale golden color.
5. Add the lemon juice, mustard, pepper, and cayenne. Simmer and stir well for 10 minutes over a low flame.
6. Heavily butter a large, shallow baking pan (or copper pan) and place the shrimp in a single layer.
7. Bake uncovered for 5 minutes.
8. Spoon the melted butter-onion mixture over the shrimp, bake for 7 minutes more or until the shrimp are just cooked (pink and tender), basting the shrimp very well 2 or 3 times.

Serving: Serve at once, either in the baking dish or a preheated serving platter. Sprinkle the parsley over the shrimp and *voilà*, one of the most delicious dishes you will ever serve or eat (but only if you are allowed to). If you are serving this as a main course, offer Boiled Rice* with it.

Szechuan Shrimp

Indoors or out, these serve 14 as a first course or 16 as a main course

To be eaten only by those people who have shrimp included in their "permitted foods."

42 raw jumbo shrimp, shelled, deveined, and butterflied

¾ cup fresh lemon juice mixed with enough ice water to cover the shrimp

MARINADE:

1½ inches ginger root, freshly grated

8 cloves garlic, pressed

¾ cup salt-free chili sauce

1 cup peanut oil

1 teaspoon finely minced fresh sweet basil

1 tablespoon seasoned salt substitute (optional)

⅓ teaspoon cayenne (or to taste)

1 tablespoon salt-free chili powder

GARNISH: 2 tablespoons finely minced fresh parsley

1. Soak the shrimp for 1 hour in the lemon juice and ice water.
2. Rinse them in fresh ice water and pat them dry with paper towels.
3. Pour half the marinade in a large flat pan and place the shrimp in a single layer in it.
4. Pour the remainder of the marinade over them, cover tightly, and marinate for 2 to 3 hours.
5. Toss them thoroughly with the marinade so they are well coated.
6. *For outdoor cooking:* Skewer the shrimp and broil them over red-hot charcoals for about 4 to 6 minutes or just until the shrimp are cooked (pink and tender), basting twice with the marinade.
7. *For indoor cooking:* Pour a little of the marinade in the bottom of a flat broiling pan and place the shrimp on top. Broil 4 inches from the broiler flame for 3 to 4 minutes or until the shrimp are just cooked (pink and tender), basting twice with the marinade.

Serving: For a first course: Place 1 tablespoon of the hot marinade into preheated individual *au gratin* dishes and place 3 shrimp in each dish. Garnish with parsley. Offer Garlic Toast* nestled in white napery in your favorite basket.

For a main course: Transfer the shrimp and the marinade into a preheated deep serving platter. Garnish with parsley. Serve over Boiled Rice.*

Sautéed Sole

Serves 6

This is superb as is or with a variety of sauces such as Sauce Velouté or Sauce Provençale.*

**6 large sole fillets (approxi-
    mately 8 ounces each)**
**³/₄ teaspoon freshly ground
    white pepper**
¹/₂ cup unbleached flour
2 eggs, moderately beaten
**¹/₂ cup salt-free cornflake
    crumbs**

4 tablespoons Clarified Butter*

**GARNISH: Fresh parsley sprigs
    and lemon wedges**

1. Preheat the oven to 180°.
2. Place the fillets between sheets of wax paper, gently flatten them, taking care not to bruise. Sprinkle with white pepper. Dust the fillets with flour, dip them in egg, and then in cornflake crumbs.
3. In a very large skillet heat the clarified butter over a medium-high flame until it is very hot, add the fillets, a few at a time, taking care that they do not touch. Sauté quickly for about 3 minutes on each side, or until the crumbs are a light golden color and the fish flakes to the touch of a fork. (When you turn the fish, use a large spatula so as not to break the fillets.)
4. Transfer to a baking pan lined with a triple thickness of paper towels. Place it in the oven to keep warm until all the fillets are sautéed.

Serving: Transfer the fish to a preheated large platter and garnish with parsley and lemon wedges. Serve with a variety of Steamed Vegetables* and your favorite fish sauce.

Fillet of Sole with Mushrooms and Cream

Serves 4

³/₄ cup Court Bouillon*
¹/₂ cup dry white wine
2 pounds sole fillets (approximately 8 ounces each)
3¹/₂ to 4 tablespoons sweet butter
1 onion, finely chopped
1 pound small mushrooms, thinly sliced lengthwise
3 tablespoons unbleached flour
1 teaspoon freshly ground white pepper

1¹/₂ inches ginger root, freshly grated
¹/₂ cup heavy cream (or triple strength low sodium dry milk)

GARNISH: 1 lemon, sliced into ¹/₄-inch rounds sprinkled with 3 tablespoons finely chopped fresh parsley

1. Preheat the oven to 180°.
2. Place the court bouillon in a fish poacher, cover, and bring to a boil over a medium-high flame.
3. When boiling, reduce the flame to low, add the wine and sole, and simmer for approximately 8 minutes or until the fish flakes easily when touched with a fork.
4. Remove the fish, place in a very well-buttered ovenproof serving dish, and place in the oven to keep warm.
5. Continue to let the fish stock and wine mixture cook uncovered over a medium flame until it has cooked down to 1 cup.
6. In the meantime, melt the butter in a heavy skillet over a medium flame and sauté the onion until it is translucent. Add the mushrooms and stir well. Sauté for 4 minutes, stirring often.
7. Slowly add the flour, stirring constantly, until the flour is thoroughly blended with the onions and mushrooms.
8. Stir in the pepper and the ginger, slowly add the 1 cup of the stock-wine mixture, stirring constantly. Cook the sauce until it is smooth and reaches a low boil.
9. Turn the flame to low and slowly stir in the cream (or triple strength low sodium milk), making sure that the cream does not boil.

Serving: Remove the sole from the oven, spoon the sauce over it, and garnish with the parsley-lemon slices. Serve at once.

Poached Fillet of Sole

Serves 4 to 6

This is a very simple, quick, delicate, and delicious dish that may be served as is or dressed up by offering a variety of sauces.

1½ cups Court Bouillon*
2½ pounds sole fillets (approxi-
     mately 6 pieces)

GARNISH:
Paprika
½ cup finely minced fresh
     parsley
1 lemon, cut into ½-inch rounds

1. Place the court bouillon in a fish poacher, cover, and bring to a boil over a medium-high flame.
2. Place the fillets on the rack of the poacher.
3. When the court bouillon is boiling, lower the rack containing the fillets into the liquid. Reduce the flame to low, and simmer for approximately 10 minutes or until the fish flakes easily to the touch of a fork.

Serving: Transfer the sole to a preheated serving platter, spoon a little of the court bouillon (approximately ½ cup) over the fish, sprinkle lightly with paprika, and garnish with freshly chopped parsley and the rounds of lemon. In a separate bowl offer Sauce Aïoli* or Lemon Butter* or Horseradish Cream Sauce* or any other salt-free sauce that you might prefer.

Fillet of Sole, Stuffed

Serves 12

I am sure you are thinking, "Is she kidding? This recipe will take forever." Actually it is not complicated and not much more time consuming
than many recipes that look shorter. Take heart and do try it ... the
results are well worth the effort.

**16 sole fillets (approximately 8
to 10 ounces each), 4 of
them finely minced**
**½ teaspoon freshly ground
white pepper**
⅓ cup fresh lemon juice
2½ tablespoons sweet butter
**1 large Spanish onion, finely
minced**
**1 pound small mushrooms – ½
pound finely minced, ½
pound sliced paper-thin
lengthwise**
**3 tablespoons finely minced
fresh chives**
**2 tablespoons finely minced
fresh parsley**
½ cup water
1½ tablespoons sweet butter

**2½ teaspoons seasoned salt sub-
stitute (optional)**
**¾ teaspoon (or more) freshly
ground white pepper**
4 tablespoons unbleached flour
**6 tablespoons sweet butter,
melted**
4 tablespoons fresh lemon juice
3 tablespoons unbleached flour
**½ cup dry vermouth mixed with
¾ cup Court Bouillon***
**¾ cup heavy cream (or triple
strength low sodium dry
milk)**
⅛ teaspoon cayenne (optional)
**½ teaspoon freshly ground
white pepper**
**2 tablespoons finely minced
fresh chives**

1. Into the fillets rub the pepper, place them in a large plastic bag. Pour
in the lemon juice and seal the bag tightly. Refrigerate, then marinate for
at least 2 hours, turning the bag 3 or 4 times during the marinating period.
Place the minced fish in a bowl, cover, and refrigerate.

2. Melt the 2½ tablespoons of butter in a heavy skillet over a medium
flame, and sauté the onion until it is translucent.

3. Add the minced mushrooms (reserving the sliced mushrooms for the
sauce), stir well, and sauté for 4 minutes.

4. Add the chives, parsley, and minced fish. Stir constantly for ½ minute or until all the ingredients are well blended. Remove the skillet from
the heat.

5. In a small saucepan add the ½ cup of water and 1½ tablespoons of
butter. Bring to a boil over a medium flame while stirring constantly with a
wooden spoon.

6. Add the salt substitute, pepper, and the 4 tablespoons of flour, a little at a time, while beating the mixture vigorously with a wooden spoon. Continue to beat until the mixture is thick and smooth. Remove from the heat.

7. Stirring the flour mixture constantly, slowly add the fish-mushroom mixture. Set aside.

8. Preheat the oven to 375°.

9. Drain the fillets and lay them on a sheet of waxed paper.

10. Spread some of the fish-mushroom-butter mixture on each of the 12 fillets, roll them up, jelly-roll fashion, starting from the tail. Fasten the roll-ups with toothpicks or skewers or tie a string around each.

11. Heavily butter an ovenproof and flameproof baking dish.

12. Place the roll-ups in the baking dish and pour the 6 tablespoons of melted butter and the lemon juice over them.

13. Cover the dish with aluminum foil and bake for approximately 15 minutes or until the fillets are no longer translucent and the fish flakes easily to the touch of a fork.

14. Remove them to an *au gratin* pan or to a deep serving platter just large enough to hold them standing up, and remove the toothpicks or skewers or string. Cover the container with aluminum foil and keep it warm on the back of the stove.

15. Add the 3 tablespoons of flour to the pan juices in the baking dish a little at a time, stirring constantly over a very low flame until well blended.

16. Slowly add the vermouth-court bouillon mixture, stirring constantly until the sauce is thickened and smooth.

17. Add the sliced mushrooms to the sauce, stir well, and simmer for 6 minutes or until all the ingredients are piping hot.

18. Slowly add the cream, cayenne, pepper, and chives, stirring constantly for 3 minutes (making absolutely sure that the cream is warmed but does not boil). Remove from the flame.

Serving: Nap the stuffed sole with one third of the sauce and put the remaining sauce into a preheated serving bowl or tiny tureen. Serve at once.

Sole Provençale à la Crème

Serves 4 to 6

Have you had fish on the wharf in St. Tropez? Then you will surely remember that mouth-watering aroma of garlic and herbs when you serve this.

6 large sole fillets (approxi-
    mately 8 ounces each)
1/2 teaspoon freshly ground
    white pepper
1/3 cup fresh lemon juice
2 1/2 tablespoons sweet butter at
    room temperature
5 tablespoons finely minced fresh
    chives
12 shallots, finely minced
6 cloves garlic, finely minced
1 cup tomatoes, peeled, seeded,
    and chopped
1/2 teaspoon freshly ground
    white pepper

1/8 teaspoon cayenne
2 teaspoons salt substitute (op-
    tional)
1/2 cup Court Bouillon*
1/3 cup dry white wine
2 teaspoons cornstarch
2/3 cup heavy cream (or triple
    strength low sodium dry
    milk)

GARNISH: 1 1/2 tablespoons
    minced fresh parsley

1. On the fillets sprinkle the pepper and place them in a plastic bag. Pour the lemon juice over them and seal the bag tightly. Refrigerate. Marinate for at least 2 hours, turning the bag 3 or 4 times during the marinating period.

2. Drain the fillets and roll them up, starting with the tail, and secure the ends with wooden toothpicks.

3. In a medium-size flameproof baking dish or deep skillet, melt the butter over a low flame, sauté the chives, shallots, and garlic for 5 minutes.

4. Add the tomatoes, pepper, cayenne, and salt substitute, stir well.

5. Arrange the rolled fillets over the mixture and pour the court bouillon and wine over them. Raise the flame to high and bring the liquid to a boil.

6. Reduce the flame to low-medium and cook for about 8 to 10 minutes or until the fish flakes easily to the touch of a fork (gently turn the rolled fillets after 5 minutes of cooking so that each side cooks for approximately 5 minutes).

7. Transfer them to a preheated platter, cover with aluminum foil, and keep warm on the back of the stove.

8. Raise the flame to medium-high, stirring the sauce constantly for 3 minutes until it is slightly reduced. Stir in the cornstarch and cook until it is thoroughly absorbed and the sauce has thickened.

9. Turn the flame to low and slowly add the cream (or triple strength low sodium dry milk), stirring constantly. Continue to simmer, stirring all the while, for 3 or 4 minutes or until the cream is thoroughly warmed and the sauce is piping hot (make sure the cream does not boil).

Serving: Spoon the sauce over the fillets and garnish with the parsley. Serve at once.

Grilled Sole à la Suisse

Serves 4

Cheese lovers will surely find this Swiss-inspired fish dish not only a pleasure to the eye but a delight to the palate.

8 sole fillets (approximately 4 to 6 ounces each)
3/4 teaspoon freshly ground white pepper
1/2 cup fresh lemon juice
6 tablespoons sweet butter, melted (or corn oil)
4 tablespoons homemade Mayonnaise*
2 teaspoons seasoned salt substitute (optional)

1 teaspoon freshly ground white pepper
1 very large Spanish onion, sliced paper thin
2 large beefsteak tomatoes, thinly sliced
1 large wedge (about 1 pound) salt-free Gouda cheese, grated

1. Rub the fillets with the pepper. Place them in a plastic bag and add the lemon juice. Seal tightly and refrigerate. Marinate for at least 2 hours, turning the bag 3 or 4 times during the marinating period.

2. Preheat the broiler for 10 minutes (550°).

3. Place 4 individual broiler pans in the broiler and heat them for 10 minutes.

4. Remove them and add to each pan 1 1/2 tablespoons of the melted butter (or corn oil).

5. Remove the fillets from the bag and drain. Place 2 in each pan (1 layer only and not overlapping).

6. Spread 1 tablespoon of mayonnaise over the 2 fillets in each pan, sprinkle with the salt substitute and pepper.

7. Place the pans about 4 to 5 inches from the broiler flame, broil for about 10 minutes, basting every 2 or 3 minutes, or until the fish barely flakes to the touch of a fork.

8. Remove the pans from the broiler, place a single layer of the onions over the fillets, then a single layer of the tomatoes over the onions, then the grated cheese on top.

9. Baste the cheese with the drippings in the pans, then place the pans back in the broiler (5 inches from the flame).

10. Turn the broiler heat down to 300°, broil for 4 to 6 minutes or until the cheese has melted and starts to bubble.

Serving: I hope that your individual broiler pans come with wooden planks or ceramic holders. Place the pans into their holders and serve at once.

Fish Tempura

Serves 7 to 8

A Japanese specialty, translated for low sodium needs.

4 pounds sole fillets cut into 2-inch strips

2½ teaspoons seasoned salt substitute (optional)

1 teaspoon freshly ground white pepper

½ cup lemon juice, freshly squeezed

1½ quarts peanut or vegetable oil

Tempura Batter (on opposite page)

1. Sprinkle the fish strips with the salt substitute and pepper. Place them in a plastic bag. Pour in the lemon juice and seal the bag tightly. Refrigerate. Marinate for at least 2 hours, turning the bag 3 or 4 times during the marinating period.

2. When you are ready to prepare the *tempura,* heat the oil in a deep-fat fryer (or very deep heavy skillet) over a medium-high flame to 360°.

3. Preheat the oven to 180°.

4. While the oil is heating, drain the fish and thoroughly pat dry between a double thickness of paper towels.

5. Spear the strips of fish with a fork, dip them into the batter, then drain for 1 to 2 minutes on wax paper to remove excess batter.

6. When 4 or 5 pieces have drained, drop them into the hot oil and fry them for about 5 minutes or until golden brown.

7. Place them on a baking sheet lined with a double thickness of paper towels, put in the oven to keep warm and let drain.

8. Repeat Steps 4, 5, and 6 until all the fish is dried and drained.

Serving: Place the fish *tempura* on a preheated serving platter garnished with thin lemon slices and small bunches of parsley. Offer either Mideastern Yogurt Sauce,* Hawaiian Sauce,* or Herb Mayonnaise.*

TEMPURA BATTER

3 egg yolks
2 cups ice water
2¹/₂ cups unbleached flour, sifted
       3 times with 1 teaspoon
       salt-free baking powder

1. Put the egg yolks and ice water into a bowl that fits into a larger bowl half filled with ice cubes.

2. Beat the mixture with a hand mixer or wire whisk until thoroughly blended.

3. Slowly add the sifted flour, and fold it in with a wooden spoon (you should see particles of flour on top of the batter). Do not overmix.

POULTRY
The Houdini of Cooking

Poultry

In Europe chickens are still bought live or freshly killed, retaining their wonderful natural flavor. But, I'm sad to say, the state of poultry in this country has suffered a setback since it became big business in the past two decades. There was a time when children accompanied their mothers or grandmothers to the live poultry markets that dotted the cities, or to farms in the country. Instead of scampering about after chickens, today, for the most part, children are reduced to looking in the storage cases of supermarkets at packaged, limp, tasteless chickens or parts thereof. Few people other than religious Jewish housewives and traditional Italian cooks manage to find the sources of truly fresh poultry. It's a shame, because chickens are low in calories, in fat, and in price relative to other meats, and they are very high in protein. However, if at all possible, do buy your chickens from the farm or from a butcher shop that gets daily farm deliveries. In many cities there is just no way to do this, so if you are relegated to supermarket purchasing, make friends with the butcher and have him notify you when "fresh" chickens are being delivered. Remember that the "fresh" chicken you buy at the supermarket is only a very distant cousin to the fresh chicken you buy from the farm.

Chicken is often eaten in our home because of its low calories, low price, low cholesterol, and high qualities of versatility. With a little effort (and sometimes with much more than a little effort) it can, with myriad herbs and spices, sauces, fruits, and vegetables, be magically transformed into the delicious and varied cuisines of Northern and Southern Italy, the *haute cuisine* of Paris and Lyon, or the earthly and divine specialties of the French Provence, the piquant and unusual flavor combinations in our dishes of Morocco, Turkey, and India or those of Peking, Canton, and Szechuan.

Contrary to this exotica, a simple broiled chicken, using a bird one and one half to two pounds, split, rubbed with garlic and freshly ground pepper, and brushed with sweet butter mixed with herbs, is a staple in our household. We take it to work as a cold picnic lunch, accompanied simply by a fresh tomato, or we raid the refrigerator on a Sunday night after a day at the beach and make a delightful supper of cold broiled chicken, accompanied by homemade Mayonnaise,* which is always in our refrigerator, Garlic Herb Toast,* a salad of arugula, watercress, buttercrunch lettuce, cold beans, tomatoes, or whatever vegetable leftovers appeal to us, tossed with a Vinaigrette Dressing* and well chilled white wine. What a joy!

Most of my recipes call for the fryer size — about two to three pounds — which can also be used for broiling, grilling, and roasting. I use a stewing chicken or fowl for soups and fricassees. It is usually an older bird, sometimes called a yearling, sized anywhere from three and one half pounds up.

My butcher can supply me with fresh ducklings and ducks if I order them a week in advance, but I know that in most parts of the country they can rarely be bought fresh anymore, so a word should be said here about defrosting. Leave the bird in the freezer wrapper and let it thaw in the refrigerator for about twenty-four hours. This method retains more of the flavor than thawing under running water or thawing at room temperature and inhibits the growth of bacteria. Giblets should be removed immediately after thawing.

Turkey, the traditional American bird, is of course the star of our Thanksgiving holiday menu. It is the most inexpensive of the economical poultry category and, while not as delicate or versatile as chicken, it has a hearty and delicious flavor all its own. Somehow, I can never decide which I enjoy more; the regal bird dressed in all its glory on the fourth Thursday of November, or the leftovers at Friday lunch featured in a divine sandwich on Russian Black Bread* spread with either Mayonnaise* or Russian Dressing* and completed with crisped Boston lettuce or thinly sliced cucumbers.

I'm sure you will notice, when you have read many of the recipes, my penchant for garlic. But, if the thought of using five cloves of garlic disturbs you, it is possible to cut down the amount without disastrous results. My own taste buds crave the staccato of garlic and the subtle excitement of a mélange of herbs and the not so subtle excitement of spices. I find, too, that when my guests ask for a recipe and I tell them how much garlic, herbs, or spices I have just used, they stare in wonderment, and I never fail to hear "I can't believe it." So if you are timid in your taste, start with less garlic, herbs, and spices called for and build up to "full flavor."

Once dinner is prepared, do not diminish it by lack of presentation. Depending on the dish, it should be housed to perfection, be it on a Georgian silver tray, a pottery tureen, a faience platter, or an earthenware casserole. Every time I travel I keep an eagle eye out for interesting casseroles and serving platters and bowls. I especially adore the Portuguese pottery for chicken, and gleaming white china tureens add sparkle to a table set with patterned cloths from Provence and masses of chunky candles. I must confess to being an avid collector, a compulsive shopper, and an overweight traveler, as anyone who has ever traveled with me can tell you. But it's not the clothes that make me overweight. I can manage with three to four changes on a two-week business trip to Europe. It's the china, the pottery, the brass, and the copper that I just can't resist. And the irony is that when I admonish myself with a "No, you don't need it. Where will you put it?" I'm always sorry, for one always finds room for something beautiful. When it isn't filled with food, it may hold flowers or cookies or candy, or mail in the foyer. It may simply stand as a beautiful *objet d'art* enhancing my baker's rack, or perhaps hang in my kitchen, or it may find a home on my desk in our bedroom, imparting continuing pleasure long after "that" dinner has been served.

Almond Chicken

Serves 6

5 tablespoons sweet butter
4 cloves garlic, pressed
2 chickens, 3½ to 4 pounds, cut into eighths and skinned
5 tablespoons dry sherry
2 tablespoons brandy
2 large onions, finely chopped
¼ cup finely chopped fresh parsley
½ teaspoon paprika
2 tablespoons seasoned salt substitute (optional)

⅔ teaspoon freshly ground white pepper
4 tablespoons cornstarch
4 cups cold Chicken Stock*
⅔ cup heavy cream, warmed (or triple strength low sodium dry milk)
2 teaspoons dried tarragon
⅔ cup toasted, slivered almonds

1. Using a very large skillet, melt the butter over a medium flame and add the garlic and chicken. Brown the pieces on all sides and remove to a platter.

2. To the skillet, add the sherry, brandy, onions, parsley, paprika, salt substitute, and pepper. Cover and cook for 5 minutes over a low-medium flame.

3. Dissolve the cornstarch in the stock and add it to the skillet, using a medium-high flame. Stir constantly until the sauce comes to a low boil. Add the chicken, cover, and cook over a medium flame for 1 hour or until the chicken is tender. Remove to a heated serving platter.

4. To the skillet, add the cream and tarragon, stir until the sauce is blended and very hot. Do not bring to a boil. Spoon the sauce over the chicken and sprinkle with the almonds.

Serving: A marvelous accompaniment to this, for both the palate and the eye, is hot Brandied Peaches* filled with Steamed Green Peas.*

Baked Chicken and Baked Chicken Breasts

Serves 4 to 6

This is a mainstay in our house and can be dressed up for company with a variety of sauces.

2 chickens, 2½ pounds, skinned and quartered

MARINADE:
2 teaspoons freshly ground white pepper
2 teaspoons seasoned salt substitute (optional)
2 large onions, finely chopped
4 cloves garlic, finely chopped
⅓ cup corn oil
½ cup dry white wine

INGREDIENTS:
3 eggs, well beaten
1½ cups crushed salt-free cornflakes, mixed with 1 teaspoon finely ground white pepper
1 teaspoon dry mustard (optional)
⅛ teaspoon cayenne (optional)
4 teaspoons seasoned salt substitute (optional)

GARNISH: Parsley

1. Wash the chicken and pat dry. Rub the pepper and salt substitute (optional) into it.

2. Place the pieces in a large plastic bag and add the onions, garlic, oil, and wine. Seal the bag tightly and rotate it well. Refrigerate it for at least 3 hours, rotating the bag 3 or 4 times during the marinating period.

3. Preheat the oven to 350°.

4. Pour ⅛ inch of oil in 2 large baking pans and place them in the oven to heat.

5. Drain the chicken, discard the marinade, and pat dry with paper towels.

6. Dip the chicken into the egg, then into the seasoned cornflakes and lay on wax paper.

7. When coated and the baking pans are very hot, put the chicken, flesh side down, into them.

8. Bake for 25 minutes. Then, turn the pieces, flesh side up, and bake for 30 to 35 minutes more, or until the chicken is brown, crisp, and tender.

Serving: If there is any oil clinging to the chicken, drain it for 2 minutes between paper towels. Put on a preheated silver tray and garnish with the parsley. Serve at once, accompanied by Apricot Mustard Sauce,* Horseradish Cream Sauce,* Hawaiian Sauce,* or Ginger Red Pepper Relish.*

NOTE: For baked chicken breasts use 4 whole breasts, split, skinned, boned, and pounded to less than ½-inch thickness. Follow the above recipe but bake the breasts for 35 minutes (turning them once during the baking period) or until they are brown, crisp, and tender.

Baked Chicken and Rice à la Crème

Serves 8

I suggest that you use one or two attractive copper or pottery *au gratin* baking dishes so that they may be brought piping hot from the oven to the sideboard. In addition to being functional and attractive, there will be no pots to wash at the conclusion of dinner . . . what a joy!

3 chickens, 2½ pounds each, cut into eighths (or 3½ pounds chicken breasts, skinned, boned, and pounded thin)
½ cup corn oil
Unbleached flour
4 tablespoons sweet butter
4 cloves garlic, finely minced
15 shallots, finely minced
¾ teaspoon freshly ground white pepper
½ tablespoon dried tarragon
1 pound fresh small mushrooms, thinly sliced lengthwise
4 cups Boiled Rice* (preferably natural brown rice)

2 cups grated salt-free Gouda cheese
2 cups grated salt-free Cheddar cheese
2 cups heavy cream (or triple strength low sodium dry milk)
1 cup dry sherry
1½ cups blanched, slivered almonds

GARNISH: 2½ tablespoons minced fresh parsley

1. Coat the chicken with a little of the oil, then dredge it in the flour.
2. Pour the remaining oil in a heavy skillet and heat over a medium-high flame.
3. Brown the chicken on all sides until golden brown (adding more oil if necessary).
4. Set the chicken aside on a platter and discard the oil left in the skillet.
5. Melt the butter in the skillet over a medium flame and sauté the garlic, shallots, tarragon, and mushrooms until the shallots and mushrooms are barely tender. Remove from the heat.

6. Preheat the oven to 375°.

7. In a well-buttered, large and attractive baking dish (or baking pans) layer in the chicken, then layer in the mushroom-shallot mixture, rice, and cheeses.

8. Mix the cream (or triple strength low sodium dry milk) and sherry together and spoon over the cheese.

9. Sprinkle the almonds on top and bake in the oven for 30 to 40 minutes or until the almonds are a deep golden brown and the cheese is melted and bubbling.

Serving: Sprinkle with chopped parsley and serve.

Baked Chicken Mornay

Serves 4 to 8

4 chicken breasts, split, skinned, boned, and pounded thin
2 eggs, lightly beaten, seasoned with 1 teaspoon salt substitute (optional), 1 teaspoon freshly ground white pepper
Cornflakes, salt-free, crushed

½ stick sweet butter (or more)
½ cup corn oil
2 cups (hot) Mornay Sauce*

GARNISH: 3 tablespoons finely minced fresh chives

1. Preheat the oven to 350°.

2. Dip the chicken breasts into the seasoned eggs, dredge them in the cornflakes.

3. In a large skillet, heat the butter and oil over a medium-high flame and sauté the chicken breasts until they are golden brown.

4. Transfer them to a well-buttered, attractive ovenproof casserole. Place them in one layer, not overlapping, and spoon the Mornay sauce over them. Cover.

5. Bake for 15 minutes covered, then 15 minutes uncovered, or until the sauce is bubbling hot.

Serving: Sprinkle the chives over the sauce and serve at once.

Broiled Chicken

Serves 4 to 6

2 chickens, 2½ pounds each, halved or quartered

MARINADE:
2 teaspoons white pepper, freshly ground
2 teaspoons salt substitute (optional)
2 large onions, finely chopped
4 cloves garlic, finely chopped
⅓ cup corn oil
¾ cup dry white wine

BUTTER SAUCE:
½ cup sweet butter
Juice of 2 lemons
2 cloves garlic, pressed (optional)
2 teaspoons dried tarragon (optional)

GARNISH: Sprigs of watercress

1. Wash the chicken and pat dry. Rub the pepper and salt substitute into it.

2. Place it in a large plastic bag and add the onions, garlic, oil, and wine. Seal the bag tightly and rotate it well. Refrigerate for at least 3 hours, rotating the bag 3 or 4 times during the marinating period.

3. Preheat the broiler to 550°.

4. Drain the chicken (but do not dry) and place it on a broiler rack skin side down.

5. Broil 4 inches from the flame for 12 minutes, basting twice. Baste either with the marinade or with the butter sauce.

6. Turn the chicken over (skin side up), and broil for 12 minutes more or until the skin is crisp and the chicken is tender, basting 3 times.

Serving: Transfer the chicken to a preheated platter garnished with watercress and serve at once.

NOTE: I always skin chicken, but since most of my guests prefer it with the skin on, I included the skin in this recipe. I think it tastes better without the skin, but the decision obviously is yours.

Cantonese Chicken with Lettuce Leaves

Serves 4 to 6

1½ cups ground Poached
   Chicken Breasts* (skinned)
3 tablespoons cornstarch
2 teaspoons seasoned salt substitute (optional)
¾ cup cold water
12 egg whites

2 tablespoons peanut oil
2¾ cups Chicken Stock,* mixed
   with ⅓ cup dry sherry and
   3 tablespoons cornstarch
16 large outer leaves from 2
   heads of iceberg lettuce

1. In a large glass bowl mix the chicken with the cornstarch and salt substitute until thoroughly blended.

2. Stirring constantly, add a tablespoon of water at a time until each spoonful is absorbed and all the water is used (do not add the water too quickly or the mixture will not bind). Set aside.

3. Using an electric mixer beat the egg whites on high speed until stiff but not dry. Stir ¼ of the egg whites into the chicken mixture. Fold in the remainder of the egg whites.

4. Preheat the oven to 180°.

5. In a large, heavy skillet or in a wok heat the peanut oil over a medium flame until hot but not smoking. Pour in the chicken mixture and immediately remove the skillet from the flame. Stir rapidly with chopsticks or a wooden spoon and mix thoroughly.

6. Return the skillet to a medium flame and cook just until the mixture sets (do not brown).

7. Spoon the mixture into a shallow ovenproof casserole and place it in the oven.

8. In a heavy saucepan heat the chicken stock mixture over a medium-high flame, stirring often until the sauce becomes thick and reaches a bubbling boil.

Serving: Spoon the sauce over the chicken. Serve with the lettuce leaves in a separate bowl. Each person will spoon some of the chicken (about 1½ to 2 tablespoons) onto a lettuce leaf. Over the chicken one can spoon Hawaiian Sauce,* Hot Mustard Sauce,* or sprinkle on the Spicy Sesame Oil* – or all three if a sweet and pungent taste is desired. Then fold the lettuce leaf over the mixture. Using one's fingers is a must in order to eat this delectable dish.

I suggest serving Meat Balls Chinoise* or Spicy Chicken Quiche* or Chicken Curry Soup* as a first course. For dessert I suggest either Cold Lemon Soufflé* or Strawberry à la Crème.* This is one of our all-time favorite dinners.

Chicken and Scampi, Marinara

Serves 10 to 12

If shrimp are a no-no, this dish is almost as good when prepared only with the chicken and sauce.

3 chickens, 2½ pounds each cut
    into eighths, skinned
2 teaspoons freshly ground black
    pepper
3 cloves garlic, crushed
⅓ cup olive oil mixed with ¼
    cup lemon juice, freshly
    squeezed

½ cup olive oil (or corn oil)
½ cup dry white wine
2 quarts (hot) Marinara Sauce*
2 pounds Boiled Shrimp*

GARNISH: ½ cup minced fresh
    parsley

1. Into the skin of the chicken rub the pepper and garlic. Place the pieces in a large plastic bag and pour in the oil-lemon juice mixture. Seal the bag tightly. Refrigerate for at least 3 hours, turning the bag 3 or 4 times during the marinating period.

2. Drain the chicken and pat dry with paper towels.

3. In a very large, heavy skillet, heat the oil over a medium-high flame and brown the chicken on all sides. Remove it.

4. Pour off the excess oil and deglaze the pan with the white wine. Replace the chicken, and pour the marinara sauce over it.

5. Cover and cook over a low-medium flame for approximately 40 minutes or until the chicken is tender.

6. Transfer it to a preheated serving platter and keep warm.

7. Add the boiled shrimp to the sauce. Stirring constantly, heat them for 2 minutes or until piping hot.

Serving: Spoon the shrimp and the sauce over and around the chicken, sprinkle with the minced parsley, and serve at once. This dish is a natural with Boiled Rice.*

Chicken Casserole

Serves 6 to 8

For a cold winter night.

2 chickens, 3½ pounds each, cut into quarters, skinned
1 teaspoon freshly ground white pepper
½ cup corn oil
⅛ teaspoon cayenne
3 large onions, thinly sliced
6 cloves garlic, pressed
6 tomatoes, peeled, seeded, and chopped
2 bay leaves
¼ cup chopped fresh parsley
1 teaspoon oregano
2 teaspoons sweet basil

12 carrots, sliced ½ inch thick
18 tiny new potatoes
3 cups dry white wine
8 medium zucchini, sliced ½ inch thick
½ pound fresh green beans, tips off
2 tablespoons corn oil
1 pound small mushrooms, sliced thinly lengthwise
⅓ cup dry sherry

GARNISH: 3 tablespoons finely minced fresh parsley

1. Rub the pepper into the chicken. In a large, heavy skillet heat the oil over a medium-high flame and brown the chicken on all sides until it is a deep golden color. Transfer to a flameproof casserole.

2. Using the same skillet, add the cayenne, onions, and garlic and stir until the onions are pale golden. Remove the vegetables with a slotted spoon to a bowl. Discard the oil and return the onion-garlic mixture to the skillet. Add the tomatoes, bay leaves, parsley, oregano, and sweet basil and stir well.

3. Spoon the mixture over the chicken. Add the carrots, potatoes, and wine to the casserole, cover, and cook on a low-medium flame for 30 minutes. Add the zucchini and green beans and cook for 20 minutes.

4. Meanwhile, heat the 2 tablespoons of oil in a heavy skillet and sauté the mushrooms until barely tender. Add the sherry and stir well.

5. Add to the casserole and cook for 10 minutes. Remove the bay leaves.

Serving: Sprinkle the parsley over the chicken and serve at once.

Chicken Concubine

Serves 6

Don't push the panic button! Many ingredients? Yes! Difficult to make?
Nay! And it certainly is delicious. So take a deep breath and let's cook.

3 pounds chicken breasts,
boned, skinned, and
pounded to about ³/₈ inch
thick
4 egg whites, lightly beaten
2 tablespoons seasoned salt substitute (optional)
1¹/₂ teaspoons freshly ground
white pepper
3 tablespoons Cointreau liqueur
5 tablespoons peanut oil (divided
in half)
6 cloves garlic, pressed
1 pound small fresh mushrooms,
thinly sliced lengthwise
12 large dried mushrooms,
soaked for 1 hour or until
soft, sliced into thin strips

6 scallions, sliced into paper-thin
rings
³/₄ pound fresh snow peas
1¹/₂ inches ginger root, finely
minced
¹/₂ cup Chicken Stock*
3 tablespoons cornstarch mixed
with 3 tablespoons cold
water
Juice of 1 large lemon
Juice of 2 large oranges
2¹/₂ tablespoons honey
1 pound shelled fresh peas, parboiled

1. Slice each chicken breast into strips about ¹/₂ inch wide.
2. Mix them with the egg whites, salt substitute, pepper, and 1¹/₂ tablespoons of the Cointreau. Set aside.
3. In a wok or a large skillet, heat 2¹/₂ tablespoons of oil over a
medium-high flame. Add the garlic, fresh and dried mushrooms, and
scallions. Stir-fry until the vegetables are lightly cooked but still very
crisp.
4. Add the snow peas and stir-fry for 1¹/₂ minutes more.
5. Remove the vegetables from the wok and place in a bowl.
6. Heat the remaining oil in the wok and add the chicken mixture and
the ginger. Stir-fry over a medium-high flame until it is no longer translucent and the chicken is tender. Remove the wok from the flame.
7. Pour the chicken stock into a small saucepan and heat over a high
flame until very hot, then stir in the cornstarch mixture and blend thoroughly.
8. Add the lemon juice, orange juice, the remainder of the Cointreau,

and the honey. Raise the flame to high and bring the mixture to a boil, stir-ring constantly.

9. Boil for 1 minute or until slightly thickened. Remove from heat.

10. Return the wok to the stove. Add the stir-fried vegetables and the parboiled peas to the chicken, stir-fry over a medium-high flame for 1 minute.

11. Pour in the sauce and stir-fry for 2 minutes more.

Serving: Transfer the chicken concubine to a preheated casserole or copper *au gratin* pan. Serve with Boiled Rice* and individual bowls of: unsweetened pineapple chunks, freshly grated coconut, toasted, slivered almonds, green onions, sliced into paper-thin rings, and Apricot-Mustard Sauce.*

Chicken Curry

Serves 10 to 12

If you are a lover of hot curry, this recipe is for you. If not, well, just move on to the next recipe.

8 tablespoons sweet butter

6 whole chicken breasts, split, skinned, and boned, cut into strips 1 by 2 inches

3 large onions, finely minced

8 cloves garlic, finely minced

4 sour green apples, peeled, cored, and coarsely chopped

5 tablespoons salt-free curry powder

5 tablespoons Chutney*

2 inches ginger root, finely grated

3/4 teaspoon freshly ground white pepper

1/4 teaspoon cayenne (or to taste)

1 1/2 tablespoons seasoned salt substitute (optional)

3 cups Chicken Stock*

2 1/2 cups milk (or low sodium dry milk)

3 tablespoons cornstarch or arrowroot, mixed with 4 tablespoons cold milk (or low sodium dry milk)

12 carrots, parboiled and sliced 1/2 inch thick crosswise

20 tiny white onions, parboiled

1 1/2 cups shelled fresh green peas, steamed but still very crisp

GARNISH: 1/3 cup finely minced fresh parsley

1. Melt the butter in a large, heavy skillet over a medium flame and sauté the chicken until no longer translucent.

2. Transfer to a large flameproof casserole.

3. To the butter in the skillet, add the onions, garlic, and apples, sauté over a medium flame, adding more butter if necessary until the onions are a pale golden color.

4. With a slotted spoon, remove the ingredients and add them to the chicken in the casserole. Mix well.

5. Add the curry powder to the remaining butter and cook for 2 minutes over a medium-low flame, stirring constantly, taking care not to burn the curry.

6. Mix the curry butter with the chutney, ginger, pepper, cayenne, salt substitute, and chicken stock. Add to the casserole and blend thoroughly with the other ingredients.

7. In a saucepan, heat the milk (or low sodium dry milk) over a low-medium flame (do not boil). Add the cornstarch mixture. Stir with a wire whisk until there are no lumps and the milk is slightly thickened.

8. Pour this into the chicken mixture and stir well.

9. Cover and cook over a low-medium flame for 25 minutes.

10. Add the carrots and onions and lightly mix all the ingredients.

11. Cover and cook over a low flame for another 20 minutes or until the chicken is tender and the sauce is thickened.

12. Add the cooked peas, mix, and cook uncovered for 2 minutes more.

Serving: Sprinkle the parsley over the curry and serve at once. Serve with Boiled Rice* and small bowls of condiments such as:

    Chutney*
    Peanuts (salt-free, of course)
    Blanched and slivered almonds, toasted
    Pineapple chunks (dietetic, naturally)
    Coconut, freshly grated
    Green onions, chopped
    Raisins
    Bananas, sliced and soaked in lemon juice
    Dried apricots and prunes, minced and soaked for 3 days in dry sherry

Chicken Diable à la Crème

Serves 8

2 4-pound Boiled Chickens,*
  skinned, boned, and cut
  into small cubes
6 tablespoons sweet butter
8 cloves garlic, pressed
½ cup finely chopped fresh
  parsley
1½ tablespoons dried mustard
¼ teaspoon cayenne
1 to 2 teaspoons salt-free chili
  powder
4 tablespoons unbleached flour
1 cup milk, scalded (or low sodium dry milk)
1 cup warmed strong Chicken
  Stock*

¾ cup warmed dry sherry
¾ cup heavy cream (or triple
  strength low sodium dry
  milk)
1 tablespoon salt substitute (optional)
1 teaspoon freshly ground white
  pepper
1½ tablespoons dried dill weed
1 cup Bread Crumbs*
3 tablespoons sweet butter, softened
1 tablespoon dry mustard
⅛ teaspoon cayenne
1 teaspoon Spanish paprika

1. Place the chicken in a large mixing bowl.

2. In a medium-size saucepan, melt 2 tablespoons of the butter over a medium flame, add the garlic, and sauté for 2 minutes. Stir in the parsley and sauté for 3 more minutes.

3. Stirring constantly, add the mustard, cayenne, chili powder, remaining butter, and flour. Cook for 4 minutes, stirring constantly. Slowly add the milk (or low sodium dry milk), chicken stock, and sherry, stirring all the while. Turn the flame to low and simmer for 3 minutes.

4. Remove the sauce from the flame and, stirring constantly, slowly add the cream (or triple strength low sodium dry milk), salt substitute, pepper, and dill.

5. Preheat the oven to 300°.

6. Fold the sauce into the chicken and spoon into a lightly buttered, large ovenproof *au gratin* dish. Sprinkle with the bread crumbs.

7. Blend the butter, mustard, and cayenne together and dot the bread crumbs with the mixture. Sprinkle with the paprika. Cover tightly with aluminum foil and bake for 10 minutes, covered. Remove the foil and bake for 10 minutes more.

8. Preheat the broiler to 550°.

9. Broil the chicken 5 inches from the flame for approximately 3 minutes or until the crumbs are well browned and the mixture is bubbling slightly.

Serving: This can also be baked in individual ramekins or scallop shells and served as a wonderful first course.

Chicken Fricassee

Serves 8

3 chickens, 3½ pounds each, cut into eighths, skinned

MARINADE:
½ cup lemon juice
5 cloves garlic, crushed
2 large onions, thinly sliced
1 tablespoon freshly ground black pepper
½ cup finely chopped fresh parsley

INGREDIENTS:
2 cups unbleached flour
⅓ cup sweet butter
¼ cup peanut oil
1 large onion, finely chopped
2 cloves garlic, pressed

4 cups boiling strong Chicken Stock*
6 tablespoons sweet butter
6 tablespoons unbleached flour
½ cup heavy cream (or triple strength low sodium dry milk)
1½ cups milk (or low sodium dry milk)
4 egg yolks
1 teaspoon freshly ground black pepper
3 tablespoons dry sherry

GARNISH: 4 tablespoons finely chopped fresh parsley

1. Place the chicken in a plastic bag with the marinade ingredients. Seal tightly. Refrigerate for at least 3 hours, turning the bag 2 or 3 times during the marinating period.

2. Drain the chicken and pat dry thoroughly with paper towels. Discard the marinade.

3. Place the flour in a plastic bag. Add a few pieces of chicken at a time and shake. Set the flour-coated chicken on a rack.

4. Heat the butter and oil in a large flameproof casserole over a medium-high flame and brown the chicken, a few pieces at a time, on all sides. Transfer to a platter and keep warm.

5. When all the pieces have been browned, discard the oil, butter mixture, and return the chicken to the casserole and add the onion, garlic, and chicken stock. Cover, turn the flame to low, and simmer for 45 minutes.

6. Preheat the oven to 180°.

7. Remove the chicken to an ovenproof serving platter and keep it warm in the oven.

8. Strain the liquid from the casserole and keep it warm in a saucepan over a very low flame.

9. Melt the butter in another saucepan over a low flame, and, stirring constantly, slowly add the flour. Stir and cook until the *roux* is browned. Remove from the flame and with a wire whisk slowly beat in the warmed liquid.

10. In a mixing bowl, lightly beat the cream (or triple strength low sodium dry milk), milk (or low sodium dry milk), egg yolks, pepper, and sherry with a wire whisk until it is thoroughly combined. Beat 1/2 cup of the *roux* into the cream mixture.

11. Place the saucepan with the *roux* on a very low flame and, beating constantly with a wire whisk, slowly add the cream mixture.

Serving: Spoon the sauce over the chicken. Garnish with the parsley, and serve with Boiled Rice.*

Chicken Mole

Serves 6 to 8

This dish is an adaptation of a Mexican recipe that supposedly dates back to the early 1700s. It is most often made in Mexico with a small turkey, but we prefer it with chicken.

2 3-pound chickens, cut into eighths, skinned

5 cloves garlic, crushed

1 1/2 teaspoons black pepper, coarsely ground

1 tablespoon seasoned salt substitute (optional)

1/4 cup olive oil

2 fresh, small hot red or green chili peppers (sliced paper thin)

Unbleached flour for dredging

1/2 cup olive oil (or corn oil)

1/2 cup white wine

2 green peppers, seeded, cored and cut into 1 inch strips

6 cloves garlic, peeled

2 slices White Bread,* toasted and cut into strips

3/4 cup blanched almonds

3 large size tomatoes, quartered, or a 1-pound can salt-free tomatoes, drained

2 fresh, small hot red or green chili peppers, cut in half

3/4 cup raisins

2 large onions, quartered

2 teaspoons sesame seeds

1 teaspoon cinnamon

1/8 teaspoon cayenne

1 teaspoon freshly ground black pepper

2 1/2 teaspoons salt substitute (optional)

2 ounces bittersweet chocolate,
   grated
1 cup grated carrots
$1/3$ cup olive oil

2 cups Chicken Stock*
18 prunes (optional)
$1/2$ cup blanched whole almonds

1. Rub all the parts of chicken well with garlic, pepper, and salt substitute.

2. Place in a plastic bag, sprinkle pieces with olive oil and chili. Seal the bag tightly. Refrigerate for at least 4 hours, rotating the bag 2 or 3 times during the marinating period.

3. Discard the marinade, dredge the chicken in the flour, and set aside.

4. In a large, heavy skillet heat the oil over a medium-high flame and brown the chicken pieces on all sides. (You will probably have to do this in 3 to 4 batches.)

5. Transfer the chicken to a well-greased ovenproof *au gratin* or roasting pan in a single layer.

6. Preheat the oven to 325°.

7. Pour off the excess fat from the pan, deglaze the pan with the white wine, and set aside.

8. Grind together the green peppers, garlic, white toast, almonds, tomatoes, red or green chili peppers, raisins, onions, and sesame seeds.

9. Transfer to a large bowl and stir in the cinnamon, cayenne, black pepper, salt substitute, chocolate, and carrots.

10. Pour the oil into the deglazed pan, heat over a medium flame for 3 minutes, and stir in all the ingredients from the bowl. Lower the flame and, stirring constantly, simmer for 4 minutes.

11. Slowly add the chicken stock, continuing to stir constantly until all the stock is combined with the ground ingredients.

12. Spoon this mixture over and around the chicken pieces. Place the prune around the chicken. Cover the pan tightly with foil and bake for 40 minutes. Remove the foil, sprinkle on the almonds, and bake for 10 minutes.

Serving: Since I bake the chicken mole in a copper *au gratin* pan, it is served directly from that pan. If your baking container is not attractive enough, transfer the chicken to a slightly deep platter and arrange the prunes around it, then sprinkle on the almonds.

Chicken Moroccan Style

Serves 8 to 10

3 fryers, 3½ pounds each, cut
    into eighths, skinned
1 teaspoon freshly ground white
    pepper
2 cloves garlic, split
½ to ⅔ cup Clarified Butter*
3 large onions, finely minced
8 cloves garlic, finely minced
6 tablespoons unbleached flour
Pineapple juice drained from the
    16-ounce can crushed pine-
    apple given below
Juice of 3 lemons
½ cup orange juice
6 tablespoons honey, heated
2½ inches fresh ginger root,
    finely minced

1½ teaspoons dry mustard
3 cups dry red wine
1½ teaspoons freshly ground
    white pepper
1 tablespoon dried cumin
2 cups pitted prunes
1 16-ounce can crushed unsweet-
    ened pineapple, drained
2 cups dried apricots
5 tart green apples, peeled,
    cored, and cut into eighths
¼ teaspoon cayenne
½ cup honey
¼ cup sweet butter
1 cup blanched almonds

1. Rub the chicken well on all sides with the pepper and garlic and let it stand at room temperature for 30 minutes.

2. Brown the chicken in clarified butter in a heavy flameproof or ovenproof casserole over a medium flame, transfer to a platter.

3. In the same casserole, sauté the onions and garlic until the onions are golden brown. Add the flour and cook until it is well blended and slightly browned, stirring constantly.

4. Preheat the oven to 300°.

5. Add the pineapple, lemon, and orange juices, honey, ginger, dry mustard, wine, pepper, cumin, prunes, pineapple, apricots, apples, and cayenne to the casserole, stirring well. Arrange the chicken on top, cover tightly, and bake for 1 hour.

6. Remove the cover, brush the chicken with the honey, and bake uncovered for 30 minutes more, brushing with the honey as you turn the pieces.

Serving: In a small skillet, melt the butter and sauté the almonds until they are golden brown. Remove the almonds with a slotted spoon and sprinkle them over the chicken and serve with parsleyed Boiled Rice.*

Chicken Tetrazzini

Serves 6 to 8

Chicken, cream, and pasta. A perfect marriage of exquisite textures and *molto* calories.

2 tablespoons sweet butter
4 tablespoons olive oil
1/2 cup rice flour
1 tablespoon seasoned salt substitute (optional)
1 teaspoon freshly ground white pepper
1/4 teaspoon cayenne (or to taste)
3 1/2 cups boiling Chicken Stock*
3 tablespoons sweet butter
3 tablespoons olive oil
1 pound mushrooms, sliced lengthwise
4 cloves garlic, minced
3 egg yolks, lightly beaten
3 tablespoons dry sherry
2/3 cup heavy cream (or triple strength low sodium dry milk)

2 Boiled Chickens,* 3 1/2 pounds each, meat only (or the meat only of 4 whole Poached Chicken Breasts,* cut into small pieces)
3/4-pound packaged thin green noodles (or the thinnest spaghetti)
3/4 cup grated salt-free Gouda cheese
2 tablespoons sweet butter

GARNISH:
1/2 cup slivered almonds, toasted
2 tablespoons minced fresh chives mixed with 1 tablespoon finely minced fresh parsley

1. In a heavy saucepan, heat the butter and olive oil over a medium flame. Add the flour, salt substitute, pepper, and cayenne, stirring with a wire whisk until all the ingredients are thoroughly blended.

2. Slowly add the chicken stock to this mixture and beat vigorously until the sauce is smooth and thick. Place the saucepan on a Flame-Tamer and turn the flame to low.

3. In a skillet heat the 3 tablespoons of sweet butter and 3 tablespoons of olive oil over a medium flame. Add the mushrooms and garlic, sauté until the mushrooms begin to brown, stir very often.

4. Stirring the lightly beaten egg yolks, add a little of the sauce to the egg yolks. Then add this mixture to the saucepan of hot sauce, stirring constantly.

5. Continuing to stir, add the sherry, cream (or triple strength low sodium dry milk), chicken, and mushrooms until all the ingredients are well blended (3 to 4 minutes).

6. Preheat the oven to 350°.

7. Cook the green noodles to your taste (*al dente,* etc.).

8. In a buttered casserole, place alternate layers of the green noodles and sauce, cover, and bake for 20 to 25 minutes.

9. Preheat the broiler to 500°.

10. Remove the casserole from the oven, uncover, add the grated cheese, and dot with the sweet butter.

11. Place the casserole under the broiler (about 4 inches from the flame) for 3 to 4 minutes or until the cheese is bubbling hot.

Serving: Sprinkle the almonds, chives, and parsley on the top and serve at once.

Chicken with Chestnut Sauce

Serves 6

1 teaspoon freshly ground white pepper
1 teaspoon dried thyme
2 chickens, 3½ pounds each, cut into eighths
½ cup corn oil
2 large onions, finely chopped
4 cloves garlic, finely chopped
1 cup Chicken Stock*
1 cup dry white wine
½ cup dry sherry
Juice of 1 lime
Juice of 1 lemon
2 pounds boiled chestnuts, peeled

¼ cup dry sherry
½ cup blanched almonds
3 tablespoons sweet butter
1 pound mushrooms, thinly sliced lengthwise
½ cup heavy cream (or triple strength low sodium dry milk)
2 tablespoons sweet butter
½ cup slivered almonds

GARNISH: 2 tablespoons finely minced fresh parsley

1. Mix the pepper and thyme together and rub well into the chicken.

2. In a heavy skillet, heat the oil over a medium-high flame and sauté the chicken until golden. Remove the chicken with a slotted spoon to a flameproof casserole.

3. In the same skillet, sauté the onions and garlic, stirring constantly, until pale golden.

4. Add the chicken stock, white wine, sherry, lime and lemon juices, stir well, and pour over the chicken. Cover and cook over a low-medium flame for 1 hour or until the chicken is tender.

5. While the chicken is cooking, place the chestnuts and the sherry in a blender (on medium speed) or in a food processor (using the steel blade) and purée. Set aside.

6. Finely mince the blanched almonds and mix them with the chestnuts and the sherry.

7. Using a heavy skillet, melt the 3 tablespoons of butter over a low-medium flame and sauté the mushrooms until brown and tender, stirring constantly. Remove the mushrooms with a slotted spoon to a bowl. Discard the butter and return the mushrooms to the skillet.

8. Add the cream (or triple strength low sodium dry milk) and heat thoroughly. Stir often, taking care not to boil the cream. Add the chestnut purée and slivered almonds.

9. When the chicken is tender, remove it from the casserole to a preheated platter, gently stir in the mushroom and chestnut purée into the casserole.

10. Return the chicken to the casserole and simmer over a very low flame for 5 to 6 minutes.

11. While the chicken is simmering, melt the 2 tablespoons of butter in a skillet over a low-medium flame and sauté the almonds until golden, stirring constantly.

Serving: Using a slotted spoon, sprinkle the almonds over the chicken and sprinkle with parsley.

Chicken with a Vegetable Sauce

Serves 4 to 6

$1/2$ cup olive oil
1 stick sweet butter
2 chickens, $2^{1}/_{2}$ pounds each, cut into eighths, skinned
2 green peppers, seeded and coarsely chopped
2 red peppers, seeded and coarsely chopped
2 large onions, finely minced
1 pound mushrooms, thinly sliced lengthwise
6 cloves garlic, finely minced

$1/3$ cup dry white wine
4 medium large tomatoes, peeled, seeded, and chopped
$1^{1}/_{2}$ cups dry white wine
$1/8$ cup finely minced fresh basil
1 tablespoon seasoned salt substitute (optional)
1 teaspoon freshly ground white pepper

GARNISH: 2 tablespoons finely minced fresh chives

1. In a heavy skillet heat the oil and the butter over a medium flame.

2. Cook the chicken on all sides until golden brown and transfer it to a platter.

3. Turn the flame to low-medium. Add the peppers, onions, mushrooms, and garlic to the pan. Stir well and sauté until all the vegetables are tender. Using a slotted spoon, transfer the vegetables to a bowl. Pour off the excess oil and butter and deglaze the pan with the wine. Return the vegetables to the skillet. Add the tomatoes, wine, basil, salt substitute, stir well.

5. Place the chicken back into the pan and cover.

6. Cook over a low-medium flame for 40 minutes, or until the chicken is tender.

7. Preheat the oven to 180°.

8. Transfer the chicken to a heated platter and keep warm in a 180° oven.

9. Bring the flame up to high and, stirring constantly, reduce the vegetable mixture until most but not all of the liquid has evaporated (about 8 to 10 minutes).

Serving: Remove the chicken from the oven and spoon the sauce over the chicken. Sprinkle the chives on top of the sauce and serve at once.

Chicken Supreme

Serves 6 to 10

This recipe is a great favorite of mine because not only is it elegant but it may be prepared in advance. If you do so, allow it to stand at room temperature for 45 minutes before baking.

6 chicken breasts, split, skinned, boned, pounded thin

MARINADE:
1 teaspoon freshly ground white pepper
1½ tablespoons seasoned salt substitute (optional)
4 cloves garlic, pressed
1 large onion, sliced paper thin
½ cup dry white wine
¼ cup corn oil

¼ cup lemon juice, freshly squeezed

2 to 3 eggs, well beaten
½ pound salt-free Gouda cheese (optional)
Cornflakes, salt-free, crushed
Peanut oil

SAUCE:
1½ sticks sweet butter
6 cloves garlic, pressed

15 shallots, minced

2½ pounds very small
   mushrooms, thinly sliced
   lengthwise

1 large bunch fresh parsley,
   finely minced

1½ teaspoons dried tarragon

¾ teaspoon freshly ground
   white pepper

1 tablespoon seasoned salt substitute (optional)

½ cup dry white wine

½ cup cognac

1½ cups heavy cream (or triple
   strength low sodium dry
   milk) mixed with 2 tablespoons cornstarch

GARNISH: ⅓ cup finely minced
fresh parsley

1. Place the chicken breasts with the marinade in a plastic bag. Seal tightly. Refrigerate for at least 6 hours, rotating the bag 3 or 4 times during the marinating period.

2. Drain and pat dry with paper towels.

3. Dip the breasts into the eggs, then into the cheese, then into the cornflakes.

4. In a large skillet heat the peanut oil over a medium-high flame and sauté the breasts on both sides until they are golden brown. Drain on double thickness of paper toweling.

5. In a large, heavy skillet, melt the butter over a medium flame and sauté the garlic and shallots, stirring constantly, until the shallots are translucent.

6. Add the mushrooms and sauté until barely tender.

7. Add the parsley, tarragon, pepper, salt substitute, wine, and cognac.

8. Mix thoroughly and stir all the ingredients for 3 to 4 minutes.

9. Add the cream (or triple strength low sodium dry milk) and cornstarch mixture slowly, stirring constantly, for 4 minutes. Remove the skillet from the flame.

10. Preheat the oven to 300°.

11. In a well-buttered large ovenproof baking dish lay the chicken in a single layer (you may have to use 2 dishes) and spoon the sauce over it.

12. Bake for 30 minutes or until bubbling hot.

Serving: The dishes that you baked the chicken in should be attractive enough to bring to the sideboard. If so, sprinkle the parsley over the chicken supreme and proudly present it to your guests. Serve it with wild rice.

Honeyed Chicken

Serves 6

2 chickens, 2 to 2½ pounds
　　each, quartered (skin on or
　　off as you prefer)

MARINADE:
½ cup peanut oil
¼ cup dry sherry
Juice of 2 large lemons
2 inches ginger root, finely
　　grated
6 cloves garlic, finely minced
1 large onion, finely minced

1 tablespoon seasoned salt sub-
　　stitute (optional)
¾ teaspoon freshly ground
　　white pepper

6 to 10 tablespoons honey (or to
　　taste)

GARNISH:
10 lemon wedges
Sprigs of fresh parsley

1. Place the chicken in a large bowl. Add the marinade and mix thoroughly. Cover tightly and refrigerate for at least 6 hours, turning the chicken every 2 hours to coat well (see Note).

2. When ready to cook, preheat the oven to 350°.

3. Pour the marinade into a large roasting pan.

4. Place the chicken, skin side down, on top of the marinade and bake for 20 minutes, basting twice.

5. Turn the chicken and bake for 20 minutes more, basting twice.

6. Preheat the broiler to 500°.

7. Remove the chicken from the oven. Turn the chicken over (skin side down) and brush on half of the honey.

8. Broil the chicken about 5 inches from the flame for 10 minutes.

9. Turn it and brush with the remaining honey.

10. Broil for about 10 minutes more or until the skin is crisp but not dried or burned.

Serving: Transfer the chicken to a preheated serving platter and garnish with the lemon wedges and parsley. Serve Brandied Peaches* and Stir-Fried Broccoli* to complete a taste and color sensation.

NOTE: Instead of using a bowl, place the chicken parts, with the marinade, in a plastic bag. Seal tightly. Refrigerate for at least 6 hours, rotating the bag 3 or 4 times during the marinating period.

Chicken Marengo

Serves 6

If you like chicken and vegetables, this recipe is unequivocally for you.

2 chickens, 2 to 2½ pounds
  each, cut into eighths,
  skinned
1 large lemon, quartered
¾ cup rice flour (or unbleached
  flour)
¾ teaspoon freshly ground
  black pepper
2 teaspoons dried tarragon
1 tablespoon seasoned salt substitute (optional)
⅓ cup olive oil
1 stick sweet butter
2 tablespoons cornstarch or arrowroot
1½ cups dry white wine
4 to 6 cloves garlic, minced
1 pound mushrooms, thinly
  sliced lengthwise

4 large potatoes, peeled and
  quartered
18 baby carrots, or 8 regular
  carrots, cut into 2-inch
  pieces
3½ cups fresh tomatoes, peeled,
  seeded and coarsely
  chopped (or 3½ cups salt-
  free canned tomatoes,
  coarsely chopped, Italian
  plum tomatoes preferably)
1 teaspoon dried dill weed
¾ teaspoon black pepper
⅛ teaspoon cayenne

GARNISH: 3 tablespoons finely
  minced fresh parsley

1. Preheat the oven to 350°.
2. Rub the chicken all over with the cut lemon.
3. Mix the flour, pepper, tarragon, and salt substitute together, dredge the chicken in the mixture.
4. Heat the oil and butter in a large skillet over a medium flame and brown the chicken on all sides. Then remove it to a large copper *au gratin* pan (or any other heavy, large skillet, heavy roasting pan, or baking pan that is attractive enough to serve from). Discard all but 2 tablespoons of the oil and butter.
5. Add the cornstarch to the remaining oil and butter in the skillet and mix vigorously with a wire whisk while slowly adding the wine.
6. Add the garlic and mushrooms to the sauce and mix until well blended. Remove the skillet from the flame.
7. Place the potatoes and the carrots around and in between the chicken parts.
8. Mix the tomatoes, dill weed, pepper, and cayenne together. Add the

garlic and mushroom sauce. Stir well and spoon the mixture all over the chicken and vegetables.

9. Cover tightly with a heavy lid or with double layers of aluminum foil and bake for 45 to 50 minutes or until the chicken is tender.

Serving: Uncover and sprinkle with the minced parsley and serve.

High-Hat Chicken Soufflé

Serves 6 to 8

2 cups Cream Sauce*
1¼ cups white meat of Boiled
  Chicken* or Poached
  Chicken Breasts,* finely
  chopped
½ cup chopped pecans
¼ cup grated raw carrots
¼ cup grated onion
⅛ cup minced fresh parsley

⅛ cup minced fresh chives
6 egg yolks
¾ teaspoon freshly ground
  white pepper
¼ teaspoon cayenne
¼ teaspoon paprika
1 tablespoon fresh lemon juice
6 egg whites

1. In a large saucepan bring the cream sauce to a low boil over a medium flame, stirring constantly. Slowly add the chicken, pecans, carrots, onion, parsley, and chives. Continue stirring until all ingredients are very hot, then turn the flame to low.

2. Beat the egg yolks with a wire whisk until they are light and fluffy, slowly add 4 tablespoons of the cream mixture, beating the egg yolks all the time.

3. Slowly pour the egg yolk mixture into the cream mixture, stirring constantly. When all the egg yolks are absorbed, cook for 2 minutes or until the sauce has thickened. Then stir in the pepper, cayenne, paprika, and lemon juice. Remove to a mixing bowl and let the mixture cool for 30 to 40 minutes.

4. Preheat the oven to 325°.

5. Prepare a 2-quart soufflé dish with a 4-inch heavy-duty aluminum foil soufflé collar (see Index), tightly secured with masking tape. Lightly butter the inside of the collar.

6. Using an electric mixer on high speed, beat the egg whites until they are stiff but not dry. Mix ¼ of the egg white into the creamed chicken mixture and gently fold in the remainder of the egg whites.

7. Spoon the mixture into the soufflé dish (it should fill about ⅔ of the dish). Bake for 50 minutes or until the soufflé is firm. Remove the collar and serve at once.

Serving: Serve with either an additional 2 cups of Cream Sauce* (to which 3 tablespoons of chives have been added) or Mushroom Almond Sauce.*

NOTE: I have successfully converted this to a fish soufflé, substituting flaked poached salmon or fillet of sole, halibut, bass, or a combination of all four. This is especially useful after you have served cold poached fish the night before, since the very expensive leftover bits and pieces can then be turned into another *tour de force* . . . for an exceedingly elegant and festive dinner.

Orange Chicken

Serves 6

²/₃ teaspoon freshly ground
    white pepper
²/₃ teaspoon cinnamon
¹/₄ teaspoon ground cloves
1 teaspoon cumin
¹/₂ teaspoon ground coriander
6 cloves garlic, minced
2 chickens, 3 to 3¹/₂ pounds
    each, cut into eighths,
    skinned
¹/₃ cup peanut oil
1 large Bermuda onion, finely
    chopped
2 inches ginger root, finely
    grated

2 tablespoons sweet butter
¹/₂ cup slivered almonds
12 pitted prunes
¹/₄ cup white raisins
¹/₂ teaspoon saffron powder
2 tablespoons cornstarch,
    blended thoroughly with the
    juice of 8 oranges
1 cup dry white wine
¹/₂ cup dry sherry

GARNISH: 3 tablespoons finely
    minced fresh parsley

1. Mix the pepper, cinnamon, cloves, cumin, coriander, and garlic together. Rub well into the chicken pieces.

2. Using a heavy skillet, heat the oil over a medium-high flame and sauté the chicken until golden. Remove the chicken to a flameproof casserole, leaving the drippings in the skillet.

3. In the same skillet, sauté the onion and ginger until the onion is golden. Spoon all of this over the chicken.

4. Using the same skillet, heat the butter over a medium flame and sauté the almonds, stirring constantly, until they are a pale golden color (take care not to burn them). Spoon them and the butter over the chicken.

5. To the casserole, add the prunes, raisins, saffron, orange juice mix-

ture, and wine. Cover and turn the flame to low. Cook for about 1 hour and 10 minutes or until the chicken is tender.

6. Add the sherry and cook for 5 more minutes.

Serving: Garnish the casserole with the parsley and serve with Boiled Rice.*

Piquant Coq Au Vin with Vegetables

Serves 8 to 10

3 fryers, 3½ pounds each, cut into eighths, skinned
Juice of 3 lemons
½ cup dry white wine
¼ cup corn oil
4 cloves garlic, crushed
¼ teaspoon cayenne
½ cup corn oil (or more if necessary)
6 large carrots, finely minced
12 shallots, finely minced
6 cloves garlic, finely minced
2 large onions, finely minced
6 tablespoons unbleached flour
4 cups dry vermouth
6 tablespoons finely minced fresh parsley
2 teaspoons dried chervil

1 teaspoon dried thyme
1 teaspoon dried marjoram
1 teaspoon dried dill weed
¼ teaspoon cayenne
6 tablespoons brandy
½ teaspoon freshly ground black pepper
24 baby carrots
24 tiny white onions
¼ cup corn oil
2 pounds tiny mushrooms, thinly sliced lengthwise
¾ cup dry sherry

GARNISH: ½ cup finely minced fresh parsley

1. Place the chicken in a plastic bag with the lemon juice, wine, ¼ cup of oil, garlic, and cayenne. Seal the bag tightly. Refrigerate for at least 3 hours, turning the bag 2 or 3 times during the marinating period.

2. In a large flameproof casserole, heat the ½ cup of oil over a medium flame and sauté the carrots, shallots, garlic, and onions until the onions are a deep golden color, stirring often. With a slotted spoon remove the vegetables to a bowl.

3. Drain the chicken and pat dry with paper towels.

4. Brown it on all sides in the casserole in which you cooked the vegetables, adding more oil if necessary. Remove the chicken to a second bowl.

5. To the casserole, add the flour and stir it until it is thoroughly mixed and browned. Then add the vermouth, parsley, chervil, thyme, marjoram, dill, cayenne, brandy, and pepper. Mix thoroughly.

6. Return the vegetables to the casserole and stir well. Add the chicken and cover tightly. Cook over a low-medium flame for 20 minutes, add the carrots and onions, and continue cooking for 45 minutes more.

7. In a skillet, heat the ¼ cup of oil over a low-medium flame and brown the mushrooms in it. Using a slotted spoon, transfer them to the casserole.

8. Add the sherry to the mushrooms, cover, and cook for 5 minutes more.

Serving: Sprinkle the parsley over the *coq au vin*. Fabulous and festive when served with wild rice; excellent, too, with brown rice.

Poached Chicken Breasts

Serves 2 to 4

2 whole chicken breasts, split, skinned, and boned (see Note)
Bones and wings from the breasts

2 cups strong Chicken Stock* (approximately)

1. Place the chicken breasts in a heavy saucepan with the bones and the wings. Pour in the chicken stock. (It should completely cover the chicken; if not, add more stock.)

2. Turn the flame to low and simmer for 25 minutes or until the chicken breasts are tender.

NOTE: If you prefer your chicken breasts thinner, pound them between 2 pieces of wax paper until they reach the desired thickness. This is generally not done when poaching chicken breasts, but I prefer to do it when I am serving the chicken breasts bathed in a sauce such as Almond Tarragon* for our main course. However, I do not pound the chicken breasts if they are going into a recipe calling for cubed or diced white meat.

Boiled Chicken

Yields 2 cooked chickens and
approximately 8 quarts of
chicken soup

The chicken from this recipe can be used in any other recipe calling for
boiled or cooked chicken. In addition, the soup from this recipe may be
used as stock in any other recipes calling for chicken stock (see Notes
below).

**2 chickens, 4 to 4½ pounds
     each, skinned, with all the
     giblets except the liver
     (which will make soup
     slightly bitter)**
**8 chicken necks, skinned (op-
     tional)**
8 chicken wings (optional)
**15 carrots, scraped and cut into
     2-inch pieces**
**4 large Bermuda onions, peeled
     and cut into eighths**
1 small bunch fresh parsley
12 leeks, cut into 3-inch slices
4 to 6 cloves garlic, split

**3 large red sweet peppers,
     seeded and quartered (op-
     tional)**
3 sprigs fresh dill
⅛ teaspoon cayenne (optional)
**2½ teaspoons freshly ground
     white pepper**
**2½ tablespoons seasoned salt
     substitute (optional)**
8 quarts water

GARNISH:
**For the soup: 2 tablespoons
     freshly minced parsley**
**For the chicken: sprigs of water-
     cress**

1. Put all the ingredients in a large heavy stock pot, cover, and bring to
a boil over a medium flame.
2. Turn it to low and simmer for 2 to 2½ hours or until the chicken and
vegetables are tender.
3. Remove the chicken and reserve it for later use, as suggested below
in serving or in any other recipe calling for boiled or cooked chicken.
4. Strain the soup through a fine sieve and discard the vegetables.

Serving: The soup: Defat the soup by:
   (a) Skimming the fat off the top of the soup with a large shallow spoon
while it is still hot
   (b) Putting the soup in a bowl in the freezer for 1 hour and then skimming off the fat (which will have risen to the top and already begun to
congeal), then reheat it to piping hot
   (c) Refrigerating the soup overnight, then skimming the fat off the top
and reheating it to piping hot.

Place the defatted piping-hot soup into a preheated tureen or individual bowls and garnish it with the parsley.

Serving: The chicken: If you are serving the chicken hot, cut it into quarters, arrange the pieces on a preheated serving platter, garnish with watercress, and offer fresh horseradish on the side.

If you are serving the chicken cold, arrange the quartered chicken on a chilled serving platter, garnish with watercress, and offer any of the following sauces as an accompaniment: Fresh Horseradish,* Cranberry Orange Relish,* Curry Mayonnaise,* or Chili Garlic Almond Sauce.*

NOTES: 1. If you are reserving the soup as stock to be used at a later date, place the defatted soup into half-pint, pint, or quart plastic containers, seal tightly, and place in the freezer.

2. If you want a stronger, more concentrated stock, return the strained, defatted stock to the pot and cook uncovered over a low flame for 2 hours or until the strong stock is two thirds the volume of the original stock (this may be done before or after freezing).

Rolled Stuffed Chicken Breasts

Serves 4 to 8

2 cups Duxelles*
2 eggs, lightly beaten
$^1/_2$ cup matzoh meal (or salt-free cornflake crumbs or Bread Crumbs*)
4 tablespoons finely minced fresh parsley
1 to 1$^1/_2$ teaspoons freshly ground white pepper
1 tablespoon seasoned salt substitute (optional)
$^1/_3$ cup grated salt-free Gouda cheese (optional)
$^1/_2$ cup finely minced onions, sautéed in 2 tablespoons sweet butter
2 cloves garlic, pressed

4 whole chicken breasts, split into 8 pieces, skinned, boned, and pounded paper thin
12 tablespoons sweet butter, melted
$^3/_4$ cup dry white wine
3 tablespoons Pernod
1 teaspoon dried tarragon
1 tablespoon cornstarch, mixed thoroughly with 1 cup heavy cream (or triple strength low sodium dry milk)

GARNISH: 3 tablespoons finely minced fresh parsley

1. Preheat the oven to 350°.

2. Mix the Duxelles, eggs, matzoh meal, parsley, pepper, salt substitute, cheese, onions, and garlic together to form a stuffing. (You may have to add a little more matzoh meal if the stuffing is too soft.)

3. Lay the flattened chicken breasts on wax paper and spoon some of the stuffing onto each.

4. Roll them up and secure the ends with toothpicks.

5. Pour 4 tablespoons of the butter into a baking dish and lay in the chicken rolls, leaving space between them.

6. Spoon ½ tablespoon of the melted butter over each and place the baking dish in the oven.

7. Bake for 35 minutes or until the rolls are tender, basting with the butter every 7 minutes or so.

8. Transfer the rolls to a heated serving platter and keep them warm on the back of the stove.

9. Pour 4 tablespoons of the pan juices into a small, heavy saucepan, add the wine, Pernod, and tarragon.

10. Place the saucepan over a medium-high flame and, stirring constantly, bring the sauce just to the boiling point (do not boil).

11. Turn the flame to low and slowly stir in the heavy cream (or triple strength low sodium dry milk) and cornstarch mixture.

12. Stirring constantly, simmer until the sauce begins to thicken slightly and the cream is thoroughly heated (approximately 5 minutes).

Serving: Spoon the sauce over the chicken, sprinkle with the parsley, and serve at once.

Roast Stuffed Capon

Serves 4 to 6

1 8-pound capon
Juice of 2 lemons
¾ teaspoon freshly ground
    black pepper
1 clove garlic, split
8 cups Apricot Prune Stuffing*
6 tablespoons melted sweet
    butter

1 large onion, very finely minced
2 cloves garlic, very finely
    minced
½ cup very finely minced fresh
    parsley
1½ cups dry vermouth

³/₄ cup heavy cream (or triple
    strength low sodium dry
    milk)
2 teaspoons arrowroot
¹/₂ cup dry sherry

GARNISH:
Orange and lemon slices soaked
    for 2 hours in Grand
    Marnier
Sprigs of watercress

1. Preheat the oven to 325°.

2. Rub both the skin and cavity of the capon well with the lemon juice, pepper, and garlic.

3. Stuff the capon loosely with approximately 8 cups of the apricot prune stuffing. Tie or use skewers to close the opening. Brush with 1¹/₂ tablespoons of the melted butter.

4. In a flameproof roasting pan melt the remaining butter over a medium flame, sauté the onions and garlic until the onions are a deep golden color. Add the parsley and stir for 2 minutes, then add the vermouth and cook for 3 minutes more.

5. Place the capon in the roasting pan, breast side up, and cover with a piece of cheesecloth that has been soaked in either melted butter or oil. Roast the capon for about 3¹/₂ hours or until tender, basting every half hour over the cheesecloth.

6. About 30 minutes before the capon is done, remove the cheesecloth and baste every 5 to 10 minutes, allowing the breast to brown well.

7. Remove to a heated platter and allow it to sit for a few minutes to settle the juices.

8. Skim the fat off the gravy in the roasting pan, and slowly add the cream (or triple strength low sodium dry milk) and the arrowroot, stirring constantly. When well blended, stir in the sherry, and when the sauce has thickened and is piping hot, pour into a gravy boat.

Serving: Remove the string or skewers from the capon, place it on a heated platter, and garnish with the orange and lemon slices and sprigs of watercress. I sometimes cut the capon into eighths in the kitchen, mound the stuffing in the center of a heated platter, arrange the pieces of capon attractively around it, and garnish as above.

Crisp Duckling Bigarade

Serves 4 to 6

2 4-pound ducklings
1 clove garlic, peeled and split
2 teaspoons freshly ground black
  pepper
1 lemon, cut into eighths
1 orange, cut into eighths
1/2 cup dry white wine
3 tablespoons cognac
1 1/4 cups orange juice
1/3 cup fresh lemon juice
1/2 cup strong Chicken Stock*

Rind of 1 orange, cut into julienne strips
Rind of 1 lemon, cut into julienne strips
1/4 cup wine vinegar
1/3 cup sugar (or equivalent)
2 navel oranges, sectioned
1/3 cup sugar (or equivalent)
1/4 cup Grand Marnier
Sprigs of watercress for garnish

1. Preheat the oven to 325°.
2. Wash the ducklings well, inside and out, and pat dry with paper towels.
3. Rub them all over with the garlic, then the pepper into the skin.
4. Place the lemon and orange pieces inside the cavity, then truss the ducklings with string.
5. Place them on a rack in a roasting pan and place in the oven.
6. Roast the ducklings for 2 hours and 45 minutes or until the birds are a golden brown. Prick the skin with a fork 2 or 3 times during the roasting in order to get a very crispy skin. Pour off the grease during the roasting.
7. When the ducklings are cooked and crisp, remove the string, also the lemons and oranges in the cavity. Transfer the ducklings to a heated serving platter and keep warm on the back of the stove.
8. Deglaze the pan with the wine and cognac, pour the mixture into a saucepan. Add the orange and lemon juice and the orange rind. Stir well and simmer over a medium flame for 10 minutes.
9. In the meantime, place the vinegar and sugar in a small saucepan. Simmer over a low flame, stirring constantly, until the sugar is dissolved.
10. Stir this mixture into the orange and lemon mixture. Turn the flame to low-medium and cook for an additional 7 or 8 minutes.
11. In the meantime, place the sectioned oranges in a broiler pan, sprinkle on the sugar and broil for 4 minutes 4 inches from the flame. Place the sections around the ducklings.
12. When the sauce is finished, add the Grand Marnier pour over the ducklings.

Serving: Garnish the platter with small sprigs of watercress and proudly bring it to the dining table to be carved and served.

NOTE: On most occasions, although the presentation is not quite as impressive, I section the ducklings in our kitchen, then pour the sauce on and arrange the orange slices and the watercress around the sections.

Roast Duck

Serves 4 to 6

This is our daughter Patricia's favorite dish. As you will see, it is very simple to prepare and does require a long roasting period. Naturally, I do not suggest preparing this during the hot summer months unless you are one of the blessed few who have air-conditioned kitchens.

2 ducks (approximately 5 pounds each)
2 teaspoons freshly ground black pepper
2 cups fresh lemon juice
2 cloves garlic, split
1 teaspoon freshly ground black pepper
2 large onions, peeled and scored

2 large apples, cored but not peeled
Juice of 2 oranges, mixed with ³/₄ cup dry white wine and ¹/₄ cup Grand Marnier
¹/₂ to ³/₄ cup honey

1. Wash the ducks thoroughly inside and out, pat dry with paper towels. Rub the pepper into the skin and the cavity.
2. Place them with the lemon juice in a heavy plastic bag and seal tightly.
3. Place the bag in the refrigerator for at least 4 hours, turning the bag every hour, so that the ducks are constantly being marinated by the lemon juice.
4. Preheat the oven to 350°.
5. Remove the ducks from the bag and thoroughly pat them dry with paper towels.
6. Rub them inside and out with the garlic and pepper.
7. Place 1 onion and 1 apple in the cavity of each duck. Place them breast side up, on a roasting rack placed in a roasting pan.

8. Roast them for 2 hours (draining the fat every half hour).

9. Continue to roast for another hour, now basting every 20 minutes with the mixture of orange juice, wine, and Grand Marnier.

10. Remove from the oven and heavily brush with the honey.

11. Place them back on the rack and roast for 30 to 45 minutes more, or until the skin is very crisp.

Serving: Transfer the ducks to a preheated serving platter and garnish with sprigs of parsley. Offer Chinese Sweet and Sour Sauce* and Rice Chinoise.*

Our Traditional Thanksgiving Turkey

Serves 24

Though this is described as serving twenty-four people, we have so many other dishes with this that it easily serves thirty-two.

As in most traditions, the first time one does something may set a precedent; the second time, a repeat action; and by the third time many people call it tradition. Thus, our traditional Thanksgiving turkey became that in such a manner. However, by now, we are truly convinced that it is tradition since we have celebrated Thanksgiving over the past twenty-two years with our bird cooked this way.

1 24-pound turkey
2 lemons, halved
3 cloves of garlic, split
2 teaspoons coarsely ground white pepper
1 tablespoon seasoned salt substitute (optional)
3 large very tart green apples, cored
3 1-pound cans of salt-free tomatoes
4 very large Spanish onions, sliced
8 carrots, cut into thirds
2 large green peppers, cored, seeded, and cut into 1-inch-wide strips

7 cloves of garlic, split
3 cups Chicken Stock*
2 cups dry white wine
2 yams, peeled and sliced into 1/2-inch thickness
1/2 cup fresh lemon juice
1/3 cup brown sugar (or equivalent)
2 teaspoons coarsely ground white pepper
2 1/2 tablespoons seasoned salt substitute (optional)
Turkey giblets

1. Preheat the oven to 300°.

2. Wash the turkey thoroughly and pat dry with paper towels.

3. Rub the cut lemons all over the skin and inside. Squeeze the lemon juice through a strainer into a bowl and pour into the cavity.

4. Rub the skin and cavity with the garlic.

5. Rub the pepper and salt substitute into the skin and cavity.

6. Place the apples in the cavity and close with skewers or sewn thread. Truss the bird. (I suggest this because it is then easier to handle.)

7. In a large roasting pan place the tomatoes, onions, carrots, green peppers, garlic, chicken stock, wine, yams, lemon juice, brown sugar, pepper, and salt substitute. Stir all the ingredients thoroughly.

8. Lay the bird, breast side up, on top of the mixture, place all the giblets, except the liver, around it. Cover tightly.

9. Place in the oven and roast for 3 hours.

10. Remove the cover and roast for 3 more hours, basting every half hour with the liquid.

11. Set the bird on a very large platter and keep warm on the back of the stove.

12. Purée the remaining ingredients in the pan, except the giblets, in batches in your blender or food processor. As each batch is blended, pour it into a heavy medium-size saucepan. When the process is completed, stir the gravy, taste, and correct the seasoning if needed. Heat the gravy over a medium flame for 3 to 4 minutes or until piping hot.

Serving: Remove the skewers or thread and the apples from the cavity. Transfer the bird to a large silver or porcelain tray and garnish the turkey with bunches of baby watercress and tiny lady apples. Pour the gravy into a large heated gravy boat or bowl and transport your "traditional Thanksgiving turkey and gravy to the table." If your husband is a grand carver, this is a most impressive way of serving your turkey. However, since we have such a large crowd of family and friends at our Thanksgiving, Dick generally carves the turkey before and lays out the white meat on one side of a massive silver tray and the dark meat on the other. The drumsticks are placed facing each other in the center, their ends, extending to the border of the tray, are appropriately covered with paper frills.

The garnish is, as with the whole bird, watercress, with the addition of a large apple candle which is lit and nestled on a huge bunch of watercress in the center of the tray between the two drumsticks.

Roast Turkey

Serves 16 to 18

One of our favorite holiday dinners.

1 18-pound turkey	1 cup melted butter
4 cloves garlic, pressed	Turkey giblets (excluding the
1 tablespoon coarsely ground	liver)
black pepper	4 cups strong Chicken Stock*
3 cups thinly sliced onions	5 tablespoons butter
1 cup strong Chicken Stock*	5 tablespoons unbleached flour
1/3 cup dry white wine	1 cup heavy cream (optional)

1. Preheat the oven to 300°.

2. Rub the pressed garlic into the skin and inside the cavity of the turkey. Repeat the procedure with the pepper.

3. Place 1 cup of onions in the cavity, then with skewers, truss the bird with string.

4. Place the 2 remaining cups of onions on the bottom of a large roasting pan. Add the chicken stock and wine and stir well.

5. Place the turkey in the roasting pan, breast side up. Brush the breast, legs, and wings with the butter. Place the giblets around the turkey.

6. Dip a double thickness of cheesecloth in the melted butter and place it over the turkey.

7. Roast for 3½ hours (uncovered), basting the turkey with the pan juices every half hour.

8. After 3½ hours remove the cheesecloth and roast for another half hour or until the breast is well browned and the turkey is tender.

9. Transfer the turkey to a heated tray or pan and remove the skewers, string, and the onions in the cavity, and keep warm.

TO MAKE THE GRAVY:

10. Remove as much fat as possible from the pan and pour the remaining liquid through a strainer into a heavy saucepan. Add the chicken stock and heat over a low flame.

11. In the meantine, melt the butter over a medium flame in a medium-sized heavy skillet and, stirring the butter constantly, slowly add the flour. Continue to stir until all the flour is absorbed and blended. Still stirring constantly, add the turkey-chicken stock and cook for 4 to 5 minutes.

12. If you like a very rich gravy, at this point add the cream—very, very slowly, while stirring constantly—and continue to cook for 3 minutes after all the cream has been added (take care, however, that the sauce doesn't boil).

Serving: Transfer the turkey to a heated serving tray and garnish with bunches of parsley and grapes, alternating them around the turkey, or with bunches of watercress and Brandied Peaches* stuffed with Cooked Prunes.* Place the gravy in a preheated gravy boat and present your guests with a sight and taste delight.

BEEF, LAMB, AND VEAL
The Heart of the Matter

Meat

Gone are the meat-and-potato men of my father's era, replaced by husbands, sons, and lovers careful of their waistlines, cholesterol, sodium counts, and good health in general.

The United States, once considered the largest consumer of beef per capita, has relinquished that title to the South Americans, who still cling to their beef-eating ways. There has been a steady decline in the amount of meat, and beef in particular, consumed in this country, and it's fortunate, or perhaps coincidental, since beef, lamb, and veal are uncommonly high priced.

Beef and lamb are high in saturated fats and it is for this reason that you will find in this chapter a larger selection of recipes for veal, a meat comparatively low in saturated fats but, sad to say, higher in price. I have included a few choice beef and lamb recipes, long-time favorites, and have taken the liberty of excluding many others since I don't believe in consuming beef and lamb on a regular basis. Very often I substitute chicken in recipes calling for lamb, beef, or veal, but I must admit that many recipes are not interchangeable and in some cases where I do make the "switch" the recipe suffers a little in translation. However, Stuffed Peppers,* Moussaka,* Veal Chops à la Crème,* Veal Scaloppine Farci,* and Lamb Curry* are quite successful when chicken is substituted. Use your imagination when substituting chicken for beef, lamb, and veal in your own recipes.

Having eaten red meat only once or twice a year for many, many years, I find I've lost my taste for it. Not so, I admit, for caviar and smoked Scotch salmon . . . and, sadly, there just aren't any substitutes for these unique delicacies. I often console myself with the fact that Scotch salmon at $23 to $35 a pound and Iranian caviar ranging in price from $125 to $250 for 14 ounces wouldn't be part of my regular eating habits anyway, but at gala parties, where friends offer these luxuries in abundance, I find myself wrestling with temptation. Thank goodness for better judgment, which convinced me that a moment of pleasure will require too high a price to be paid for days to come. Forgive my digressing to days gone by, while discussing beef, lamb, and veal, but occasionally I do become nostalgic for a few bygone goodies.

And now, as the saying goes, "On with the show!" . . . starring veal and featuring beef and lamb.

Stuffed Peppers

Serves 4 to 8, depending on the appetite of your family and guests

8 very large green peppers
1/4 cup corn oil
1 large onion, finely chopped
4 cloves garlic, finely minced
1 1/2 pounds lean chuck, finely ground

2 1/2 cups Boiled Rice*
1/4 teaspoon cayenne
1/2 teaspoon paprika
2 1/2 cups Tomato Sauce*
2 tablespoons corn oil

1. Slice 1/4 inch off the peppers from the core side and remove the core and seeds.

2. In a large skillet heat the 1/4 cup oil over a medium flame. Add the onion and garlic and sauté until the onion is pale gold.

3. Add the chuck and sauté only until it loses its raw color, stirring constantly. Do not overcook.

4. Remove from the heat and add the boiled rice, cayenne, and paprika. Stir well.

5. Preheat the oven to 350°.

6. Add 1/2 to 2/3 cup of the tomato sauce and mix well. The mixture should be well moistened.

7. Using the 2 tablespoons corn oil, grease a deep baking dish that is just large enough to hold the peppers standing upright and touching each other. Fill the peppers with the cooked mixture, spooning some of the tomato sauce over each stuffed pepper. Pour the remaining sauce between the peppers. Cover tightly with aluminum foil.

8. Bake for 30 minutes covered. Then remove the foil and bake for 15 minutes more, or until the peppers are tender.

Serving: It is preferable to use shallow soup plates when serving stuffed peppers. However, if there are none presently in your cupboards, panic not. Use your dinner plates, taking care not to spoon too much sauce over each stuffed pepper.

Stuffed Cabbage

Serves 16 as a first course and 8
as a main course

16 large cabbage leaves
2 cups canned salt-free tomatoes
3 tablespoons salt-free tomato
    paste
1 teaspoon dried dill
1 teaspoon salt-free chili powder
3/4 teaspoon paprika
1 cup dry red wine
2 pounds lean chuck, finely
    ground
1 large onion, finely chopped

5 tablespoons finely chopped
    fresh parsley
6 cloves garlic, pressed
1 1/2 teaspoons dried thyme
1/8 to 1/4 teaspoon cayenne
3 heaping tablespoons wheat
    germ
3 eggs, well beaten
1 teaspoon freshly ground black
    pepper

1. Cook the cabbage leaves in a deep pot two thirds full of boiling water. Cook for 3 minutes, drain, and dry them between double thickness of paper towels. Set aside.

2. Using a blender or food processor, purée the tomatoes, tomato paste, dill, chili powder, and paprika. Add the wine and blend for 10 seconds more.

3. Pour one third of the tomato mixture into an attractive ovenproof baking dish large enough to hold the cabbage rolls close together in a single layer. Set aside.

4. Preheat the oven to 350°.

5. Mix the chuck, onion, parsley, garlic, thyme, cayenne, wheat germ, eggs, and pepper. Divide the mixture into 16 parts and place 1 part in the center of each cabbage leaf.

6. Roll the leaves and fold over the ends, or fold envelope style. Place the stuffed cabbage rolls, folded ends facing down, into the prepared baking dish in a single layer. Spoon the remaining tomato mixture over the stuffed cabbage rolls. Cover the baking dish tightly with aluminum foil.

7. Bake for 50 minutes covered. Remove the foil and bake for 10 minutes more.

Serving: For a first course, place 1 stuffed cabbage roll on each plate and spoon a little of the sauce over it. If serving as a main course, serve 2 stuffed cabbage rolls to each person.

NOTE: If you like your stuffed cabbage sweet and sour, add 1/2 cup of freshly squeezed lemon juice and 3 1/2 tablespoons of brown sugar (or substitute equivalent) to step 2.

Stuffed Tomatoes à la Grecque

Serves 8, 12, or 16

Vary the size of the tomatoes, depending upon the course in which you are planning to serve stuffed tomatoes à la grecque. For example, as a main course for 8, use very large tomatoes; as a first course for 12, use medium-size tomatoes; and as a buffet dish for 16, or for a brunch, use small tomatoes.

8 very large (or 12 medium-size, or 16 small), firm ripe tomatoes
¼ cup olive oil
1 cup finely chopped onions
8 cloves garlic, finely chopped
1 pound veal, finely ground
1 pound lean chuck, finely ground
¼ teaspoon cayenne
2 teaspoons seasoned salt substitute (optional)
1½ teaspoons cumin
2 tablespoons salt-free tomato paste

1 cup Boiled Rice,* puréed in a blender or food processor
¼ cup fresh lemon juice
⅓ cup finely minced fresh parsley
2 tablespoons minced fresh mint (optional)
⅔ cup finely grated salt-free Gouda cheese
½ cup pignoli (pine nuts)
¾ cups strong Chicken Stock* mixed with ¾ cup dry white wine, and heated

1. Cut ½ inch off the tops of the tomatoes and reserve. Slice off the stem part of the tomato (cutting off as little as possible and making sure you leave a thick enough shell).

2. Scoop out the tomato pulp. Chop and reserve it. Turn the tomatoes over (base side up) and drain on paper towels.

3. In a large, heavy skillet heat the oil over a medium flame and sauté the onions and garlic until the onions are translucent. Add the ground veal and chuck and stir constantly until lightly browned. Stir in the cayenne, salt substitute, cumin, and tomato paste. Turn the flame to low and simmer uncovered for 20 minutes.

4. Stir in the puréed rice, lemon juice, parsley, mint, cheese, and pignoli.

5. Preheat the oven to 325°.

6. In an ovenproof au gratin or baking dish, place the tomatoes base side down and fill them with the meat-rice mixture. Cover the tomatoes with the reserved tops.

7. Pour the hot wine-stock mixture around the tomatoes and bake large

tomatoes for 40 minutes (30 minutes for medium-size tomatoes; 20 minutes for small tomatoes).

Serving: These are excellent either hot or cold.

If serving hot: Serve directly from the au gratin dish after removing them from the oven.

If serving cold: Arrange the tomatoes on an attractive green pottery plate or silver serving tray and garnish with small bunches of parsley.

Beef Stroganoff

Serves 6

3 pounds beef fillet, cut into ¹/₂-inch-thick slices
4 tablespoons Clarified Butter*
1 large onion, very finely minced
3 cloves garlic, pressed
2 pounds fresh mushrooms, sliced thinly lengthwise
2 tablespoons finely minced fresh parsley
¹/₈ teaspoon cayenne
1 teaspoon dried tarragon (optional)
³/₄ teaspoon freshly ground white pepper

2 teaspoons salt substitute (optional)
¹/₂ teaspoon Spanish paprika
¹/₈ teaspoon freshly grated nutmeg
1¹/₂ cups Sour Cream* (or substitute Yogurt*) (see Note)
¹/₈ to ¹/₄ cup cognac

GARNISH: ¹/₄ cup finely minced fresh parsley

1. Pound the meat with a wooden or metal mallet until it is about ¹/₄ inch thick and cut it into strips ¹/₂ inch by 2 inches.

2. Preheat the oven to 180°.

3. In a heavy skillet melt the 4 tablespoons of butter over a medium flame and sauté the onion and garlic until the onion is golden brown. Remove the onion and garlic with a slotted spoon to an attractive ovenproof au gratin pan of copper or pottery.

4. Raise the flame to medium high and sauté the beef until it is browned on both sides (about 5 to 6 minutes) and add it to the onion and garlic. Place the au gratin pan in the oven to keep warm.

5. In the same skillet, using a medium flame, sauté the mushrooms until moderately brown.

6. Add the parsley, cayenne, tarragon, white pepper, salt substitute, paprika, and nutmeg. Sauté for 3 minutes, stirring constantly.

7. Slowly add the sour cream (or yogurt), stirring gently all the time. When thoroughly heated (but not boiled), stir in the cognac. Turn the flame to low and simmer for 8 minutes, stirring often.

Serving: Remove the au gratin pan from the oven, spoon the sauce over the beef, garnish with parsley, and serve at once. I generally accompany this with Parsley Almond Rice Ring,* the center of which is filled with Steamed Baby or Julienne Carrots* bathed in 1 tablespoon of melted sweet butter.

NOTE: If yogurt is substituted for the sour cream hang the yogurt in cheesecloth over a bowl for at least 90 minutes to remove the excess liquid.

Old-Fashioned Beef Stew

Serves 8

As with all stews, this hearty dish is at its best when prepared one day in advance.

2 teaspoons freshly ground black pepper
4 pounds very lean chuck, cut into 1½-inch cubes
¼ cup fresh lemon juice
1½ cups dry red wine
4 cloves garlic, split
3 tablespoons olive oil
4 tablespoons sweet butter
5 onions, finely chopped
4 cloves garlic, finely minced
2 teaspoons seasoned salt substitute (optional)
1 teaspoon freshly ground black pepper
Unbleached flour
2 cups Beef Stock*
2 cups dry red wine

24 little white onions
24 baby carrots (or 12 regular carrots)
2 green cabbages, cut into fourths
1 teaspoon dried thyme

ADD THE NEXT DAY:
16 small new potatoes, parboiled (or barely Steamed*)
1 pound green peas, parboiled (or barely Steamed*)
1 pound green beans, parboiled (or barely Steamed*)

GARNISH: 3 tablespoons finely chopped fresh parsley

1. Rub the pepper into the meat and place it in a large plastic bag. Pour in the lemon juice and the wine and add the garlic. Seal the bag tightly. Refrigerate for 3 to 4 hours, rotating the bag two or three times during the marinating period.

2. In a large, heavy skillet heat the oil and butter over a medium flame. Sauté the onions and garlic until the onions are golden brown, stirring often. Transfer the onions and garlic, using a slotted spoon, to heavy large pot.

3. Add the salt substitute and pepper and mix well.

4. Drain the meat, discarding the marinade, and pat dry with paper towels. Dredge lightly in the flour. Brown on all sides in the same skillet used to sauté the onions and garlic. (You will probably have to brown the meat in two or three batches.) Transfer the meat, using a slotted spoon, to the pot containing the browned onions and garlic.

5. Add the stock and the wine. Cover the pot tightly. Turn the flame to high and bring the liquid to a boil. Reduce the flame to low and simmer for 1 hour.

6. Add the onions, carrots, and cabbage. Sprinkle with the thyme and stir well. Cover and cook until the meat is tender and the vegetables are cooked (approximately 45 minutes).

7. Remove the pot from the heat and let the stew cool. Transfer to a deep bowl. Cover tightly and refrigerate overnight.

8. One hour before serving, remove the stew from the refrigerator and skim off all the fat.

9. Place the stew in a large, heavy pot, add the potatoes, and stir well. Cover tightly, turn the flame to medium high, and bring to a boil. Add the peas and beans and stir well. Cover and cook for 10 minutes more over a low-medium flame, or until the peas and beans are tender but still slightly crisp.

Serving: Transfer the stew to a preheated deep platter or a huge au gratin pan, arranging the vegetables and meat in an attractive and colorful pattern. Spoon the gravy over all and sprinkle with the parsley. A perfect accompaniment to this is warm Crusty Peasant Rye Bread* or French Bread* cut into 1-inch-thick slices . . . a great way to sop up the delicious gravy.

Braised Short Ribs

Serves 6

Prepare this one day in advance for the tastiest and most fat-free results.

4 pounds lean short ribs, cut
    into 3-inch pieces
1 tablespoon coarsely ground
    black pepper
6 cloves garlic, split into fourths
2 cups dry red wine
4 tablespoons corn oil
3 large onions, finely chopped
4 cloves garlic, finely minced
Unbleached flour

2½ cups Beef Stock*
3 cups dry red wine
3 tablespoons fresh lemon juice
3 tablespoons salt-free tomato
    paste

GARNISH: 3 tablespoons finely
    chopped fresh parsley

1. Rub the pepper into the short ribs. Place the ribs in a large plastic bag. Sprinkle in the split garlic and pour 2 cups wine over the beef and garlic. Seal the bag tightly and refrigerate at least 3 hours, rotating the bag two or three times during the marinating period.

2. In a large, heavy skillet heat the oil over a medium flame. Sauté the onions and minced garlic until the onions are a golden brown, stirring often. Transfer the onions and garlic, using a slotted spoon, to a large, heavy pot.

3. Drain the ribs, discarding the marinade, and pat dry with paper towels. Dredge lightly in the flour. In the same skillet used to brown the onions and garlic, brown the ribs on all sides over a medium-high flame. (You will probably have to do this in two or three batches.) Transfer the ribs to the pot containing the onions and garlic.

4. Add the beef stock, 3 cups wine, lemon juice, and tomato paste. Stir well and cover tightly. Turn the flame to high and bring the liquid to a boil. Reduce the flame to low and simmer for 2 to 2½ hours, or until the meat is very tender.

5. Remove the pot from the flame and let the ribs cool. Transfer the ribs and the gravy to a deep bowl, cover tightly, and refrigerate overnight.

6. One hour before serving, remove the ribs from the refrigerator and skim off all the fat.

7. Place the ribs and gravy in an attractive heavy flameproof casserole. Cover. Turn the flame to medium high and bring the liquid to the boiling point. Reduce the flame to low and simmer for 10 minutes.

Serving: Sprinkle the ribs with parsley and proudly bring the casserole to the table. Place 2 ribs in each shallow soup bowl, ladle on gravy, and serve.

Offer Thin Garlic Herb Toast* or French Bread,* sliced, spread with Garlic Herb Butter* and heated in a 350° oven until piping hot and the butter is thoroughly melted (approximately 15 minutes).

Mandarin Spicy Steak

Serves 4 to 6

This dish is delicious, quick, and easy and its only drawback is that it must be served immediately after cooking. If one of your guests must have "just one more cocktail" . . . don't serve it.

1½ tablespoons peanut oil
⅛ to ¼ teaspoon cayenne
½ to ¾ teaspoon cumin
½ teaspoon coriander
2 teaspoons seasoned salt substitute (optional)
2 teaspoons garlic powder
2 teaspoons brown sugar (or substitute equivalent)
2½ tablespoons cornstarch
2½ pounds sirloin, cut into paper-thin slices, approximately ⅛ inch by 2 inches

⅓ cup peanut oil
4 teaspoons finely minced fresh ginger
3 green onions (scallions) cut into 1-inch pieces
2 1-pound cans unsweetened pineapple chunks, drained
¼ cup sherry

GARNISH: ½ cup whole blanched almonds, toasted

1. In a large mixing bowl mix the 1½ tablespoons peanut oil, cayenne, cumin, coriander, salt substitute, garlic powder, brown sugar and cornstarch together.
2. Add the sirloin slices and coat well.
3. In a large, heavy skillet (or wok) heat the ⅓ cup of peanut oil over a medium-high flame. Add the sirloin slices, ginger, and the green onions and stir-fry 1 minute.
4. Add the pineapple chunks and sherry while continuing to stir-fry and cook for ½ to ¾ minute.

Serving: Transfer the steak to a heated platter and spoon the ginger, green onions, pineapple chunks, and the sauce over the sirloin slices. Sprinkle the almonds on top. Serve at once.

This dish quite naturally goes wonderfully with rice. I also offer a small tray of condiments for those who like it especially hot. The condiments are Spicy Sesame Oil,* freshly grated ginger, dried crushed red pepper, and cumin.

Brisket with a Horseradish Sauce

Serves 8 to 10

1/3 cup corn oil
1 5- to 6-pound brisket (first cut)
2 large onions, grated
4 cloves garlic, crushed
6 carrots, grated
3 tablespoons minced fresh parsley
2 cups red wine
8 salt-free beef bouillon cubes dissolved in 3 cups boiling water
1/8 teaspoon cayenne
3/4 teaspoon freshly ground black pepper
2 teaspoons seasoned salt substitute (optional)

4 tablespoons sweet butter
1/2 cup minced onions
4 tablespoons unbleached flour
3 cups liquid from the pot, strained (see Note)
1/4 to 1/3 cup freshly grated horseradish root
3/4 cup heavy cream (or triple-strength low sodium dry milk)
1/2 cup dry sherry

GARNISH: 4 tablespoons finely minced fresh parsley

1. In a large, heavy skillet heat the oil over a high flame and sear the meat on both sides. Remove the brisket to a waterless cooker or a flameproof heavy casserole.

2. Lower the flame under the skillet to medium and sauté the grated onions and garlic until the onions are golden.

3. Add the carrots and 3 tablespoons parsley and stir-fry for 2 minutes. Remove the vegetables with a slotted spoon and add them to the meat. Add the wine, bouillon, cayenne, pepper, and salt substitute.

4. Cover the cooker (or casserole) and place it over a high flame until the liquid comes to a boil. Reduce the flame to low and simmer the meat for 2½ to 3 hours, or until the brisket is tender.

5. Remove the brisket to a cutting board and let it rest for at least 30 minutes, or until it has cooled considerably. Slice it thinly. Strain the liquid and skim off the fat. Reserve the liquid.

6. In a heavy saucepan melt the butter over a medium flame and sauté the minced onions until golden.

7. Add the flour, stirring constantly until it is well blended with the onions. Stir in 3 cups of the strained reserved liquid, blending well, and then blend in the grated horseradish.

8. Reduce the flame to low medium and add the cream or triple strength low sodium dry milk, stirring constantly. Simmer for 8 minutes.

9. Pour a little of the sauce into a flameproof au gratin pan. Add the sliced brisket, overlapping the slices, and then pour the remainder of the sauce over the meat. Heat for 8 to 12 minutes over a low flame, or until the meat is piping hot, taking care not to let the sauce boil.

Serving: Sprinkle the brisket with parsley and serve. Boiled Rice* is a natural accompaniment.

NOTE: The remaining reserved liquid may be used in any recipe calling for Beef Stock.* If you prefer your brisket cold: Follow the recipe through Step 5. (Eliminate in your ingredients all those following seasoned salt substitute.) Refrigerate your brisket until well chilled. Serve it with Chili Garlic Almond Sauce,* Curry Mayonnaise,* or Fresh Horseradish.* Tony prefers his cold brisket with dry mustard (dissolved in cider vinegar) and an all-time cold buffet favorate is cold sliced brisket marinated in Mustard Vinaigrette Dressing.*

Lamb Curry

Serves 6 to 8

4 tablespoons corn oil
3 pounds boned lamb shoulder, cut into 1¹/₂-inch cubes
2 tart green apples, peeled, seeded, and finely chopped
2 large onions, finely chopped
6 cloves garlic, finely minced
1 large sweet potato, cut into 1-inch cubes
2 cups Chicken Stock,* boiling
10 pitted prunes
2¹/₂ tablespoons salt-free curry powder
1 teaspoon cumin

1¹/₂-inch piece ginger root, grated
2 teaspoons seasoned salt substitute (optional)
¹/₄ to ¹/₃ teaspoon cayenne (or to taste)
3 tablespoons finely chopped fresh parsley
¹/₄ cup white raisins
1 cup milk (or low sodium dry milk)
3 tablespoons cornstarch
¹/₂ cup cold water

1. In a large, heavy skillet heat the oil over a medium-high flame and brown the lamb cubes on all sides. Remove the lamb from the skillet.
2. Lower the flame and add the apples, onions, garlic, and sweet potato. Stir-fry until the onions are translucent.
3. Return the lamb to the skillet and add the boiling chicken stock, the

prunes, curry powder, cumin, ginger, salt substitute, cayenne, and parsley. Cover and simmer for 35 minutes, or until the lamb is tender.

4. Add the raisins and simmer for 5 minutes more. Remove all the ingredients, except the liquid, to a preheated deep serving platter.

5. Stir the milk into the pan liquids. Dissolve the cornstarch in the cold water, stirring well, and pour into the sauce. Turn the flame to high. Stir thoroughly until the sauce is smooth and thickened. Pour the sauce over the lamb.

Serving: Serve with Boiled Rice* and offer the following condiments in separate bowls:

    Chopped green onions (scallions)
    Heated unsweetened canned pineapple chunks
    Chutney*
    Toasted blanched almonds
    Fresh coconut, grated
    Unsalted peanuts

Lamb Casserole

Serves 6

1/4 cup corn oil
2 large onions, sliced paper thin
4 cloves garlic, pressed
3 pounds boned lamb shoulder, fat removed and cut into 1-inch cubes
2 1/2 tablespoons sweet butter
3 tablespoons flour
1 3/4 cups Beef Stock*
1 1/2 cups tomatoes, skinned, seeded, and coarsely chopped
2 teaspoons seasoned salt substitute (optional)

1 teaspoon freshly ground black pepper
1/8 teaspoon cayenne
1 pound mushrooms, sliced thinly lengthwise
5 potatoes, peeled and thinly sliced
1/2 cup sherry

GARNISH: 3 tablespoons finely minced fresh parsley

1. Heat the oil in a large, heavy skillet over a medium flame. Sauté the onions and garlic until the onions are pale golden brown. With a slotted spoon, transfer the onions to an ovenproof casserole.

2. Brown the lamb in the skillet on all sides and transfer the lamb with a slotted spoon to the casserole.

3. Preheat the oven to 350°.

4. In a small, heavy saucepan heat the butter over a medium flame and, stirring constantly, slowly add the flour until all the flour is absorbed and browned.

5. Stirring the roux constantly, slowly add the beef stock and cook until thickened. Add the tomatoes, salt substitute, pepper, and cayenne and stir well.

6. Pour the stock-tomato mixture over the lamb in the casserole. Add the mushrooms and potatoes and stir well.

7. Stir in the sherry. Cover tightly.

8. Cook in the oven for 1 hour and 15 minutes, or until the lamb is tender and the vegetables are cooked.

Serving: Uncover the casserole, sprinkle with parsley, and serve.

NOTE: As with most other stews, soups, and casseroles, you may prepare this the day before and refrigerate it. Two hours before you are going to serve, remove the casserole from the refrigerator, skim off any fat, and let the casserole stand at room temperature for 1 hour and 15 minutes. Heat in a 325° oven for 45 minutes or until it is piping hot. Garnish with minced parsley and serve.

Moussaka

Serves 8 to 12

This three-step recipe is a divine Greek specialty and well worth the effort.

STEP 1: *LAMB SAUCE:*

3 tablespoons olive oil
2 large onions, finely chopped
2½ pounds lean lamb, ground
3 large ripe tomatoes, peeled
   and diced
1½ tablespoons salt-free tomato
   paste
2 tablespoons finely chopped
   fresh parsley

1 teaspoon freshly ground black
   pepper
1 tablespoon seasoned salt substitute (optional)
⅛ teaspoon cayenne
⅓ cup dry red wine
⅔ cup Tomato Sauce*

1. In a large skillet heat the olive oil over a low flame and sauté the onions until limp and translucent.

2. Add the lamb and, stirring well, sauté until browned.

3. Stir in the tomatoes, tomato paste, parsley, pepper, salt substitute, cayenne, and wine. Cook for 10 minutes.

4. Stir in the tomato sauce and cook for 50 minutes, or until the sauce is thick, stirring occasionally.

STEP 2: *CHEESE SAUCE:*

6 tablespoons sweet butter
⅓ cup unbleached flour
1 quart milk (or low sodium dry
   milk)
½ teaspoon freshly ground
   white pepper

⅓ teaspoon freshly grated
   nutmeg
3 large egg yolks, well beaten
⅔ cup grated salt-free Swiss
   cheese

1. In a saucepan melt the butter over a medium flame and, beating constantly with a wire whisk, slowly add the flour until it forms a smooth paste.

2. Continue stirring with the whisk and slowly add the milk, pepper, and nutmeg. Still stirring with the whisk, cook about 7 minutes more, or until the sauce is smooth and slightly thickened.

3. With the wire whisk, beat ⅓ cup of this sauce into the egg yolks, a little at a time, and then beat the egg yolk mixture into the remaining sauce.

4. Cook over a very low flame, whisking occasionally, until the sauce is thick (approximately 25 minutes).

5. Whisk in the cheese until it is melted and thoroughly blended.

STEP 3: *TO COMPLETE THE MOUSSAKA:*

5 medium eggplants, washed well and cut lengthwise into ⅛-inch slices; soaked for 45 minutes in 1 cup unsweetened pineapple juice

3 cups corn oil

⅔ cup Bread Crumbs*

3 large ripe tomatoes, peeled and cut into ⅛-inch rounds

1¼ cups grated salt-free Gouda cheese

1. Drain the eggplants and dry them between double thickness of paper towels.

2. Heat the oil in a larrge, heavy, very deep skillet over a medium flame and deep-dry the eggplant slices until golden. Drain the fried eggplant on paper towels.

3. Preheat the oven to 350°.

4. Butter an ovenproof and flameproof baking dish 13 by 9 by 12 inches and pack the bread crumbs tightly on the bottom. On top of the bread crumbs arrange layers of half the sliced eggplant, half the lamb sauce, half the sliced tomatoes, and half the grated cheese. Repeat this procedure until all the "layering" ingredients are used up, and then spoon the cheese sauce over all and bake for 30 minutes.

5. Preheat the broiler to 500°.

6. Place the baking dish 4 inches from the flame and broil until the cheese sauce is bubbling and golden brown (about 3 to 4 minutes). Remove from the broiler and let stand at room temperature for 20 minutes.

Serving: Place the baking dish in a wicker basket that will hold a container of this size and cut the moussaka into 3-inch squares. Either serve your guests or let them help themselves.

Moroccan Lamb Stew

Serves 6 to 8

3½ pounds boneless leg of lamb (or lamb shoulder), trimmed of all the fat and cut into 1-inch cubes
1 cup Yogurt*
1 tablespoon salt-free curry powder
2 tablespoons fresh lemon juice
4 cloves garlic, pressed
1 teaspoon freshly ground white pepper
2½ teaspoons seasoned salt substitute (optional)
7 tablespoons olive oil
1½ cups finely chopped onions
5 cloves garlic, pressed
5 tablespoons unbleached flour
2 teaspoons dry mustard
¾ teaspoon freshly ground black pepper
⅛ to ¼ teaspoon cayenne (optional)

1½- to 2½-inch piece ginger root, finely minced
½ teaspoon cinnamon
5 teaspoons honey
2½ cups Chicken Stock*
1 16-ounce can unsweetened pineapple chunks (including the juice)
1½ tablespoons fresh lemon juice, mixed with 4 table-spoons honey, heated

GARNISH:
½ cup unsweetened flaked coconut (preferably fresh)
½ cup whole blanched almonds
1 cup raisins steeped for 1 day, at least, in ⅓ cup apricot brandy (1 to 2 weeks is far better)
Sprigs of fresh mint (optional)

1. Place the lamb cubes in a large plastic bag.
2. Place the yogurt in a mixing bowl and add the curry powder, lemon juice, 4 cloves garlic, white pepper, and salt substitute. Stir thoroughly and pour the mixture over the lamb.
3. Seal the plastic bag tightly and rotate it three to four times. Refrigerate for at least 4 hours, rotating the bag every hour.
4. Drain the lamb and pat dry between double thickness of paper towels.
5. In a heavy, deep, large skillet, heat 4 tablespoons of the oil over a medium-high flame. Add the lamb and brown well on all sides. With a slotted spoon, transfer the lamb to a plate and set aside.
6. Discard the oil and lamb drippings from the skillet and heat the remaining oil in the skillet over a low-medium flame.
7. Sauté the onions and 5 cloves garlic, stirring often until the onions are translucent. Add the flour and stir constantly for 4 minutes.
8. Add the mustard, black pepper, cayenne, ginger, cinnamon, and 5

teaspoons honey. Stir constantly for 2 minutes (or until the honey is liquidy and all the ingredients are completely blended).

9. Add the lamb and the chicken stock. Stir all the ingredients thoroughly, cover tightly, and simmer for 45 minutes.

10. Stir in the pineapple chunks and the juice. Cover tightly and simmer for another 15 to 20 minutes, or until the lamb is very tender.

11. Drizzle in the heated lemon juice-honey mixture and stir well. Simmer uncovered for 5 minutes, stirring often.

Serving: Transfer the stew to a preheated deep serving platter or au gratin dish and garnish it with the coconut, almonds, and raisins. Place the sprigs of fresh mint around the lamb. Serve with Boiled Rice.*

Broiled Lamb on Skewers

Serves 4 to 6

This is especially delicious when barbecued outdoors . . . but for those of us without a back yard or a barbecue grill this way of preparing lamb on skewers is almost as good.

2 pounds boneless leg of lamb
   (or lamb shoulder), cut into
   1½-inch cubes
1½ teaspoons finely ground
   black pepper
2½ teaspoons cumin (optional)
3 tablespoons fresh lemon juice
⅓ cup olive oil
1 onion, finely chopped

4 cloves garlic, finely minced
20 tiny white onions
20 cherry tomatoes
20 very small mushrooms, caps
   only
2 large green peppers, cut into
   1½-inch squares
Olive oil

1. Rub the lamb well with the pepper and place in a large plastic bag. Sprinkle in the cumin, lemon juice, ⅓ cup olive oil, onion, and garlic. Seal the bag tightly. Refrigerate for 6 hours, rotating the bag five or six times during the marinating period.

2. Preheat the broiler to 550°.

3. Place the lamb on 15- to 18-inch skewers, alternating it with the onions, tomatoes, mushroom caps, and peppers.

4. Place the skewers on a broiler pan and broil 4 to 5 inches from the flame for approximately 35 minutes, or until the lamb is cooked through. Rotate the skewers frequently and brush after each rotation with olive oil.

Serving: Transfer the skewers to a preheated platter. At the table lift one skewer at a time and push the lamb and vegetables off onto each plate. Spoon some Parsley Almond Rice Ring* onto each plate and proudly serve your lamb kabobs.

Roast Leg of Lamb
Italian Country Style

Serves 6 to 8

This is generally not served with gravy, but if that is your bent, I have tried to accommodate you. (See Note at the end of this recipe.)

1 5-pound leg of lamb (bone in) and all fat removed
2 teaspoons coarsely ground black pepper
4 cloves garlic, split
1/4 cup fresh lemon juice
2 onions, finely chopped
1/2 cup olive oil
2 cloves garlic, cut into paper-thin slivers
1 1/2 teaspoons dried rosemary
1 teaspoon finely ground black pepper

1/2 cup olive oil
12 very small white onions
6 large potatoes, peeled and sliced lengthwise into fourths

GRAVY:
1 1/2 cups boiling strong Chicken Stock* (or strong Vegetable Stock*)

GARNISH: Sprigs of fresh rosemary (optional)

1. Rub the pepper into the lamb and place it in a large plastic bag. Sprinkle in the split garlic, lemon juice, onions, and 1/2 cup olive oil. Seal tightly and rotate the bag three or four times. Refrigerate for 5 hours, rotating the bag three or four times during the marinating period.

2. Preheat the oven to 450°.

3. Drain the lamb and pat it dry with paper towels. Make small deep slashes in the lamb and insert the slivers of garlic. Rub the rosemary and finely ground pepper into the lamb.

4. Place the lamb in a deep roasting pan and brush it with 1/2 cup oil. Roast uncovered for 1 to 1 1/2 hours (depending upon whether you like your lamb rare or well done), basting it often and turning it two or three times during the roasting period.

5. Place the onions and the potatoes around the lamb 40 minutes before it has finished roasting. Baste the vegetables with the pan drippings, turning them once.

6. Remove the fat that has accumulated on top of the liquid.

Serving: Transfer the lamb to a preheated serving platter and let it rest for 15 to 20 minutes before carving. Keep the onions and potatoes warm until you are ready to serve. Then surround the lamb with the vegetables and garnish with sprigs of fresh rosemary.

NOTE: *For Gravy:* After the lamb and vegetables are removed, deglaze the pan with 1½ cups boiling strong Chicken Stock* or strong Vegetable Stock.* Cook over a high flame for 15 minutes or until the stock is concentrated and reduced by a third, stirring often. Pour this into a gravy boat and serve.

Rack of Lamb Persillée

Serves 6

In this day and age it almost costs a king's ransom to buy the double rack of lamb. So, if you serve it as rarely as we do, enjoy every bit of it and don't be embarrassed to "lick your chops."

1 double rack of lamb, 6 to 8 pounds, trimmed of fat and with the bones prepared French style; namely, scraping all the meat away, down to 1½ inches from the bottom of the lamb bones. (My butcher generally prepares this for me.)
½ cup corn oil
3 large carrots, grated
1 large onion, finely minced
4 cloves garlic, crushed
½ teaspoon dried thyme (optional)

1 bay leaf
1 cup dry white wine
6 tablespoons sweet butter
1 cup white Bread Crumbs*
6 shallots, very finely minced
½ cup finely minced fresh parsley
¾ teaspoon freshly ground black pepper
¼ cup melted sweet butter

GARNISH: Sprigs of parsley

1. Preheat the oven to 350°.
2. Tie the ribs with kitchen string (this will keep them tight and prevent their spreading during the roasting period). Wrap the scraped ends of the bones tightly in aluminum foil.

3. In a large, heavy skillet heat the oil over a high flame and sear the lamb on all sides.

4. Put the carrots, onion, garlic, thyme, bay leaf, and wine in a roasting pan. Stir well. Lay the rack of lamb, skin side down, on top of the mixture.

5. Roast for 45 to 50 minutes, basting every 10 to 12 minutes with the pan juices.

6. While the lamb is roasting, melt and brown the 6 tablespoons of butter in a heavy skillet over a medium-high flame. Turn the flame to low-medium and sauté the bread crumbs and shallots until the shallots are tender (approximately 7 minutes). Add the parsley and pepper and stir the mixture well. Remove from the flame.

7. When the lamb has finished roasting, remove it from the oven and place it on an ovenproof platter. Pat the shallot-crumb mixture tightly on top of the rack of lamb, spoon the melted butter over the mixture, and return to the oven for 6 minutes. Remove the string.

Serving: Transfer your exquisite rack of lamb to a preheated serving platter, garnish with the parsley sprigs, and bring it to the table at once. Slice and serve it while it is still hot.

Veal Casablanca

Serves 6

12 dried pitted prunes
12 dried apricots
1½ cups dry sherry
4 tablespoons corn oil
3 pounds boneless veal shoulder, cut into 1½-inch cubes
6 cloves garlic, pressed
⅔ teaspoon cinnamon (or more to taste)
1½ teaspoons cumin

2-inch piece ginger root, finely grated
1 teaspoon freshly ground black pepper
1 cup strong Chicken Stock*
2 tablespoons sweet butter
⅔ cup blanched almonds
½ cup honey (or more to taste) heated to a syrup

1. Soak the prunes and apricots in the sherry overnight.

2. In a large, heavy skillet heat the oil over a medium flame and brown the pieces of veal on all sides (you may have to do this in two or three batches).

3. Place the veal, garlic, cinnamon, cumin, ginger, pepper, chicken stock, prunes, apricots, and sherry in a flameproof uncovered casserole and bring the liquid to a boil over a medium-high flame.

4. Turn the flame to low, cover the casserole, and simmer for approximately 1 hour and 10 minutes, or until the veal is tender.

5. In a frying pan, melt the butter over a low-medium flame and, stirring constantly, sauté the almonds until they are barely a pale golden color. Add the honey, mix well, and simmer for 3 minutes, stirring constantly.

6. Spoon the honey-almond mixture into the casserole and gently stir all the ingredients. Cover and simmer for 5 minutes more.

Serving: If your casserole is attractive, serve directly from that. If not, transfer the ingredients to a preheated deep serving platter.

Veal Paprikash Casserole

Serves 6

3 pounds boneless veal shoulder, cut into 1½-inch cubes
½ cup unbleached flour, mixed with 1 teaspoon freshly ground white pepper
⅓ cup Clarified Butter*
4 cloves garlic, finely minced
1 large onion, finely minced
4 tablespoons finely minced fresh parsley
4 carrots, finely grated
1 teaspoon dried rosemary
1 teaspoon dried tarragon
½ teaspoon dried marjoram

1½ teaspoons seasoned salt substitute (optional)
⅛ teaspoon cayenne
⅔ cup dry vermouth
1½ cups strong Chicken Stock*
1 cup heavy cream (or triple-strength low sodium dry milk), heated
2 teaspoons Hungarian paprika

GARNISH: ¼ cup finely minced fresh chives

1. Dredge the veal in the flour-pepper mixture.

2. Using a large, heavy flameproof casserole, melt the butter over a low flame. Add the veal and sauté it very slowly until it barely browns, stirring often. Remove the veal pieces to a platter.

3. Add the garlic, onion, parsley, and carrots and sauté for 5 minutes, stirring often.

4. Sprinkle in the rosemary, tarragon, marjoram, salt substitute, and cayenne. Stir in the vermouth and the strong chicken stock. Simmer for 10 minutes.

5. Return the veal pieces to the casserole. Cover tightly and simmer for 1 hour and 15 minutes, or until the veal is tender.

6. Remove the cover from the casserole and slowly add the cream or milk, stirring the veal and sauce gently.

7. Sprinkle in the paprika, lightly mix all the ingredients together, and cover. Simmer for 5 minutes. (See Note.)

Serving: Spoon the veal and sauce over Boiled Rice,* which has been apportioned into individual shallow soup plates, and garnish with the chives.

NOTE: If substituting the triple-strength low sodium dry milk for the cream, mix it with 1 tablespoon cornstarch. Simmer the casserole for 10 minutes, instead of 5, and stir often (but gently) or until the sauce has thickened.

Veal Stew Mykonos

Serves 8

It is essential that this stew be made the day before serving to allow the flavors to blend.

COOKING THE DAY BEFORE:
4 pounds boneless veal shoulder, cut into 2-inch cubes
¾ cup unbleached flour (approximately)
½ cup sweet butter (approximately)
2 large onions, finely minced
8 cloves garlic, finely minced
½ cup finely minced fresh parsley
1 teaspoon dried thyme
½ teaspoon Spanish paprika
1½ teaspoons freshly ground white pepper
2 bay leaves
2 cups dry white wine
3 cups Veal Stock*

24 tiny white onions
24 baby carrots
¼ cup sweet butter
2 pounds small mushrooms

COOKING THE NEXT DAY:
⅓ cup sweet butter
4½ tablespoons unbleached flour
3 cups liquid from the pot the veal was cooked in
5 egg yolks, beaten
¼ cup dry sherry
¼ cup minced fresh parsley
¼ cup minced fresh chives

GARNISH: ¼ cup minced fresh chives

COOKING THE DAY BEFORE
1. Dredge the veal cubes in the flour and shake off the excess.

2. Heat approximately ½ cup sweet butter in a heavy skillet over a medium flame and lightly brown the veal. Remove the veal with a slotted spoon to a flameproof casserole.

3. Add the onions and garlic to the skillet and sauté until the onions are golden.

4. Add the parsley, thyme, paprika, pepper, and bay leaves and stir well. Continue stirring while pouring in the wine and the veal stock. Bring the liquid to a boil, then pour it over the veal and cover tightly. Turn the flame to low and simmer for 45 minutes.

5. Add the onions and carrots to the pot and simmer another 40 minutes, or until the veal and vegetables are tender but not soft.

6. While the veal is cooking, melt ¼ cup butter in a heavy skillet over a medium flame and sauté the mushrooms until quite dark. Add the mushrooms to the stew, stir well, and remove from the flame.

7. When the stew is cool, remove the bay leaves and discard. Transfer the veal and vegetables to a bowl and cover tightly. Pour the liquid into a bowl and cover tightly. Refrigerate overnight.

COOKING THE NEXT DAY

8. One hour before serving, remove the veal, vegetables, and liquid from the refrigerator.

9. Skim any fat off the liquid. Place it in a saucepan and bring it to a boil over a high flame.

10. In another saucepan, melt the butter over a low-medium flame and slowly stir in the flour until it is thoroughly blended, then slowly stir in 3 cups of the boiling liquid. Place the remaining liquid in a flameproof casserole and add the veal and vegetables. Cover tightly and turn the flame to medium. Heat for 20 minutes or until piping hot.

11. In the meantime, stir the sauce from Step 10 with a wire whisk until it is smooth and boiling.

12. Then with the wire whisk beat half of the sauce, a little at a time, into the egg yolks and then slowly add this egg yolk mixture to the sauce on the stove, beating the sauce constantly until all of the egg yolk mixture has been absorbed and the sauce has thickened. Add the sherry, parsley, and chives. Stir well and pour the sauce over the veal and vegetables.

13. Turn the flame under the casserole to low and simmer until everything is piping hot.

Serving: Sprinkle the chives on top of the stew and bring the casserole to your dining table. Place a 1-inch slice of toasted French Bread* in the bottom of each shallow soup bowl. Spoon some of the veal, vegetables, and sauce over the bread. Pass more of the toasted bread accompanied by Garlic Butter.*

Stuffed Breast of Veal

Serves 4 to 6

STUFFING:
1/2 stick sweet butter
1 large onion, finely minced
5 cloves garlic, finely minced
2/3 cup matzoh meal
3 eggs
1/2 to 1 teaspoon dried oregano
    (optional)
1/2 to 1 teaspoon dried sweet
    basil (optional)
5 tablespoons finely minced
    fresh parsley
2 1/2 teaspoons salt substitute (op-
    tional)
3/4 teaspoon freshly ground
    white pepper
1 cup grated salt-free Gouda
    cheese

VEAL:
1 breast of veal (4 to 5 pounds),
    trimmed of all fat and pre-
    pared with a deep pocket

2 large carrots, grated
1 large onion, finely minced
1 bay leaf
4 cloves garlic, pressed
1 teaspoon dried oregano
1 teaspoon dried sweet basil
2 cups dry white wine
1 teaspoon freshly ground white
    pepper
4 tablespoons salt-free tomato
    paste
1 16-ounce can salt-free tomato
    juice
2 1/2 tablespoons olive oil
1 teaspoon Spanish paprika

GARNISH: sprigs of watercress

STUFFING

1. In a heavy skillet melt the butter over a medium flame. Add the onion and garlic and sauté until the onion is translucent. Add the matzoh meal and stir constantly until the butter is absorbed. Remove from the flame.

2. In a large bowl beat the eggs well, then stir in the onion-matzoh meal mixture. Stir in the oregano, basil, parsley, salt substitute, pepper, and cheese. Mix thoroughly.

3. Fill the pocket of the veal with the stuffing and either close the ends with skewers or sew with heavy thread.

VEAL

4. Preheat the oven to 300°.

5. In a heavy roasting pan place the carrots, onion, bay leaf, garlic,

oregano, basil, wine, pepper, tomato paste, and tomato juice. Mix thoroughly. Lay the veal on top of this, bone side down.

6. Rub the top of the veal with the olive oil and sprinkle on the paprika. Cover the roasting pan tightly.

7. Roast for 2½ hours, basting every ½ hour.

8. Uncover the veal and continue to roast for another ½ hour, or until the veal is very tender and brown on top. Take the veal out of the oven and remove the skewers.

9. Transfer the veal to a large cutting board (bone side up) and slice between the bones. Lay the pieces on a large ovenproof platter. Place in a 180° over to keep warm.

10. Pour the gravy into a saucepan and place it in the freezer for 20 minutes. Remove the fat that has accumulated on top. Heat the gravy over a medium flame.

Serving: When the gravy is piping hot, pour it into a gravy boat. Remove the platter of veal from the oven and garnish it with the watercress.

Veal Shanks Provençale

Serves 6 to 10

Prepared with a delectable sauce of puréed vegetables.

7 tablespoons Clarified Butter*
6 veal shanks, cut into 3-inch pieces
1½ cups dry white wine
2 cups Veal Stock* (or Vegetable Stock*)
6 large carrots, sliced thinly
2 large onions, coarsely chopped
2 large sweet potatoes, peeled and sliced paper thin
⅓ cup chopped fresh parsley
6 cloves garlic, pressed
3 large firm, ripe tomatoes, peeled, seeded, and coarsely chopped

1 teaspoon freshly ground white pepper
2 teaspoons seasoned salt substitute (optional)
1½ teaspoons dried rosemary
1 teaspoon dried chervil
1 teaspoon dried sweet basil (optional)
Juice of 2 lemons
1½ to 2½ teaspoons brown sugar (or substitute equivalent)

GARNISH: ⅓ cup chopped fresh parsley

1. In a heavy flameproof casserole melt the clarified butter over a

medium-high flame and brown the veal on all sides. Transfer to a platter.

2. To the casserole, add the white wine, stock, carrots, onions, sweet potatoes, parsley, garlic, tomatoes, pepper, salt substitute, rosemary, chervil, sweet basil, lemon juice, and brown sugar and stir well. Return the veal shanks to the casserole, standing them upright on top of the vegetables. Cover tightly and simmer over a low-medium flame for 1½ hours, or until the veal is tender. Remove the veal shanks to a preheated au gratin pan (standing upright) and keep them warm on the back of the stove.

3. Remove the fat that has accumulated on top of the liquid.

4. Purée the vegetables and liquid in a blender or food processor and then return to the casserole. Turn the flame to high and stir the purée until it just comes to a low boil. Spoon over the veal shanks.

Serving: Garnish the veal shanks with parsley. Offer a Crusty Peasant Rye Bread* or French Bread* which has been sliced, spread generously with Garlic Butter,* wrapped in aluminum foil, and baked for 20 minutes in a 350° oven. (For a very hard crust, bake the bread uncovered on a cookie sheet.)

Veal Marsala

Serves 6

3 pounds veal scaloppine, sliced
  very thinly
1 cup finely grated salt-free
  swiss cheese (optional)
1 cup unbleached flour
⅛ teaspoon cayenne
2 teaspoons dried tarragon
2 tablespoons finely chopped
  fresh parsley
½ teaspoon freshly ground
  white pepper

½ teaspoon dried rosemary
6 tablespoons Clarified Butter*
1 cup Marsala wine
1 teaspoon dried oregano
2 tablespoons chopped fresh
  parsley
Juice of 1 large lemon
1½ teaspoons sugar (or substitute equivalent)

1. Place the veal between sheets of wax paper and pound them paper thin with a wooden or metal mallet.

2. Press some cheese into each side of the veal (optional, but delicious). Mix flour with cayenne, tarragon, finely chopped parsley, pepper, and rosemary. Dredge veal in the seasoned flour.

3. In a large, heavy skillet melt the butter over a low-medium flame and

gently brown the veal on both sides. Transfer to a heated serving platter and keep warm on the back of the stove.

4. Add the wine to the skillet, stir well, and simmer for 10 minutes, stirring often. Add the oregano, chopped parsley, lemon juice, and sugar. Simmer and stir for 3 minutes.

Serving: Pour the sauce over the scaloppine and serve at once.

Osso Buco

Serves 6 to 8

This dish is a specialty of the Lombardy area and most specifically of Milan.

Veal shanks, unfortunately, are not easy to come by. If necessary, ask your butcher to save them for you when he is able to get them, and to keep them in his freezer. When he has 2 or 3, you will be able to prepare and serve this delectable treat.

If you are a collector of kitchen and serving gadgets, treat yourself to marrow forks, a complete frivolity, but a decidedly elegant and useful utensil for this most special dish.

6 veal shanks, split into 3-inch-long pieces
1½ teaspoons freshly ground black pepper
Unbleached flour
¼ cup sweet butter
¼ cup cup olive oil
15 shallots, finely chopped
3 to 4 cloves garlic, finely minced
2 cups dry white wine

2 large ripe tomatoes, peeled, seeded, and very finely chopped
2 tablespoons salt-free tomato paste
6 carrots, scarped and finely grated
1½ cups Veal Stock,* hot

GARNISH:
2 teaspoons finely grated lemon rind
3 teaspoons finely minced fresh parsley

1. Sprinkle the shanks with pepper, dredge very lightly in the flour, and set aside.

2. In a heavy skillet, large enough to hold the shanks standing upright, thus preventing the marrow from falling out, heat the butter and oil over a medium flame and sauté the shallots and garlic until the onion is a deep golden brown. With a slotted spoon, remove the onion and garlic and reserve.

3. Turn the flame to medium high and brown the shanks on all sides (you may have to do this in two batches). Discard the butter and oil.

4. Place the onion and garlic back in the skillet and add the wine, tomatoes, tomato paste, and carrots. Stir well. Add the stock and stir again.

5. Turn the flame to low and stand the shanks upright on top of the onion-tomato mixture.

6. Cover the skillet tightly and simmer until the meat is very tender (approximately 1½ to 2 hours).

7. Remove the fat that has accumulated on top of the liquid.

Serving: Transfer the meat to a preheated platter, spoon the sauce over the shanks, sprinkle with the lemon rind and parsley and serve at once. Offer Rice Milanese* and crusty French Bread.* (The delectable marrow is scooped out and spread on the bread, to add the finishing touch to a rare delicacy.)

Veal Scaloppine Farci

Serves 6 to 8

3 pounds veal, cut from the leg and sliced paper thin (approximately 2 inches square)

⅓ cup Clarified Butter*

⅔ cup finely minced onions

3 cloves garlic, pressed

½ cup finely grated carrots

⅔ cup finely chopped mushrooms

⅛ teaspoon cayenne

2 teaspoons seasoned salt substitute (optional)

1 teaspoon freshly ground white pepper

6 tablespoons finely chopped fresh parsley

2 teaspoons dried tarragon

½ cup wheat germ

1 cup grated salt-free Gouda cheese

3 eggs, well beaten

1 cup unbleached flour, for dredging

3 eggs, lightly beaten

½ cup salt-free cornflake crumbs

6 tablespoons Clarified Butter*

1 cup heavy cream (or triple-strength low sodium dry milk)

1 cup dry white wine

2 tablespoons cornstarch

8 tablespoons dry sherry

¼ cup chopped fresh parsley

3 tablespoons chopped fresh chives

1. Place the veal between slices of wax paper and pound them paper thin with a wooden or metal mallet.

2. In a heavy skillet melt ⅓ cup of clarified butter over a medium flame and sauté the onions and garlic until the onions are translucent. Stir in the carrots, mushrooms, cayenne, salt substitute, pepper, parsley, and tarragon. Remove the skillet from the heat.

3. Add the wheat germ. Stir in the cheese and the well-beaten eggs and mix thoroughly. (This stuffing should have a thick but not dry consistency. If it is too dry, add a little heavy cream. If it is too wet, add a little more wheat germ.)

4. Lay out the veal pieces on wax paper. Divide the stuffing mixture evenly among the scaloppine and smooth it out to ½ inch from the edges. Roll up the scaloppine, jelly-roll fashion, and fasten each one with a small metal skewer or wooden toothpick.

5. Dredge the stuffed scaloppine in the flour and dip them into the lightly beaten eggs. Then roll in the cornflake crumbs.

6. In a heavy flameproof casserole, melt ¾ cup of clarified butter over a medium flame and sauté the scaloppine until they are a light golden brown.

7. When the veal is brown, turn the flame down to low and add the cream (or milk) and the wine. Cover and simmer gently for 40 minutes or until the veal is tender.

8. While the veal is cooking, dissolve the cornstarch in the sherry. Stir well.

9. When the veal is cooked, take out the skewers (or toothpicks) and remove to a heated serving platter (seam side down) and keep warm. Stir the cornstarch mixture into the casserole, blending it thoroughly with the sauce. Stir in the ¼ cup of parsley and the chives and continue to cook for 6 more minutes, or until the sauce has thickened, stirring constantly.

Serving: Spoon some of the sauce over the scaloppine and pour the remainder into a heated gravy boat. Serve at once.

Veal Chops à la Crème

Serves 6

6 large veal chops, about 1 inch thick
1/2 cup unbleached flour
3 eggs, beaten well with 5 tablespoons cold water
2 cups crushed salt-free corn-flake crumbs
2 teaspoons seasoned salt substitute (optional)
2/3 teaspoon freshly ground white pepper
1/8 teaspoon cayenne
1/8 teaspoon dried rosemary
1/2 teaspoon dried chervil
1/2 teaspoon dried tarragon
3 teaspoons finely chopped fresh parsley
4 tablespoons Clarified Butter*

1 1/3 cups heavy cream (or triple-strength low sodium dry milk)
1 cup strong Veal Stock* (or strong Vegetable Stock*)
2 tablespoons finely chopped fresh chives
2 tablespoons finely chopped fresh parsley
2 1/4 tablespoons cornstarch
1/2 cup dry sherry

GARNISH:
12 very thin lemon slices, dipped in 1/4 cup finely chopped fresh parsley

1. Place the veal chops between wax paper and pound the meat gently, using a large wooden or metal mallet, until it is 1/2 inch thick.

2. Mix cornflake crumbs with salt substitute, pepper, cayenne, rosemary, chervil, tarragon, and parsley.

3. Dredge the cutlets in the flour, dip them in the eggs, then dredge them in the seasoned cornflake crumbs.

4. Preheat the oven to 300°.

5. Using a large, heavy skillet, melt the clarified butter over a medium flame and sauté the chops until they are very lightly browned on both sides. Transfer them to a baking pan large enough to hold them in a single layer.

6. Pour the cream (or milk) and stock into the skillet. Stir in the chives and parsley and cook for 15 minutes, or until piping hot, stirring often. Spoon the sauce over the veal. Cover the baking pan tightly with aluminum foil.

7. Bake for 10 to 15 minutes, or until the veal is tender. Do not overcook.

8. Transfer the veal to a preheated serving platter and keep it warm, on the back of the stove.

9. Transfer the sauce to a heavy saucepan and heat it over a low flame.

10. Dissolve the cornstarch in the sherry and, stirring vigorously with a wire whisk, slowly add to the sauce. Cook for 5 to 7 minutes, or until the sauce has thickened and is smooth, stirring constantly.

Serving: Spoon a little sauce over each chop and garnish with 2 parsley-lemon slices. Pour the remaining sauce into a preheated gravy boat. Serve at once.

Vitello Tonnato

Serves 4 as a main course or 8 as a first course

This is one of my favorite dishes. Until I evolved this recipe I was unable to enjoy it, for no restaurant would prepare this for me without salt, salted tuna, anchovies, and capers . . . all of which bear the sign "poison" to someone on a low sodium regimen! Therefore I hope you will enjoy this recipe as much as my family has.

2¹/₂ pounds boneless leg of veal, rolled and tied
¹/₂ cup ice water
¹/₂ cup fresh lemon juice
1¹/₂ cups dry white wine
2 carrots, finely grated
1 large onion, finely chopped
Juice of large lemon
2 bay leaves
1¹/₂ teaspoons freshly ground white pepper
1 7- to 7¹/₂-ounce can tuna (packed in water, no salt added)

2 teaspoons salt substitute (optional)
1 teaspoon freshly ground white pepper
¹/₈ teaspoon cayenne
1 egg yolk
1¹/₂ teaspoons fresh lemon juice
1¹/₂ teaspoons dry mustard
¹/₃ cup olive oil

GARNISH:
1 lemon, thinly sliced
3 tablespoons finely minced fresh parsley

1. Place the veal in a large plastic bag. Pour in the water and ¹/₂ cup lemon juice. Seal the bag tightly, rotate two or three times, and refrigerate for 1 hour. Drain the veal and pat dry.

2. In a heavy pot put the wine, carrots, onion, juice of 1 lemon, bay leaves, and 1¹/₂ teaspoons of pepper. Place the veal on top of this and cover tightly.

3. Turn the flame to medium, bring the liquid to a boil, then turn the

flame to low and simmer until the veal is tender (approximately 2 hours).

4. Remove the veal from the pot and cool. Refrigerate until cold (approximately 2½ hours).

5. Mash the tuna with the salt substitute, 1 teaspoon of pepper, and the cayenne. Set aside.

6. Place 1 egg yolk in a blender or food processor and beat for twenty seconds, then slowly add 1½ teaspoons of lemon juice and mustard. Add the oil drop by drop until it has a thick but fluid consistency. Add the tuna mixture and blend for 15 seconds.

Serving: Slice the veal very thinly and place it on a large serving platter. Spoon the sauce over the veal. Cover tightly with plastic wrap or aluminum foil and refrigerate at least 8 hours. Garnish with thin lemon slices and sprinkle with the minced parsley.

VEGETABLES
Food of All Seasons

Vegetables

I must admit that it is difficult to be enthusiastic about vegetables in this country owing in large measure to the deplorable state in which we are forced to accept them from some of our supermarkets. When I am on a business trip in France, a day doesn't go by that I don't stop at one of the innumerable and fabulous vegetable markets that dot the streets. It is with great wonderment that I stare at the brilliant palette of color and the artistic array of eggplants, green beans, tiny carrots, broccoli, cauliflower, tomatoes, lettuce in every conceivable variety, radishes, zucchini, bright red peppers, and bunches of baby watercress.

For most people who have to make do with the produce from our supermarkets, planning and shopping and ingenuity in preparation are most definitely required. Find out on which days your supermarket receives its fresh produce and plan your green grocery shopping for those days. If you are buying seasonal vegetables buy only those that are at the height of their season and don't settle for less than perfect vegetables, seasonal or otherwise.

Actually, living in New York City has an enormous advantage over many small towns and other large cities far from the farming areas. In New York we have a slew of specialty produce markets and, while they are quite expensive, their quality is excellent. Although the cost may actually seem high, it isn't, for the waste that accompanies poor vegetables skyrockets their price.

However, even in New York City the winter months provide very little in the way of exciting seasonal vegetables, such as asparagus, good tomatoes, and cauliflower . . . unless you are willing to pay the king's ransom. Thus, these seasonal foods are consumed with great pleasure when they are plentiful and less expensive.

In the summer, if you are fortunate enough to have a garden, join the millions of Americans and plant a large assortment of vegetables. Your budget will benefit and the thrill of accomplishment and taste in eating home-grown produce is well worth the effort. However, if you do not have a garden, see if you can become a sharecropper with someone who does. Or do what I do: haunt the farmers' markets and cajole your friends with gardens in to sharing their bounty with you. In turn, perhaps you can repay their kindness with something they'd enjoy, such as home-baked breads, a wonderful casserole, or a delectable soup.

My three rules for vegetables regardless of season are:

1. Use the best produce available.
2. Don't overcook them.
3. Serve them immediately.

Wherever possible I steam vegetables, preserving both vitamins and color, and my trusty steamers see hardy duty. Another way of preparing vegetables, one that preserves not only their vitamins and their flavors, is the Chinese method of stir frying, using small quantities of oil, and vegetables cut into small uniform pieces to hasten cooking. Coated with the oil and cooked quickly, they retain their color, flavor, and crispness. On the other hand, long slow cooking is essential for puréed vegetables, which lend an interesting texture to heavier entrees.

We usually combine vegetables on platters, making sure that the colors and textures complement each other. Therefore, if steamed vegetables are in the offing, each one is steamed individually. The effect is beautiful, the taste is superb, and the work is not difficult. It is true that there are a few more pots to wash, but the results are well worth the nuisance.

With light main courses, it is nice to serve exciting vegetables with an interesting sauce; or on those nights when a vegetarian dinner is planned with its assortment of colorful vegetables, we generally serve one of the vegetables in a cheese sauce such as a Mornay* or with Hollandaise.* On these occasions offer one of your warm home-baked breads, accompanied by sweet butter. In any case, whether the vegetables are an accompaniment or the main course itself, they are exceedingly nutritious and when prepared with tender loving care can become the highlight of lunch or dinner.

Equipment, Rules and Method for Steaming Vegetables

Such as: broccoli, brussels sprouts, cauliflower, green beans, green peas, and carrots.

EQUIPMENT:
1. A heavy saucepan.
2. A metal steamer or strainer, or a colander with legs that will stand securely in the saucepan to insure that the "steamer basket" is suspended at least 1 inch above the bottom of the pot.

RULES:
1. Make sure that the vegetables are the freshest possible, firm and unbruised.
2. Wash the vegetables thoroughly and drain them.
3. Steam one vegetable at a time in a saucepan to insure the height of flavor from each vegetable.

1. Fill the saucepan with water to within 1/4 inch from the steamer basket and lay the vegetable in the steamer, strainer, or colander.
2. Cover the saucepan and turn the flame to high. Bring the water to a boil. Reduce the flame to medium and cook as follows:

For Broccoli flowerets, Brussels Sprouts, Cauliflower flowerets, or Green Beans: Keep the saucepan covered for 5 minutes. then uncover and continue to cook on a medium flame for 6 to 8 minutes, or until barely tender but still very crisp.

For Green Peas: Keep the saucepan covered for 3 minutes, then uncover and continue to cook on a medium flame for 5 to 6 minutes, or until barely tender but still very crisp.

For Whole Carrots: Keep the saucepan *covered the entire time* and cook for 9 to 10 minutes, or until barely tender but still very crisp.

For Julienne Carrots: Keep the saucepan *covered the entire time* and cook for 1 1/2 to 2 minutes, or until barely tender but still very crisp.

NOTE: The investment in the steamers is quite nominal. They cost from $1.98 to $4.98 and can be purchased in most hardware and house-wares stores. In all honesty, the steamers I purchased at $1.98 are just as good as the ones I purchased at $4.98. I would suggest investing in three to four so you can cook your garden array of vegetables at the same time.

Stir-Fried Chinese Vegetables

Serves 4 to 6

3½ tablespoons peanut oil
4 cloves garlic, finely minced
8 Chinese dried mushrooms,
soaked in warm water for
20 minutes and cut into
strips
2 green onions (scallions), thinly
sliced
2 cups shredded Chinese cabbage
¾ cup thinly sliced water chestnuts (canned in water, no
salt)

¾ cup thinly sliced bamboo
shoots (canned in water, no
salt)
¾ pound snow peas, tips and
string removed
1½ tablespoons dry sherry
2 teaspoons Spicy Sesame Oil*
(optional)

1. Heat the peanut oil in a wok or heavy frying pan over a high flame. Add the garlic, mushrooms, and green onions and stir-fry for 10 to 15 seconds.

2. Add the cabbage and stir-fry for 1 minute.

3. Add the water chestnuts, bamboo shoots, and snow peas. Mix all the ingredients well and stir in the sherry.

4. Cover the wok and cook for 1 minute.

5. Remove the cover, stir in the spicy sesame oil, and remove from the flame.

Serving: Transfer the vegetables to a heated platter or bowl and serve at once.

Stir-Fried Green Beans with Garlic

Serves 4

1 pound green beans, tips off
and cut into 1½-inch pieces
3 tablespoons peanut oil
3 cloves garlic, pressed
2 tablespoons dry sherry

½ teaspoon sugar (or substitute
equivalent)
½ teaspoon freshly ground
black pepper

1. Parboil the string beans for 2½ minutes, drain, and rinse under cold water.

2. Heat the oil in a wok or heavy frying pan over a high flame. Stir-fry the garlic for 10 seconds.

3. Add the string beans and stir-fry for 2 minutes.

4. Add the sherry, sugar, and pepper, then stir-fry 1½ minutes.

Serving: Transfer the beans to a heated platter or bowl and serve at once.

Stir-Fried Broccoli

Serves 4

2 tablespoons peanut oil
3 cloves garlic, finely minced
1 large bunch broccoli, tough
    ends removed, stems cut
    into ½-inch diagonal slices,
    and top of broccoli cut (or
    broken) into small flowerets

COMBINE:
⅔ cup strong Chicken Stock* or
    Beef Stock*

1 teaspoon sugar (or substitute
    equivalent)
⅛ teaspoon cayenne
½ teaspoon freshly ground
    black pepper
1½-inch piece fresh ginger root,
    finely minced
1 tablespoon dry sherry
2 teaspoons cornstarch

1. Heat the oil in a wok or heavy frying pan over a high flame until it begins to smoke. Turn the flame to low and add the garlic. Stir well and add the broccoli. Turn the flame to high and stir-fry for 3 minutes.

2. Stir the stock mixture well and add it to the broccoli.

3. Stir-fry for 1 minute.

4. Cover the wok and cook for approximately 2½ minutes, or until the sauce is slightly thickened.

5. Uncover and remove from the flame. Stir thoroughly.

Serving: Transfer the broccoli to a heated platter or shallow bowl and serve at once.

Asparagus al Dente

Serves 14 as an hors d'oeuvre, 8 as a first course, or 12 as a vegetable accompanying the main course

After many experiments I discovered that this is the perfect way to achieve crisp and crunchy asparagus.

4 pounds of very, very thin asparagus (approximately with the diameter of a drinking straw)

1. Fill a large pot (approximately 8 quarts) halfway with water and bring to a rolling boil over a high flame.

2. While the water is coming to a boil, prepare the asparagus. Break off the ends where they break most easily and discard them. Wash thoroughly.

3. When the water is at a rolling boil, submerge the asparagus, let the water come back to a boil, and cook uncovered for 1 minute only!

4. Immediately transfer the asparagus to a colander and run cold water over them for 5 minutes. This stops the cooking process and also "sets" the color. This procedure is sometimes referred to as "refreshing the asparagus."

5. Pat the asparagus dry between double thickness of paper towels. Arrange them on a serving platter, cover with foil or plastic wrap, and refrigerate for at least 2 hours.

Serving: Serve these cold as an hors d'oeuvre, offering either Mideastern Yogurt Sauce,* Sauce Aïoli,* or Curry Mayonnaise* as the dip. They are also superb as a first course with Mustard Vinaigrette,* or as a vegetable slightly heated in a sparse amount of melted Clarified Butter.*

NOTE: Most cooks feel that the asparagus should be peeled to the tips. Since this recipe calls for extremely thin asparagus (which I prefer), that procedure is unnecessary. It is also unnecessary to tie the asparagus in bunches and stand them upright in the boiling water (which is exactly what most other recipes direct); since it takes the same amount of time for the tips and stems of these very very thin asparagus to cook.

Asparagus Mornay

Serves 8 as a first course or 12 as an accompaniment to the main course

4 pounds very thin asparagus, cooked as directed for Asparagus al Dente* through Step 4 only. Drain thoroughly and pat dry between double thickness of paper towels.
1 cup Mornay Sauce,* hot
¹/₂ cup salt-free Gouda Cheese

1. Preheat the broiler to 450°.
2. Arrange the asparagus in a heavily buttered, flameproof, shallow au gratin pan.
3. Spoon the mornay sauce over the top third of the asparagus (i.e., the tips and about 2 inches). Sprinkle the cheese on top of the sauce.
4. Place the asparagus 5 inches from the flame and broil for 3 to 4 minutes, or until the cheese is melted and bubbling.

Serving: Serve at once.

Asparagus Polonaise

Serves 8 for a first course or 12 as an accompaniment to the main course

4 pounds very, very thin asparagus, cooked as directed for Asparagus al Dente,* through Step 4 only. Drain thoroughly and pat dry between double thickness of paper towels.
¹/₂ cup Clarified Butter*

3 tablespoons Bread Crumbs*
3 tablespoons finely grated (or sieved) hard-boiled egg yolk
3 tablespoons finely grated (or sieved) hard-boiled egg white
3 tablespoons finely minced fresh parsley

1. Arrange the asparagus in a heavily buttered, flameproof, shallow au gratin pan.

2. In a small heavy skillet melt the clarified butter over a medium flame. Add all of the remaining ingredients to the melted butter and sauté for 3 minutes.

3. Spoon the sauce over the top third of the asparagus (i.e., the tips and about 2 inches).

4. Place the asparagus 5 inches from the flame and broil for 3 to 4 minutes, or until piping hot (take care not to burn the asparagus).

Serving: Serve at once.

Cooked Artichokes

Serves 8

Artichokes are a higher sodium vegetable. So please, with this, as with all other things . . . check with your physician.

8 large artichokes	**2 cloves garlic, finely mashed**
2½ quarts very cold water	**6 tablespoons fresh lemon juice**
2½ tablespoons white vinegar	**3 tablespoons olive oil (or corn**
⅔ cup finely minced onions	**oil)**

1. Cut the stem off each artichoke and pull off the bottom row of tough leaves.

2. Lay each artichoke on its side and cut off ½ inch from the top. With scissors, trim off ¼ to ½ inch of the tops of all the artichoke leaves and spread the leaves slightly.

3. As you finish preparing each artichoke drop it into a large bowl containing the 2½ quarts of cold water acidulated with the vinegar.

4. Into a heavy saucepan large enough to hold all the artichokes in an upright position, pour enough water to come up to 2 inches. Add the onions, garlic, lemon juice, and oil and bring the water to a boil. Boil for 3 minutes.

5. Reduce the flame to low-medium and carefully place the artichokes in the water, standing in an upright position. Cover and cook for 50 minutes, or until tender.

6. Remove the artichokes and place them upside down on a rack to drain. (I put my rack in a roasting pan to facilitate this step.)

7. When the artichokes are thoroughly drained, spread the leaves and pull out the choke.

Serving: Serve at once with Lemon Butter Sauce;* or refrigerate for at least 4 hours and serve cold with an Herb Vinaigrette Dressing* or Mayonnaise.*

Artichoke plates are a fabulous luxury . . . but if you do not have them, put each artichoke in a small deep bowl and place the bowl on a dessert-size plate, on which you have laid a paper doily. You may either spoon the sauce into the center of the artichoke or place it in individual tiny bowls, so that each person may dip to his heart's content.

NOTE: If you are going to stuff the cooked artichokes with Chicken Salad* for a main course, spread the leaves open to a greater degree and pull out the choke (while the artichokes are still very warm) as this will better accommodate the filling. Offer the Herb Vinaigrette Dressing* or the Mayonnaise* in individual tiny bowls next to each person's dinner plate.

Tomatoes Stuffed with Mushrooms, Rice, and Peas

Serves 8 as a first course, or use 12 medium-size tomatoes and serve as an accompaniment to the main course

8 large (or 12 medium-size) firm, ripe tomatoes
1/4 cup corn oil
1/2 pound tiny mushrooms, stems chopped, caps thinly sliced
1 cup fresh Steamed Green Peas*
1 1/2 cups Boiled Rice,* warm
2 tablespoons finely chopped fresh parsley

2 teaspoons salt substitute (optional)
1/8 teaspoon cayenne
1/2 cup heavy cream (or triple-strength low sodium dry milk), heated
1 cup white Bread Crumbs*
2 tablespoons sweet butter, melted

1. From the core side, cut a large hollow into each tomato. Invert the tomatoes and let them drain for 20 minutes.

2. Heat the oil in a frying pan over a medium flame and sauté the mushrooms, stirring often, until they begin to turn brown.

3. Remove the mushrooms with their juice to a mixing bowl, add the peas and rice, and mix well. Stir in the parsley.

4. Add the salt substitute and the cayenne to the cream or milk, stir, and then mix well with the mushroom mixture.

5. Preheat the oven to 350°.

6. Invert the tomatoes and place them in a well-buttered baking dish. Fill with the mixture, mounding it slightly.

7. Press some of the bread crumbs into each mounded stuffed tomato, brush with the melted butter, and bake for 15 minutes.

Serving: As a first course, place a tomato on each plate. They naturally look wonderful on green leaf-shaped plates.

As the main course, use an attractive baking dish and serve directly from that.

Tomatoes Stuffed with Mushrooms au Gratin

Serves 6 as a first course or 12 as a vegetable

6 large, firm, ripe tomatoes
3 tablespoons corn oil
1/8 cup (heavy virgin) olive oil
1/8 cup corn oil
2 medium Bermuda onions, finely chopped
8 cloves garlic, finely minced
1 pound small fresh mushrooms (ends off and thinly sliced lengthwise)
10 dried mushrooms, soaked, dried, and chopped
1/2 cup finely chopped fresh parsley
1/4 cup finely chopped fresh chives
1 tablespoon finely chopped fresh dill

2 tablespoons seasoned salt substitute (optional)
1/8 to 1/4 teaspoon cayenne
1 teaspoon freshly ground black pepper
1/2 cup white Bread Crumbs* (or matzoh meal)
1/3 cup wheat germ
2 eggs, well beaten
1/2 pound salt-free Swiss cheese, grated
1/2 pound salt-free Gouda cheese, grated
4 tablespoons sweet butter, melted

GARNISH: Sprigs of fresh parsley

1. Preheat the oven to 350°.

2. Slice 1/2 inch off the core side of each tomato and slice 1/8 inch from the other end, thus giving the tomatoes a firm base to stand on (. . . on either end). Cut the tomatoes in half crosswise.

3. With a small spoon, scoop out the seeds, pulp, and juice, taking care not to disturb the bottom or sides of the tomato "cases."

4. Drizzle the 3 tablespoons of oil evenly over the 12 tomato halves on the cut side.

5. Put the tomatoes in a buttered baking dish, cut side up, and bake 20 minutes.

6. In the same baking dish, invert the tomatoes and let them drain, allowing them to steep in their own juice.

7. Preheat the broiler to 550°.

8. In a large heavy skillet, over a medium flame, heat the olive oil and corn oil.

9. Sauté the onions, garlic, fresh and dried mushrooms until the onions take on a translucent color.

10. Push the mixture aside and stir-fry the parsley and chives for 2 minutes.

11. Add the fresh dill, salt substitute, cayenne, black pepper, bread crumbs, and wheat germ.

12. Stir until all the ingredients are well blended, then simmer for 2 to 3 minutes.

13. Remove the mixture from the frying pan into a large mixing bowl and slowly fold in the beaten eggs and the salt-free Swiss cheese.

14. Pour the liquid from the tomatoes into a well-buttered flameproof baking pan and place the 12 tomato halves in the pan (right side up), touching each other.

15. Divide the filling mixture evenly among the 12 tomato halves and mound.

16. Divide the salt-free Gouda cheese evenly over the tomato halves, pressing gently on the mounded filling.

17. Drizzle 1 teaspoon of the melted sweet butter over each tomato half and broil 6 inches from the flame for 4 to 5 minutes, or until the cheese is melted and bubbly.

Serving: As a first course, place 2 tomato halves on each plate and garnish with sprigs of parsley.

As a vegetable: A. Serve directly from the baking pan, if it is attractive enough.

B. Surround your chicken, fish, or meat, if prepared without sauces.

C. Transfer the tomatoes to a preheated platter and garnish with the parsley.

Curried Stuffed Tomatoes

Serves 8

I don't have to tell you that summer's firm, ripe tomatoes make this a very special treat.

4 large, firm, ripe tomatoes
2 tablespoons peanut or corn oil
$^1/_3$ cup peanut or corn oil
1 large Bermuda onion, finely minced
4 cloves garlic, finely minced
$^1/_2$ cup coarsely minced parsley
2 tablespoons salt-free curry powder
1 teaspoon cumin
$3^1/_2$ teaspoons seasoned salt substitute (optional)

$^1/_4$ teaspoon cayenne (optional)
$^1/_4$ teaspoon freshly ground white pepper
$^1/_2$ teaspoon salt-free chili powder
$^1/_2$ cup white Bread Crumbs* (or matzoh meal)
1 pound fresh Steamed Green Peas*
3 tablespoons peanut or corn oil

1. Preheat the oven to 350°.
2. Slice about $^1/_2$ inch off the core end of each tomato and slice $^1/_8$ inch off the other end, thus giving the tomatoes a firm base to stand on (. . . on either end). Cut the tomatoes in half crosswise.
3. With a small spoon, scoop out the seeds, pulp, and juice, taking care not to disturb the bottom or sides of the tomato "cases."
4. Drizzle the 2 tablespoons of oil evenly over the 8 tomato halves on the cut side.
5. Put the tomatoes into a greased baking dish, cut side up, and bake for 20 minutes.
6. In the same baking dish, invert the tomatoes and let them drain, allowing them to steep in their own juice.
7. Preheat the broiler to 550°.
8. In a large heavy skillet heat the $^1/_3$ cup of oil over a medium flame.
9. Sauté the onion and garlic until the onion is a pale golden color.
10. Push the onion and garlic aside and stir-fry the parsley until it starts to crisp.
11. Add the curry, cumin, salt substitute, cayenne, white pepper, chili powder, and bread crumbs.
12. Stir well until all the ingredients are thoroughly blended.
13. Fold in the steamed green peas.
14. Turn the tomatoes right side up and place them in a well-buttered flameproof baking pan.

15. Divide the filling mixture among the 8 tomato halves and mound.

16. Drizzle the stuffed tomatoes with the 3 tablespoons of oil (approximately 1 teaspoon per stuffed tomato) and broil 6 inches from the flame for 5 to 6 minutes, or until bubbly.

Serving: If your baking pan is attractive enough, serve directly from that. If not, transfer the tomatoes to a heated serving platter.

Curried Corn and Tomatoes à la Crème

Serves 8

¹/₃ cup corn oil

1 large onion, finely chopped

2 green peppers, finely chopped

¹/₂ cup chopped fresh parsley

2 1-pound cans salt-free tomatoes, finely chopped (discard juice)

2 1-pound cans salt-free corn (discard liquid)

²/₃ cup heavy cream (or triple-strength low sodium dry milk)

1¹/₂ tablespoons salt-free curry powder

¹/₈ to ¹/₄ teaspoon cayenne

4 teaspoons seasoned salt substitute (optional)

1 teaspoon freshly ground white pepper

3 eggs, lightly beaten

1¹/₂ cups soft Bread Crumbs*

1¹/₂ cups crushed salt-free cornflakes

3 tablespoons melted sweet butter

1. In a heavy skillet heat the oil over a medium flame and sauté the onion and peppers until tender and lightly browned.

2. Add the parsley and sauté for 2 minutes, stirring constantly.

3. Preheat the oven to 350°.

4. Mix the tomatoes, corn, and the onion mixture together.

5. In a bowl combine the cream or milk, curry powder, cayenne, salt substitute, pepper, eggs, and bread crumbs. Mix well.

6. Add the cream mixture to the corn, tomato, and onion mixture and stir. Pour the mixture into a greased ovenproof casserole.

7. Sprinkle with the cornflake crumbs. Spoon the melted butter over the conflake crumbs.

8. Cover. Put the casserole in a pan containing 2 cups of very hot but not boiling water and bake for 20 minutes.

9. Remove the cover and bake 10 minutes more.

Serving: Bring the casserole to the table and serve.

NOTE: You may add 1 cup grated cheese after 25 minutes of baking and then place the casserole 4 inches from the broiler set at 550° and broil until the cheese is melted and bubbly (about 4 minutes).

Tomato Purée: Method 1

(Using fresh tomatoes)
Yields approximately 1 quart

10 large ripe tomatoes, skinned, cored, and finely chopped (see Note), retaining all the juice

1½ tablespoons natural sugar (or substitute equivalent)

½ cup dry white wine

½ to 1 teaspoon freshly ground white pepper

1 large onion, finely chopped (optional)

In a heavy saucepan bring the tomatoes, sugar, wine, pepper, and onion to a boil over a medium flame, stirring often with a wooden spoon. Turn the flame to low and cook until the tomatoes are reduced to a thick purée, approximately 45 minutes; stir often with a wooden spoon.

NOTE: To skin tomatoes:

1. Plunge into boiling water for 1 minute, if on the soft side, and for 2 minutes, if firm.

2. Drain, remove core, and peel off skin with a sharp knife, starting from the core opening.

Tomato Purée: Method 2

(Using salt-free canned
tomatoes)
Yields approximately 1 quart

2 16-ounce cans salt-free toma-
toes, drained and finely
chopped (or salt-free Italian
plumb tomatoes)
¹/₄ cup juice from the drained
canned tomatoes
1 tablespoon natural sugar (or
substitute equivalent)

¹/₃ cup white wine
¹/₂ to 1 teaspoon freshly ground
white pepper
1 large onion, finely chopped
(optional)

In a large heavy saucepan bring the tomatoes, tomato juice, sugar, wine, pepper, and onion to a boil over a medium flame, stirring often with a wooden spoon. Turn the flame to low and cook until the tomatoes are reduced to a thick purée, approximately 45 minutes; stir often with a wooden spoon.

NOTE: If you are using the purée as a vegetable and not as part of another recipe, you may add a variety of spices such as fresh salt-free curry powder, paprika, salt-free chili powder, chopped fresh parsley, chopped chives, and a little melted butter.

For an Italian flavor, add in the last 15 minutes of cooking minced fresh parsley, fresh or dried sweet basil, dried oregano, crushed garlic, and a little olive oil.

If you like a very thick purée, add ¹/₂ to 1 cup of soft Bread Crumbs* in the last 15 minutes of cooking.

Tomato Pudding

Serves 4 to 8

1 quart Tomato Purée* or 2 16-ounce cans salt-free tomato purée
1/3 cup dry vermouth
3 tablespoons natural sugar (or substitute equivalent)
1 tablespoon finely chopped fresh chives
1 tablespoon chopped fresh parsley
1 tablespoon finely chopped fresh basil

2 teaspoons seasoned salt substitute (optional)
1 teaspoon freshly ground black pepper
1/4 cup peanut oil
1 large onion, finely chopped
4 cloves garlic, finely chopped
2 1/4 cups soft white Bread Crumbs*
1/4 cup melted sweet butter

1. In a heavy saucepan heat the tomato purée over a medium-high flame just until it reaches a boil, stirring often with a wooden spoon.

2. Add the vermouth, sugar, chives, parsley, basil, salt substitute, and pepper. Stir well. Turn the flame to low and cook for 10 minutes.

3. While this is cooking, heat the oil in a heavy skillet over a medium flame and sauté the onion and garlic until the onion is pale golden, stirring frequently.

4. Add the onion mixture to the tomato mixture, blending everything thoroughly. Cook for 5 minutes.

5. Sprinkle the bread crumbs into an ovenproof casserole and pour the butter over them.

6. Pour the tomato and onion mixture on top of this and cover very tightly. Bake for 45 minutes.

Serving: Serve directly from the casserole.

Sweet and Sour Cabbage and Tomatoes

Serves 8

1/3 cup corn oil
8 cups finely shredded cabbage
1 large onion, finely chopped
2 large green peppers, finely
    chopped
2 cups Tomato Purée* or 1 1-
    pound can salt-free tomato
    purée
1 teaspoon dried tarragon (op-
    tional)
2 tablespoons finely chopped
    fresh dill

1/8 teaspoon cayenne
1 teaspoon caraway seeds (or
    you can pulverize them to a
    powder in a dry blender)
    (optional)
Juice of 4 lemons
2½ to 3½ tablespoons natural
    sugar (or substitute equiv-
    alent)
3/4 teaspoon freshly ground
    black pepper

1. In a heavy saucepan heat the oil over a low-medium flame and sauté the cabbage, onion, and peppers for 10 minutes, stirring often.

2. Add the tomato purée, tarragon, dill, cayenne, caraway seeds, lemon juice, sugar, and pepper. Stir well to combine. Turn the flame to low and cook for 20 minutes, stirring often.

Serving: Transfer the mixture to a preheated au gratin dish or bowl and serve at once.

Red Cabbage Extraordinaire

Serves 8

1/4 cup corn oil
2 large onions, finely chopped
8 carrots, grated (optional)
1 very large red cabbage, finely
    shredded
1 cup dried prunes
1 cup dried apricots
2 large tart green apples, peeled
    and cut into 1/2-inch slices

Juice of 4 lemons
Juice of 3 oranges
3 tablespoons natural sugar (or
    substitute equivalent)
1½ cups dry red wine
1 teaspoon freshly ground black
    pepper
3½ teaspoons caraway seeds
    (optional)

1. In a large, heavy saucepan heat the oil over a medium flame and sauté the onions until they are translucent.

2. Add the carrots, cabbage, prunes, apricots, apples, lemon juice, orange juice, sugar, wine, pepper, and caraway seeds. Stir well and cover tightly. Bring the flame up to high for 5 minutes and then turn it to low and cook for 1½ hours.

Serving: Transfer the mixture to a preheated attractive bowl and serve.

Purée of Green Beans

Serves 8

4 tablespoons sweet butter
1 large onion, finely chopped
½ cup hot water
½ cup warm dry white wine
¼ cup warm dry sherry
½ teaspoon dried dill (or 1 tablespoon finely chopped fresh dill)
½ teaspoon dried basil (or 1 tablespoon finely chopped fresh basil)
1 tablespoon salt substitute (optional)

⅛ teaspoon cayenne
½ to 1 teaspoon freshly ground white pepper
3 pounds green beans, stems removed
⅓ cup heavy cream (or triple-strength low sodium dry milk) mixed with ½ cup milk (or low sodium dry milk)
2 tablespoons sweet butter

1. In a heavy saucepan melt the butter over a low-medium flame and sauté the onion until golden.

2. Add the water, wine, sherry, dill, basil, salt substitute, cayenne, and white pepper and bring to a boil.

3. Add the beans, turn the flame to low-medium, and simmer for 20 minutes, or until the beans are tender and almost all of the liquid has evaporated.

4. Purée the mixture in a blender or food processor. Transfer the purée to a large mixing bowl.

5. Using a wire whisk, slowly beat in the cream-milk mixture, a little at a time, until the puréed beans are soft, quite moist, but not soupy.

6. Melt the 2 tablespoons of butter over a medium-low flame in a he flameproof au gratin pan and add the puréed green beans. Stir constantly until the purée is piping hot.

Serving: Bring the au gratin pan to the table and serve at once.

Chestnut Vegetable Purée

Serves 4 to 6

5 tablespoons sweet butter
5 carrots, finely chopped
1 large onion, finely chopped
4 tablespoons unbleached flour
½ cup milk (or low sodium dry
    milk)
½ cup dry white wine
3 tablespoons finely chopped
    fresh parsley
2 teaspoons dried tarragon
2 cups raw peas, shelled

2 cups boiled chestnuts, finely
    chopped
2 teaspoons salt substitute
1 teaspoon freshly ground white
    pepper
2 tablespoons sweet butter,
    melted
⅓ cup heavy cream (or triple-
    strength low sodium dry
    milk)
⅛ cup dry sherry

1. In a heavy saucepan melt the 5 tablespoons of butter over a medium flame. Add the carrots and onion and sauté for 5 minutes, stirring often.

2. Slowly add the flour, stirring constantly until it is thoroughly blended with the carrots and onion.

3. Add the milk, wine, parsley, tarragon, and peas. Cover and simmer over a low flame for 20 minutes, or until the peas are tender.

4. Add the chestnuts, salt substitute, and pepper. Stir well. Cover and simmer for 3 to 4 minutes.

5. Purée the mixture in a blender or food processor in 2 or 3 batches.

6. Return the purée to the saucepan, add the melted butter, cream or milk, and sherry. Turn the flame to low and with a wire whisk beat all the ingredients until they are thoroughly blended and the purée is piping hot, very moist but definitely not soupy.

Serving: Transfer the purée to a preheated ceramic bowl and serve at once.

Purée of Cauliflower

Serves 6 to 8

¹/₄ stick sweet butter
2 large Bermuda onions, finely
   chopped
2 cloves garlic, crushed
Juice of large lemon
1 tablespoon salt substitute (optional)
1¹/₄ teaspoons freshly ground
   white pepper

2 large Steamed Cauliflowers*
   separated into flowerets (see
   Note)
¹/₂ cup heavy cream (or triple-
   strength low sodium dry
   milk) mixed with ¹/₂ cup
   milk (or low sodium dry
   milk)
2 tablespoons sweet butter

1. In a large, heavy skillet melt the butter and sauté the onions and garlic until translucent.

2. Add the lemon juice, salt substitute, and pepper and mix thoroughly.

3. Put the cauliflowers and the onion mixture in a blender or food processor and purée in 2 or 3 batches. Transfer to a large mixing bowl.

4. Using a wire whisk, slowly beat in the cream-milk mixture, a little at a time, until the purée is creamy but not soupy.

5. In a heavy skillet melt the 2 tablespoons of butter over a low flame. Add the purée and stir constantly until hot and very smooth.

Serving: Transfer the purée to a preheated au gratin pan and serve.

NOTE: If you prefer, the cauliflower may be boiled until it is tender, rather than steamed.

Purée of Peas au Beurre

Serves 6 to 8

A good accompaniment to Rack of Lamb Persillée.*

2 tablespoons sweet butter
1 large onion, finely chopped
1½ cups hot water
½ cup warm dry vermouth
½ teaspoon crushed dried rosemary
¼ teaspoon crushed dried chervil

3½ teaspoons salt substitute (optional)
¾ teaspoon freshly ground white pepper
3½ pounds fresh peas, shelled
4 tablespoons sweet butter, softened
2 tablespoons sweet butter

1. In a heavy saucepan melt 2 tablespoons of butter over a medium flame and sauté the onion until golden.

2. Add the water, vermouth, rosemary, chervil, salt substitute, and pepper. Turn the flame to high and bring the liquid to a boil.

3. Lower the flame to medium, add the peas, and simmer uncovered for 20 minutes, or until the peas are very tender and about three fourths of the liquid has evaporated.

4. Purée the mixture in a blender or food processor (in 2 or 3 batches).

5. Beat in the softened butter.

6. Melt the remaining 2 tablespoons of butter in a heavy saucepan and add the purée of peas. Turn the heat to medium-low and stir constantly until the purée is hot.

Serving: Transfer to a preheated silver bowl and serve at once.

NOTE: If the purée is not creamy enough add ¼ cup heavy cream (or triple-strength low sodium dry milk) a little at a time, until it is creamy but not soupy.

Broccoli Soufflé

Serves 8

A soufflé is rather easy to make. On a particular occasion, however, I goofed badly. It was the time I served soup as a first course and Rack of Lamb Persillée* accompanied by this broccoli soufflé as the main course. The problem I ran into was a guest who was an exceptionally slow eater but a very big talker. By the time she finished the soup and her story, the soufflé had fallen and the rack of lamb was overcooked. What an expensive disaster! As a result, I now have three simple rules: Rule 1: I serve a hot soufflé as a first course. Rule 2: If I'd like to serve the soufflé with the main course there can be no first course and I time the soufflé according to the meat. Rule 3: I serve soufflé as a dessert. Ah . . . but you'll have to wait for that.

4 to 5 cups Steamed Broccoli*
6 tablespoons sweet butter
2 tablespoons finely chopped
   shallots
3 cloves garlic, pressed
6 tablespoons unbleached flour
1 cup Chicken Stock,* mixed
   with 1 cup heavy cream (or
   triple-strength low sodium
   dry milk)

6 egg yolks, well beaten
1/8 teaspoon cayenne
2 1/2 teaspoons seasoned salt substitute (optional)
1/2 teaspoon freshly ground
   white pepper
1/2 teaspoon paprika
3/4 cup grated salt-free Gouda
   cheese
6 egg whites

1. Purée the broccoli in a blender or food processor, making sure it measures 2 cups after puréeing.

2. In a skillet melt the butter over a medium flame and sauté the shallots and garlic for 2 minutes.

3. Stirring constantly, slowly add the flour until it is well blended.

4. Continue to stir and very slowly add the stock-cream mixture.

5. Continue stirring until the mixture comes to a boil and then, still stirring, add the broccoli purée.

6. Slowly add to the egg yolks 4 tablespoons of the purée. Reduce the flame to low and slowly stir the egg mixture into the remaining purée.

7. Continue to stir for 1 1/2 minutes or until thickened.

8. Add the cayenne, salt substitute, pepper, paprika, and cheese and cook for 2 minutes more.

9. Remove from the heat and cool (approximately 30 to 40 minutes).

10. Preheat the oven to 325°.

11. Well grease a 10-inch ring mold.

12. Beat the egg whites until stiff peaks form and they hold their shape.

13. Mix one fourth of the egg whites into the broccoli mixture to lighten it, then gently fold in the remaining egg whites.

14. Spoon the mixture into the ring mold. Place the ring mold in a pan of hot water (the water should come up to approximately half the mold) and bake for 45 minutes.

Serving: Place a preheated round platter on top of the soufflé and quickly invert onto the round platter. Fill the center of the soufflé with Creamed Mushrooms* and serve at once.

Chestnut Soufflé

Serves 8

Our family is crazy about chestnuts . . . and this is one of our favorites.

3 tablespoons sweet butter
16 shallots, finely chopped
5½ tablespoons unbleached
    flour
⅛ teaspoon cayenne
¼ teaspoon Spanish paprika
1 tablespoon salt substitute (op-
    tional)
3 tablespoons finely chopped
    fresh parsley

1½ tablespoons finely chopped
    fresh chives
2 cups chestnuts, boiled, peeled,
    and puréed
1 cup heavy cream (or triple-
    strength low sodium dry
    milk)
6 egg whites

1. In a heavy saucepan melt the butter over a low flame and sauté the shallots until translucent, stirring often. Add the flour slowly, stirring constantly until everything is thoroughly blended. Add the cayenne, paprika, salt substitute, parsley, and chives.

2. Stir in the chestnuts and blend all the ingredients thoroughly. Slowly add the cream or milk, stirring constantly. Cook 6 to 7 minutes, but make sure that the liquid does not come to a boil.

3. Transfer the mixture to a large mixing bowl and cool thoroughly (30 to 45 minutes).

4. Preheat the oven to 325°.

5. Beat the egg whites until stiff peaks hold their shape and mix one fourth of the egg whites into the purée to lighten it, then gently fold in the remaining egg whites.

6. Spoon the soufflé mixture into a greased 9-inch ring mold and set it in a pan of hot water (water should come two thirds up the side of the mold). Bake for 45 minutes.

Serving: Place a preheated round platter on top of the soufflé and quickly invert onto the round platter. Fill the center of the soufflé with different vegetables, e.g., sautéed mushrooms and onions or Steamed Green Peas* lightly buttered. Then spoon Mushroom Almond Sauce* over the soufflé.

Mushroom Soufflé

Serves 6 to 8

3 tablespoons sweet butter
3 tablespoons unbleached flour
10 to 12 shallots, very finely chopped
4 cloves garlic, pressed
1 pound mushrooms, very finely chopped
2 tablespoons chopped fresh parsley
4 egg yolks
1/2 teaspoon paprika

2 1/2 teaspoons seasoned salt substitute (optional)
3/4 teaspoon freshly ground black pepper
1 cup heavy cream
4 egg whites
1/8 teaspoon cream of tartar

GARNISH: 1/3 cup finely chopped fresh parsley

1. In a large, heavy skillet melt the butter over a low-medium flame. Add the flour and brown very slightly, stirring constantly.
2. Add the shallots, stirring constantly, and sauté for 2 minutes. Add the garlic, mushrooms, and parsley and sauté for 2 minutes more, continuing to stir. Remove from the flame and cool.
3. While the mushroom mixture is cooling, using a wire whisk, lightly beat the egg yolks, paprika, salt substitute, and pepper in a mixing bowl and set aside.
4. Using an electric mixer on medium-high speed, beat the cream until peaks form and hold their shape. Refrigerate.
5. In another bowl, beat the egg whites with the cream of tartar on high speed until stiff. Refrigerate.
6. Beat the egg yolk mixture into the cooled mushroom mixture.
7. Preheat the oven to 325°.
8. Butter a 9-inch ring mold.

9. Fold the cream into the mushroom mixture. Gently fold the egg whites into the mushroom-cream mixture. Spoon the mixture into the buttered mold and cover with a well-buttered piece of wax paper.

10. Place the mold in a pan of hot water (water should come two thirds up the side of the mold) and bake for 1 hour.

Serving: Place a preheated round platter on top of the soufflé and quickly invert on the platter. Sprinkle with the parsley and serve at once.

Creamed Mushrooms

Serves 6 to 8

4 tablespoons sweet butter
2 pounds small mushrooms,
    thinly sliced lengthwise
4 tablespoons finely minced
    onion
3 cloves garlic, pressed
2¹/₂ teaspoons fresh lemon juice
4 tablespoons unbleached flour
¹/₂ cup milk (or low sodium dry
    milk)
¹/₂ cup heavy cream (or triple-
    strength low sodium dry
    milk)

³/₄ cup strong Vegetable Stock*
¹/₂ teaspoon Spanish paprika
¹/₈ teaspoon cayenne
¹/₂ teaspoon freshly ground
    black pepper
4 tablespoons sherry
1 tablespoon finely chopped
    fresh parsley
2 teaspoons finely chopped fresh
    chives
¹/₂ teaspoon dried marjoram

1. In a large skillet melt the butter over a medium-high flame and sauté the mushrooms for 3 minutes.

2. Add the onion and garlic, stir well, and sauté 2 more minutes.

3. Lower the flame to medium and add the lemon juice. Stirring constantly, slowly add the flour until it is thoroughly blended.

4. Continue to stir and slowly add the milk, cream, and vegetable stock. Cook until the mixture comes to a very low boil.

5. Stir in the paprika, cayenne, pepper, sherry, parsley, chives, and marjoram. Cook for 3 more minutes on a very low flame, stirring constantly.

Serving: Transfer the creamed mushrooms to a preheated silver bowl and serve at once.

Mushrooms Stuffed with Rice

Serves 8 to 12

4½ tablespoons sweet butter
4 tablespoons minced onion
4 cloves garlic, pressed
24 mushroom stems, finely
    chopped
2 tablespoons finely chopped
    fresh parsley
1 cup Boiled Rice,* warm
2 teaspoons dry sherry
1-inch piece fresh ginger root,
    grated
2 tablespoons unsweetened pine-
    apple juice

2 tablespoons apricot preserves,
    heated
2 teaspoons salt-free Dijon mus-
    tard
⅛ teaspoon cayenne
24 large mushroom caps
3 tablespoons melted sweet
    butter
½ cup coarsely chopped
    blanched almonds

GARNISH: Sprigs of fresh
parsley

1. In a heavy, medium-size skillet melt the 4½ tablespoons of butter over a medium flame and sauté the onion and garlic until translucent. Add the chopped mushroom stems and cook, stirring often, until the mushrooms are very dark brown. Add the parsley, stir, and cover. Cook for 5 minutes. Remove from the heat.

2. Add the boiled rice to the onion-mushroom mixture and blend thoroughly.

3. Combine the sherry, ginger, pineapple juice, apricot preserves, mustard, and cayenne and blend into the rice mixture.

4. Preheat the broiler to 550°.

5. Arrange the mushroom caps on a lightly buttered cookie sheet, cap side down, and brush with a little melted butter. Broil 4 inches from the flame for 4 minutes.

6. Turn the caps up and stuff and mound them with the rice mixture. Press the almonds on top of each mound, brush with melted butter, and broil 6 to 7 inches from the flame, until the almonds are golden brown and the mixture is piping hot.

Serving: Transfer the mushrooms to a preheated serving tray, garnish with sprigs of parsley, and serve at once.

NOTE: If you want to make the stuffing in advance, remove it from the refrigerator, add ⅛ cup melted butter, cover, and bake in a 250° oven for 30 minutes, or until very warm. Then proceed with Step 4.

Green Bean, Mushroom, Pepper, and Cheese Casserole

Serves 10 to 12

If you would like a meatless main course, this certainly fills the bill. It will, under these circumstances, only serve 4.

2 pounds green beans, stems removed
3 tablespoons Clarified Butter*
1/2 cup finely minced onions
3 cloves garlic, finely minced
1 1/2 pounds mushrooms, sliced thinly lengthwise
2 green peppers, cored, seeded, and thinly sliced
2 red peppers, cored, seeded, and thinly sliced
1/4 cup finely chopped fresh chives
1/2 teaspoon Spanish paprika

1 1/2 teaspoons seasoned salt substitute (optional)
1/8 teaspoon cayenne
3/4 cup grated salt-free Swiss cheese
1/2 cup heavy cream (or triple-strength low sodium dry milk)
3/4 cup Chicken Stock* or Vegetable Stock*
1/3 cup dry sherry
3/4 cup grated salt-free Gouda cheese

1. Preheat the oven to 350°.
2. Put the beans into a lightly buttered casserole.
3. In a large, heavy skillet melt the clarified butter over a medium-high flame and sauté the onions, garlic, and mushrooms, green and red peppers, chives, paprika, salt substitute, and cayenne for 4 minutes. Pour the mixture into the casserole. Sprinkle the Swiss cheese on top of the mixture and pour the cream and the stock over all.
4. Cover tightly and bake for 45 minutes.
5. Preheat the broiler to 500°.
6. Sprinkle the sherry and the Gouda cheese over the casserole and broil 5 inches from the flame for 5 minutes, or until the cheese is bubbling hot.

Serving: Serve at once.

Eggplant Napoli

Serves 8 to 12

I never plan this dish in advance, but rather prepare it whenever I am fortunate enough to find tiny baby eggplants at the vegetable market, or when friends who grow them share their bounty with me. This is obviously a summer dish since this recipe requires fresh herbs and beefsteak tomatoes, as well as the eggplants.

12 tiny baby eggplants
¹/₈ cup olive oil, mixed with
    ¹/₈ cup corn oil
1 giant sweet Spanish onion
    (about 1¹/₄ pounds), very
    finely chopped
4 cloves garlic, pressed
3 very large beefsteak tomatoes,
    peeled and finely chopped
    (or 1 16-ounce can salt-free
    tomatoes, drained and
    finely chopped)

2 teaspoons natural sugar (or
    substitute equivalent)
¹/₃ cup cider vinegar
2¹/₂ teaspoons seasoned salt sub-
    stitute (optional)
2 teaspoons finely chopped fresh
    basil
1 teaspoon finely chopped fresh
    oregano
³/₄ cup pignoli (pine nuts)
¹/₃ cup raisins, light or dark (op-
    tional)

1. Make 3 deep slits lengthwise in each eggplant.

2. Heat the oil in a large, heavy skillet over a medium flame and brown the eggplants on all sides. Remove with a slotted spoon and set aside.

3. Add the onion and garlic to the oil and sauté until the onion is golden.

4. In a mixing bowl stir together the tomatoes, sugar, vinegar, salt substitute, basil, oregano, pignoli, and raisins.

5. Return the eggplants to the skillet, add the tomato mixture, and cover tightly. Turn the flame to low and simmer for 30 minutes, or until the eggplants are very tender.

Serving: This is superb piping hot but, although it is not *de rigueur,* I adore it after it has been refrigerated overnight.

Eggplant Casserole

Serves 6 to 8

2 large eggplants
2 cups unsweetened pineapple
  juice
$^{1}/_{8}$ cup olive oil
1 large onion, finely minced
4 cloves garlic, pressed
4 cups Tomato Purée*
1$^{1}/_{2}$ tablespoons seasoned salt
  substitute (optional)
1 teaspoon freshly ground black
  pepper

1 tablespoon brown sugar (or
  substitute equivalent)
3 tablespoons finely chopped
  fresh parsley
$^{1}/_{3}$ cup olive oil
1$^{1}/_{2}$ cups grated salt-free Gouda
  or Swiss cheese (or a mix-
  ture of both)
$^{1}/_{2}$ cup wheat germ
3 tablespoons butter cut into
  tiny pieces

1. Cut eggplants into $^{1}/_{4}$-inch slices and soak in the pineapple juice for 30 minutes.

2. Remove the eggplant from the pineapple juice, drain, and dry between double thickness of paper towels.

3. In a large, heavy skillet heat $^{1}/_{8}$ cup of the oil over a medium flame and sauté the onion and garlic until the onion is pale gold.

4. Add the Tomato Purée,* salt substitute, pepper, brown sugar, and parsley, stirring constantly. Cook for 5 minutes. Remove from the heat and transfer the mixture to a bowl.

5. In the same skillet heat the second $^{1}/_{3}$ cup of olive oil over a medium-high flame and brown the eggplant very quickly on both sides. As the eggplant is browned, lay it on double thickness of paper towels to drain.

6. Heat the oven to 350°.

7. In a well-buttered casserole lay a single layer of eggplant. Spoon over it some of the tomato mixture, then sprinkle with some cheese. Continue to layer until all the eggplant, tomato mixture, and cheese are used up, ending with the cheese.

8. Sprinkle the wheat germ over the top layer of cheese and dot with the pieces of butter.

9. Bake for 1 hour.

Serving: Serve at once.

Aubergines Farcies

Serves 6 as a vegetable

This is a marvelous vegetable dish that I often serve with Baked Chicken.* It is also a favorite as a main course with my vegetarian friends.

3 medium-size eggplants
1 cup unsweetened pineapple
    juice
$1/8$ cup corn oil
$1/8$ cup olive oil
1 large Bermuda onion, coarsely
    chopped
3 cloves garlic, finely chopped
1 pound small mushrooms,
    sliced lengthwise
8 Steamed Carrots* cut into $1/4$-
    inch slices
$1/4$ cup finely chopped fresh
    parsley

$1/4$ to $1/3$ teaspoon cayenne
2 tablespoons seasoned salt sub-
    stitute (optional)
$1/2$ teaspoon dried dill (or $1 1/2$ ta-
    blespoons finely chopped
    fresh dill)
1 teaspoon freshly ground black
    pepper
$2/3$ cup grated salt-free Swiss
    cheese
$1/2$ cup grated salt-free Gouda
    cheese
2 tablespoons melted sweet
    butter

1. Cut the eggplants in half lengthwise and with a sharp knife deeply score the cut sides, taking care not to cut the skin.

2. Place the pineapple juice in a large pan, add the eggplants, cut side down, and let them stand in the juice for 30 minutes. (This will help take the bitterness out of the eggplant. The pineapple juice is a good substitute for salt, which is generally used for this purpose.) Pat the eggplants dry with paper towels.

3. In a large, heavy skillet heat the corn and olive oil over a medium-low flame and sauté the eggplants, cut side down, for 5 minutes. Cover and cook for 15 minutes, then turn (being very careful not to pierce the skin), cover again, and continue cooking for 15 minutes more.

4. Transfer the eggplants to a well-greased flat ovenproof baking dish.

5. In the same skillet used to cook the eggplants, sauté the onion and garlic until the onion is a pale yellow, adding more corn oil if necessary.

6. Push the onion and garlic aside and sauté the mushrooms until they are quite dark.

7. Add the carrots, parsley, cayenne, salt substitute, dill, and pepper. Stir the mixture well and cook for 5 more minutes.

8. Scoop out the eggplant pulp with a spoon, taking care not to bruise the skin, and chop the pulp well.

9. Preheat the broiler to 550°.

10. Add the eggplant pulp to the vegetable mixture and stir all the ingredients until well blended. Remove the pan from the heat.

11. Add the Swiss cheese to the mixture and stir well.

12. Stuff and mound the eggplant shells with the mixture and sprinkle the Gouda cheese on top. Drizzle 1 teaspoon of butter on top of the cheese in each shell.

13. Place the baking dish 6 inches from the broiler flame and broil for about 6 to 8 minutes, or until the cheese is melted and bubbling.

Serving: Place the baking dish into a silver or pottery or wicker holder and serve at once.

— *Stuffed Acorn Squash*

Serves 8

1½ cups unsweetened pineapple juice

4 large acorn squash, well scrubbed, cut in half lengthwise and seeded

3 tablespoons sweet butter, melted

5 large green apples, cored, peeled, and cut into small chunks

3 tablespoons natural sugar (or substitute equivalent)

Juice of 2 lemons

1 16-ounce can unsweetened pineapple chunks with the juice

1¼ teaspoons cinnamon

½ teaspoon freshly grated nutmeg

½ cup sherry

1 cup Cooked Prunes*

1 cup Cooked Apricots*

3 tablespoons butter, cut into tiny pieces

1. Preheat the oven to 325°.

2. Into a baking dish large enough to hold the 8 squash halves pour the pineapple juice (make sure there is at least ¼ inch of liquid in the bottom of the pan) and place the squash, cut side down, in the juice.

3. Bake the squash for 30 minutes.

4. Into another baking dish pour the melted butter, spoon in the apple chunks, and cover. Bake for 20 minutes.

5. In a large mixing bowl mix together the sugar, lemon juice, pineapple chunks and juice, cinnamon, nutmeg, sherry, prunes, and apricots. Fold in the apple chunks.

6. Turn the squash halves cut side up and fill the centers with the mix-

ture. Dot with the pieces of butter. (If there is less than ¼ inch of liquid in the pan, add more unsweetened pineapple juice.)

7. Bake at 325° for 30 minutes, or until the squash is quite tender. Run under the broiler for 3 minutes 4 inches from the flame.

Serving: If you like it hot, serve at once.

If you like it cold, cool for 1 hour and then refrigerate overnight. This is our favorite way to serve stuffed acorn squash during the long hot summer.

Stuffed Zucchini Boats au Gratin

Serves 8 to 12

12 small zucchini, scrubbed but not peeled
⅓ cup corn oil
1 large onion, finely chopped
½ pound mushrooms, finely chopped
¾ to 1 cup Boiled Rice,* puréed in a blender
2 teaspoons salt substitute (optional)
¾ teaspoon freshly ground white pepper
1 teaspoon dried tarragon

⅓ cup heavy cream (or triple-strength low sodium dry milk)
2 eggs, slightly beaten
⅛ teaspoon cayenne
½ cup grated salt-free Gouda cheese
½ cup grated salt-free Swiss cheese
3 tablespoons butter, cut into tiny pieces
¾ cup dry vermouth

1. Cut tips from the ends of the zucchini. Immerse in a large pot of boiling water and cook for 2 minutes. Remove from the pot and drain well on double thickness of paper towels.

2. In a large skillet heat the oil over a medium flame and sauté the onion and mushrooms until the onion is a pale golden color.

3. In a large mixing bowl combine the puréed rice, salt substitute, pepper, tarragon, cream, eggs, cayenne, and Gouda cheese.

4. Slice the zucchini in half lengthwise and scoop out the pulp. Add the pulp to the ingredients in the mixing bowl.

5. Preheat the oven to 350°.

6. Stuff the zucchini boats, mounding them slightly. Sprinkle with the grated Swiss cheese and dot with the butter.

7. Pour the vermouth into a shallow roasting pan or a large ovenproof baking dish and arrange the zucchini boats next to each other.

8. Bake for 20 to 25 minutes.

9. Run under the broiler 4 inches from the flame for 3 to 4 minutes, or until the cheese bubbles.

Serving: Serve at once, and listen to the cheers!

NOTE: This recipe may be prepared in the morning through Step 8 (without preheating the oven, of course). Refrigerate the boats and then allow them to come to room temperature for 30 minutes before baking. If you prefer to take them out of the refrigerator and bake them immediately, it will take about 35 to 40 minutes.

Vegetable Kabobs

Serves 10 to 12

5 large green peppers, cut into
   chunks
2 large or 3 medium-size eggplants, peeled and cut into
   chunks
3 large onions, cut into chunks
40 medium-size mushroom caps
1/2 cup corn oil
1/8 cup cider vinegar
1/8 cup dry vermouth
1/8 teaspoon cayenne

2 teaspoons dry mustard
1 teaspoon dried basil
1 teaspoon dried dill
1 teaspoon dried tarragon
1 teaspoon freshly ground black
   pepper
5 large very firm tomatoes, cut
   into wedges, or 40 cherry
   tomatoes
1/4 cup olive oil

1. Place the peppers, eggplants, onions, and mushrooms in a fairly large plastic bag.
2. In a mixing bowl beat the corn oil, vinegar, vermouth, cayenne, mustard, basil, dill, tarragon, and black pepper with a wire whisk until thoroughly blended.
3. Pour the mixture over the vegetables. Seal the bag tightly and refrigerate for at least 3 hours, rotating the bag three or four times during the marinating period.
4. Drain the vegetables and reserve the marinade.
5. Preheat the oven to 350°.
6. Using 10-inch skewers, spear the vegetables, including the tomatoes, alternating them for an attractive color presentation, leaving the skewers empty for 1 1/2 inches at each end.
7. Place the skewers on a 7-inch shallow baking dish with the ends

(which have no vegetables) hanging over the edges (this makes rotating the skewers an easy task).

8. Add the olive oil to the marinade and mix thoroughly.

9. Baste the vegetables well with the marinade. Rotate the skewers often and thoroughly baste after each rotation. Bake until the vegetables are tender but still hold their shape (approximately 25 minutes).

Serving: Arrange the kabobs on a large heated serving platter. At the table, using a large serving fork, push the vegetables off the skewers onto individual plates.

If you would like this for your main course, serve the kabobs over a bed of Boiled Rice.* It will serve 4 to 6.

Baked Onion Shells Filled with Mushrooms and Peas

Serves 8

8 large "flat-ended" barely steamed onions
1/2 cup corn oil
1 pound mushrooms, finely chopped
4 tablespoons unbleached flour
1/2 cup heavy cream (or triple-strength low sodium dry milk)
1/2 teaspoon freshly ground white pepper
2 1/4 teaspoons salt substitute (optional)
1/3 cup sherry
2 cups peas, parboiled or Steamed*

SAUCE:
2 tablespoons sweet butter

2 tablespoons unbleached flour
1 cup milk (or low sodium dry milk) mixed with 1/2 cup heavy cream (or triple-strength low sodium dry milk)
1/2 pound mushrooms, finely chopped
1/8 teaspoon cayenne
1/2 to 3/4 cup dry sherry
1/4 cup finely chopped fresh parsley
2 teaspoons dried tarragon
1/2 teaspoon dried thyme
3/4 teaspoon dried rosemary
3/4 teaspoon freshly ground white pepper
3 tablespoons sweet butter, cut into tiny pieces

1. Cut a deep wide well in each onion, leaving a 3/4-inch shell, and chop the pulp finely.

2. Heat the oil in a heavy skillet over a medium flame and sauté the chopped onion and 1 pound of the mushrooms until the mushrooms are tender and the onion is slightly golden in color.

3. Sprinkle in the flour, a little at a time, and stir the mixture constantly until the flour is totally absorbed.

4. Slowly add the cream, pepper, and salt substitute, stirring all the time, and do the same with the sherry.

5. Gently fold in the peas.

6. Stuff and mound the onion shells with the mixture. (See Note, if there is too much filling left over.)

SAUCE:

7. In a skillet, melt the butter over a medium flame and add the flour, a little at a time, stirring constantly.

8. Slowly add the milk-cream mixture and continue stirring until the sauce is very hot and thickened but not boiling. Add the mushrooms and cook 3 minutes, stirring constantly.

9. Lower the flame slightly and add the cayenne, sherry, parsley, tarragon, thyme, rosemary, and pepper, stirring constantly. When everything is well blended, cook 2 minutes more.

10. Preheat the oven to 350°.

11. Pour the sauce from the frying pan into an ovenproof baking dish.

12. Place the onions, standing upright and touching each other, in the baking dish.

13. Dot the stuffed onions with butter and bake for 1 hour and 30 minutes, or until the onions are tender.

Serving: Remove the baking dish from the oven and bring it to the table. Spoon some sauce over each stuffed onion.

NOTE: If there is too much filling left over, I mix it with the sauce at the end of Step 9. It is most unorthodox to do this . . . but who cares? It tastes delicious.

Ratatouille

Serves a crowd

You'll faint when you see the number of bowls used . . . but it is worth it, for what a presentation it makes!

¹/₃ cup corn oil
¹/₃ cup olive oil
2 large Bermuda onions, cut into small chunks
8 cloves garlic, finely minced
2 large eggplants cut into 1-inch cubes (skin on)
12 small zucchini, cut into ¹/₂-inch slices
10 medium-size very firm tomatoes, skinned and cut into ¹/₄-inch slices
1¹/₂ pounds mushrooms, sliced lengthwise
¹/₂ to ¹/₃ teaspoon cayenne
2 tablespoons seasoned salt substitute (optional)

¹/₃ cup dry vermouth
²/₃ cup salt-free tomato juice
3 tablespoons natural sugar (or substitute equivalent)
1 tablespoon finely minced fresh dill
4 teaspoons finely minced fresh basil
4 teaspoons finely minced fresh tarragon
1 teaspoon dried oregano
4 cloves garlic, pressed
Juice of 2 lemons
1 teaspoon freshly ground black pepper
¹/₄ cup olive oil

1. In a large, heavy skillet heat the corn oil and ¹/₃ cup of olive oil over a medium flame.

2. Sauté the onions and garlic until the onions are golden in color, stirring frequently. Remove the onions and garlic to a bowl, using a slotted spoon.

3. In the same skillet, sauté the eggplants until lightly brown on both sides. Remove the eggplants to another bowl, using a slotted spoon.

4. In the same skillet, sauté the zucchini on both sides until lightly browned. Remove the zucchini to a third bowl, using a slotted spoon.

5. If there is not enough oil in the skillet add more. Place the tomatoes in the skillet and cook for 1 minute on each side. Remove them to still another bowl, using a slotted spoon.

6. Add the mushrooms to the skillet and sauté until tender and medium brown in color. Remove the mushrooms to a fifth bowl, using a slotted spoon.

7. Stir into the juice and oil in the skillet the cayenne, salt substitute, vermouth, tomato juice, sugar, dill, basil, tarragon, oregano, garlic, lemon juice, pepper, and ¹/₄ cup of olive oil. Blend all the ingredients thoroughly.

8. Preheat the oven to 300°.

9. Pour ⅓ cup of the spice and herb mixture into the bottom of an ovenproof glass casserole.

10. Layer in one fourth each of the onions, eggplants, zucchini, tomatoes, and mushrooms. Then repeat the layers three more times.

11. Pour the remaining spice-herb mixture over the ratatouille.

12. Cover tightly and bake for 30 to 40 minutes.

13. Uncover and bake at 450° for 10 more minutes.

Serving: If you want it hot, remove the casserole from the oven and serve at once.

If you like it cold, refrigerate it for at least 24 hours before serving.

Vegetable Croquettes

Serves 8

⅓ cup corn oil
1 pound mushrooms, finely minced
2 large onions, finely minced
2 large green peppers, finely minced
5 large carrots, grated
5 cloves garlic, pressed
⅛ to ¼ teaspoon cayenne
2 teaspoons salt substitute (optional)
Juice of 1 lemon
½ teaspoon dried sweet basil
½ teaspoon dried tarragon
2 tablespoons dry sherry

1 teaspoon freshly ground black pepper
4 large boiled potatoes, mashed
3 or 4 eggs, well beaten
Wheat germ
3 cups crushed cornflake crumbs
¼ teaspoon cayenne
½ teaspoon dried tarragon
½ teaspoon dried sweet basil
½ teaspoon freshly ground white pepper
2 eggs, mixed with 4 tablespoons milk (or low sodium dry milk)
Corn oil

1. In a large frying pan heat ⅓ cup of oil over a medium flame. Add the mushrooms, onions, green peppers, carrots, garlic, cayenne, salt substitute, lemon juice, sweet basil, tarragon, sherry, and black pepper. Stir well, cover, and cook over a low-medium flame for 15 minutes, or until the vegetables are tender but not brown.

2. Purée the vegetables in a blender or food processor.

3. In a large bowl mix the mashed potatoes with the vegetable purée. Stir in 3 or 4 eggs and add wheat germ a little at a time until the mixture has enough consistency to hold its shape.

4. Shape the mixture into oval patties or cylinders (1 inch in diameter by 3 inches long).

5. Mix the cornflake crumbs with the cayenne, tarragon, basil, and pepper. Pour into a large pie plate.

6. Beat 2 eggs lightly with the milk and pour into another pie plate.

7. Roll the patties or cylinders in the crumb mixture, then in the egg mixture, then in the crumb mixture again. Refrigerate for a few hours, or until you are ready to fry them.

8. Preheat the oven to 180°.

9. In a heavy skillet heat enough oil, over a medium-high flame, to cover the bottom of the pan to a depth of about ½ inch.

10. Carefully fry the croquettes until golden on all sides. As the croquettes have been fried, place them in a baking pan lined with double thickness of paper towels. Place the pan in the oven.

Serving: Transfer the croquettes to a heated serving platter and serve at once.

Boiled Rice

Yields approximately 6 cups

I generally use natural brown rice, since I prefer the flavor, texture, and vitamin content. However, this recipe will do just as well with a white short- or long-grain rice, which in all honesty are both lower in sodium than the natural brown rice (i.e., 4 ounces natural brown rice, cooked, has 6 milligrams of sodium while the same amount of cooked white rice has 1 milligram of sodium).

3⅛ cups water
1¾ cups rice

1. In a saucepan bring the water to a boil over a high flame.

2. Slowly add the rice, stirring constantly. Bring the water to a boil again. Cover. Turn the flame to low and simmer the rice for 18 to 20 minutes for white rice and 30 to 35 minutes for brown rice.

3. Flake the rice with a fork.

4. If you are *not* concerned about the starch content, *do not do the following:* When the rice is cooked, run hot sink water over it until the water runs clear and return it to the pot. Cover. Place the pot on a Flame-Tamer. Turn the flame to low and simmer for approximately 10 minutes, or until the rice is dry and the grains have separated. Flake the rice with a fork. Almost all the starch will be washed away, but sadly so will a great deal of the nutrients.

NOTE: You may substitute Chicken Stock,* Beef Stock,* Veal Stock,* or Court Bouillon* for the water; but then ignore Step 4.

You may add 1½ tablespoons of butter, cut into small pieces, to the boiled rice. In that case, place the rice in an ovenproof baking dish (after it's been boiled), dot with the butter, and let it heat in a 200° oven for 20 minutes, flaking the rice often with a fork.

Baked Spanish Rice

Serves 6 to 10

4 tablespoons corn or peanut oil
1 large onion, chopped
4 cloves garlic, pressed
1 pound small mushrooms, sliced paper-thin lengthwise
2 large green peppers, coarsely chopped
2 large red peppers, coarsely chopped
5 cups Boiled Rice*
2 16-ounce cans salt-free tomatoes, drained and chopped (reserve liquid)

1½ teaspoons natural sugar (or substitute equivalent)
3½ teaspoons salt substitute (optional)
⅛ teaspoon cayenne
1 teaspoon freshly ground white pepper
½ teaspoon Spanish paprika
1 cup grated salt-free Cheddar (or Gouda) cheese (optional)
½ cup Bread Crumbs*
4 tablespoons sweet butter, cut into tiny pieces

1. Heat the oil in a large skillet over a medium flame and sauté the onion and garlic until the onion is translucent. Add the mushrooms, stir well, and sauté for 10 minutes, stirring often. Add the green and red peppers, stir well, and sauté 7 minutes, stirring often.

2. Add the sautéed vegetables to the rice and mix thoroughly in a large mixing bowl.

3. Combine the tomatoes, sugar, salt substitute, cayenne, pepper, paprika, and ⅓ cup of the reserved tomato liquid.

4. Add the tomato mixture to the rice mixture and mix well. Stir in the cheese.

5. Preheat the oven to 350°.

6. Heavily butter an ovenproof baking dish and spoon in the rice mixture. Sprinkle the bread crumbs over the rice mixture and dot with the butter. Bake for 30 to 40 minutes or until the liquid is absorbed into the rice.

Serving: Remove from the oven and serve at once.

Rice Milanese

Serves 4

4 tablespoons sweet butter
1 medium-size onion, finely
   chopped
1 cup long-grain rice
4 cups of Chicken Stock,* boiling, mixed with ⅛ teaspoon
   saffron
¾ cup finely grated salt-free
   Gouda cheese

1 teaspoon freshly ground white
   pepper
⅛ teaspoon cayenne
1 teaspoon salt substitute (optional)

1. In a heavy saucepan melt the butter over a medium flame and sauté the onion until it is translucent. Add the rice and, stirring constantly, cook for 2 minutes.

2. Pour the boiling chicken stock-saffron mixture slowly over the rice, stirring constantly, then add the cheese, pepper, cayenne, salt substitute, and stir well. Cover the saucepan.

3. Place the saucepan on a Flame-Tamer over a medium-low flame and cook the rice for 1 hour to 1 hour and 15 minutes, flaking the rice with a fork every 10 to 15 minutes.

Serving: Transfer the rice to a heated ceramic or silver bowl and serve while it is still piping hot.

Saffron Rice Pilaf

Serves 8

7 tablespoons sweet butter
2 cups raw long-grain rice
2 teaspoons salt substitute (optional)
1 teaspoon freshly ground white
   pepper

1½ teaspoons crushed saffron
   (steeped in 1 cup warm
   water for ½ hour)
4 cups strong Chicken Stock*

1. Preheat the oven to 350°.

2. Melt the butter in a flameproof or ovenproof baking dish over a medium flame. Add the rice.

3. Stir the rice constantly and cook until it is a golden brown.

4. Stir in the salt substitute, pepper, saffron with the water, and the chicken stock. Cover and bake for 1 hour to 1 hour and 15 minutes, or until the rice is tender and all the liquid has been absorbed. Fluff the rice with a fork.

Serving: Remove the casserole from the oven and either serve the rice directly from the casserole or transfer it to a preheated serving bowl.

Parsley Almond Rice Ring

Serves 4 to 6

This may be filled with a variety of vegetables, such as mushrooms, peas, a combination of both, Creamed Mushrooms,* or Steamed Carrots* drizzled with melted sweet butter.

4 tablespoons Clarified Butter*
3/4 cup sliced blanched almonds
4 tablespoons minced fresh parsley
2 1/2 tablespoons minced fresh chives

1/2 teaspoon freshly ground white pepper
4 cups warm Boiled Rice* which has been cooked in strong Chicken Stock* (but not washed after cooking)

1. In a large saucepan melt the butter over a medium flame and sauté the almonds until a pale gold.

2. Lower the flame and add the parsley, chives, and pepper, stirring constantly. Sauté for 3 minutes.

3. Preheat the oven to 350°.

4. Remove the saucepan from the flame and add the rice. Fluff with a fork while mixing it thoroughly with the other ingredients.

5. Spoon the rice mixture into a well-greased 7-inch ring mold.

6. Place the mold in a pan of hot water (the water should come halfway to the top of the ring mold) and bake for 20 to 25 minutes.

7. Loosen the rice by running a spatula or sharp knife around the inside edge of the mold.

Serving: Place a heated round silver or ceramic tray on top of the mold and quickly invert. Fill the center of the ring with any vegetable of your choosing or with sprigs of parsley.

Rice à la Chinoise

Serves 12

12 cups Beef Stock* or Chicken
    Stock*
3 cups raw long-grain rice
3 tablespoons peanut oil
1/2 cup peanut oil
6 large onions, chopped
6 cloves garlic, pressed
2 bunches scallions, sliced into
    paper-thin rings
6 large carrots, coarsely grated
2 tablespoons seasoned salt sub-
    stitute (optional)

1 teaspoon freshly ground white
    pepper
1/8 teaspoon cayenne
2 pounds fresh peas, parboiled
    or Steamed,* hot
10 eggs; fried like an omelet,
    cooled, and sliced into strips
    1 by 2 inches

GARNISH: 1/3 cup finely chopped
    fresh parsley

1. Bring the stock to a boil in the top part of a large double boiler, over a medium-high flame.

2. While the stock is heating, put enough water into the bottom part of the double boiler to come to within 1/2 inch of the top part of the double boiler. Bring the water to a boil over a medium-high flame.

3. Place the top part of the double boiler (filled with the boiling stock) into the bottom. Add the rice, cover, and reduce the flame to medium. Cook until the rice is tender (approximately 50 minutes). While the rice is cooking, flake it frequently with a fork.

4. Add the 3 tablespoons of peanut oil, flake the rice with a fork, and cook uncovered for 10 minutes more.

5. In a large heavy skillet heat the 1/2 cup of peanut oil over a medium flame and sauté the onions and garlic until the onions are translucent. Stir in the scallions, carrots, salt substitute, white pepper and cayenne and continue to sauté for 6 minutes more, or until the vegetables are cooked but still slightly crisp, stirring frequently.

6. Combine rice and vegetables.

7. Fold the peas and egg strips into the rice and vegetable mixture.

Serving: Transfer the rice to a large preheated serving dish and sprinkle on the parsley. Serve at once.

Mashed Potato and Cheese Balls

Serves 8 to 10

8 large boiled potatoes
6 tablespoons sweet butter,
   softened
2½ teaspoons seasoned salt substitute (optional)
1 teaspoon freshly ground white
   pepper
⅛ teaspoon cayenne
½ cup milk (or low sodium dry
   milk)
¾ cup grated salt-free Gouda
   cheese
3 tablespoons heavy cream (or
   triple-strength low sodium
   dry milk)

3 egg yolks, beaten and mixed
   with 1 teaspoon salt-free
   baking powder
¼ cup finely minced fresh parsley (optional)
2 eggs beaten with 4 tablespoons
   cold water
3 cups salt-free cornflakes,
   crushed
Melted sweet butter

1. Preheat the oven to 350°.
2. In a large mixing bowl mash the potatoes thoroughly. Using an electric mixer on medium speed, beat in the butter, salt substitute, pepper,
cayenne, milk, cheese, cream, egg yolks, baking powder, and parsley.
3. Continue beating until the mixture is thoroughly blended and fluffy.
4. Shape the mixture into small balls (approximately 1½ inches) and
roll in the cornflakes, then in the egg mixture, and then back into the
cornflakes.
5. Butter a baking sheet, place the potato balls on the sheet, and drizzle
a little of the melted butter over each. Bake for 40 minutes.

Serving: Transfer the potato balls to a heated platter and serve at once.

Stuffed Potato Boats with Vegetables

Serves 10 to 12

6 very large baked potatoes
4 tablespoons sweet butter
3 medium-size onions, finely
  chopped
1 pound mushrooms, finely
  chopped
1 teaspoon freshly ground black
  pepper
3½ teaspoons seasoned salt substitute (optional)
6 large carrots, peeled and
  grated

1½ cups peas, parboiled or
  Steamed*
½ cup milk (or low sodium dry
  milk)
⅓ cup heavy cream (or triple-
  strength low sodium dry
  milk)
⅛ teaspoon cayenne
1 cup grated salt-free Cheddar
  or Swiss cheese (optional)
3 tablespoons melted butter

1. Cut the potatoes in half lengthwise
2. Scoop out the pulp, leaving a ¼-inch case, including the skin, and mash well. Set aside.
3. In a large, heavy skillet melt the 4 tablespoons butter over a medium flame, add the onions and mushrooms, and sauté until both are tender, stirring frequently.
4. Add the pepper, salt substitute, and carrots. Stir well and sauté another 3 minutes. Remove from the heat and fold in the peas.
5. In a saucepan, over a medium flame, heat the milk, cream, and cayenne, stirring constantly. Do not boil. Remove from the heat.
6. Mix the cream mixture into the mashed potatoes and then fold this into the vegetable mixture.
7. Preheat the oven to 350°.
8. Stuff and mound the potato shells with the vegetable-potato mixture. If using cheese, press the cheese into the mounds.
9. Drizzle on the melted butter and place the potatoes in a well-greased baking dish. Bake for 20 minutes.
10. Preheat the broiler to 550°.
11. Run the stuffed potatoes under the broiler 4 inches from the flame and broil for 3 or 4 minutes, or until the cheese bubbles.

Serving: If the baking dish is attractive, serve the stuffed potatoes directly from it . . . it is the easiest and best way. However, if you must, transfer the boats to a heated serving platter, taking care that they retain their shape.

NOTE: If you want to prepare these the day before, or in the morning, follow Steps 1, 2, 3, 4, 5, 6, and 8. Forty-five minutes before you want to serve, follow Step 9 but bake at 300° for 35 to 40 minutes and drizzle more heavily with the melted butter, then run under the broiler as in Step 11.

Potato Pancakes

Yields 14 3-inch pancakes or 35 "silver-dollar" size

Using a food processor, these are a snap to prepare.

6 large potatoes
2 eggs
2¹/₂ tablespoons unbleached flour, sifted
¹/₂ teaspoon salt-free baking powder

1 medium-size onion, grated
1¹/₂ teaspoons salt substitute (optional)
¹/₂ to ³/₄ teaspoon freshly ground white pepper
Corn oil for frying

1. Peel the potatoes and cut them into eighths, placing them in a bowl of ice water as each one is peeled and cut.

2. Drain the potatoes and grate them in the food processor, using the shredding blade. Place the grated potatoes in a bowl of ice water.

3. Beat the eggs, then add the flour, baking powder, onion, salt substitute, and pepper.

4. In a large, heavy skillet heat ¹/₄ inch of oil over a medium flame.

5. While the oil is heating, drain the potatoes in a strainer and press out all of the excess liquid.

6. Combine the egg mixture with the potatoes and mix well. Drop by scant tablespoons into the hot oil. Brown the pancakes on both sides and drain them on paper towels.

Serving: These should be served at once, but they may be kept warm in a 180° oven if necessary.

Crusty Potato Pie

Serves 8 to 12

8 very large Idaho potatoes
4 tablespoons sweet butter (at
   room temperature)
2½ teaspoons salt substitute (optional)

1½ teaspoons freshly ground
   white pepper
½ pound sweet butter, melted

1. Preheat the oven to 400°.
2. Peel and slice the potatoes in thin rounds and place them in ice water.
3. Butter 2 9-inch pie plates, using 2 tablespoons of butter for each.
4. Drain the potatoes and thoroughly dry them between double thickness of paper towels.
5. Arrange a layer of potatoes on the bottom of each pie plate (each slice slightly overlapping the other), sprinkle with salt substitute and pepper, and pour a little of the melted butter over the layer. Continue layering until all the potatoes are used up.
6. Bake for 45 minutes, or until the potatoes are crusty and browned.

Serving: Run a sharp knife around the inside edge of the pie plates. Place a heated round platter on top of each pie plate and quickly invert the pies on the heated round platters. Bring the platters to the table and serve at once, cutting each pie into 4 or 6 wedge-shaped pieces.

Potato and Cheese Casserole

Serves 8

8 large potatoes
3½ cups milk (or low sodium
    dry milk), scalded
4 eggs, beaten
4 cloves garlic, pressed
2½ teaspoons salt substitute (op-
    tional)

¾ teaspoon freshly ground
    white pepper
1 pound salt-free Gouda cheese,
    grated
5 tablespoons sweet butter

1. Preheat the oven to 350°.
2. Peel and slice the potatoes thinly into rounds and place the slices in ice water.
3. Using an electric mixer on medium speed, beat the scalded milk, a little at a time, into the eggs and then beat in the garlic, salt substitute, and white pepper.
4. Butter a 2½-quart casserole, using 2 tablespoons of butter.
5. Drain the potatoes thoroughly.
6. Layer in half of the potatoes. Pour half of the egg mixture over the potatoes and sprinkle on half of the cheese. Then layer the remainder of the potatoes, egg mixture, and cheese. Dot with the remaining butter and bake for 50 minutes.

Serving: Place the casserole in a silver or wicker holder or on a heatproof tray and bring it to the table. Serve at once.

SAUCES
Exotica

Dressings, Sauces, and Relishes

Sauces are the low sodium cook's greatest boon. Mixed green salads become exciting taste sensations when lightly tossed with Basic,* Mustard,* or Herb Vinaigrette Dressing.* Broiled Fish,* Poached Fillet of Sole,* or Broiled Chicken,* delicious but often bland, come alive when bathed in such sauces as Mushroom Almond,* Lemon Butter,* or Marinara,* to mention but a few. However, if you prefer "sauce on the side" for your fish or chicken, Chili Garlic Almond,* Horseradish Cream,* or Sauce Aïoli* will give you the paradox of the smoothness of velvet and the kick of a mule. Let us say your taste runs to the sweet and sour or piquant flavor; then try the Hawaiian Sauce* or Ginger Red Pepper Relish.* If you crave hot and spicy sensations, try the Spicy Sesame Oil,* Red Hot Oil,* or Hot Red Pepper Oil.* However, beware of "fire mouth" . . . a little goes a long, long way!

One of my great losses, when I started to cook low sodium food, fifteen years ago was mayonnaise. Hellman's had always been a mainstay of mine for salads and sauces calling for mayonnaise, and then, alas, I realized I had to give up an old friend. I searched for months to find a good replacement, ultimately lowering my standards for just a decent one. None that were edible were on the shelves of the dietetic sections in the supermarkets, gourmet stores, or health food stores. First I tried "doctoring" them and then, giving up in disgust, I realized how silly I had been to waste my time in fruitless searching. The solution to my mayonnaise problem was staring me in the face . . . my trusty blender. From the original Mayonnaise* recipe there evolved other sauces such as Curry Mayonnaise* and Russian Dressing.* Once this was accomplished, many old trusted mayonnaise-based recipes were experimented with and converted into low sodium delights.

A colloquial and rather mundane expression, "Sauce is the spice of life," is certainly an exaggeration, but sauces surely help to transform otherwise pedestrian fare into tantalizing taste treats. Experimentation with sauces presents one of the greatest challenges as well as the greatest rewards to the gourmet cook. Enjoy these recipes and experiment with your own adored and trusted recipes, in order to create many new low sodium Epicurean delights.

Basic Vinaigrette Dressing

Yields approximately 1¼ cups

This will keep indefinitely in your refrigerator, but you must shake it vigorously before using.

1 cup olive or corn oil
¼ cup wine vinegar (or fresh
   lemon juice)
1 teaspoon freshly ground black
   pepper

2 to 3 cloves garlic, pressed
2 teaspoons seasoned salt substitute (optional)

1. Place all the ingredients in a medium-size glass bowl. Beat with a wire whisk until thoroughly blended (approximately 4 minutes).
2. Pour into a glass jar, cover tightly, and store in the refrigerator.

Mustard Vinaigrette Dressing

Yields approximately 1¼ cups

Shake vigorously before using.

1 teaspoon dry mustard
2 teaspoons seasoned salt substitute (optional)
1 teaspoon freshly ground black
   pepper

1 cup olive or corn oil
¼ cup wine vinegar (or fresh
   lemon juice)
1 tablespoon dry vermouth
4 cloves garlic, pressed

1. Mix the mustard, salt substitute, and pepper in a medium-size glass bowl. Using a wire whisk, beat in 2 tablespoons of the oil.
2. Add 3 tablespoons of the vinegar and continue to beat until the mustard is dissolved and all ingredients are thoroughly blended.
3. Beat in the remainder of the oil and vinegar and add the vermouth and garlic.
4. Pour into a glass jar, cover tightly, and store in the refrigerator.

Herb Vinaigrette Dressing

Yields approximately 1½ cups

Since fresh herbs are used, I would suggest using this dressing within a few days. Many of my friends, all wonderful cooks, violently disagree, citing pesto sauce as an example of fresh herbs and oil which will last for months in the refrigerator. It is all a matter of taste and there really is no correct answer. So let your taste buds be the final judge. In any case, shake vigorously before using.

1¼ cups Mustard Vinaigrette
  Dressing*
⅔ tablespoon finely minced
  fresh parsley
⅔ tablespoon finely minced
  fresh chives

⅔ tablespoon finely minced
  fresh dill
⅔ tablespoon finely minced
  fresh sweet basil
2 teaspoons sugar (or substitute
  equivalent)

1. Place all the ingredients in a medium-size glass bowl and beat with a wire whisk until all are thoroughly blended.
2. Pour into a glass jar, cover tightly, and refrigerate.

Mayonnaise

Yields approximately 2½ cups

We think it's as good as Hellman's and that says a lot.

2 eggs plus 2 egg yolks (at room
  temperature)
1 teaspoon dry mustard
⅛ teaspoon cayenne
4 teaspoons seasoned salt substitute (optional)

1 teaspoon freshly ground white
  pepper
4 tablespoons fresh lemon juice
2 cups peanut oil (or 1 cup olive
  oil mixed with 1 cup corn
  oil)

1. Place the eggs and egg yolks in a blender or food processor fitted with the steel blade.
2. Add the mustard, cayenne, salt substitute, pepper, lemon juice, and ¼ cup of the oil. (Cover the blender.)
3. Turn the blender or food processor on and mix until all the ingre-

dients are blended (about 10 seconds). (Uncover the blender.) With the motor still running, pour in the remaining oil in a very, very slow and steady stream (see Note 1) until all the oil is absorbed (see Note 2).

NOTE 1: The very, very slow addition of the oil to the egg mixture is the key to making a thick and creamy mayonnaise. Should you add the oil to quickly your mayonnaise will become watery. So please take the time required when adding the oil.

NOTE 2: If your blender does not have a very high-powered motor, you might find that after adding three fourths of the remaining oil, the mayonnaise will not absorb any more. In that event, transfer the mayonnaise to the bowl of your electric mixer. Beat the mayonnaise on high speed for 30 seconds and then very, very slowly add the remainder of the oil. Continue beating until the last drop of oil has been totally absorbed and the mayonnaise is very thick and creamy.

Herb Mayonnaise
also called Green Mayonnaise

Yields approximately 1¼ cups

1 cup Mayonnaise*
2 tablespoons very finely minced
    fresh parsley
2 tablespoons very finely minced
    fresh chives

4 teaspoons very finely minced
    fresh dill

Place the mayonnaise, parsley, chives, and dill in a bowl. Mix thoroughly and refrigerate at least 1 hour before using.

Curry Mayonnaise

Yields approximately 1 cup

1 cup Mayonnaise*
2¼ tablespoons salt-free hot
   curry powder

⅛ teaspoon cayenne
¼ to ½ teaspoon Spanish
   paprika

Place the mayonnaise in a glass mixing bowl and, using a wire whisk, beat in the remaining ingredients until all is thoroughly blended.

Russian Dressing

Yields approximately 2½ cups

2 cups Mayonnaise*
3 tablespoons salt-free tomato
   paste
⅓ cup salt-free chili sauce
3 to 4 cloves garlic, pressed
⅛ teaspoon cayenne

1 tablespoon freeze-dried chives
1 teaspoon salt-free chili powder
2 teaspoons seasoned salt substitute (optional)
¾ teaspoon finely ground white
   pepper

Place all the ingredients in a glass bowl and beat very gently with a wire whisk until thoroughly blended, pale pink and smooth.

Sauce Aïoli

Yields approximately 2½ cups

Garlicky, spicy, and divine with Bourride,* Boiled Fresh Shrimp,* and Fish Chowder Bon Marché.*

**5 egg yolks (at room tempera-
ture)**
10 cloves garlic, minced
**1 teaspoon dry mustard (op-
tional)**
4 tablespoons fresh lemon juice
**1 teaspoon freshly ground white
pepper**

**¼ teaspoon cayenne (or more to
taste)**
**4 teaspoons seasoned salt substi-
tute (optional)**
**1 teaspoon Spanish paprika (op-
tional)**
**2 cups olive oil (or 1 cup olive
oil and 1 cup corn oil)**

1. Place the egg yolks in a blender or food processor fitted with the steel blade.

2. Add the garlic, mustard, lemon juice, pepper, cayenne, salt substitute, Spanish paprika, and ½ cup of olive oil. (Cover the blender.)

3. Turn the blender or food processor on and mix until all the ingredients are blended (about 10 seconds). (Uncover the blender.) With the motor still running, pour in the remaining oil in a very, very slow stream (see Note 1), until all the oil is absorbed (see Note 2).

NOTE 1: The very, very slow addition of the oil to the egg yolk mixture is the key to making a thick and creamy sauce aïoli. Should you add the oil too quickly, your sauce will become watery. So please take the time required when adding the oil.

NOTE 2: If your blender does not have a very high-powered motor, you might find that after adding three fourths of the remaining oil the sauce will not absorb any more. In that event, transfer the sauce to the bowl of your electric mixer. Beat the sauce on high speed for 30 seconds and then very, very slowly add the remainder of the oil. Continue beating until the last drop of oil has been totally absorbed and the sauce is very thick and creamy.

Chili Garlic Almond Sauce

Yields approximately 4 cups

A superb and very spicy sauce to use with cold sliced meats such as Brisket,* Baked Chicken,* or Sautéed Sole,* as well as a dressing for Tuna and Vegetable Aspic.*

5 egg yolks (at room temperature)

4 tablespoons fresh lemon juice

12 cloves garlic, minced

2 tablespoons salt-free hot chili powder

1/4 to 1/2 teaspoon cayenne

4 teaspoons seasoned salt substitute (optional)

2 cups olive oil (or 1 cup olive oil and 1 cup corn oil)

1 1/2 cups finely chopped blanched almonds

1. Place the egg yolks in a blender or food processor fitted with the steel blade. Add the lemon juice, garlic, chili powder, cayenne, salt substitute, and 1/4 cup of the oil. (Cover the blender.)

2. Turn the blender or food processor on and mix until all the ingredients are well blended (about 10 seconds). (Uncover the blender.) With the motor still running, pour in the remaining oil in a very, very slow stream (see Note 1) until all the oil is absorbed (see Note 2).

3. When the sauce is thick and creamy and all the oil has been absorbed, transfer it to a mixing bowl and fold in the almonds (see Note 3).

NOTE 1: The very, very slow addition of the oil to the egg yolk mixture is the key to making a thick and creamy sauce. Should you add the oil too quickly, your sauce will become watery. So please take the time required when adding the oil.

NOTE 2: If your blender does not have a very high-powered motor, you might find that after adding three fourths of the remaining oil the sauce will not absorb any more. In that event, transfer the sauce to the bowl of your electric mixer. Beat the sauce on high speed for 30 seconds and then very, very slowly add the remainder of the oil. Continue beating until the last drop of oil has been totally absorbed and the sauce is very thick and creamy.

NOTE 3: If you have transferred the sauce to the mixing bowl (Note 2) simply fold the almonds into the sauce at the completion of beating.

Sour Cream

Yields approximately 1 quart

This sour cream will keep in the refrigerator for approximately 4 to 6 weeks. The longer it remains in the refrigerator, the thicker it becomes.

1 quart heavy cream
Juice of 4 large lemons

1. Pour the heavy cream into a 1½-quart glass jar. Stir in the lemon juice.
2. Cover three fourths of the mouth of the jar with aluminum foil (leaving one fourth exposed to the air).
3. Let it stand in a cool, dry place for 24 hours.
4. Stir the mixture with a large wooden spoon. Cover tightly and refrigerate for at least 72 hours before using.

Crème Fraîche

Yields approximately 1 quart

Although this is not the true French crème fraîche (their cream is so different from ours), it is a marvelous adaptation. In any case, this will keep in the refrigerator for about 1 month. It becomes thicker and better as it stands.

1 quart heavy cream
3 tablespoons plus 1 teaspoon
    buttermilk (no salt added)

1. Put the cream and buttermilk in a 1½-quart glass jar. Cover tightly and shake very well.
2. Let the mixture stand at room temperature 2 days, or until it has thickened considerably.
3. Refrigerate at least 2 days before using.

Plain Yogurt

Yields 1 quart

1 quart milk (or low sodium dry   4 ounces store-bought plain
    milk)   yogurt

1. Place the milk in a heavy saucepan and bring it to a boil over a medium-high flame. Remove it from the flame and let it cool to room temperature (approximately 72°).

2. Place the yogurt and one fourth of the cooled milk into a wide-neck 1½-quart glass jar. Stir until the yogurt and milk are thoroughly blended.

3. Pour the remaining milk into the jar and stir well. Cover tightly.

4. Cover the jar with 4 sheets (or more) of plastic wrap, envelop the jar in a turkish towel, and let it stand in a warm place (about 72°).

5. After 24 hours (or, for a more tart yogurt, 36 hours) remove the plastic wrap and the towel.

6. Refrigerate for at least 12 hours before using.

NOTE: You may use 4 ounces of this yogurt as the starter the next time you make yogurt. Then 4 ounces of that yogurt as the starter, and so on, and so on.

Yogurt Dill Sauce

Yields approximately 3½ cups

If using fresh dill, I like to use this sauce within 1 week.

1 pint Plain Yogurt*   4 teaspoons seasoned salt substi-
½ pint Sour Cream* (at least 1   tute (optional)
    week old)   6 cloves garlic, pressed
2 tablespoons fresh lemon juice   3 tablespoons finely minced
3 tablespoons olive oil   fresh dill (or 2 to 3 tea-
1 teaspoon freshly ground white   spoons dried dill weed)
    pepper

1. Place all the ingredients in a large glass bowl and gently beat with a wire whisk until thoroughly blended.

2. Spoon the sauce into a 1-quart glass jar. Cover tightly and refrigerate.

Mideastern Yogurt Sauce

Yields approximately 1 quart

Because this recipe calls for fresh mint and fresh parsley, I like to use it within 1 week.

1½ cups Plain Yogurt*
2 cups Mayonnaise*
6 cloves garlic, pressed
1 teaspoon freshly ground white pepper
2 teaspoons seasoned salt substitute (optional)
⅛ to ¼ teaspoon cayenne

3 to 4 tablespoons fresh lemon juice
3 tablespoons olive oil
2 tablespoons finely minced fresh parsley
4 tablespoons finely chopped fresh mint
⅔ cup pignoli (pine nuts)

1. Place all the ingredients except the pignoli in a large glass bowl and gently beat with a wire whisk until thoroughly blended.
2. Fold in the nuts.
3. Spoon the sauce into a 1-quart glass jar. Cover and refrigerate.

Bengal Yogurt Sauce

(2½ cups)

2 cups Plain Yogurt*
3 tablespoons finely minced fresh chives
6 large cloves garlic, pressed
2 tablespoons finely minced green onions (scallions)
1 tablespoon salt-free curry powder (or more to taste)
1 teaspoon cumin (or more to taste)

¼ teaspoon cayenne (or more to taste)
2 teaspoons seasoned salt substitute (optional)
Juice of medium-size lemon
⅓ cup olive oil
1½-inch piece ginger root, finely grated and sautéed in
1 tablespoon olive oil until lightly browned

Mix all the ingredients thoroughly. Chill at least 4 hours, although it is actually better to make this the day before and chill overnight.

Clarified Butter

Yields approximately 3 cups

This is superb for sautéeing foods, as it burns much less rapidly than regular butter. To substitute clarified butter for regular butter, use two thirds the amount called for; e.g., if 3 tablespoons sweet butter are called for in a recipe, use 2 tablespoons clarified butter.

2 pounds sweet butter, cut into
pieces

1. In a heavy saucepan melt the butter over a very low flame. Skim off the foam as it rises to the top.
2. When there is a clear yellow liquid on the top and a white and brown residue on the bottom, remove the saucepan from the heat and let the butter cool.
3. Pour the yellow liquid only through a very fine strainer lined with doubled cheesecloth into clean glass jars. Cover tightly. Take care not to disturb the residue at the bottom.
4. Refrigerate the clarified butter. It will keep almost indefinitely.

Garlic Butter

Yields approximately 1 cup

¹/₂ pound sweet butter (at room
temperature)
8 cloves garlic, pressed

¹/₂ teaspoon freshly ground
white pepper

1. Using an electric mixer on the lowest speed, blend all the ingredients together.
2. Place the butter in a small crock or bowl and refrigerate for at least 10 minutes before serving.

Garlic Herb Butter

Yields approximately 1 cup

This recipe may be used in various ways—for instance, as a spread on sliced home-baked breads. It can be heated to replace sweet butter when broiling fish or scrambling eggs. It can be placed in a crock to be served instead of sweet butter at your buffet table, and on and on and on.

$^1/_2$ **pound sweet butter (at room temperature)**
2 teaspoons finely minced fresh dill
2 teaspoons finely minced fresh tarragon
$2^1/_2$ tablespoons finely minced fresh parsley

$2^1/_2$ tablespoons finely minced fresh chives
4 cloves garlic, pressed
1 teaspoon freshly ground white pepper (optional)

1. Using an electric mixer on the lowest speed, blend all the ingredients together.
2. Place the butter in a small crock or bowl and refrigerate for 10 minutes before serving.

Mint Butter

Serves 12

This is an excellent accompaniment to home-baked bread, especially when leg of lamb is being served.

1 cup sweet butter, at room temperature
3 teaspoons fresh lemon juice

$^1/_3$ cup very finely minced fresh mint leaves

1. Using an electric mixer on low speed, beat the butter until very soft.
2. Continue beating slowly, adding the lemon juice drop by drop until all the lemon juice is absorbed.
3. Add the mint leaves and beat them into the butter.
4. Chill and shape into balls, or spoon the butter into French butter crocks and chill for at least 10 minutes.

Lemon Butter Sauce

Yields approximately 1½ cups

1 cup Clarified Butter*   **⅛ teaspoon cayenne (optional)**
½ cup fresh lemon juice

1. Melt the clarified butter in a heavy saucepan over a low-medium flame.
2. Add the lemon juice and cayenne.
3. Stir, blend well, and serve immediately.

NOTE: If you like your sauce less piquant, use less lemon juice.

Cream Sauce

Yields approximately 2 cups

This sauce is also called (or known as) White Sauce and Béchamel Sauce ... but a "rose by any other name" ...

4 tablespoons sweet butter   **¾ teaspoons freshly ground**
4 tablespoons unbleached flour   **white pepper**
1 cup milk (or low sodium dry   **2 teaspoons salt substitute (op-**
   milk)   **tional)**
1 cup heavy cream (or triple-
   strength low sodium dry
   milk)

1. In a heavy saucepan melt the butter over a very low flame. Slowly add the flour, stirring constantly with a wire whisk.
2. When the flour is thoroughly blended (but not browned) slowly add the milk and cream, beating vigorously with the wire whisk. Add the pepper and salt substitute and continue to beat until the sauce is thick and smooth.

NOTE: For a thinner cream sauce, follow the above recipe but use only 1 tablespoon of butter and 1 tablespoon of flour to each cup of milk or cream.

Curry Cream Sauce

Yields approximately 2¼ cups

2 cups Cream Sauce*
2 tablespoons onion, sautéed and
    drained
2 tablespoons salt-free curry
    powder

⅛ teaspoon cayenne
2 teaspoons fresh lemon juice

While stirring sauce vigorously with a wire whisk, add remaining ingredients.

Mustard Cream Sauce (Hot)

Yields approximately 2 cups

2 cups Cream Sauce*
2 tablespoons dry mustard dis-
    solved in 2 tablespoons hot
    water

While stirring sauce vigorously with a wire whisk, add remaining ingredients.

Mornay Sauce

Yields approximately 3 cups

2 cups Cream Sauce*
⅓ cup grated salt-free Swiss
    cheese
⅓ cup grated salt-free Gouda
    cheese

3 tablespoons sweet butter (op-
    tional) at room temperature
⅛ teaspoon cayenne
1 teaspoon dry mustard (op-
    tional)

1. Place the cream sauce in a very heavy saucepan. Turn the flame to low and, beating constantly with a wire whisk, slowly add the Swiss cheese, Gouda cheese, butter, cayenne, and mustard.

2. Beat the sauce constantly with the wire whisk until it is piping hot and the cheese is thoroughly melted and absorbed.

Sauce Nantua

Yields 2 cups

I have three comments to make about this sauce:

1. It is not an authentic Nantua, which would be made with pulverized crayfish shells. This is obviously an absolute no-no.

2. As with any recipe containing shrimp, I implore you to check with your doctor to determine whether you are allowed to eat it.

3. With shrimp so astronomically high in price, and if in fact you are permitted to eat this sauce, eat very slowly and savor every morsel.

Now that we have my confessions and admonitions out of the way, let's get on with the preparation.

1 cup Cream Sauce*
¼ cup heavy cream (or triple-strength low sodium dry milk)
½ cup Boiled Fresh Shrimp,* or Boiled Flash Frozen Shrimp* finely ground
½ cup Boiled Fresh Shrimp,* or Boiled Flash Frozen Shrimp* coarsely chopped

2 teaspoons seasoned salt substitute (optional)
¾ teaspoon freshly ground white pepper
2 tablespoons brandy

1. Put the cream sauce and the cream in a heavy saucepan. Turn the flame to low and stir the sauce constantly until it is hot. (Do not boil.)

2. Add both the ground and coarsely chopped boiled shrimp, salt substitute, pepper, and brandy. Continue to stir until all ingredients are well blended and piping hot. (At no time should the sauce boil.)

Sauce Velouté

Yields approximately 2½ cups

6 tablespoons sweet butter
8 tablespoons unbleached flour
3 cups Chicken Stock* Clarified*

3 tablespoons dry vermouth (optional)

1. In a heavy saucepan melt the butter over a low flame.
2. Stirring briskly with a wire whisk, slowly add the flour.
3. When the flour is absorbed into the butter (but not browned), beat in the stock.
4. Place the saucepan on a Flame-Tamer and simmer the sauce for approximately 45 minutes, or until it is reduced by a third and is very thick and creamy. Stirring often with the wire whisk is a necessity in order to achieve a velvety sauce.
5. Beat in the dry vermouth and simmer for 15 minutes more.

NOTE: You may substitute Fish Stock* Clarified* if you are preparing a fish recipe.

Almond Tarragon Sauce

Yields approximately 3½ cups

I have used this sauce to spark up Baked Chicken* as well as Sautéed Sole.* I have also spooned it over an omelette . . . it was superb.

4 tablespoons sweet butter, cut into cubes
4 tablespoons unbleached flour
⅛ to ¼ teaspoon cayenne
2½ teaspoons dried tarragon
¾ teaspoon freshly ground white pepper
1 tablespoon seasoned salt substitute (optional)

1 cup cream (or triple-strength low sodium dry milk)
1 cup milk (or low sodium dry milk)
2 tablespoons sweet butter
⅔ cup slivered blanched almonds
½ cup dry sherry or
½ cup brandy

1. Fill the bottom half of a double boiler with water to within 1 inch of the top section, and bring to a boil over a high flame.

2. Reduce the heat to low and melt the 4 tablespoons of butter in the top section of the double boiler, stirring occasionally with a wire whisk.

3. Gradually add the flour, stirring constantly. When well blended, add the cayenne, tarragon, white pepper, and salt substitute. Continue stirring for another minute.

4. Very slowly add the cream and the milk, stirring constantly until the sauce thickens. Turn the flame to low and simmer for 3 to 4 minutes.

5. In a small skillet melt the 2 tablespoons of butter over a low flame and lightly brown the almonds until they are a pale golden color. Add them slowly to the sauce in the double boiler, stirring constantly.

6. Simmer for another minute, then stir in the sherry or brandy and continue to simmer for 3 to 4 minutes more, stirring constantly.

Mushroom Almond Sauce

Yields approximately 6 cups

4 to 5 tablespoons sweet butter
1½ pounds very small
    mushrooms, thinly sliced
    lengthwise
⅔ cup sliced blanched almonds
5 to 6 tablespoons unbleached
    flour
1¼ cups heavy cream (or triple-
    strength low sodium dry
    milk)

1¼ cups milk (or low sodium
    dry milk)
¼ teaspoon cayenne
1 tablespoon seasoned salt sub-
    stitute (optional)
2 tablespoons finely chopped
    fresh parsley
½ teaspoon dried marjoram
6 tablespoons dry sherry

1. Melt the butter in a heavy skillet over a low-medium flame and sauté the mushrooms until they begin to brown. Remove the mushrooms with a slotted spoon to a bowl.

2. Sauté the almonds in the same skillet until very light golden brown, stirring often.

3. Return the mushrooms to the pan and slowly sprinkle in the flour, stirring constantly. Still stirring, slowly add the cream, milk, cayenne, salt substitute, parsley, and marjoram.

4. Turn the flame to low and, stirring constantly, cook the sauce until it begins to thicken. Slowly add the sherry, continuing to stir. Cook for 5 minutes more, stirring constantly until all the ingredients are blended and the sauce is quite thick.

Horseradish Cream Sauce

Yields approximately 6 cups

Excellent as an accompaniment to cold poached fish such as Salmon* and Bass* ... and my family also loves it with very thinly sliced cold Brisket.*

4 eggs, separated (at room temperature)
5 tablespoons Fresh Horseradish*
1/2 teaspoon freshly ground white pepper

Juice of 1 large lemon
1 tablespoon seasoned salt substitute (optional)
2 tablespoons finely chopped fresh chives (optional)
1 pint heavy cream (very cold)

1. Using an electric mixer on medium speed, beat the egg yolks until they are pale yellow. Beat in the horseradish, then beat in the pepper, lemon juice, salt substitute, and chives.

2. Using an electric mixer on high speed, beat the egg whites until stiff peaks form and they hold their shape.

3. Using an electric mixer on medium-high speed, beat the cream until peaks form and hold their shape.

4. Fold the egg whites into the cream. Spoon a fourth of this into the egg yolk mixture and gently stir to combine all the ingredients and also to lighten the mixture. Fold the remaining egg white-cream mixture into the egg yolk mixture and transfer to a serving bowl. Cover tightly. Refrigerate at least 4 hours before serving.

Hollandaise Sauce

Yields 1 cup

"The Traditional Way"

3 egg yolks (at room temperature)
1/2 teaspoon freshly ground white pepper
3/4 teaspoon salt substitute

1 tablespoon cold water
1/2 cup sweet butter (at room temperature)
1 1/2 tablespoons fresh lemon juice (or more to taste)

1. Fill the bottom of a double boiler with water to within 1 inch of the top part. Place the bottom of the double boiler over a medium flame until the water is hot but not boiling. Turn the flame to low so the water will remain hot but never boil.

2. Place the top part of the double boiler in the bottom and add the egg yolks, pepper, salt substitute, and water.

3. Beat with a wire whisk until the egg yolks are light and fluffy.

4. Add the butter in small quantities, constantly beating vigorously with the whisk. (Do not add more butter until the last addition has been thoroughly absorbed and the sauce has thickened.)

5. Beat in the lemon juice.

6. Remove the top of the double boiler from the bottom and cover the sauce. The sauce can remain this way for at least ½ hour before serving and should then be transferred to a warm serving bowl.

Food Processor Hollandaise

Yields 2 cups

This is an absolute joy! It is mistake-proof, quick, easy, and effortless. While it is considered cheating by those of the "formal cooking school," it is cheered by those of us who want gourmet cooking the easy way.

6 egg yolks, at room temperature

3 to 4 tablespoons fresh lemon juice

1 teaspoon freshly ground white pepper

1½ teaspoons salt substitute (optional)

⅛ teaspoon cayenne

1 cup sweet butter, melted and kept hot

1. Place 6 egg yolks, lemon juice, pepper, salt substitute, and cayenne in the food processor container with the steel blade.

2. Turn the processor on and off, and then on again.

3. Very slowly pour the hot melted butter in the tube in a steady stream until all the butter has been absorbed.

4. Transfer the sauce to a warm serving dish.

NOTE: If you are not serving the sauce immediately, cover it and place the dish over hot but not boiling water. Serve the sauce within ½ hour, if possible.

Sauce Mousseline

Yields approximately 2 cups

This is simply a combination of warm Hollandaise Sauce* and whipped cream. It is delicate and delicious and very fattening. Sauce mousseline is generally served with Poached Salmon Chaud Au Froid,* or any other warm poached fish such as Sole* or Bass.*

When you are ready to serve the fish:

Fold ½ cup very cold whipped   1½ cups warm Hollandaise
    cream into   Sauce*

Sauce Newburg

Serves 8 well and 6 generously

This sauce may be spooned over warm poached fish such as Salmon,* Bass,* Sole,* or served on the side.

5 tablespoons sweet butter, cut into small cubes
5 tablespoons unbleached flour
⅛ to ¼ teaspoon cayenne
1 teaspoon freshly ground white pepper
1 teaspoon dry mustard
2 teaspoons salt substitute (optional)

1¼ cups heavy cream (or triple-strength low sodium dry milk)
1¼ cups milk (or low sodium dry milk)
4 egg yolks (at room temperature)
4 tablespoons dry sherry
3 tablespoons brandy

1. Fill the bottom half of a double boiler with water to within 1 inch of the top section and bring to a boil over a high flame.

2. Reduce the heat to low and melt the butter in the top section of the double boiler, stirring occasionally with a wire whisk.

3. Gradually add the flour, stirring constantly. When well blended add the cayenne, white pepper, mustard, and salt substitute, stirring well to blend. Continue stirring for 2½ to 3 minutes.

4. Very slowly add the cream and milk, stirring constantly. Remove the top of the double boiler and allow the mixture to cool for 5 minutes.

5. While the mixture is cooling, using an electric mixer on medium

speed, beat the egg yolks in a mixing bowl until frothy and slowly pour the cream mixture, a little at a time, into the eggs. While beating constantly, continue adding the cream mixture until it is thoroughly blended with the eggs.

6. Return the sauce to the top of the double boiler and add the sherry and brandy, stirring well to blend.

7. Return the top part of the double boiler to the bottom and heat over a medium flame for 2 to 3 minutes, stirring constantly. (Make sure the water in the bottom does not boil.)

Tomato Sauce

Yields approximately 6 cups

I generally triple this recipe and freeze it in pint containers.

3 tablespoons olive oil
1 medium-size onion, finely
    minced
4 cloves garlic, finely minced
2 1-pound cans salt-free toma-
    toes, chopped (include
    juice), or 6 large fresh
    tomatoes, skinned and
    chopped, or 2 1-pound cans
    salt-free Italian plum toma-
    toes.
1 can salt-free tomato paste

$^1/_8$ teaspoon cayenne
2 to 3 teaspoons natural sugar
    (or substitute equivalent)
$^3/_4$ teaspoon freshly ground
    black pepper
$4^1/_2$ teaspoons seasoned salt sub-
    stitute (optional)
1 cup salt-free tomato juice
1 teaspoon dried sweet basil
$^1/_2$ teaspoon dried oregano
1 bay leaf

1. In a heavy enamel saucepan heat the oil over a medium flame and sauté the onion and garlic until the onion is pale gold. Add the chopped tomatoes, tomato paste, cayenne, sugar, pepper, salt substitute, and tomato juice. Stir well.

2. Lower the flame and cook uncovered for 50 minutes, stirring fairly often.

3. Add the sweet basil, oregano, and the bay leaf. Stir well and cook for 20 minutes more. (The sauce should be fairly thick and reduced by a third.)

NOTE: When cooking tomatoes, I always try to avoid tin and metal in gen-
    eral, as I feel that the tomatoes take on a slightly acid-bitter taste.
    Therefore, an enamel saucepan is stressed and I heartily suggest
    using a wooden spoon to stir.

Marinara Sauce

Yields about 5 quarts

I make this in large quantities and then freeze it in pint and quart plastic containers. It makes life very easy to be able to take your sauce from the freezer, heat it, and add rice, spaghetti, leftover cooked fish, chicken, or whatever for a delicious meal in minutes.

½ cup corn oil or ¼ cup corn oil mixed with ¼ cup olive oil

10 large onions, thinly sliced

3 large green peppers, seeded and cut into thin strips

3 large red peppers, seeded and cut into thin strips

8 cloves garlic, crushed

2½ pounds small mushrooms, cut lengthwise into thin slices

8 1-pound cans salt-free tomatoes, coarsely chopped, or and coarsely chopped, or 8 1-pound cans salt-free Italian plum tomatoes.

4 cans salt-free tomato paste

1 cup dry red wine (optional)

Juice of 2 large lemons

3 tablespoons natural sugar (or substitute equivalent)

¼ to ½ teaspoon cayenne

2 to 3 teaspoons freshly ground black pepper

3½ tablespoons seasoned salt substitute (optional)

½ cup olive oil

3 bay leaves

1 tablespoon dried sweet basil

1 teaspoon dried oregano

1. In two 15-inch heavy skillets heat the oil (¼ cup in each) over a medium flame and in one sauté the onions, peppers, and garlic until the onions are pale gold and the peppers are tender, stirring often.

2. In the other skillet sauté the mushrooms until they are dark brown and tender, stirring often.

3. Using a huge enamel pot, combine the chopped tomatoes with their juice, tomato paste, wine, lemon juice, sugar, cayenne, pepper, salt substitute, and ½ cup olive oil. Mix well and bring to a low boil over a medium flame. Turn the flame to low and simmer uncovered 1 hour, stirring frequently.

4. Add the onions, peppers, garlic, mushrooms, bay leaves, basil, and oregano. Stir well and continue to simmer uncovered for another 30 minutes. Remove the bay leaves. (The sauce should be fairly thick.)

NOTE I: You may either use at once, cool and refrigerate, or cool and freeze. This sauce will keep up to 1 week in the refrigerator.

NOTE 2: When cooking tomatoes, I always try to avoid tin and metal in general as I feel the tomatoes take on a slightly acid-bitter taste. Therefore, an enamel pot is stressed and I heartily suggest using a wooden spoon to stir.

Sauce Provençal

Yields approximately 1 quart

4 tablespoons olive oil
1 medium-size onion, finely
    minced
6 cloves garlic, pressed
1/3 cup unbleached flour
3 1/2 cups dry white wine, heated
    over a low flame for 20
    minutes
4 tablespoons salt-free tomato
    paste

4 teaspoons seasoned salt substi-
    tute (optional)
1 teaspoon freshly ground white
    pepper
2 teaspoons "herbes de Pro-
    vence" or make your own
    by using a blend of rose-
    mary, thyme, fennel, sage,
    oregano, basil, and chervil

1. In a heavy sauce pan, heat the olive oil over a medium flame and sauté the onion and garlic until the onion is a light gold, stirring often.

2. Lower the flame, stir in the flour, and continue to stir for 3 to 4 minutes, or until the flour is thoroughly blended with the onion and garlic.

3. Add the wine and beat vigorously with a wire whisk until the mixture is thick and smooth.

4. Add the tomato paste and whisk the mixture for another 2 to 3 minutes. Add the salt substitute, pepper, and herbs and simmer for 20 minutes.

NOTE: If you want an extra smooth sauce you may either purée it in a blender or food processor or strain it through a fine sieve.

Spicy Sesame Oil
(Szechuan Style)

Yields ½ cup

This will keep at least 2 months if stored in a cool place.

3 fresh small hot red peppers
½ cup sesame oil

1. Remove the stems and seeds from the peppers and slice them into 1-inch strips.
2. In a wok or a heavy skillet heat the oil over a high flame and stir-fry the peppers for 2 minutes.
3. Remove from the flame and let cool.
4. Pour the oil and peppers into a glass jar and cover tightly. Let the mixture stand for 5 days in a cool place. Then remove the peppers and re-cover the jar tightly. The oil is now ready for use.

Red Hot Oil

Yields approximately ½ cup

Follow the directions for Spicy Sesame Oil,* substituting corn oil or peanut oil for the sesame oil.

Hot Red Pepper Oil
(Otherwise known as "Fire Mouth")

Yields approximately ¾ cup

½ cup peanut oil   **¼ cup sesame oil**
1½ to 2 tablespoons cayenne

1. In a wok or a heavy small skillet heat the oil over a medium-high flame until it is hot (approximately 375°).

2. Remove it from the flame and stir in the cayenne. Cool at least 30 minutes.

3. Add the sesame oil and blend it thoroughly with the other ingredients.

4. Line a fine sieve with double thickness of cheesecloth and place it over a large measuring cup. Pour in the oil.

5. When all of the oil has dripped into the measuring cup, pour it into a glass jar and cover tightly.

Fresh Horseradish

Yields approximately 2½ quarts

The fresher the horseradish, the stronger the taste. So beware of the first week. This horseradish will still retain a lot of its flavor, though some of its strength will be diminished by the time you use the last bit at the end of eight weeks. Some of my more finicky friends tell me that really fresh horseradish should not be used after two weeks, for it loses much of its pungency. This may be true, but I couldn't face the agony of those teary eyes more than once every eight weeks. And, without question, this is still far better tasting and more pungent after eight weeks than the store-bought variety.

3 pounds fresh horseradish root, peeled and cut into small cubes

1 quart white vinegar (approximately)

2 tablespoons sugar (or substitute equivalent) (approximately)

1. Place 1 cup of the vinegar in the glass container of a blender. Add 2½ cups of the horseradish cubes and 1 to 2 teaspoons of the sugar.

2. Blend on high speed until the horseradish is finely grated and well blended with the vinegar and sugar.

3. Repeat Steps 1 and 2 until all the horseradish is used.

NOTE 1: Store in tightly covered glass jars in the refrigerator.

NOTE 2: To make horseradish in a food processor, place the horseradish pieces up to ½ inch from the top of the steel blade. Pour in enough vinegar to almost cover the horseradish. Add 1 teaspoon of sugar (or substitute equivalent) and process until the horseradish is finely grated and thoroughly blended with the vinegar and sugar. Repeat until all the horseradish is used.

Spicy Cocktail Sauce

Yields approximately 1 cup

³/₄ cup salt-free chili sauce
4 tablespoons Fresh Horseradish*
¹/₂ to ³/₄ teaspoon Hot Red
  Pepper Oil* or ¹/₈ to ¹/₄ teaspoon cayenne

¹/₂ teaspoon salt-free hot chili
  powder
¹/₂ teaspoon freshly ground
  black pepper
1¹/₂ tablespoons fresh lemon
  juice

1. Place all the ingredients in a glass bowl and lightly beat with a wire whisk until thoroughly blended.
2. Place in a glass jar and cover tightly.

NOTE: Store in the refrigerator. (This will keep for many weeks.)

Hawaiian Sauce

Yields approximately 3 cups

1¹/₂ cups salt-free chili sauce
1¹/₂ cups unsweetened pineapple
  juice
2 tablespoons fresh lemon juice
2 tablespoons brown sugar (or
  substitute equivalent)
2 teaspoons salt-free chili
  powder

1 teaspoon dry mustard
³/₄ teaspoon Hot Red Pepper
  Oil* or ¹/₄ teaspoon cayenne
6 cloves garlic, pressed
2-inch piece fresh ginger root,
  finely grated
1¹/₂ tablespoons cornstarch
¹/₂ cup pineapple juice

1. In a heavy saucepan heat the chili sauce, 1¹/₂ cups of pineapple juice, lemon juice, brown sugar, chili powder, dry mustard, hot red pepper oil or cayenne, garlic, and ginger over a low-medium flame until piping hot, stirring often.
2. Mix the cornstarch with the ¹/₂ cup of pineapple juice until it is thoroughly absorbed.
3. Pour ¹/₃ cup of the hot sauce into the cornstarch mixture, stirring constantly. Slowly pour the cornstarch mixture into the remaining hot sauce and stir until all is well blended.
4. Simmer on a low flame for 15 to 20 minutes, stirring fairly often, until the mixture is thick and smooth.

Hot Mustard Sauce

Yields approximately 1½ cups

2 tablespoons peanut oil
6 cloves garlic, crushed
1½-inch piece ginger root, grated
4 teaspoons dry mustard dissolved in
⅓ cup dry sherry

1 cup Chicken Stock* mixed with
2 tablespoons cornstarch
¾ teaspoon freshly ground white pepper
⅛ teaspoon cayenne (optional)

1. In a wok or heavy skillet heat the peanut oil over a high flame until it smokes. Remove it from the heat and let it cool.
2. In the meantime, mix the garlic, ginger, mustard, and sherry together.
3. Place the wok containing the peanut oil back on the stove and heat until it is very hot over a medium-high flame.
4. Add the garlic mixture and stir-fry for 1 minute.
5. Add the chicken stock and cornstarch, pepper, and cayenne and stir-fry until the sauce thickens.

Apricot Mustard Sauce

Yields approximately 2 quarts

It's quick, it's easy and it's wonderful as an accompaniment to Broiled Chicken* or Baked Chicken* . . . or as one of the sauces you serve with Chicken Concubine* or Chicken Curry.*

2 16-ounce cans unsweetened pineapple (drained)
3 8-ounce jars apricot preserves
¾ cup Cooked Apricots* (optional)

6 tablespoons salt-free Dijon-style mustard (or more to taste)

1. In a blender or food processor fitted with the steel blade place half of the pineapple, half of the apricot preserves, half of the cooked apricots, and half of the mustard.

2. Mix until thoroughly puréed and blended (approximately 2 minutes).
3. Pour the sauce into a glass jar and cover tightly.
4. Repeat with the remaining half of the ingredients.

NOTE: Store in the refrigerator. It will keep for months.

Cantonese Sauce

Yields 1½ cups

2 tablespoons peanut oil
1 teaspoon garlic powder
5 tablespoons dark rice vinegar
4 tablespoons brown sugar (or
    substitute equivalent)
2 tablespoons salt-free tomato
    paste

1 teaspoon dried ginger
1 teaspoon Beef Stock*
2 tablespoons cornstarch
½ cup sweet, salt-free water-
    melon rind, finely chopped,
    with the juice

1. In a wok or a medium-size heavy skillet heat the peanut oil over a high flame until it smokes. Remove the wok from the flame.
2. Place the garlic powder, vinegar, sugar, tomato paste, and ginger in a bowl. Beat with a wire whisk until thoroughly blended. Set aside.
3. In a glass bowl mix the beef stock with cornstarch and beat with a wire whisk until smooth.
4. Place the peanut oil back on a high flame and heat. Add the watermelon rind and stir-fry for ½ minute. Add the garlic powder mixture and stir thoroughly. Bring to a boil. Once boiling, cook for 1½ minutes, stirring constantly.
5. Continuing to stir, slowly add the beef stock mixture until it is all blended with the other ingredients.
6. Stir-fry the sauce until it thickens (approximately 3 minutes).

Chinese Sweet and Sour Sauce

Makes 3 cups

3 tablespoons peanut oil
4 cloves garlic, crushed
1 medium-size green pepper,
  finely chopped
3 large carrots, grated
5 teaspoons sugar (or substitute
  equivalent)
½ cup rice vinegar
2 tablespoons cornstarch mixed
  with

½ cup cold water
1 16-ounce can peaches, packed
  in water, drained and
  puréed
1 16-ounce can apricots, packed
  in water, drained and
  puréed

1. Heat the oil in large skillet over a medium flame. Add the garlic, green pepper, and carrots and stir-fry for 3 minutes.

2. Stir in the sugar and the vinegar. Add the cornstarch mixture and cook for 2 minutes, stirring constantly.

3. Add the peaches and the apricots and stir the sauce constantly until thick and piping hot (approximately 6 minutes).

Whole Cranberry and Orange Sauce

Serves 10 to 12

¾ cup water
¾ cup orange juice
1½ to 2 cups sugar (or substitute equivalent)

1 tablespoon finely grated
  orange rind
4 cups cranberries, washed and
  picked over

1. Place the water, orange juice, sugar, and orange rind in a heavy saucepan. Stirring constantly, bring the liquid to a boil over a high flame. Lower the flame and simmer.

2. Place the cranberries in the "syrup" and cook for approximately 10 minutes, or until the cranberries pop open.

Cranberry Orange Relish

Serves 10 to 16

1 quart cranberries, washed and
  picked over
2 large navel oranges, cut into
  fourths and seeded

2 cups sugar (or substitute
  equivalent)

1. Grind the cranberries and oranges. Put them in a large bowl and thoroughly blend in the sugar.

2. Place the relish in a 1½-quart glass jar, cover tightly, and refrigerate.

NOTE: Do not use for at least 2 days. This will keep in your refrigerator for at least 8 days.

Chutney

Yields approximately 2½ cups

2 large tart green apples, peeled,
  cored, finely chopped, and
  soaked in
2 tablespoons fresh lemon juice
1 medium-size onion, finely
  chopped
½ cup raisins (brown)
⅓ cup apple cider vinegar
⅓ cup brown sugar (or substitute equivalent)

¼ cup water
2½ teaspoons salt-free curry
  powder
1-inch piece fresh ginger root,
  finely grated (or more to
  taste)
⅛ teaspoon ground cloves
1 teaspoon ground cinnamon
3 to 4 cloves garlic, pressed
¼ cup dry sherry

1. Mix all the ingredients together until they are thoroughly blended.

2. Place the mixture in a heavy saucepan over a Flame-Tamer and cook over a low flame for 1 hour to 1 hour and 20 minutes, or until all the ingredients are very tender and thoroughly blended, stirring quite often.

3. Store the chutney in an airtight jar in the refrigerator. This will keep for many weeks.

Ginger Red Pepper Relish

Yields approximately 5 cups

This is an excellent accompaniment to Beignets,* Hawaiian Chicken,* Meat Balls Chinoise,* and curried dishes.

1½ pounds sweet red peppers, skinned (or unskinned) (see Note)
⅓ cup olive oil
2 cups minced onions
6 cloves garlic, pressed
2 cups fresh ripe tomatoes, skinned and finely chopped
3-inch piece fresh ginger root, finely grated
¾ cup brown or natural sugar (or substitute equivalent)
¼ cup wine vinegar
¼ cup dry sherry
2½ teaspoons salt-free hot curry powder (optional)
⅛ to ¼ teaspoon cayenne
⅔ cup Cooked Apricots,* drained and coarsely chopped
½ teaspoon dry mustard dissolved in
2 tablespoons cold water`

1. Remove the seeds from the peppers and cut them into thin strips about ¼ inch by 1½ inches.

2. In a heavy skillet heat the oil over a medium flame and sauté the onions, garlic, and peppers until the onions are golden brown. Cover, turn the flame to low, and simmer for 20 minutes.

3. In a large casserole place the tomatoes, ginger, brown or natural sugar, vinegar, sherry, curry, cayenne, apricots, and mustard. Mix well.

4. Preheat the oven to 300°.

5. Add the onion mixture to the casserole and stir well. Cover and bake for 2½ to 3 hours, or until thick.

NOTE: The peppers are good both ways, but if you like a smoother relish, definitely skin them. The simplest way to remove the skin is to place a long fork (such as the type used for outdoor barbecues) into the pepper. Turn the flame to high and hold the pepper over the flame until the skin is charred on all sides. Place the charred peppers into a brown paper bag and close tightly. When the peppers have cooled, remove them from the bag and peel off the charred outer skin. (If you don't have a gas stove or if you don't feel like "grilling" each pepper, place them in a 450° oven and bake until the skin is charred; cool in the same manner as stated before.)

August Corn and Tomato Relish

Yields approximately 6 cups

This was named as such because the only time I make it is at the height of the home-grown corn and tomato season (which happens to be synonymous with August). This relish will keep for three weeks, I guess . . . but it never lasts more than ten days in our house.

3 large onions, ground

2 large green peppers, seeded and ground

3 cups sweet corn kernels (approximately 16 small ears)

8 cloves garlic, pressed (optional)

2 large beefsteak tomatoes, peeled, seeded, and chopped

$1/2$ cup sugar (or substitute equivalent)

$1/4$ cup fresh lemon juice

$1/2$ cup apple cider vinegar

1 teaspoon turmeric

$1/4$ teaspoon cayenne (or more to taste)

1 teaspoon freshly ground black pepper

4 teaspoons seasoned salt substitute (optional)

2 teaspoons dry mustard

1. Place the onions, peppers, corn, garlic, and tomatoes in a large pot.

2. Put the sugar, lemon juice, vinegar, turmeric, cayenne, pepper, salt substitute, and mustard in a bowl and beat with a wire whisk until thoroughly blended. Pour over the vegetables in the pot.

3. Turn the flame to high and stir constantly until the liquid comes to a boil. Reduce the flame to low, cover and cook for 1 hour.

4. While the mixture is hot, spoon it into a glass jar, cover tightly, and cool.

NOTE: Refrigerate for at least 3 days before using.

BREADS

Accompaniments

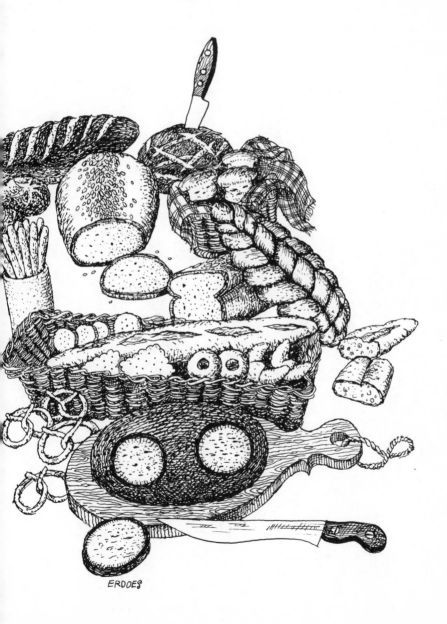

ERDOES

Breads, Crackers, Muffins, and Stuffings

BREADS: When I first was put on a salt-free diet, bread was the last thing I was thinking about. However, as the months and years passed I suddenly realized that the only bread available to me was a packaged white bread which I found after a long, arduous search in one market and one gourmet store. Suddenly, because it was forbidden fruit, I developed the wildest craving for the staff of life. With great joy and glee, one of the many health food stores that I frequented called to tell me they had a marvelous new bread that was "salt free." When I got to the store and read the label, I found it had a large proportion of sea salt. Crestfallen, I left the store. It was at that time that I started to teach myself bread making. Fortunately for me, some of my good friends were excellent home bread bakers and we started a salt-free experimental bread kitchen. The recipes in this chapter represent a wide variety of interesting breads, muffins, crackers, and stuffings.

There is nothing more delicious than the aroma that will permeate your home as fresh bread is being baked. Your guests will ooh and aah at your expertise and will revel in reflections of an era gone by when every good homemaker baked her own wonderful breads.

There are a few general rules that you should keep in mind:

1. Yeast doughs are very sensitive and must be in a draft-free place. In many instances I have suggested covering the dough with turkish towels. Another trick to employ is to use a large clean plastic bag. Place the container with the dough into the bag. Allow enough room for the dough to rise and seal the bag. This certainly guarantees a draft-free nesting place for your dough.

2. If you are fortunate enough to have two ovens, a wonderful place to allow bread to rise would be in one of your ovens, preheated for 5 minutes to 110° and then turned off. Let the oven cool down for 20 minutes and then place your dough in an approximately 85° oven for its rising period.

3. The surface you knead and roll your dough on must, of course, be immaculately clean. You can use a Formica counter or table, or a huge marble or wooden board that can be stored in a utility closet.

4. It is wonderful to be able to eat freshly baked homemade bread

shortly after it comes from the oven, but if you want to freeze your bread, rest assured it freezes beautifully if you double-wrap it in heavy-duty aluminum foil, label, and date it; and place it in a double thickness of plastic bags sealed airtight. This will prevent moisture getting to your bread. To defrost, remove it immediately from its wrappings and set it on a dry surface. Right before serving, pop the bread back in a 225° oven and let it come back to its original hot crusty state. Frozen bread should be used within six months.

5. The type of Melba Toast* that you will find in this chapter is similar to one I had purchased for years at one of New York's finest gourmet shops. It cost an arm and a leg. Of course, despite its cost, I haven't been able to use it in years because it contains salt, so I hope you will find this as much of a treat as we have.

CRACKERS: Fourteen years ago low sodium crackers were practically unobtainable. There were two brands, however, and although they had very little taste, they were a lot better than nothing.

Then one day a friend called to tell me she had found a recipe for crackers; and since it was a rainy Saturday, and neither of us was working, why didn't we make crackers? At the end of the day I was "crackers," for our recipe, without salt, was a total bust. Talk about dreary? Then you know exactly how those crackers tasted.

Through further experimentation and many failures, four flavorful and interesting crackers evolved. These will keep for quite a while if stored correctly (see Crackers, General Rules*). They are tasty enough to be eaten by themselves and are naturally a wonderful accompaniment to soups and salads. Crisp and crunchy, two or three are a marvelous pick-up at that fading hour of 4 P.M.

MUFFINS: Store-bought muffins without salt did not exist years ago. In all honesty, they are not an integral part of our menus. However, we do have an assortment of muffins at Sunday brunches and appreciate them no end when traveling long distances by plane. It is most comforting, at these times, to know that some delicious muffins are neatly tucked away. Sadly, but more often than not, the stewardess responds to my inquiry of "I have ordered a salt-free meal. May I have it please?" with "Oh, I'm *so* sorry, Mrs. Brenner, it is not on board. There must have been a foul-up in the computer." Without question, my muffins taste most delicious at these times and certainly help to make a six- to eight-hour plane trip both tolerable and palatable; not to mention my satiated salivary glands.

STUFFINGS: Although certainly not low in calories, I must admit that stuffings are great favorites of mine. And besides, who could ever think of Thanksgiving dinner without stuffing? And isn't striped bass a little more

special with a Mushroom Herb Stuffing for Fish*? And Roasted Capon,*
generally a rather mundane dish: isn't it transformed into an exciting dinner when Apricot Prune Stuffing* nestles in its cavity?

White Bread

Makes 2 loaves

Certainly not one of your more exciting breads . . . nonetheless a good
classic basic bread.

1 cup scalded milk (or low
  sodium dry milk)
2½ tablespoons honey
¼ cup vegetable shortening
1 cup lukewarm water (about
  110°)
2 packages active dry yeast
2 teaspoons honey

6 to 7 cups sifted unbleached
  flour
1 teaspoon finely ground white
  pepper
2½ teaspoons salt substitute
  (optional)
¼ cup sweet butter, melted

1. To the saucepan in which you scalded the milk add the 2½ tablespoons of honey and the shortening, stirring together with a wooden
spoon until the shortening is totally blended. Let the mixture cool to lukewarm (110° approximately).
2. Pour the cup of lukewarm water into a large warm mixing bowl
(rinse the bowl with very hot water and thoroughly dry it) and spinkle in
the yeast and the 2 teaspoons of honey. Stir until the yeast is dissolved
and then let the mixture stand in a warm place (about 80°) for 5 to 6 minutes, or until the yeast has blended with the water.
3. Beat the milk mixture into the yeast mixture, using an electric mixer
on low speed. Then turn the speed up to low-medium and beat in 3½ cups
of flour, a little at a time. Add the pepper and salt substitute and continue
beating until all the flour is absorbed and the dough is smooth.
4. Add 3 more cups of the flour, a little at a time, and stir with a wooden
spoon until a dampened dough is formed. Cover and let the dough stand in
a warm place (80°) for 12 minutes.
5. Turn the dough out onto a lightly floured board and knead it for approximately 10 minutes, or until it is smooth and elastic (adding more flour
if necessary). Form the dough into a ball and place it in a well-buttered
large bowl. Roll the ball over so that all sides have touched the butter.
6. Cover the bowl with a turkish towel and let it rise in a warm draft-

free place (85° to 90°) for approximately 40 minutes, or until it has doubled in bulk (see Note).

7. Punch the dough down and turn it out onto a board and let it rest for
10 minutes, covered with wax paper.

8. Butter two loaf pans (9 by 5 by 3 inches).

9. Cut the dough in half and shape into two loaves. Place the loaves,
seam side down, in the loaf pans.

10. Cover the pans with a turkish towel, or place in plastic bags (see
Note), and let the dough rise until double in bulk in a warm draft-free
place (85°) for approximately 40 to 50 minutes.

11. Preheat the oven to 375°.

12. Brush the loaves with the melted butter and bake for 1 hour and 10
minutes to 1 hour and 20 minutes, or until the loaves are a dark golden
brown and sound hollow when tapped with the fingertips.

13. Turn the bread onto a wire rack to cool thoroughly.

NOTE: Instead of using a turkish towel, place the bowl in a large, clean
plastic bag. Allow enough room for expansion and seal the bag.
Proceed as above.

Challah

Makes 2 loaves

Although this is the traditional Sabbath bread in many Jewish homes, one
of my dear Italian-Catholic friends taught me how to bake it. This wonderful bread is the bread of tradition in her family.

2 cups milk (or low sodium dry milk)	**2 packages active dry yeast**
¹/₃ cup sweet butter	**¹/₄ cup honey**
¹/₄ cup water	**3 eggs, plus 1 egg, separated**
¹/₄ teaspoon powdered saffron	**4 to 6 tablespoons poppy seeds**
4¹/₄ to 5 cups sifted unbleached flour	

1. Stirring constantly, heat the milk, butter, water, and saffron in a
medium-size heavy saucepan over a very low flame until the butter is
melted and the temperature of the ingredients is quite warm (about 125°).
Remove from the flame.

2. Spoon 3 cups of flour into a large mixing bowl, and add the yeast and honey. Turn an electric mixer to low-medium speed and slowly add the milk mixture. Continue beating for 1 minute while scraping the sides of the bowl with a rubber spatula.

3. Beat in 1 egg at a time until all 3 eggs are absorbed into the mixture and then beat in the egg white from the separated egg, scraping the sides of the bowl with a rubber spatula.

4. Turn off the mixer and, using a wooden spoon, blend in enough additional flour to make a soft dough.

5. Turn the dough onto a floured board and knead, adding a little more flour only if necessary, until the dough is satiny and smooth and no longer sticks to the board (approximately 10 minutes).

6. Shape the dough into a ball and place it in a well-buttered bowl. Roll the dough over so that all sides are buttered. Cover with a turkish towel and let the bread rise in a warm draft-free place (85° to 90°) until it doubles in bulk (approximately 1½ hours). (See Note.)

7. Punch the dough down and turn it out onto a floured board. Divide it into two parts. Separate each part into three equal pieces and roll out each piece evenly to 15 or 16 inches in length. Braid the three lengths by pinching the top edges together, then braiding them to the end. Undo the pinched end and braid that.

8. Place the challahs on a well-greased baking sheet (15 by 18 inches).

9. Beat the reserved egg yolk with 2 teaspoons of water and brush the tops of the challahs. Sprinkle with poppy seeds. Cover with wax paper and then a towel; let rise in a warm, draft-free place (85° to 90°) for approximately 50 minutes, or until double in bulk.

10. Preheat the oven to 375°.

11. Bake for 30 to 35 minutes, or until the challahs are golden brown and sound hollow when tapped with the fingertips.

12. Transfer to a wire rack to cool.

NOTE: Instead of using a turkish towel, place the bowl in a large clean plastic bag. Allow enough room for expansion and seal the bag. Proceed as above.

French Bread

Makes 1 loaf

With great embarrassment, I must admit that without a Corning Bake-around (a glass tube which sits in a metal rack and gives a perfect cylindrical, though slightly fat, shape to French bread), I have been unable to get a beautiful-looking French bread. I have tried and developed innumerable recipes and, while most were delicious to the taste, they were not pleasing to the eye. Therefore I present you with the following recipe, which is both delicious in texture and taste and a delight to behold, the only drawback being the investment for the Bakearound.

1 package active dry yeast
2 teaspoons sugar (or honey, which I prefer)
1/4 cup warm water (approximately 110°)
3/4 cup warm water (approximately 110°)
1 tablespoon vegetable shortening
1 tablespoon sweet butter
1/2 teaspoon white pepper

2 teaspoons salt substitute (optional)
3 to 3 1/2 cups unbleached flour mixed with
1/4 cup soy flour (this adds more protein and aids in the rising)
1 egg white, unbeaten
Sweet butter, at room temperature, for greasing
1 tablespoon cornmeal

1. Sprinkle the yeast and sugar into 1/4 cup of warm water in a small bowl. Stir 2 to 3 times and set aside for 10 to 12 minutes.

2. Using a large mixing bowl, pour in the 3/4 cup of warm water and add the shortening, butter, pepper and salt substitute and 1 cup of the flour mixture. Using an electric mixer, beat until smooth.

3. While continuing to beat, add the yeast mixture, the egg white, and the remaining flour, a little at a time, until a stiff dough is formed.

4. Turn the dough out onto a floured board and knead until it is smooth and elastic and no longer sticky (approximately 10 minutes).

5. Cover the bowl with a turkish towel and let the dough rise in a warm draft-free place (85° to 90°) for approximately 40 minutes, or until double in bulk (see Note).

6. Punch the dough down and turn it out onto a very lightly floured board. Knead lightly for 2 to 3 minutes.

7. Roll the dough and shape it into a strip 3 by 18 inches. Mark it lightly into thirds. Fold one third over the center third and pinch the edge to seal it. Then fold the remaining third over the other two thirds and seal well.

8. Butter the Bakearound tube and dust it thoroughly with the corn-meal. Center the dough in the Bakearound tube and butter the ends of the loaf. Place the Bakearound tube in the rack and drape double thicknesses of damp paper towels over each end. Allow the dough to rise in a warm draft-free place until double in bulk (about 1½ to 2 hours or less time in a warm oven).

9. Preheat the oven to 425°.

10. Remove the damp paper towels and bake the bread for 10 minutes. Lower the temperature to 350° and bake for 35 minutes more. Slide the bread onto a wire rack to cool.

NOTE: Instead of using a turkish towel, place the bowl in a large clean plastic bag. Allow enough room for expansion and seal the bag. Proceed as above.

Whole Wheat Bread

Makes 2 loaves

1 cup milk
¼ cup molasses
3 tablespoons sweet butter at
    room temperature
1½ teaspoons freshly ground
    black pepper (optional)
1 tablespoon salt substitute (op-
    tional)

1¼ cups lukewarm water
    (approximately 110°)
2 packages active dry yeast
3 tablespoons honey
6 cups sifted stone-ground
    whole wheat flour
¼ cup sweet butter, melted

1. Scald the milk in a small saucepan over a medium flame. Remove from the flame and add the molasses, 3 tablespoons of butter, black pepper, and salt substitute. Stir until everything is dissolved.

2. Pour the water into a huge warm mixing bowl. Sprinkle the yeast over the water, then, stirring constantly, slowly add the honey and continue to stir until everything is dissolved.

3. Pour in the milk mixture, stirring constantly.

4. Continuing to stir, slowly add 5 cups of the flour. Add enough of the remaining 1 cup of flour to form a soft dough, but stiff enough to leave the sides of the bowl.

5. Turn the dough onto a well-floured surface and knead for approximately 8 minutes, or until the dough is smooth and not sticky.

6. Roll the dough into a ball and place it in a large, heavily buttered

bowl. Turn the dough over in the bowl so that the greased side is up. Cover with a turkish towel and let it rise in a warm place (85° to 90°) for approximately 1½ hours or until double in bulk (see Note).

7. Punch the dough down and roll it over so that the smooth side is on top. Cover with the towel and let it rise for another 30 minutes.

8. Turn the dough out onto a lightly floured surface and divide in half. Cover with the towel and let it rest for 10 minutes.

9. Shape the dough into loaves and place in two well-buttered loaf pans (9 by 4 by 2½ inches). Set the pans in a warm place and cover with the towel. Let the bread rise until double in bulk (see Note), approximately 1 hour and 15 minutes.

10. In the meantime preheat the oven to 450° for 15 minutes.

11. Brush the tops of the loaves with the melted butter and bake the bread for 10 minutes. Reduce the heat to 350° and bake 45 minutes more, or until it is well browned and sounds hollow when lightly tapped with the fingertips.

12. Turn out onto wire racks and cool thoroughly.

NOTE: Instead of using a turkish towel, place the bowl in a large clean plastic bag. Allow enough room for expansion and seal the bag. Proceed as above.

Hearty Black Bread with Bran, Herbs, and Spices

Makes 2 round loaves

3½ cups unsifted rye flour
2¼ cups unbleached flour
½ cup soy flour
1½ teaspoons honey
1½ cups coarse bran
3 tablespoons caraway seeds
3 tablespoons instant coffee (powder or freeze dried)
2 tablespoons onion powder
2 tablespoons dried dill weed
2 teaspoons dry mustard
1 teaspoon freshly ground black pepper

2 teaspoons salt substitute (optional)
2 teaspoons dried basil
1 teaspoon dried tarragon
½ teaspoon fennel seed
2 packages active dry yeast
2½ cups water
¼ cup cider vinegar
¼ cup dark molasses
2 squares unsweetened chocolate
¼ cup sweet butter
1 teaspoon cornstarch
½ cup water

1. Mix the rye, unbleached, and soy flours together.

2. Place 2⅓ cups of the flour mixture in a large mixing bowl. Stir in the honey, bran, caraway seeds, coffee, onion powder, dill, mustard, pepper, salt substitute, basil, tarragon, fennel seed, and undissolved yeast. Blend thoroughly.

3. Place the 2½ cups of water, the vinegar, molasses, chocolate, and butter in a small saucepan and heat over a low flame until the mixture is warm (120°).

4. Using an electric mixer on low speed, add the liquid ingredients, a little at a time, to the dry ingredients, until all the liquid is absorbed. Turn the mixer up to medium speed and beat for 3½ minutes, scraping the sides of the bowl constantly.

5. Slowly add ½ cup of the flour mixture to the bowl and raise the speed to high; continuing to scrape the sides of the bowl, mix 2 minutes more.

6. Stir in the remaining flour mixture, a little at a time, and continue to mix with your hands until the dough leaves the sides of the bowl. (The dough will be quite stiff.)

7. Turn the dough out onto a lightly floured board and knead for approximately 6 to 8 minutes, or until it is smooth and elastic.

8. Form the dough into a ball and place it in a well-buttered bowl. Roll the dough in the bowl so that the ball is buttered all over. Cover the bowl with a turkish towel and put it in a warm draft-free place (about 85°) and let it rise until double in bulk (about 1½ to 2 hours). (See Note.)

9. Punch the dough down and turn it out onto a lightly floured board. Divide it in half and form each half into a ball. Place the balls into two well-buttered and lightly floured 8-inch round cake pans.

10. Cover the pans with the towel and let the dough rise in a warm draft-free place until double in bulk (approximately 1 hour and 15 minutes to 1 hour and 45 minutes see Note).

11. Preheat the oven to 350° and bake the bread 45 to 50 minutes, or until the loaves sound hollow when tapped with the fingertips.

12. About 15 minutes before the bread is done, place the cornstarch and water in a small heavy saucepan. Turn the flame to medium and cook until the mixture comes to a rolling boil, stirring constantly. Then continue to stir and cook the mixture another 2 minutes on a medium flame.

13. When the bread is baked, immediately brush each loaf with the cornstarch mixture and return the loaves to the oven. Bake 3 to 5 minutes, or until the glaze is set.

14. Remove the pans from the oven and turn the loaves out onto wire racks to cool.

NOTE: Instead of using a turkish towel, place the bowl in a large, clean plastic bag. Allow enough room for expansion and seal the bag. Proceed as above.

Russian Black Bread

Makes 2 round loaves

If you have ever longed for black bread (without salt) . . . here it is.

¹/₂ cup cornmeal
¹/₃ cup cold water
³/₄ cup boiling water
1 teaspoon freshly ground black
    pepper (optional)
2 teaspoons salt substitute (op-
    tional)
1 tablespoon sweet butter, at
    room temperature
2¹/₂ squares unsweetened choco-
    late, melted
¹/₄ cup instant coffee (powdered
    or freeze dried)

¹/₄ cup warm water
2 packages active dry yeast
2 cups dark rye flour
1 cup stone-ground whole wheat
    flour
1¹/₂ cups unbleached flour
¹/₂ cup soy flour
1 cup very warm water (about
    120°)
³/₄ cup dark molasses
3 tablespoons cornmeal
1 egg white, slightly beaten with
    1 tablespoon water

1. In a medium-size heavy saucepan mix the ¹/₂ cup of cornmeal with the cold water. Stir in the boiling water. Turn the flame to medium and cook the mixture until it has thickened, stirring constantly.

2. Remove the mixture from the flame and stir in the butter, pepper, salt substitute, chocolate, and instant coffee. Cook for 10 minutes.

3. Pour the warm water into a very large mixing bowl, sprinkle the yeast on top of the water, and stir until the yeast has dissolved.

4. Stir the cornmeal mixture into the yeast mixture and add the rye, whole wheat, white, and soy flours, stirring constantly. Add the very warm water and the molasses and blend thoroughly.

5. Turn the dough onto a floured board and knead, adding more flour if necessary, to make a firm but elastic dough (approximately 8 minutes).

6. Divide the dough in half and shape into two balls. Place each ball in a large well-buttered bowl and roll the dough over in the bowl so that all sides are buttered.

7. Cover the dough with a turkish towel and let it rise in a warm draft-free place (85°) until double in bulk (about 1¹/₂ to 2 hours). (See Note.)

8. Punch the dough down and place each ball in a well-buttered and lightly floured 8-inch cake pan, or in two well-buttered and lightly floured 1-quart casseroles. Sprinkle 1¹/₂ tablespoons of cornmeal over each ball. Cover with the towel and let rise in a warm draft-free place until double in bulk (approximately 1 hour and 15 minutes to 1 hour and 45 minutes). (See Note.)

9. Preheat the oven to 375°.

10. Brush the bread with the egg white mixture and bake until it is very brown and sounds hollow when tapped with the fingertips (approximately 50 to 65 minutes).

11. Turn the bread out onto wire racks and cool.

NOTE: Instead of using a turkish towel, place the bowl in a large, clean plastic bag. Allow enough room for expansion and seal the bag. Proceed as above.

Rolled Cheese and Herb Bread

Makes 2 loaves

Tangy, delicious . . . and, needless to say, fattening.

1 cup scalded milk (or low sodium dry milk)
2½ tablespoons honey
¼ cup vegetable shortening
1 cup lukewarm water (about 110°)
2 packages active dry yeast
2 teaspoons honey
4½ to 6 cups sifted unbleached flour
1 pound salt-free Cheddar cheese, grated
2 tablespoons sweet butter
1 cup fresh finely minced parsley
1 cup finely minced fresh green onions (scallions)

6 cloves garlic, pressed
1 teaspoon dried oregano
2 teaspoons dried tarragon
2½ teaspoons salt-free curry powder
1½ teaspoons dried cumin
1 teaspoon dried sweet basil
2½ teaspoons dried dill weed
⅛ teaspoon cayenne
½ to ¾ teaspoon freshly ground white pepper
¾ to 1 teaspoon dry mustard
1½ to 2 tablespoons sugar (or substitute equivalent)
2 eggs, lightly beaten
1 egg yolk mixed with 1 teaspoon water

1. To the saucepan in which you scalded the milk add the 2½ tablespoons of honey and shortening. Using a wooden spoon, stir until the shortening is totally blended. Let the mixture cool to lukewarm (approximately 110°).

2. Place the lukewarm water in a large warm mixing bowl (rinse with very hot water and then thoroughly dry it). Sprinkle in the yeast and the 2 teaspoons of honey. Stir until the yeast is dissolved and then let the mix-

ture stand in a warm place for 5 to 6 minutes, or until the yeast has blended with the water.

3. Using an electric mixer on low speed, beat the milk mixture into the yeast mixture. Then turn the speed up to low-medium and add 2½ cups of the flour, a little at a time, and beat until all the flour is absorbed and the dough is smooth.

4. Beat in a little of the cheese at a time, until all the cheese is thoroughly mixed in with the dough.

5. Stir the dough with a wooden spoon and add enough of the remaining flour (approximately 2 cups), a little at a time, until a moist dough is formed. Cover with a turkish towel and let it stand in a warm draft-free place for 12 minutes (see Note).

6. Turn the dough out onto a lightly floured board and knead it for approximately 10 to 15 minutes, or until it is smooth and elastic (add more flour if necessary). Form the dough into a ball and place it in a well-buttered large bowl and roll the ball over so that all sides have touched the butter.

7. Cover the bowl with a turkish towel and let it rise in a warm draft-free place (85° to 90°) for approximately 50 minutes, or until double in bulk (see Note).

8. While the dough is rising, melt the butter in a medium-size skillet over a low-medium flame. Add the parsley, green onions, and garlic and sauté until the green onions have slightly wilted, stirring constantly. Add the oregano, tarragon, curry powder, cumin, sweet basil, dill, cayenne, white pepper, mustard, sugar, and the eggs. Sauté until all the ingredients are thoroughly blended (about 2 to 3 minutes) and remove from the flame. (Make sure you stir this constantly.)

9. Punch the dough down and turn it out onto a board and let it rest (covered with wax paper) for 10 minutes.

10. Cut the dough in half and shape each half into a ball. Roll out each ball into a rectangle ¼ inch thick by 8¾ inches wide.

11. Divide the filling into two parts and spread one part of the filling onto each rectangle to within ½ inch of the edges.

12. Tightly roll each rectangle (jelly-roll fashion) and place each one, seam side down, into a well-buttered loaf pan (1 by 5 by 3 inches), tucking the ends under, if necessary.

13. Cover the pans with a turkish towel and let the dough rise until double in bulk in a warm draft-free place (85°) for approximately 40 to 50 minutes (see Note).

14. Preheat the oven to 375°.

15. Brush the loaves with the egg yolk mixture and bake for 1 hour and 10 minutes to 1 hour and 20 minutes, or until the loaves are a dark golden brown and sound hollow when tapped with the fingertips.

16. Turn out the bread onto wire racks to cool thoroughly.

NOTE: Instead of using a turkish towel, place the bowl in a large, clean plastic bag. Allow enough room for expansion and seal the bag. Proceed as above.

Cheese Souffle Bread

Makes 2 round loaves

Unusual and delicious, especially during the cold winter months.

1 1/2 cups scalded milk (or low sodium dry milk)

2 tablespoons honey

1/8 teaspoon cayenne

1/2 teaspoon dry mustard

1/2 teaspoon freshly ground white pepper

2 teaspoons seasoned salt substitute (optional)

1/4 cup sweet butter, cut into pieces

1/4 teaspoon powdered saffron

1 cup lukewarm water (110°)

3 packages active dry yeast

1 1/2 teaspoons honey

6 cups sifted unbleached flour

12 to 16 ounces salt-free Cheddar cheese, grated

1 egg yolk, lightly beaten with 1 teaspoon cold water

1. To the saucepan in which you scalded the milk add the 2 table-spoons of honey, cayenne, mustard, pepper, salt substitute, butter, and saffron. Using a wooden spoon, stir until the butter has melted. Then let the mixture cool to lukewarm (110° approximately).

2. Place the lukewarm water in a large, warm mixing bowl (rinse the bowl in very hot water and then dry it thoroughly) and sprinkle in the yeast and the 1 1/2 teaspoons of honey. Stir well to dissolve. Let it stand in a warm place for 5 minutes, or until the yeast is well blended with the water and honey.

3. Using an electric mixer on low speed, beat the yeast mixture and slowly add the milk mixture. Turn the beater up to low-medium and add 3 cups of the flour, a little at a time. Beat until all the flour is absorbed and the dough is smooth.

4. Add the cheese, a little at a time, beating on medium speed until all the ingredients are totally blended.

5. Stir in the remaining flour, a little at a time, with a wooden spoon, until a soft dough is formed. Let the dough rest for 12 to 15 minutes.

6. Turn the dough out onto a lightly floured board and knead until it is smooth and elastic (about 10 to 12 minutes).

7. Form the dough into a ball and place it in a well-buttered bowl. Roll the dough over so that the butter touches all sides of the ball. Cover the bowl with a turkish towel and let the dough rise in a warm draft-free place (85°) until double in bulk (about 50 to 55 minutes). (See Note.)

8. Punch the dough down, turn it out into a lightly floured board, and knead it lightly for 2 minutes.

9. Cut the dough in half and shape it into two balls. Place each ball in a well-greased 2-quart soufflé dish. Brush the dough well with melted butter and cover with a turkish towel. Allow the dough to rise in a warm draft-free place (85°) until it has doubled in bulk, approximately 45 to 55 minutes.

10. Preheat the oven to 400°.

11. Brush the loaves with the egg yolk mixture and bake 55 to 65 minutes, or until they are a dark golden brown and sound hollow when tapped with the fingertips.

12. Turn onto a wire rack to cool.

NOTE: Instead of using a turkish towel, place the bowl in a large, clean plastic bag. Allow enough room for expansion and seal the bag. Proceed as above.

Pita Bread

Makes 20

2 packages active dry yeast
2½ cups lukewarm water (110°)
2 teaspoons honey
1 to 1½ teaspoons dry mustard
1 teaspoon freshly ground white pepper
2½ teaspoons salt substitute (optional)
1½ tablespoons garlic powder
2 tablespoons onion powder
6¾ cups unsifted unbleached flour

1. Put the yeast in a large mixing bowl. Pour in the water and honey and stir well. Let the mixture stand 5 to 8 minutes, or until the yeast has blended with the other ingredients.

2. Using an electric mixer on low speed, beat the mustard, pepper, salt substitute, garlic powder, and onion powder into the yeast mixture. Then beat in 5¼ cups of the flour, a little at a time, or until a soft dough is formed.

3. Place the remaining flour on a board in a small mound and make a well in the center. Place the soft dough in the well and knead all the dough for 12 to 18 minutes, or until it forms a clean and firm dough. Shape the dough into a ball.

4. Place the dough in a well-buttered bowl and roll the ball around so that all sides are buttered. Cover the bowl with a turkish towel and let rise in a warm draft-free place (80° to 85°) for 40 minutes or until double in bulk (see Note).

5. Punch the dough down and turn it out onto a board. Knead it for 7 to 8 minutes and return it to the bowl. Cover it again with the towel and let it rise, once again in a warm draft-free place, until double in bulk (approximately 30 minutes). (See Note.)

6. Roll the dough out to approximately 4 by 20 inches and divide it into 20 equal parts.

7. Butter two or three baking sheets well.

8. Preheat the oven to 500°.

9. Press each part of the dough between the palms of your hands to form a circle of approximately 3½ to 4 inches in diameter by ¼ to ⅜ inch thick.

10. Place the dough "patties" on the baking sheets 3 inches apart and bake for 10 to 12 minutes, or until a light golden color and puffed.

11. Remove the pita to wire racks, cool for 10 minutes, and then slice them three fourths through horizontally to form a pocket for your filling.

NOTE: Instead of using a turkish towel, place the bowl in a large, clean plastic bag. Allow enough room for the dough to expand and seal the bag. Proceed as above.

Street Corner Garlic Pretzels

Makes 12 pretzels

These are similar to the pretzels you can buy on New York street corners in the freezing winter months, but without the salt. They will evoke an image of the vendor selling his pretzels and chestnuts to the rushing and hungry passers-by.

2 cups unbleached flour
2 cups stone-ground wheat flour
1 package active dry yeast
2½ teaspoons garlic powder
¾ teaspoon freshly ground white pepper
1 teaspoon salt substitute (optional)

½ to ¾ teaspoon dry mustard (optional)
2½ teaspoons onion powder
1⅓ cups water
3 tablespoons corn oil
1½ tablespoons honey
¼ cup dried minced onion mixed with ¼ cup dry garlic flakes

1. Combine the flours.

2. To 1½ cups of the flour mixture add the yeast, garlic powder, white pepper, salt substitute, dry mustard, and onion powder.

3. Heat the water in a small heavy saucepan over a medium flame to warm (about 125°). Remove it from the flame and stir in the oil and honey.

4. Add the warm liquid to the flour and herb mixture and, using an electric mixer on medium speed, beat for 3 minutes.

5. Add enough additional flour to make a fairly stiff dough.

6. Preheat the oven to 400°.

7. Knead the dough until it is smooth (about 5 to 6 minutes) and cut it into 12 equal pieces.

8. Roll each piece into a 16-inch rope and roll in combined minced onion and garlic flakes. Shape each rope into a pretzel.

9. Butter two baking sheets well.

10. Place the pretzels on the baking sheets and bake 25 to 30 minutes, or until lightly browned.

11. Turn the pretzels onto a wire rack to cool.

Herb Bagels

Makes 12

Our friends say they like these bagels better than any they have purchased. I hope they are telling me the truth.

2 packages active dry yeast
4¼ to 4½ cups sifted unbleached flour
1½ cups likewarm water (100°), mixed with
3 tablespoons sugar (or substitute equivalent)
2 tablespoons minced fresh chives
1¼ tablespoons minced fresh dill
1 teaspoon dry mustard

2 teaspoons onion powder
1 teaspoon dried oregano
1½ teaspoons garlic powder
1 teaspoon freshly ground white pepper
1½ teaspoons salt substitute (optional)
1 teaspoon dried sweet basil
1 gallon water
1 tablespoon sugar (or substitute equivalent)

1. In a large mixing bowl combine the yeast and 2 cups of the flour. Mix well.

2. Using an electric beater on low-medium speed, slowly add the sugar-water mixture and beat for 1 minute. Beat in the chives, dill, mustard, onion powder, oregano, garlic powder, pepper, salt substitute, and basil, scraping the sides of the bowl constantly with a rubber spatula. Turn the speed up to high and beat for 4 minutes more, still scraping the sides of the bowl.

3. Stir in enough of the remaining flour to make a moderately stiff dough. Turn the dough out onto a lightly floured board and knead until the dough is smooth (about 7 to 10 minutes).

4. Cover the dough with a turkish towel and set it in a warm draft-free place (about 85°) for 15 minutes.

5. Cut the dough into 12 equal portions and, with the palms of your hands, roll each piece into a smooth ball.

6. Punch a hole in the center of each ball and pull the dough gently to enlarge the hole (should look like a doughnut).

7. Place the bagels back on the board and cover them with the turkish towel. Put the bagels in a warm draft-free place and let them rise 20 minutes.

8. While the bagels are rising, place the 1 gallon of water, with 1 tablespoon of sugar, in a large heavy pot and bring it to a rolling boil over a high flame. Turn the flame to medium-low and let the water simmer.

9. With a large slotted spoon or Chinese strainer place 4 bagels in the water and simmer for 4 minutes. Turn the bagels and simmer 4 more minutes. Remove them with the slotted spoon or Chinese strainer and drain the bagels on double layers of paper towels. Working in this manner, cook all of the bagels.

10. Preheat the oven to 375°.

11. Arrange the bagels on an ungreased cookie sheet and bake for 30 to 35 minutes, or until the bagels are well browned.

12. Remove to a wire rack to cool.

Quick and Easy Pumpernickel Bread
(no kneading)

Makes 1 loaf

1½ cups unbleached flour
2 packages active dry yeast
1½ teaspoons finely ground black pepper
2 teaspoons seasoned salt substitute (optional)
1½ teaspoons dry mustard (optional)
1½ tablespoons instant coffee
3 tablespoons caraway seeds

¼ cup molasses
¾ cup water
1 cup milk (or low sodium dry milk)
¼ cup corn oil
1 egg
2½ cups rye flour
½ to 1½ cups unbleached white flour

1. In a large mixing bowl combine the 1½ cups unbleached flour, yeast, pepper, salt substitute, mustard, coffee, caraway seeds, and molasses.
2. In a small heavy saucepan, over a low flame, heat the water, milk, and corn oil to warm (approximately 125°).
3. Using an electric mixer on low speed, slowly add the milk mixture to the flour mixture until all the milk is thoroughly absorbed. Then beat in the egg. Turn the speed to medium-high and beat for 4 minutes.
4. Stir in the rye flour with a wooden spoon and then add enough of the unbleached white flour to make a stiff dough.
5. Cover the dough with a turkish towel and let it rise in a warm draft-free place (85°) for 30 minutes (see Note).
6. While the dough is rising, butter and lightly flour a loaf pan (9 by 5 by 3 inches).
7. When the dough has risen, spoon it into the metal pan. Cover with the turkish towel and let it rise again for 18 minutes (at no time should the dough double in size).
8. Preheat the oven to 375°.
9. Bake the bread for 45 to 55 minutes, or until it is well browned and sounds hollow when lightly tapped with the fingertips.
10. Turn the bread out onto a wire rack to cool well before serving.

NOTE: Instead of using a turkish towel, place the bowl in a large, clean plastic bag. Allow enough room for expansion and seal the bag. Proceed as above.

Crusty Peasant Rye Bread
(no kneading)

Makes 1 loaf

It's easy to make and wonderful to eat. How's that for an unbeatable combination?

2½ cups rye flour
3 cups unbleached flour
2 packages active dry yeast
¾ teaspoon freshly ground black pepper
2 teaspoons seasoned salt substitute (optional)
1 teaspoon dry mustard (optional)

¼ cup brown sugar, tightly packed (or substitute equivalent)
2 tablespoons honey
4 to 5 teaspoons caraway seeds
2 tablespoons corn oil
1 cup milk (or low sodium dry milk)
1 cup water

1. Combine the rye flour and the unbleached flour.

2. In a large mixing bowl thoroughly blend 1½ cups of the flour mixture with the yeast, pepper, salt substitute, mustard, brown sugar, honey, and caraway seeds.

3. In a heavy saucepan, over a low flame, heat the oil, milk, and water to warm (approximately 125°) and stir well.

4. Using an electric mixer on low-medium speed, slowly add the milk mixture to the flour-yeast mixture, beating for 3 minutes, while scraping the sides of the bowl with a rubber spatula.

5. Slowly add ¾ cup of the remaining flour while still beating at low-medium speed. Increase the speed to high and beat 3 minutes more.

6. Stir in enough of the remaining flour mixture to make a stiff dough.

7. Cover the dough with a turkish towel, put it in a warm draft-free place (approximately 85°) and let the dough rise until double in bulk (approximately 45 minutes). (See Note.)

8. Preheat the oven to 375°.

9. Spoon the dough into a well-buttered and lightly floured loaf pan (9 by 5 by 3 inches). Bake 40 to 45 minutes, or until the crust is well browned.

10. Turn the bread out onto a metal rack and allow to cool at least 45 minutes before serving.

NOTE: Instead of using a turkish towel, place the bowl in a large, clean plastic bag. Allow enough room for expansion and seal the bag. Proceed as above.

Round Herb Rye Bread
(no kneading)

Makes 1 loaf

If you like your rye bread in the round . . .

1½ cups unbleached flour
¼ cup sugar (or substitute equivalent)
2 packages active dry yeast
1 teaspoon freshly ground black pepper
2 teaspoons seasoned salt substitute (optional)
1 teaspoon dry mustard
1 teaspoon cumin
2 teaspoons dried chives
2 teaspoons onion powder
1 teaspoon garlic powder
1½ teaspoons dried dill weed

½ teaspoon dried sweet basil
2½ tablespoons caraway seeds
1 cup water
1 cup milk (or low sodium dry milk)
¼ cup corn oil
1 egg
2½ cups rye flour
¼ to ½ cup unbleached white flour
1 egg lightly beaten with 1 tablespoon water
1 tablespoon caraway seeds

1. In a large mixing bowl blend the 1½ cups of unbleached flour, sugar, yeast, pepper, salt substitute, mustard, cumin, chives, onion powder, garlic powder, dill, sweet basil, and 2½ tablespoons of caraway seeds.

2. In a small heavy saucepan, over a low flame, heat the water, milk, and corn oil to warm (approximately 125°).

3. Using an electric mixer on low speed, slowly add the milk mixture to the flour mixture until all the milk is thoroughly absorbed. Then beat in the egg. Turn the speed to medium-high and beat for 4 minutes.

4. Stir in the rye flour with a wooden spoon. Then add enough of the remaining unbleached white flour to make a stiff dough.

5. Cover the dough with a turkish towel and let it rise in a warm draft-free place (85°) for 30 minutes (see Note).

6. While the dough is rising, butter and lightly flour a 9-inch round metal pan.

7. When the dough has risen, spoon it into the metal pan. Cover it with the turkish towel and let it rise again in a warm draft-free place for 18 minutes (at no time should the dough double in size).

8. Preheat the oven to 375°.

9. Brush the bread with the egg mixture and sprinkle the 1 tablespoon of caraway seeds on top.

10. Bake the bread for 45 to 55 minutes, or until it is a deep golden brown and sounds hollow when lightly tapped with the fingertips.

11. Turn the bread out onto a wire rack and cool it well before serving.

NOTE: Instead of using a turkish towel, place the bowl in a large, clean plastic bag. Allow enough room for expansion and seal the bag. Proceed as above.

Whole Wheat Cinnamon Nut Bread
(no kneading)

Makes 2 loaves or 38 to 60 slices of toast

A perfect toast for brunch or afternoon coffee or tea.

2 cups stone-ground whole wheat flour

1 cup unbleached flour

1½ teaspoons salt-free baking powder

4 eggs, plus 1 egg yolk

1 cup corn oil

1 tablespoon cinnamon

2 teaspoons finely grated orange peel

2 teaspoons finely grated lemon peel

1-inch piece ginger root, finely grated

1½ teaspoons vanilla

¾ cup brown sugar, tightly packed

1¼ cup chopped walnuts

1. Preheat the oven to 350°.

2. In a mixing bowl combine the whole wheat and unbleached flour with the baking powder.

3. In a large mixing bowl, using an electric mixer on low-medium speed, beat the eggs, yolk, oil, cinnamon, orange and lemon peel, ginger, and vanilla until slightly frothy. Slowly add the sugar, increasing the speed to medium. Beat in the flour mixture, a little at a time, until all the ingredients are blended.

4. Stir the walnuts into the dough.

5. Spoon the dough into two well-buttered and lightly floured loaf pans (8 by 4 by 2 inches) and bake for 45 to 55 minutes, or until the loaves are a deep golden brown and sound hollow when tapped with the fingertips.

6. Cool in the pans for 10 minutes, then turn the bread out onto wire racks and cool thoroughly about 25 to 30 minutes.

TO MAKE WHOLE WHEAT TOAST:

1. Preheat the oven to 350°.

2. Cut the bread into $1/4$ to $3/8$-inch slices and place on ungreased baking sheets. Bake for 12 to 15 minutes or until golden brown. Turn the slices and bake 10 to 12 minutes more.

3. Cool the toast for 45 minutes, then place the slices in a double plastic bag and seal tightly.

NOTE: This toast will last for many, many weeks if stored properly.

Apple Cheese Bread

Makes 1 loaf

For morning and afternoon tea or coffee.

$2^1/2$ cups sifted unbleached flour
1 tablespoon salt-free baking
    powder
$3/4$ cup sweet butter, at room
    temperature
$1/2$ cup brown sugar, tightly
    packed
4 eggs, plus 1 egg yolk
2 teaspoons cinnamon
$1/8$ to $1/4$ teaspoon cayenne
$1/2$ to 1 teaspoon cumin
$1^1/2$ teaspoons grated orange
    rind (optional)

1 teaspoon grated lemon rind
    (optional)
$1/2$ to 1 teaspoon dry mustard
$1/2$ teaspoon freshly ground
    white pepper
$1^1/2$ cups tart green apples,
    seeded, unpeeled, grated,
    and with their own juice
1 cup grated salt-free Cheddar
    cheese
$3/4$ cup chopped walnuts

1. Preheat the oven to 375°.

2. Sift the flour and baking powder together.

3. Using an electric mixer on low-medium speed, cream the butter and slowly add the brown sugar until the mixture is light and fluffy. Turning the speed to medium, add the eggs, and the yolk one at a time, beating well after each addition.

4. Beat in the cinnamon, cayenne, cumin, orange and lemon rinds, dry mustard, and pepper. When all is thoroughly blended, beat in the apples, cheese, and walnuts.

5. Beat in the flour mixture, a little at a time, until all the flour is dampened, taking care not to overbeat.

6. Pour the batter into a well-buttered and lightly floured loaf pan (9 by 5 by 3 inches). Push the batter up into the corners, leaving a light indentation in the center, and bake for 1 hour and 15 minutes to 1 hour and 25 minutes, or until a toothpick inserted in the center of the bread comes out clean.

7. Turn the bread out onto a wire rack and allow it to cool at least 45 minutes to an hour before serving.

Apricot Banana Bread

Makes 1 loaf

A delectable dessert bread.

1¾ cups sifted unbleached flour
1 tablespoon salt-free baking
  powder
1 teaspoon cinnamon
⅓ cup sweet butter, at room
  temperature
½ cup sugar, plus 2 tablespoons
  (or substitute equivalent)

2 eggs, well beaten
1½ cups mashed ripe bananas,
  sprinkled with
2 teaspoons lemon juice
1 cup chopped dried apricots
1 cup chopped walnuts

1. Preheat the oven to 350°.

2. Sift together the flour, baking powder, and cinnamon.

3. Using an electric mixer on low-medium speed, cream the butter until smooth, then add the sugar, a little at a time, and beat until the mixture is light and fluffy.

4. Add the eggs, one at a time, beating well after each addition.

5. In a separate bowl mix together the bananas, apricots, and walnuts. Beating the egg mixture on low-medium speed, add the flour mixture, a little at a time, alternating with the fruit and nut mixture, until all the ingredients are thoroughly blended and the batter is smooth.

6. Pour the batter into a well-buttered and slightly floured pan (8½ by 4½ by 3 inches) and bake 1 hour and 5 minutes to 1 hour and 15 minutes, or until a toothpick inserted into the center comes out clean.

7. Turn out onto a wire rack and allow to cool 45 minutes to an hour before serving.

Zucchini Bread

Makes 2 loaves

One summer a friend of ours grew zucchini in great abundance. We cooked and baked everything imaginable with it . . . including this bread.

3 eggs, plus 1 egg yolk
1 cup honey
1 cup corn oil
1 tablespoon vanilla
2 cups coarsely grated zucchini, with skin
2 cups unbleached flour
1 tablespoon cinnamon
1 teaspoon powdered ginger (optional)

$^1/_8$ teaspoon cayenne
2 teaspoons grated lemon rind (optional)
$8^1/_4$ teaspoons salt-free baking powder
$^1/_8$ teaspoon freshly grated nutmeg (optional)
$1^1/_2$ cups chopped walnuts

1. Preheat the oven to 375°.
2. Sift flour with cinnamon, ginger, and cayenne.
3. Using an electric mixer on low-medium speed, beat the eggs until frothy, then slowly beat in the honey, oil, and vanilla.
4. Stir in the zucchini, flour mixture, lemon rind, baking powder, and nutmeg, a little at a time. Stir in the walnuts.
5. Pour the batter into two well-buttered and lightly floured pans ($8^1/_2$ by $4^1/_2$ by 3 inches) and bake for 1 hour to 1 hour and 10 minutes, or until a toothpick inserted into the center of the bread comes out clean.
6. Turn the bread out onto wire racks and cool for at least 1 hour before serving.

Melba Toast

1 loaf frozen Crusty Peasant Rye Bread* or Round Herb Rye Bread*; Russian Black Bread* or Challah*; White Bread* or French Bread.*

1. Defrost the bread until it is three fourths defrosted. (It will still be very cold and quite hard.)
2. Preheat the broiler to 500°.

3. With a razor-sharp bread knife, slice the bread into paper-thin slices.

4. Place the slices on an unbuttered cookie sheet and broil 4 to 5 inches from the flame until the slices are well toasted and then turn and toast the other side. Remove and cool thoroughly.

5. Place the toast in double thickness of plastic bags and seal tightly.

NOTE: Toast will keep for many weeks if it is in an airtight container (or sealed double plastic bags) and kept in a cool dry place.

Thin Garlic Herb Toast

Serves 8 to 16, depending on your customers

16 very thin slices White Bread*
   or French Bread*
6 tablespoons sweet butter, sof-
   tened
5 cloves garlic, pressed
2 tablespoons finely minced
   fresh chives

1 tablespoon finely minced fresh
   parsley
¹/₈ teaspoon cayenne
¹/₄ teaspoon paprika

1. Preheat the oven to 350°.

2. Place the bread on a lightly buttered cookie sheet and toast in the oven on one side.

3. While the bread is toasting, cream the butter with the garlic, chives, parsley, cayenne, and paprika.

4. When the bread has toasted on one side, turn it over and spread the garlic herb butter evenly over each piece.

5. Return the bread to the oven for 3 minutes.

6. Preheat the broiler to 350°.

7. Place the bread under the broiler about 5 inches from the flame and broil until toasted and the butter mixture is bubbly.

Serving: Slice each piece of toast diagonally, place it in a napkin-lined basket, and serve at once.

NOTE: For Thin Garlic Toast* simply eliminate the chives and parsley.

Garlic Croutons

Makes 3 cups

½ cup Clarified Butter* or corn oil
5 cloves garlic, pressed

3 cups White Bread,* crusts removed and cut into ½-inch cubes

1. In a medium-size skillet melt the clarified butter or heat the oil over a low-medium flame and add the garlic. Stir well and sauté for 2 minutes, taking care that the garlic does not burn.
2. Turn the flame up to medium, add the bread cubes, and brown on all sides, stirring gently.
3. Drain on paper towels.

Bread Crumbs

1. Place stale White Bread* slices in a 250° oven for 10 minutes, or until thoroughly dry and crisp.
2. Break up the slices into small pieces and pulverize them into crumbs, using either a blender on medium speed or a food processor with the steel blade.

NOTE: To prevent mold, place the crumbs in a glass jar covered with triple thickness of cheesecloth secured with a rubber band. (This is an old-fashioned method but it works very well.)

Crackers

GENERAL RULES

Crackers are simple to make and similar in technique to piecrusts. Therefore, if you take the following precautions and helpful hints, your crackers will be both easy and successful.

1. Refrigerate your dough balls overnight.

2. If you use a pastry slab to roll out the dough, such as plastic or marble, place it in the freezer for 5 minutes or the refrigerator for 1/2 hour. Then lightly flour it. (If using a pastry cloth, flour it well.)

3. Make sure you roll your cracker dough in a very cool place.

4. Use a well-floured pastry stocking on your rolling pin.

5. Roll the dough in one direction, away from you, and lift the pin after each roll. Do not roll it back and forth.

6. Try a pizza cutter to cut your cracker shapes.

7. Since the dough must be very thin, care should be taken that the crackers do not burn in the oven. Watch them carefully during the last few minutes.

8. Make sure the crackers are cold, crisp, and dry before storing them in airtight jars or tins.

Poppy or Sesame Seed Crackers

Makes approximately 55 crackers

1/4 cup soy flour
1 1/2 cups unbleached flour
3 teaspoons salt-free baking powder
1 teaspoon salt substitute (optional)
1/2 teaspoon freshly ground white pepper

1/4 cup wheat germ
1 cup sweet butter, at room temperature, cut into tiny pieces
5 tablespoons cold milk (or low sodium dry milk)
1 egg white, slightly beaten
Poppy or sesame seeds

1. Sift the soy flour, unbleached flour, baking powder, salt substitute, and pepper together into a large mixing bowl. Stir in the wheat germ.

2. Cut the butter into the dough with a pastry blender.

3. Add the milk, a little at a time, while mixing vigorously with a wooden spoon until all the milk is absorbed. (This makes a very soft dough.)

4. Divide the dough into two balls. Wrap them tightly in wax paper and refrigerate at least 10 hours (preferably overnight).

5. Preheat the oven to 400°.

6. Lightly butter the baking sheets.

7. Roll out the dough (see general rules for crackers) ⅛ inch thick.

8. Cut the dough into squares, triangles, or diamond shapes (all shapes approximately 1½ inches) and brush with the egg white. Sprinkle on either the poppy or sesame seeds. Transfer the crackers to baking sheets, allowing 1½ inches between crackers.

9. Bake for 10 to 12 minutes, or until golden.

Cheese Rye Crackers

Makes approximately 60 crackers.

⅔ cup unbleached flour
1¼ tablespoons soy flour
¾ cup rye flour
2 to 3 tablespoons caraway seeds
1 teaspoon freshly ground black pepper
1 teaspoon salt-free chili powder
⅛ teaspoon cayenne
⅔ cup grated salt-free Swiss or Gouda cheese

6 tablespoons sweet butter at room temperature, cut into tiny pieces
2 tablespoons vegetable shortening
3½ to 4½ tablespoons ice water
1 egg white, lightly beaten

1. In a large mixing bowl thoroughly mix the unbleached flour, soy flour, rye flour, caraway seeds, pepper, chili powder, and cayenne.

2. Add the cheese, butter, and vegetable shortening a little at a time. Using an electric mixer on low speed, blend thoroughly.

3. Continuing to beat, add 3½ tablespoons of ice water, 1 tablespoon at a time, until the dough forms a ball. If necessary, add more ice water.

4. Divide the dough into two balls, wrap tightly in wax paper, and refrigerate overnight.

5. Preheat the oven to 350°.

6. Roll out each ball (see general rules for crackers) ⅛ inch thick and cut into diamonds or squares approximately 1½ inches in diameter. Brush tops with egg white.

7. Transfer to unbuttered baking sheets, allowing 1½ inches between crackers, and bake for 10 minutes, or until crisp and golden.

Garlic Dill Crackers

Makes approximately 55 crackers

1 cup unbleached flour, plus 1 tablespoon
¾ cup rye flour
3 teaspoons salt-free baking powder
1 teaspoon salt substitute (optional)
¾ teaspoon freshly ground black pepper
⅛ to ¼ teaspoon cayenne
2½ teaspoons garlic powder

1 teaspoon dry mustard (optional)
¼ cup wheat germ
2 teaspoons dried dill weed
2 to 4 teaspoons caraway seeds
1 cup sweet butter at room temperature, cut into tiny pieces
6 tablespoons cold milk (or low sodium dry milk)

1. Sift the unbleached flour, rye flour, baking powder, salt substitute, pepper, cayenne, garlic powder, and mustard together into a large mixing bowl.

2. Stir in the wheat germ, dill, and caraway seeds.

3. Cut the butter into the dough with a pastry blender.

4. Add the milk, a little at a time, while mixing vigorously with a wooden spoon until all the milk is absorbed. (This makes a soft dough.)

5. Divide the dough into two balls and wrap tightly in wax paper. Refrigerate overnight.

6. Preheat the oven to 400°.

7. Lightly butter baking sheets.

8. Roll out the dough (see general rules for crackers) ⅛ inch thick.

9. Cut the dough into squares, triangles, or diamond shapes (all shapes approximately 1½ inches).

10. Transfer the crackers to baking sheets, allowing 1½ inches between crackers. Bake for 10 to 12 minutes, or until golden.

Tangy Cheese and Nut Crackers

Makes approximately 48
crackers

²/₃ cup unbleached flour
1¹/₄ tablespoons soy flour
¹/₄ cup wheat germ
1 teaspoon freshly ground white
　　pepper
¹/₈ teaspoon cayenne
1¹/₂ teaspoons dry mustard
1 teaspoon garlic powder
¹/₃ cup sweet butter at room
　　temperature, cut into small
　　pieces

1¹/₂ cups grated salt-free Gouda
　　or salt-free Swiss cheese
¹/₂ cup finely chopped walnuts
　　or pecans
¹/₄ cup finely minced onion
2 teaspoons dried chives

1. In a large bowl combine the unbleached flour, soy flour, wheat germ, pepper, cayenne, mustard, and garlic powder. Mix well.
2. Using a pastry cutter, cut the butter into the flour mixture.
3. Mix in the cheese, nuts, onion, and chives.
4. Form the dough into a ball.
5. Divide the ball in half and shape each half into a log 1¹/₂ by about 7 inches long.
6. Wrap tightly in wax paper and refrigerate overnight.
7. Preheat the oven to 350°.
8. Lightly butter the baking sheets.
9. Using a razor-sharp serrated knife, slice the logs into ¹/₄-inch rounds and transfer to the baking sheets, allowing 1¹/₂ inches between crackers.
10. Bake for 12 to 14 minutes, or until a light golden brown.

Basic Muffins

Makes 12 muffins

2 cups unbleached flour
4 teaspoons salt-free baking
　　powder
¹/₄ to ¹/₃ cup sugar (or substitute
　　equivalent)

2 eggs
3¹/₂ tablespoons sweet butter,
　　melted
³/₄ cup milk (or low sodium dry
　　milk)

1. Preheat the oven to 350°.

2. If using muffin tins, butter lightly. If using paper muffin cups, arrange them in the muffin tins.

3. Combine the flour, baking powder, and sugar. Sift together into a large mixing bowl.

4. Using an electric mixer on medium speed, beat the eggs for 1½ minutes, then beat in the melted butter and milk.

5. Stir the egg mixture into the flour mixture, taking care to stir only until all ingredients are thoroughly moistened. This will be a lumpy batter and should not be overstirred.

6. Ladle the batter into the muffin tins (or cups) two thirds full.

7. Bake for 15 to 20 minutes, or until a toothpick inserted in the center comes out clean and the muffins are golden brown.

8. Turn the muffins out onto a wire rack to cool.

NOTE: To create a variety of muffins from this basic recipe:

1. *Fruit and nut muffins* (makes 12 to 14): Substitute orange or pineapple juice for the milk and add ½ cup chopped walnuts to the flour mixture before stirring in the egg mixture.

2. *Blueberry muffins* (makes 15 to 16): Add 1 cup floured blueberries to the batter before ladling into the muffin tins. As above, you may substitute fruit juice for the milk.

3. *Corn muffins* (makes 12): Use 1 cup unbleached flour and ¾ cup cornmeal instead of 2 cups flour, and proceed with basic muffin recipe.

Apricot Prune Muffins

Makes 15 to 18 muffins

¼ cup sweet butter, at room temperature

⅓ cup brown sugar, tightly packed

1 egg

1¾ cups sifted unbleached flour

4½ teaspoons salt-free baking powder

1 cup freshly squeezed orange juice

½ cup milk (or low sodium dry milk)

⅓ cup finely chopped Cooked Prunes* (well drained)

⅓ cup finely chopped Cooked Apricots* (well drained)

1. Preheat the oven to 400°.

2. If using muffin tins, butter lightly. If using paper muffin cups, place them in the muffin tins.

3. Using an electric mixer on low speed, cream the butter and sugar together. Beat in the egg.

4. Sift the flour (second sifting) and the baking powder together.

5. Add one third of the flour mixture to the butter mixture, then one third of the orange juice, then one third of the milk, stirring in the ingredients with a wooden spoon (DO NOT BEAT). Continue alternating the ingredients until all are blended, taking care not to overstir.

6. Fold in the prunes and apricots and ladle the mixture into the muffin tins (or cups) two thirds full.

7. Bake for 25 minutes, or until a toothpick inserted into the center of a muffin comes out clean and the muffins are golden brown.

8. Turn out onto a wire rack to cool.

Bran Walnut Muffins

Makes 18 muffins

2 cups sifted unbleached flour
6 teaspoons salt-free baking
   powder
2 cups coarse bran
¾ cup chopped walnuts
2 tablespoons sweet butter,
   melted

2 eggs, well beaten
½ cup honey (or more to taste)
1½ cups milk (or low sodium
   dry milk)

1. Preheat the oven to 350°.

2. If using muffin tins, butter lightly. If using paper muffin cups, place them in the muffin tins.

3. Sift the flour (second sifting) together with the baking powder.

4. Stir in the bran and the walnuts.

5. In another bowl, combine the butter, eggs, honey, and milk.

6. Stir the milk mixture into the flour-bran mixture with a wooden spoon, stirring only until the ingredients are mixed (no flour showing). Do not overstir.

7. Ladle the muffin mixture into the muffin tins (or cups) two thirds full and bake for 20 minutes, or until a toothpick inserted into the center comes out clean and the muffins are golden brown.

8. Turn the muffins out onto a wire rack to cool.

Raisin Rice Muffins

Makes 30 muffins

2 egg yolks
1 cup Boiled Rice*
1¼ cups milk (or low sodium
   dry milk)
2 tablespoons sweet butter,
   melted
1½ cups sifted unbleached flour
5 tablespoons sugar (or substitute equivalent)

½ teaspoon freshly grated nutmeg
2 to 3 teaspoons cinnamon
4½ teaspoons salt-free baking
   powder
1 cup raisins, lightly floured
2 egg whites

1. Preheat the oven to 350°.
2. Grease the muffin tins well with the vegetable shortening and heat for 10 minutes.
3. Beat the egg yolks with a wire whisk and stir in the rice, milk, and butter.
4. Sift together the flour (second sifting), sugar, nutmeg, cinnamon, and baking powder.
5. Stir the raisins into the rice mixture. Stir in the flour mixture only until all ingredients are blended and no flour shows. Do not overstir.
6. Using an electric mixer on high speed, beat the egg whites until stiff, then fold them into the muffin batter.
7. Ladle the batter into the muffin tins two thirds full and bake for 25 to 30 minutes, or until a toothpick inserted into the center comes out clean and the muffins are a deep golden brown.
8. Turn the muffins out onto a wire rack to cool.

Apple Bread Stuffing

For a 12-pound turkey, or approximately 2 quarts of stuffing

3½ tablespoons sweet butter
3 cloves garlic, finely minced
1½ cups chopped onions
3 cups tart green apples, pared, seeded, and cut into ½-inch cubes
4 cups White Bread,* crusts removed and cut into ½-inch cubes
¾ cup melted sweet butter

1 cup coarsely chopped walnuts
2 to 3 teaspoons freshly squeezed lemon juice
1 tablespoon brown sugar (or substitute equivalent)
1 teaspoon freshly ground white pepper
¼ teaspoon freshly grated nutmeg
1½ teaspoons cinnamon

1. In a large heavy skillet melt the 3½ tablespoons butter over a medium flame. Sauté the garlic and onions until the onions are translucent.

2. Remove the skillet from the flame. Stir in the apples, bread cubes, melted butter, walnuts, lemon juice, brown sugar, pepper, nutmeg, and cinnamon.

NOTE: You may either stuff the turkey with this or butter a 2-quart ovenproof casserole, cover, and bake at 300° for 20 minutes. Uncover and bake for 10 to 15 minutes, or until piping hot.

Apricot Prune Almond and Apple Stuffing

For a 25-pound bird

2 cups dried apricots
3 cups dried pitted prunes
2 cups dry red wine
2 cups water
3 tablespoons brown sugar (or substitute equivalent)
3 tablespoons Clarified Butter*
1 very large onion, finely minced

2 cups blanched almonds
3 cups apples, peeled, cored, and cut into ½- to 1-inch cubes
6 tablespoons lemon juice
½ cup of honey (heated until it is liquefied)
6 cups Boiled Rice* (see Note)

6 cups Bread Crumbs* (see
    Note)
3 well-beaten eggs
1/4 to 1/3 teaspoon cayenne

1 teaspoon freshly ground black
    pepper
2 teaspoons paprika
1 cup melted butter

1. Place the apricots, prunes, red wine, water, and brown sugar in a heavy saucepan. Bring it to a boil over a medium flame and then reduce the flame to low and simmer for 10 minutes.

2. In the meantime, in a heavy skillet melt the clarified butter over a medium flame and sauté the onion until light gold.

3. Add the almonds and sauté for 2 minutes, stirring constantly.

4. Remove from heat and transfer the onion-almond mixture to an 8-quart mixing bowl or pot.

5. Add the apples, lemon juice, and honey, a little at a time, and lightly toss after each addition.

6. Toss in the rice and the bread crumbs.

7. By now the apricots and prunes should be finished; drain them, *reserving the juice,* and chop very coarsely. Add them to the stuffing mixture.

8. To the beaten eggs add the cayenne, pepper, and paprika. Add to the stuffing mixture, stirring until well blended.

9. Add the melted butter a little at a time and stir it into the stuffing mixture until it is all absorbed.

10. If the stuffing is too dry add a little of the apricot-prune liquid until the stuffing is slightly moist but not soggy.

11. You may stuff a 25-pound turkey with this or bake in a lightly greased baking dish for 30 minutes at 300°, or until piping hot. If you make this one day ahead, take it out of the refrigerator and let stand at room temperature for 1 hour before baking.

NOTE: You may use all rice or all bread crumbs rather than both rice and crumbs if you prefer.

Mushroom Herb Stuffing for Fish

This will stuff a 5- to 6-pound fish or fill at least 12 large rolled-up fillets

6 tablespoons Clarified Butter*
2 medium-size onions, finely minced
1/2 pound mushrooms, minced
2 tablespoons finely chopped fresh parsley
1 tablespoon finely chopped fresh dill
2 teaspoon finely chopped fresh tarragon (or 1 teaspoon dried)
2 to 3 teaspoons seasoned salt substitute (optional)

1/8 teaspoon cayenne
1 teaspoon freshly ground black pepper
1 egg, lightly beaten
1 1/2 cups salt-free cornflakes (pulverized into crumbs)
2 cups Bread Crumbs*
1/2 cup light cream (more or less) (or triple-strength low sodium dry milk)

1. In a large skillet, over a medium flame, melt the butter and sauté the onions and mushrooms until tender.

2. Add the parsley, dill, tarragon, salt substitute, cayenne, and black pepper and stir thoroughly to blend. Add the egg and mix thoroughly.

3. Add the cornflake crumbs, bread crumbs, and the onion-mushroom-herb mixture. Place in a large mixing bowl and mix thoroughly, adding enough cream to moisten well.

Duxelles

Makes 2 cups

This may be used as a stuffing for fish, veal, or chicken.

2/3 cup Clarified Butter*
10 shallots, very finely chopped
2 pounds mushrooms, washed, thoroughly dried, and very finely chopped
1/2 cup very finely chopped fresh parsley

1 teaspoon freshly ground black pepper
2 teaspoons seasoned salt substitute (optional)

1. In a large heavy skillet melt the clarified butter over a low flame and sauté the shallots for 5 minutes.

2. Add the mushrooms and parsley and mix well. Simmer over a very low flame, taking care not to sauté the mushrooms. Stir fairly often. The mushrooms should darken deeply as the liquid cooks out.

3. When the mushrooms are almost black and quite dehydrated and the mixture is thick (about 1 hour and 45 minutes) add the pepper and salt substitute and stir well.

4. Cool the mixture. Place it in a mason jar and cover tightly. This will keep in the refrigerator very well for 10 days to 2 weeks.

NOTE: I generally freeze the mixture in ½-pint plastic containers, so that it is always on hand.

Our Traditional Thanksgiving Stuffing

For a 25- to 30-pound bird

⅔ cup Clarified Butter*

3 pounds small mushrooms, sliced thinly lengthwise

6 very large Bermuda onions, finely chopped

8 cloves garlic, finely minced

½ cup finely minced fresh parsley

¼ cup finely minced fresh chives

⅛ to ⅓ teaspoon cayenne

2 teaspoons freshly ground black pepper

3 tablespoons seasoned salt substitute (optional)

6 pounds chestnuts, boiled, peeled, and coarsely chopped

⅓ cup Clarified Butter*

2 cups blanched sliced almonds

10 cups cooked rice (which has been boiled in Chicken Stock*)

3 eggs, well beaten

¾ cup melted Clarified Butter*

1. In a 17-inch skillet (or two large skillets) melt the ⅔ cup clarified butter over a medium-high flame. Sauté the mushrooms until quite dark.

2. Remove the mushrooms with a slotted spoon to a 10-quart mixing bowl or pot.

3. In the same skillet sauté the onions and garlic until the onions are gold, then thoroughly mix in the parsley, chives, cayenne, black pepper, and salt substitute. Add the onion mixture to the mushrooms. Add the chestnuts and mix all the ingredients thoroughly.

4. Melt the ⅓ cup clarified butter in a saucepan over a medium flame.

Sauté the almonds, stirring constantly until a light golden color. Add to the onion-mushroom-chestnut mixture.

5. Add the rice and mix well.

6. Add the eggs and mix well.

7. Add the melted butter, a little at a time, until the stuffing is moist but not liquid.

NOTE: This will stuff a 25- to 30-pound turkey, or it can be baked in a lightly greased baking dish for 30 minutes at 300°, or until piping hot.

    If you are making this the day before, take it out of the refrigerator an hour before putting it into the oven.

Wild Rice Stuffing

This will stuff a crown roast of lamb or a 6- to 8-pound bird

2 cups boiled chestnuts, shelled
   and drained
1/2 cup finely minced onions
2 cloves garlic, pressed
1/8 cup Clarified Butter,* melted
4 tablespoons finely minced
   fresh parsley
1/8 teaspoon cayenne
3/4 teaspoon paprika
2 teaspoons dried tarragon

1 teaspoon freshly ground black
   pepper
3/8 cup Clarified Butter*
3 cups cooked wild rice
1/2 cup coarsely chopped pecans
1/2 cup coarsely chopped walnuts
1/3 to 1/2 cup heavy cream (or
   triple-strength low sodium
   dry milk)

1. Purée the chestnuts in a blender or food processor.

2. Sauté the onions and garlic in 1/8 cup of clarified butter until the onions are a pale golden color.

3. Add the parsley, cayenne, paprika, tarragon, and pepper. Stir well and remove from the heat.

4. Add the 3/8 cup of clarified butter to the mixture. Stir well and add the chestnuts. Add the wild rice, pecans, and walnuts. Mix thoroughly.

5. Slowly blend in the cream until the mixture is slightly moist, making sure not to add too much cream as the mixture should be just moist and not soggy.

NOTE: You may either stuff a roast or a bird, or you may place it in a lightly greased baking dish and bake 30 to 40 minutes at 300°.

Sweet Potato Stuffing

For a 20-pound turkey, or approximately 3 quarts of stuffing

2 tablespoons sweet butter
2 tablespoons corn oil
²/₃ cup finely chopped onions
2 to 3 cloves garlic, pressed
6¹/₂ cups boiled, mashed sweet potatoes, at room temperature
3¹/₂ tablespoons sweet butter (at room temperature), cut into small pieces
1¹/₂ teaspoons freshly ground white pepper
2 tablespoons seasoned salt substitute

1¹/₂ teaspoons ground cinnamon
¹/₃ teaspoon Hungarian paprika
¹/₄ teaspoon freshly grated nutmeg (optional)
¹/₂ cup heavy cream (or triple-strength low sodium dry milk)
¹/₃ cup pure maple syrup
3¹/₂ cups Bread Crumbs*
3 eggs, lightly beaten
1¹/₂ tablespoons finely chopped fresh parsley

1. In a very large heavy skillet heat the 2 tablespoons of butter and the oil over a medium flame and sauté the onions and garlic until the onions are translucent.

2. Add the mashed sweet potatoes and stir-fry for 2 minutes, or until the potatoes are warm. Stir in the 3¹/₂ tablespoons butter and continue to stir-fry until the butter is absorbed into the sweet potatoes (approximately 1¹/₂ minutes).

3. Remove the skillet from the flame and stir in the pepper, salt substitute, cinnamon, paprika, nutmeg, cream, maple syrup, bread crumbs, eggs, and parsley.

4. You may either stuff the turkey with this or butter a 3- to 3¹/₂-quart ovenproof casserole, cover, and bake at 300° for 30 minutes. Uncover and bake 15 to 20 minutes more, or until piping hot.

DESSERTS

Curtain Calls

Desserts

Desserts, for the "sweetaholics," are the most anticipated and treasured part of the meal. For others, who merely enjoy sweets, they are the finishing touch to lunch or dinner; and for myself, who has never had a penchant for sweets, they are something I almost always pass up, except for fresh, stewed, or baked fruit in any and all forms.

In our home, none of us actually has a sweet tooth, but since we all adore fruit and salt-free cheeses, they have become *de rigueur* at the conclusion of most evening meals.

Years ago I wouldn't have thought of giving a luncheon or dinner party without the pièce de résistance . . . the exciting and unusual dessert. Nowadays, with everyone being calorie conscious, it is only on a rare occasion that a rich dessert such as a Cold Lemon Soufflé* or a Bittersweet Chocolate Mousse* is offered in our home. Instead, our guests enjoy the fruits of the season in their natural form; sometimes accompanied by a liqueur if it is a summer fruit salad; salt-free cheese, if it's during the pear and apple season; and whipped cream when strawberries are at their peak. However, so as not to deprive the dessert lover who, despite calorie counting, craves something sweet, a tray of Lace Cookies* or Crescent Cookies* is passed after the fruit is served. Therefore, most of the rich recipes in this chapter that saw hard duty in years long since past are now served only occasionally.

Whatever your pleasure in rich desserts, rest assured these are low in sodium, but alas, they are conversely quite high in calories. As my father told me many, many years ago, "You just can't have everything" . . . and thus, dear reader, the choice of recipes is varied, but the decision as to which ones you will serve most often is, of course, entirely yours.

Pears Baked in Red Wine

Serves 6

6 large pears
2½ cups dry red wine
½ cup brown sugar (or substitute equivalent) (or more to
taste)

2 cinnamon sticks
5 cloves (optional)
6 tablespoons honey, heated but
not boiled

1. Preheat the oven to 325°.
2. Peel and core the pears but try to leave stems intact. (Core the pear from the bottom up.) Place the pears in an ovenproof baking dish standing upright but not touching.
3. Combine the wine, sugar, cinnamon, and cloves in a heavy saucepan over a low flame, stirring constantly. Do not boil.
4. Pour the wine sauce over the pears, cover, and bake for 50 minutes, basting every 10 to 20 minutes (the more often the better).
5. Spoon some of the honey over each pear and bake uncovered for 10 minutes more, or until the pears are tender.

Serving: If your baking dish is attractive, serve the pears directly from that; if not, transfer the pears to a shallow serving dish approximately 1½ to 2½ inches high. Serve the pears hot or at room temperature.

NOTE: You may substitute apples for the pears.

Bananas Flambé

Serves 6

6 large firm bananas
3 tablespoons fresh lemon juice
6 tablespoons Clarified Butter*

8 tablespoons sugar (or substitute equivalent)
½ cup brandy, heated

1. Preheat the oven to 350°.
2. Peel the bananas, slice them in half lengthwise, and sprinkle them with the lemon juice.
3. In a flameproof, overproof baking dish, such as a copper au gratin

pan, melt the butter over a medium flame and arrange the bananas in the baking dish.

4. Sprinkle the bananas with the sugar and bake them for 20 to 25 minutes, or until tender.

Serving: Bring the au gratin pan to the table. Place it on a warmer, containing denatured alcohol or Sterno and pour in the heated brandy. Ignite the brandy and *voilà!* Bananas Flambé. You may serve the bananas while they are flaming or let the flame die down and then serve. This is the method I choose, as I am very insecure about handling the bananas while they are flaming, but hopefully, "You're a better man than I am . . ."

Layered and Marinated Summer Fruit

Serves 24 (save this for a big buffet)

"Marinate" is not considered the correct adjective for fruit, whereas "macerate" is. However, I always say marinate, as macerate sounds unpleasant to my ears. I hope you will forgive my transgression.

4 large bananas, sliced
²/₃ cup fresh lemon juice
2 cups confectioner's sugar (or substitute equivalent), sifted
4 navel oranges, sectioned
1 small firm and ripe honeydew melon, peeled and scooped into balls
1 medium-firm and ripe canta- loupe, peeled and scooped into balls

8 firm and ripe nectarines cut into ¹/₄-inch slices
4 peaches, firm and ripe and cut into ¹/₄-inch slices
1¹/₂ pounds firm large green seedless grapes
1¹/₂ pints firm strawberries, hulled and sliced
3 cups dry white wine
¹/₂ cup brandy

1. Place the bananas in a flat-bottomed cylindrical glass container (I sometimes use a glass vase that is this shape). Sprinkle very well with some of the lemon juice and sprinkle on some of the sugar.

2. Add the remaining fruit in layers, sprinkling some lemon juice and sugar over each layer (i.e., arrange the oranges on top of the bananas, sprinkle some lemon juice and sugar over them, then layer on the honeydew, etc.), ending with the strawberries.

3. Pour the white wine and brandy over the layered fruit.

4. Cover tightly and refrigerate overnight.

Serving: Place the fruit on the buffet table and use an oversized, extremely long-handled serving spoon to serve it.

Summer Brandied Peaches

Yields approximately 5 quarts

This recipe is, of course, far superior to the Quick Brandied Peaches.* However, you must prepare this when peaches are at their peak, which is during the "boiler" months of July and August. So . . . if you are willing to spend the better part of a day in your kitchen, you will surely enjoy "the fruits of your labor" all winter long.

10 pounds perfect peaches, ripe   **10 cups water**
but firm (use freestone or   **10 cups sugar**
cling)   **Brandy**

1. Wash and dry the peaches. Rub off the fuzz with a coarse towel.

2. Prick each peach in two places with a fork.

3. Place the water and sugar in a large heavy pot (about 10 to 12 quarts) and heat the mixture over a low flame until it is very syrupy and comes to a low boil. Stir constantly.

4. Let the syrup boil for 3 minutes, stirring constantly.

5. Carefully lower the peaches into the syrup (see Note). Boil for approximately 6 minutes, or until they are tender. (The smaller the peaches, the less time, and naturally, the bigger they are, the more time.)

6. Place the peaches in hot Sterilized Jars* and pour in enough syrup to fill the jars three fourths full.

7. Pour the brandy to ½ inch from the top of the jars.

8. Cover with lids (check individual manufacturers directions).

9. Place a wire rack in the bottom of a very deep pot. Fill the pot with water to the height of the jars.

10. Turn the flame to high and bring the water to a rolling boil.

11. When the water is boiling, carefully lower the jars (one at a time) with canning tongs into the water, taking care to leave at least 1½ inches between the jars as well as the sides of the pot. If necessary add more boiling water, so that the jars are covered by 2 inches of water at all times during the boiling period.

12. Boil the jars for 35 minutes.

13. Carefully lift the jars out of the pot (using the canning tongs) seal the lids tightly and leave in a draft-free place for 12 hours. The jars should stand at least 1 inch apart during this period.

14. Store the jars in a cool place.

Serving: The peaches should be stored at least 6 weeks before using them. When ready to serve, if you want them hot, heat them in their own syrup in an attractive baking dish in a moderate oven and serve them for dessert; or heat them in their own syrup in a heavy saucepan and arrange them around your Roasted Turkey* or Baked Chicken* or whatever. . . .

If you want them cold, either transfer them to a serving dish and serve them with Lace Cookies* for dessert, or surround your poultry as above. You may serve them whole or split in half (remove the pit) and hot, cold, with or without syrup, or filled with whole Cranberry and Orange Sauce* or Cranberry Orange Relish,* or whipped cream, or Crème Fraîche* as an accompaniment to your main course.

NOTE: Use a very long-handled large spoon or a small strainer when placing the peaches into the boiling syrup. I stress the length of the handle because, careful as you may be when lowering the peaches, there is still the possibility of splattering the boiling syrup on yourself.

Quick Brandied Peaches

Serves 4

These brandied peaches are not as good as Summer Brandied Peaches* but . . . they're quick, easy, and not fattening, so pick you preference.

1 16-ounce can unsweetened peach halves (juice reserved)
1/2 cup unsweetened pineapple juice

3 tablespoons brandy
Honey (optional but highly recommended)

1. Preheat the oven to 275°.

2. Combine the reserved peach juice and the pineapple juice and pour it into a baking dish. Arrange the peaches, cut side up, in the dish. (There should be at least 1/3 inch of juice in the bottom of the dish.)

3. Pour the brandy into the peach cavities and drizzle ³/₄ teaspoon honey over each peach half. Bake for 1 hour.

Serving: You may serve the brandied peaches piping hot from the baking dish if it is attractive enough. If not, transfer the peaches to a preheated serving dish or surround your main course, such as Broiled Chicken* or Roasted Turkey* with the peach halves . . . they make a stunning garnish as well as a delicious accompaniment.

On some occasions, I have served the peaches after they have been chilled overnight, then filled with whipped cream or Crène Fraiche.* They are especially cooling and pleasant after a summer supper.

Cooked Apricots or Prunes

Apricots yield approximately 5¹/₂ cups. Prunes yield approximately 4 cups

These will keep very well in your refrigerator (if tightly covered) for 4 weeks.

**1 pound dried apricots (or pitted
    prunes)
2¹/₂ cups rapidly boiling water**

1. Place the apricots or prunes in a heatproof glass jar. Pour the boiling water over the fruit and cover with aluminum foil.
2. Let the fruit stand at room temperature for 1 to 1¹/₂ hours.
3. Remove the aluminum foil, cover tightly with the jar lid, and refrigerate at least 1 week before using.

Serving: Drain 1 cup of cooked apricots and 1 cup of cooked prunes, stir in ¹/₄ cup Grand Marnier, and sprinkle in ¹/₃ cup brown or natural sugar (or substitute equivalent). Mix well and spoon into 4 champagne glasses. Chill in the refrigerator for 1 hour. When ready to eat, spoon 2 tablespoons of whipped cream over each serving.

NOTE: This recipe is used as an ingredient in many other recipes but it is also delicious when used in the manner described above.

Stewed Fruit

Since I love to serve a selection of stewed fruits (generally called a compote), I often offer Cooked Apricots* and Prunes,* which are basically stewed off the stove, accompanied in the winter by stewed apples and pears. In the summer the prunes are still offered but the dried apricots are replaced with fresh apricots, peaches, and nectarines. For best results, each fruit should be stewed separately and just until tender.

**2¹/₂ cups unsweetened pineapple
  juice
1 quart pared fruit (see Note)**

1. In a heavy saucepan bring the pineapple juice to a boil over a medium-high flame.
2. Place the fruit in the boiling juice and cook just until tender. Remove from the flame and carefully spoon the fruit into large-necked jars or a deep bowl. Pour the liquid over the fruit.
3. Cool the fruit for 30 minutes, cover, and refrigerate.

NOTE: A. To pare summer fruits such as apricots, peaches, and nectarines: Bring water to a rolling boil and place the fruit in the water for approximately 1 minute, or until the skin loosens. Dip into cold water and gently pull off the skin. Cut the fruit in half and remove the pit. Place in 1 quart of cold water acidulated with ¹/₄ cup of lemon juice to keep the fruit from discoloring.

B. To pare winter fruits such as apples and pears: Using a sharp knife or a vegetable peeler, cut or scrape the skin off the fruit. Cut in half and core the fruit. Place in the water and lemon juice solution as above.

C. However, and whatever the fruit, immediately after the above process of paring, begin the stewing process.

Serving: This fruit may be served as is or drained and generously laced with Kirschwasser, or drained and served with whipped cream, Sour Cream,* or Crème Fraîche.*

Strawberries à la Crème

Serves 8

A simple and elegant dessert.

8 cups (about 2 quarts) strawberries, hulled, washed, and
thoroughly dried
1 to 1¼ cups confectioner's
sugar (or substitute equivalent)

1 pint heavy cream
⅓ cup Kirsch or Benedictine
and Brandy

1. Cut strawberries in half and sprinkle with the confectioner's sugar, tossing to incorporate the sugar. Chill for 10 to 15 minutes.

2. Using an electric mixer on medium-high speed, whip the cream until stiff peaks hold their shape.

3. Toss the Kirsch or Benedictine and Brandy into the berries and gently fold in the whipped cream. Refrigerate for 1 hour.

Serving: Divide the strawberry-cream mixture into 8 balloon glasses and place them on small crystal or faïence plates lined with doilies (optional).

NOTE: If you refrigerate your glasses first and then dip the rims into super-fine granulated sugar, it makes a very elegant presentation.

Apricot Pineapple Cream Whip

Serves 8

1 cup heavy cream
1 cup Cooked apricots,*
drained and puréed
1 cup canned unsweetened
crushed pineapple, drained

2 large egg whites
½ cup sugar (or substitute
equivalent), sifted twice
½ teaspoon vanilla
1 tablespoon fresh lemon juice

1. Using an electric mixer on medium-high speed, whip the cream until stiff peaks hold their shape. Refrigerate.

2. Beat the cooked apricots, pineapple, egg whites, sugar, vanilla, and lemon juice until light and fluffy.

3. Gently fold the whipped cream into the mixture, a little at a time.

Serving: Spoon the whip into oversized wine or parfait serving glasses and refrigerate at least 2 hours before serving.

Bittersweet Chocolate Mousse

Serves 6

It took me twenty-four tries to get the right taste and consistency to this mousse. Untold thanks to my dear husband Dick and great friends Judy and Janet, for tasting each and every one. I hope they haven't lost their taste for bittersweet chocolate mousse.

9 ounces bittersweet chocolate, cut into small pieces (such as Tobler's Swiss Bittersweet Chocolate)
1 ounce unsweetened chocolate, cut into small pieces
¹/₃ cup boiling water
3 tablespoons instant coffee
6 eggs, separated, at room temperature

¹/₃ cup sugar
¹/₄ teaspoon cream of tartar

GARNISH:
1 cup heavy cream, whipped (optional)
¹/₂ ounce unsweetened chocolate, grated (optional)

1. Fill the bottom of the double boiler with enough water to come within 1 inch from the top section. Place the chocolate (bittersweet and unsweetened), boiling water, and instant coffee in the top section. Place over a low-medium flame and, stirring occasionally, cook until the chocolate is melted, velvety, and thoroughly blended with the water and coffee.

2. Using an electric mixer on medium high speed, beat the egg yolks and sugar until they are thick and pale yellow in color.

3. Slowly add the chocolate mixture to the egg yolk mixture, while continuing to beat on medium speed until everything is thoroughly combined. Set aside.

4. Using an electric mixer on high speed, beat the egg whites with the cream of tartar until they are stiff but not dry.

5. Stir a little of the egg whites into the chocolate-egg yolk mixture (to lighten it) and then gently fold in the remainder of the egg whites.

6. Spoon the mousse into a 2-quart crystal bowl and refrigerate at least 24 hours before using.

Serving: You may serve the mousse as is, or garnish it with the whipped cream and grated semi-sweet chocolate. Place the crystal bowl on a doily-lined (optional) silver tray.

Cold Apricot Soufflé

Serves 10 to 12

¹/₂ cup cold water
¹/₂ cup unsweetened pineapple
    juice
2 packages unflavored gelatin
4 cups Cooked Apricots,* heated
    and puréed with
¹/₂ cup of the apricot liquid
3¹/₂ cups heavy cream
8 eggs, separated, at room tem-
    perature

¹/₄ teaspoon cream of tartar
1¹/₂ cups sugar (or more to
    taste)
¹/₃ cup fresh lemon juice

GARNISH:
¹/₂ cup heavy cream, whipped

1. Place the cold water and pineapple juice in the top part of a double boiler. Sprinkle on the gelatin and let it soften for 5 minutes.

2. In the meantime prepare a 2¹/₂- or 3-quart soufflé dish with a 5-inch Soufflé Collar.* Spray the inside of the collar with a vegetable spray.

3. Add the heated apricot purée to the gelatin mixture. Place the top part of the double boiler into the bottom, filled with enough scalded water to come to within 1 inch from the top part. Turn the flame to low-medium and stir the gelatin-apricot purée mixture constantly until the gelatin is totally dissolved (about 5 to 7 minutes).

4. Transfer the apricot mixture to a bowl and cool it in the refrigerator (approximately 15 minutes).

5. Using an electric mixer on medium-high speed, whip the cream until stiff peaks hold their shape. Refrigerate.

6. Using an electric mixer on high speed, beat the egg whites and the cream of tartar until stiff but not dry. Refrigerate.

7. Using an electric mixer on medium-high speed, beat the egg yolks and sugar until they are thick, creamy, and a pale lemon color. Beat in the lemon juice.

8. Add the apricot purée mixture to the egg yolk mixture, a little at a time, beating constantly until everything is thoroughly blended.

9. Using a rubber spatula, stir one fourth of the egg whites into the egg yolk-apricot purée mixture and then fold in the remaining egg whites.

10. Fold the whipped cream into the mixture. Spoon the mixture into the soufflé dish. Refrigerate for 24 hours.

Serving: Cover the top of the soufflé with the whipped cream, carefully remove the soufflé collar. Place the soufflé dish on a round silver or china tray lined with a doily (optional). Serve at once, with Apricot Sauce.*

Apricot Sauce

Serves 10 to 12

2 cups apricot preserves
1 tablespoon finely grated
  orange rind
$^1/_4$ cup unsweetened pineapple
  juice

$1^1/_4$ cups heavy cream
$^1/_2$ cup apricot brandy

1. Using an electric mixer on low speed, mix the apricot preserves only until soft.
2. Beat in the orange rind and pineapple juice.
3. Beat in the cream until it is thoroughly blended.
4. Then, stirring constantly with a wooden spoon, add the apricot brandy and mix well.

Serving: Transfer the sauce to a silver, crystal, or china bowl. Place the bowl on a doily-lined (optional) silver, crystal, or china tray. Place a small silver ladle on the tray.

Cold Grand Marnier Soufflé

Serves 6 to 8

My friends love it . . . but if you don't like Grand Marnier this certainly isn't a dessert for you.

2 packages unflavored gelatin
¹/₂ cup cold water
³/₄ cup milk
³/₄ cup Grand Marnier
3¹/₃ cups heavy cream
6 large egg whites, at room temperature
1 cup sugar
1¹/₂ teaspoons vanilla

GARNISH:
²/₃ cup heavy cream, whipped
with 1 tablespoon confectioner's sugar
1 ounce semi-sweet chocolate, grated (optional), or
1¹/₂ tablespoons grated orange rind, mixed with
1¹/₂ tablespoons confectioner's sugar (optional)

1. Prepare a 1¹/₂-quart soufflé dish with a 5-inch Soufflé Collar.* Spray the inside of the collar with a vegetable spray.

2. Soften the gelatin in the water in a small bowl.

3. Scald the milk in the top of a double boiler over a medium flame, taking care that the water in the bottom of the double boiler comes to within 1 inch of the top part and is hot but not boiling.

4. Add the gelatin mixture and cook, stirring constantly, until it is totally dissolved in the milk. Remove the mixture from the heat and slowly stir in the Grand Marnier until it is all added and thoroughly blended with the milk mixture. Transfer the mixture to a large bowl and place it in the refrigerator for approximately 10 minutes, or until it is chilled.

5. Using an electric mixer on medium-high speed, whip the cream until stiff peaks hold their shape. Refrigerate.

6. Using an electric mixer on high-speed, beat the egg whites with the sugar and vanilla until the egg whites are stiff but not dry.

7. Stir one fourth of the egg white mixture into the gelatin mixture, then fold in the remaining egg whites.

8. Fold the whipped cream into the egg white-gelatin mixture.

9. Spoon the soufflé into the prepared dish and refrigerate at least 24 hours before serving.

Serving: Cover the top of the soufflé with the whipped cream. Carefully remove the soufflé collar. Sprinkle on the grated chocolate or the orange rind. Place the soufflé dish on a silver or ceramic tray which has a doily resting on it (optional). Serve at once.

Cold Lemon Soufflé

Serves 8 to 10

It looks like a picture.

Its texture is superb.

It tastes divine . . . and it should . . . because this is the result of twenty years of testing and trying and making cold lemon soufflé.

1¼ cups cold water
2 packages unflavored gelatin
3⅓ cups heavy cream
1 teaspoon vanilla (optional)
8 large eggs, separated, at room
 temperature
1¾ cups sugar
Juice of 4 large lemons (¾ cup)

2 tablespoons finely grated
 lemon rind
¼ teaspoon cream of tartar

GARNISH:
⅔ cup heavy cream, whipped
 with
1½ tablespoons confectioner's
 sugar

1. Prepare a 2-quart soufflé dish with a 5-inch Soufflé Collar.* Spray the inside of the collar with a vegetable spray.

2. Place the water in the top part of a double boiler and sprinkle the gelatin on top of the water to soften.

3. Using an electric mixer on medium-high speed, whip the cream with the vanilla until stiff peaks hold their shape. Refrigerate.

4. Fill the bottom of the double boiler with water to within one inch from top part. Turn the flame to medium and bring the water to the scalding point. Turn the flame to low, place the top part of the double boiler into the bottom, and cook for 3 to 4 minutes, or until the gelatin is dissolved. (The water in the bottom part should not boil.) Turn off the flame.

5. Using an electric mixer on medium speed, beat the egg yolks with the sugar until they are thick, creamy, and a pale lemon color. Beat in the lemon juice and rind. Slowly add the gelatin mixture, beating all the time, until the gelatin is totally absorbed into the egg yolk-sugar-lemon mixture.

6. Using the electric mixer on high speed, beat the egg whites and cream of tartar until stiff but not dry.

7. Using a rubber spatula, mix one fourth of the egg whites into the egg yolk mixture, then fold in the remainder of the egg whites.

8. Fold the whipped cream into the egg mixture.

9. Spoon the mixture into the soufflé dish and refrigerate at least 24 hours.

Serving: Cover the soufflé top with whipped cream, remove collar, serve immediately on a doily-covered silver tray.

Pastry Crust

Makes 2 9-inch crusts

Please! DO NOT PANIC . . . this method for making a pastry crust is spoon-fed to you so that there will not be any questions or errors. It is actually not complicated and very easy to make. Take heart . . . the results are terrific.

1½ cups sifted unbleached flour
3½ to 4½ tablespoons ice water
9½ tablespoons sweet butter,
    very cold and cut into tiny
    pieces

1. Place your pastry board in the freezer for 20 minutes. Or, if you are using a marble slab, rub it with ice cubes to chill it well and dry it thoroughly.

2. Place the flour in a soft pile on the pastry board and make a well in the center of the flour.

3. Put ½ tablespoon of water into the well and about half of the butter pieces.

4. Using a pastry cutter, cut the butter and water into the flour.

5. Add another ½ tablespoon of water and the remainder of the butter and continue to cut the butter and water into the flour. (Your dough, at this point, should be slightly pebbly.)

6. While still cutting the butter and flour, add the remainder of the water needed to dampen the dough, ½ tablespoon at a time. Use a maximum of 4½ tablespoons of water.

7. When all the water needed has been added, using your hands, roll the dough into a ball, gathering the loose particles of dough that are on the board and incorporating those into the ball. (Your ball should be smooth when this procedure is completed.) *Handle the dough as little as possible.*

8. Divide the dough in half and shape each half into a round flat cake approximately 1 inch high by 3 inches wide.

9. Poke your fingers into the center of the dough, making a deep indentation. If the indentation remains, your dough will be ready for use after 20 minutes of refrigeration. However, if the indentation closes, the dough will have to be refrigerated for 3 to 4 hours at least (see Note 1).

10. Place your dough cakes in wax paper and wrap tightly. Refrigerate (see Note 2).

11. Wash off your pastry board and wipe it well. Put it in the freezer, along with your rolling pin, 20 minutes before you are ready to roll out

your dough (or, if it is marble, follow same procedure as in Step 1).

12. Flour the pastry board well and flour the rolling pin. (You may have to flour the rolling pin a few times during the rolling.)

13. To make one pastry crust, place one dough cake in the center of the cold pastry board. Press the rolling pin into the center of the dough and roll it in one direction (lengthwise) toward the other end of the board.

14. Then place the rolling pin in the center of the dough and roll out the other half of the dough in the opposite direction (lengthwise) toward the end of the board.

15. Then repeat Steps 13 and 14 . . . but going widthwise this time instead of lengthwise.

16. Your dough should be absolutely no thicker than $1/8$ inch (thinner is better) and should be $10\frac{1}{2}$ inches in diameter.

17. Butter well and very lightly flour a 9-inch Pyrex pie plate.

18. Flour your rolling pin well. Starting at one edge, roll the dough loosely over the pin and unroll it onto the pie plate.

19. Pat the dough firmly against the bottom and side of the pie plate. Pat the dough along the rim of the plate and trim off the excess with a pair of kitchen scissors or a sharp knife.

20. If you want the rim of the pie fluted:

    A. Press the rim-edge dough between your thumb and index finger, repeating this motion until the entire rim is fluted.

    B. Or press gently around the rim with the flat part of the tongs of a cake or salad fork.

NOTES: 1. It is preferable to make your dough one day in advance and refrigerate it.

2. The dough will keep well for 5 days if it is tightly wrapped in wax paper and then wrapped in aluminum foil and stored in your refrigerator.

3. The dough freezes very well if it is tightly wrapped in wax paper, then wrapped and air-sealed in aluminum foil. It will keep for months in your freezer.

4. To thaw a frozen dough you may either defrost it in the refrigerator for 24 hours or thaw it on the counter for 2 to $2\frac{1}{2}$ hours.

5. Pastry crusts should be rolled on very cold and dry surfaces such as marble or plastic pastry slabs for best results.

6. Always roll your dough in one direction, lifting the pin as you start to roll again. Never roll the dough back and forth.

7. Many people like to use a well-floured pastry stocking over the rolling pin and a heavily floured pastry cloth over the pastry board. I do not object to the floured stocking, although I do not use it, but I certainly feel that nothing substitutes for a well-chilled board . . . and if the chilled board is used the pastry cloth is superfluous.

TO BAKE A PIECRUST TO BE USED FOR A PRECOOKED FILLING:

1. Preheat the oven to 425°.
2. Prick the bottom of the crust well with a fork.
3. Place wax paper (or aluminum foil) snugly inside the pastry crust and fill with enough dried beans or rice to come to the top of the pie plate.
4. Bake for 7 minutes.
5. Remove the beans and wax paper or foil and bake for 5 minutes more.

TO MAKE A LATTICE CRUST

1. Prepare and roll the crust as described in Steps 1 through 16.
2. Cut the dough into $^3/_8$-inch-wide strips, using a pastry cutter (this will create a pinched edge).
3. Place a strip across the top of the pie from edge to edge. Then place another strip on the tip of the first strip and lay this strip in the opposite direction, from edge to edge of the pie.
4. Repeat Step 3 every $^3/_4$ inch until the entire top of the pie is a lattice from edge to edge.
5. At the edges of the pie where the lattice strips meet, brush and moisten lightly with ice water.

Apricot Prune Pie

Makes 1 9-inch pie

1 8-ounce can unsweetened crushed pineapple, with the juice
$^3/_4$ cup sugar (or substitute equivalent)
2$^1/_2$ teaspoons cornstarch
1$^1/_2$ tablespoons sweet butter
1$^1/_4$ cups Cooked Apricots,* drained and left whole, or drained and coarsely chopped

1$^1/_4$ cups Cooked Prunes,* drained and left whole, or drained and coarsely chopped
1 Pastry Crust,* in a well-buttered and lightly floured 9-inch Pyrex pie plate
1 Lattice Crust*
Egg bath: 1 egg lightly beaten with 1 tablespoon ice water

1. Preheat the oven to 425°.

2. Put the pineapple, sugar, cornstarch, and butter in a heavy saucepan. Turn the flame to medium-high and stir constantly until the mixture comes to a boil.

3. Remove the saucepan from the heat and stir the apricots and prunes into the pineapple mixture.

4. Spoon the mixture into the pastry crust. Top the pie with the lattice crust and flute the edges of the lattice and bottom crust together.

5. Using a pastry brush, brush the lattice and the fluted edge of the crust with the egg bath. (This will give the crust a glaze.)

6. Bake for 35 minutes, or until the crust is a deep golden brown.

7. Cool at least ½ hour before serving.

Serving: Transfer the pie dish into a silver or pottery pie holder. Serve along with whipped cream if you want to add a superbly delicious and definitely fattening accompaniment.

Apple Pie

Makes 1 9-inch pie

See Note for a delectable Apple Cheese Pie.* Both are long-time favorites of ours.

7 large tart green apples, peeled, cored, and cut into ¼-inch slices

2½ tablespoons fresh lemon juice

½ cup brown sugar (or substitute equivalent)

1 to 1½ tablespoons cornstarch

2 teaspoons cinnamon

¼ teaspoon freshly grated nutmeg

2 tablespoons sweet butter, cut into tiny cubes

1 Pastry Crust,* in a well-buttered and lightly floured 9-inch Pyrex pie plate

1 9-inch Pastry Crust* to be used for the top crust

Egg bath: 1 egg, lightly beaten, mixed with 1 tablespoon ice water

1. Preheat the oven to 450°.

2. Place the apples in a large glass bowl and sprinkle with the lemon juice. Sprinkle in the sugar and toss the apples.

3. Sprinkle the cornstarch, cinnamon, and nutmeg, a little at a time, over the apple mixture and toss the apples after each addition, so they will become lightly coated with the cornstarch, cinnamon, and nutmeg.

4. Layer the apples into the pastry crust and dot them with the butter. Cover the apples with the top crust. Trim off the excess crust with a sharp knife or kitchen scissors. Crimp and flute the edges of the top and bottom crust together, and brush with the egg bath.

5. Prick the top crust in 4 places with the tines of a fork (in order to permit the steam to escape) and bake for 10 minutes. Reduce the heat to 350° and bake for 50 minutes more, or until the crust is a deep golden brown.

Serving: Place the pie in a silver or ceramic pie holder and bring it to the table. The pie should be quite warm (but not hot). Serve it as is . . . and that is quite delicious . . . or offer with whipped cream or slices of salt-free Gouda or Cheddar cheese.

NOTE: TO BAKE A SUPER APPLE CHEESE PIE:

1. Preheat the oven to 450°.

2. Eliminate the top crust.

3. Bake the "topless" pie in a 450° oven for 20 to 25 minutes, or until the apples are tender and the bottom crust is a light golden brown.

4. Remove from the oven and sprinkle 1 to 1½ cups of grated salt-free Cheddar or Gouda cheese on top of the apples.

5. Place the pie in the broiler, about 4 inches from the flame, and broil for 5 to 6 minutes, or until the cheese is melted and bubbling hot.

Virginia Pecan Pie

Makes 1 9-inch pie

One of the traditional desserts for our Thanksgiving dinner.

3 eggs
¾ to 1 cup dark brown sugar
1 cup dark corn syrup
1⅛ teaspoons vanilla
3 tablespoons sweet butter, melted
¾ cup chopped pecans

1 Pastry Crust,* in a well-buttered and lightly floured 9-inch Pyrex pie plate
¾ cup pecan halves

GARNISH:
2 cups whipped cream

1. Preheat the oven to 400°.

2. In a large mixing bowl combine the eggs, sugar, corn syrup, and vanilla. Using an electric mixer on low speed, beat the ingredients until thor-

oughly blended, then slowly add the melted butter, while continuing to beat.

3. Stir in the chopped pecans.

4. Spoon the filling into the pastry shell and bake for 15 minutes.

5. Remove from the oven and arrange pecan halves attractively on top of the pie. Return the pie to the oven and bake another 20 to 25 minutes, or until the crust is golden brown and a toothpick inserted into the center of the pie comes out clean.

6. Cool the pie at least 2 hours.

Serving: Place the pie plate in a silver or ceramic server and garnish with whipped cream or offer the whipped cream in a separate serving bowl to be taken as desired by your guests.

Our Pumpkin Pie

Makes 1 9-inch pie

Could your Thanksgiving dinner ever be complete without "Our Pumpkin Pie"?

16 ounces Cooked Pumpkin*
  (see Note) or
1-pound can pumpkin (no salt)
³/₄ cup brown sugar, firmly
  packed
2 teaspoons cinnamon
¹/₂ teaspoon freshly grated nut-
  meg
¹/₂ to ³/₄ teaspoon powdered
  ginger

¹/₈ teaspoon ground cloves (op-
  tional)
3 eggs, lightly beaten
1³/₄ cups heavy cream, scalded
1 Pastry Crust* in a well-but-
  tered and lightly floured 9-
  inch Pyrex pie plate

GARNISH:
2 cups whipped cream

1. Preheat the oven to 400°.

2. In a large mixing bowl beat the pumpkin with the brown sugar, using an electric mixer on low speed, just until mixed.

3. Combine the cinnamon, nutmeg, ginger, and cloves.

4. While continuing to beat the pumpkin-sugar mixture, sprinkle in the spices and combine thoroughly.

5. Beat in the eggs until blended and continuing to beat, add the cream, a little at a time, until it is totally absorbed and the mixture is smooth.

6. Pour the pumpkin mixture into the pie shell and bake for 50 minutes,

or until the crust is a deep golden brown and a toothpick inserted in the center of the pie comes out clean.

7. Cool at least 2 hours.

Serving: Place the pie plate in a silver or ceramic server and garnish with whipped cream or offer the whipped cream in a separate serving bowl to be taken as desired by your guests.

NOTE: Cooked Pumpkin: Wash and dry a pumpkin. Cut it in half and scoop out the seeds and strings. Put in a roasting pan filled to ½ inch with orange juice. Lay the pumpkin in the pan cut side down. Bake at 350° for 1 hour or until very tender. Scoop the pumpkin from its shell and mash either with a hand ricer or in a food processor.

Key Lime Pie

Makes 1 9-inch pie

A spring and summertime favorite.

1 package unflavored gelatin
½ cup sugar
4 large egg yolks
½ cup fresh lime juice
¼ cup water
1½ teaspoons finely grated lime peel
Green food coloring (optional)
4 egg whites

½ cup sugar
1 cup heavy cream
1 9-inch baked Pastry Crust*

GARNISH:
1 cup whipped cream
1 teaspoon finely grated lime peel, mixed with 2 teaspoons sugar

1. Place the gelatin and ½ cup of sugar in a medium-size saucepan. Mix and set aside.

2. Place the egg yolks, lime juice, and water in a mixing bowl and beat for 2 minutes, using an electric mixer on low speed.

3. Stir the egg yolk mixture into the gelatin mixture. Place the saucepan over a medium flame and stir constantly until the mixture comes to a boil.

4. Remove from heat, stir in the lime peel and a few drops of food coloring (just enough to create a pale green color).

5. Transfer the mixture to a mixing bowl and refrigerate until the mixture is chilled and has begun to thicken.

6. In the meantime, beat the egg whites, using an electric mixer on

medium-high speed, until soft peaks form. Slowly add ½ cup of sugar while continuing to beat until all the sugar is absorbed and the egg whites form stiff peaks. Refrigerate.

7. Beat the cream, using an electric mixer on medium-high speed, until stiff peaks form. Refrigerate.

8. When the gelatin mixture has begun to thicken, remove it from the refrigerator and beat it with a wire whisk for 2 to 3 minutes, or until it is fluffy.

9. Fold the egg whites into the gelatin mixture and then fold in the cream.

10. Spoon the mixture into the baked pastry crust and refrigerate at least 6 hours.

Serving: Place the pie plate in a silver or ceramic server and garnish with the whipped cream, which may be smoothed over the top of the pie or piped into rosettes around the edge. Sprinkle the lime peel-sugar mixture over the whipped cream.

Apple Crisp

Serves 6

10 large tart green apples
Juice of 3 large lemons (approximately ½ cup)
½ cup brown sugar (or substitute equivalent), mixed with
⅓ cup white sugar (or substitute equivalent)

3½ teaspoons cinnamon
1 teaspoon freshly grated nutmeg
¾ cups sifted unbleached flour
10 tablespoons sweet butter, cut into small pieces
½ cup coarsely chopped pecans

1. Preheat the oven to 350°.

2. Butter well and lightly flour a 1½-quart soufflé dish or 1½-quart baking dish.

3. Peel, core, and slice the apples. Place them in a bowl and sprinkle them with lemon juice. (Do this immediately to prevent the apples from discoloring.)

4. Combine ½ cup of the mixed sugars with 2 teaspoons of the cinnamon and sprinkle over the apples. Toss the apples in order to coat them with the sugar-cinnamon mixture.

5. Layer the apples into the soufflé or baking dish.

6. Sift together the remaining ⅓ cup of mixed sugars, the remaining 1½ teaspoons of cinnamon, the nutmeg, and the flour.

7. Using a pastry blender, cut the butter into the flour mixture until it reaches a crumbly consistency.

8. Add the pecans and toss the flour mixture lightly. Sprinkle evenly on top of the apples.

9. Cover the soufflé or baking dish or deep pie plate with aluminum foil and bake for ½ hour.

10. Uncover and bake for 20 to 30 minutes more, or until the crumb crust is golden brown.

11. Cool at least 15 minutes before serving.

Serving: Place the soufflé or baking dish on a round silver, brass, copper, or heatproof ceramic tray and proudly present it to your guests. Offer whipped cream as an accompaniment.

NOTE: If you would prefer a Cheese Apple Crisp, follow the recipe as above (through Step 10), then remove from the oven and sprinkle on a mixture of ½ cup grated salt-free Cheddar cheese and ½ cup grated salt-free Gouda cheese. Return the crisp to the oven and bake uncovered for 10 minutes at 350°, then run it under the broiler approximately 4 inches from the flame, for 2 to 3 minutes, or until the cheese is thoroughly melted and bubbling hot.

Serve at once.

Carrot Cake

Makes 1 9-inch loaf

1 pound carrots, peeled and finely grated	1 teaspoon cinnamon
	2 eggs, at room temperature
1 cup unbleached flour	¾ cup corn oil
5½ teaspoons salt-free baking powder	1 cup sugar
	1 cup raisins, floured (optional)

1. Preheat the oven to 325°.

2. Sift the flour with the baking powder and cinnamon.

3. Using an electric mixer on low speed, beat the eggs and oil for 2 minutes, or until thoroughly blended. Then slowly add the sugar, continuing to beat.

4. Continuing to beat, slowly add the flour mixture just until it is blended with the egg mixture.

5. Fold in the carrots and raisins.

6. Butter well and lightly flour a Pyrex loaf pan (9 by 5 by 3 inches) and spoon in the mixture.

7. Bake for 1 hour. Cool in the pan for 30 minutes, turn out on a cake rack and cool thoroughly.

Serving: Turn the cake out onto a rectangular pottery or brass tray and serve.

Poundcake

Makes 1 round cake or 2 loaves

2¹/₂ sticks sweet butter, at room temperature, cut into small pieces

1³/₄ to 2 cups sugar (if you like a sweeter cake)

8 eggs, at room temperature

¹/₂ cup milk

¹/₂ cup orange juice

4 teaspoons vanilla

4 cups sifted cake flour

1 tablespoon salt-free baking powder

1. Preheat the oven to 350°.

2. Using an electric mixer on medium speed, cream the butter in a large bowl for 5 minutes. Slowly add the sugar and continue beating 4 minutes after all the sugar has been added.

3. Beat in the eggs, one at a time, beating well after each addition. Beat 5 minutes after all the eggs have been added.

4. While this is beating, heavily butter and lightly flour a 12-cup Bundt cake pan or two loaf pans (9 by 5 inches).

5. Add the milk, orange juice, and vanilla to the egg mixture and beat another minute.

6. Resift the flour three more times with the salt-free baking powder.

7. Turn the mixer to low speed and slowly add the flour. Continue to mix just until all the flour is thoroughly absorbed and everything is totally blended.

8. Pour the batter into the Bundt pan and bake for 1 hour, or until the cake is a golden brown and a toothpick inserted into the cake comes out clean.

9. Turn the cake out onto a cake rack to cool.

Serving: This is a wonderful plain cake to be served after a luncheon, for tea, or as one of the selections for a dessert buffet. Place your Bundt-shaped cake on a large round platter (or, if you are using loaf pans, place the two pound cakes on a large rectangular tray or each on its own tray and sprinkle heavily with sifted confectioner's sugar.

Spongecake

Makes 1 10-inch cake

10 eggs, separated and at room
 temperature
1½ cups sugar (or more to
 taste)
Juice and finely grated rind of 1
 large lemon

Juice of 1 large orange
1¾ cups twice-sifted cake flour
2 teaspoons salt-free baking
 powder
½ teaspoon cream of tartar

1. Preheat the oven to 325°.
2. Using an electric mixer on medium speed, beat the egg yolks for 10 minutes.
3. Slowly add the sugar, while continuing to beat, and when it is all blended and absorbed into the egg yolks, beat for another 10 minutes. The mixture should be extremely thick, creamy, and a very pale lemon color.
4. Add the lemon juice and rind and the orange juice, and beat for an additional 8 to 10 minutes.
5. While this is beating, sift the twice-sifted flour and the baking powder together four times.
6. Slowly add the flour to the egg yolk mixture and beat *only until the flour is absorbed* (not a minute longer).
7. Using an electric mixer on high speed, beat the egg whites with the cream of tartar until stiff but not dry.
8. Using a rubber spatula, stir one fourth of the egg whites into the batter (to lighten it) and then fold in the remainder of the egg whites.
9. Spoon the batter into an ungreased 10-inch tube spring-form pan.
10. Place the oven rack on the bottom rung and put the pan on the rack. Bake for 1 hour and 10 minutes, or until the top of the cake is a deep golden brown and springs back when lightly touched with the index finger.
11. The cake must be cooled thoroughly upside down. If your spring-form pan has legs, invert the pan and let it rest on them. If not, place the neck of a wine bottle in the tube and then invert the pan, letting it rest on the neck of the wine bottle.

Serving: When the cake is completely cooked, (approximately 2 hours) stand it right side up. Run a sharp knife around the inner edge of the pan and around the tube and push the bottom of the pan up out of the "ring." Run a sharp knife between the metal bottom and the cake. Gently lift the cake off the tube and place it on a doily-lined cake stand. The cake is delicious plain and can also be split into thirds, widthwise, filled, and then frosted all over. It makes a very high and very impressive Super Special Strawberry Cream Cake* or Zuppa Inglese.*

NOTE: If you are making the spongecake in advance (before it is filled and frosted), be sure to place it in a large airtight plastic bag to keep it moist as it has a tendency to dry out if not completely covered.

Super Special Strawberry Cream Cake

Serves 8 to 12

This cake evolved for our son Tony's sixth birthday. He wanted a "super special cake" . . . and knowing that he loved whipped cream and strawberries . . . and pecans . . . and bananas . . .

2 cups heavy cream
1 teaspoon vanilla
1/2 cup confectioner's sugar
3/4 cup coarsely chopped strawberries
1 banana, mashed with
1 tablespoon fresh lemon juice

1/2 cup pecans, chopped medium fine
1 Spongecake,* cut into 3 equal layers

GARNISH:
12 large strawberries whole

1. Using an electric mixer on medium-high speed, beat the cream with the vanilla until it begins to thicken. Slowly add the sugar, beating constantly until stiff peaks hold their shape.
2. Combine the strawberries, banana-lemon juice mixture, and the pecans.
3. Fold the cream into the fruit-nut mixture.
4. Place a layer of the spongecake on a tall cake stand and spread with one fourth of the cream mixture.
5. Place the second layer on top of the filling and spread with one fourth more of the filling, then lay the last layer on top of this.
6. Spread the top, center, and sides with the remaining cream mixture.
7. Place in the refrigerator until you are ready to serve.

Serving: Garnish with the whole strawberries, and proudly bring your creation to the table. Is it time to sing: H-a-p-p-y B-i-r-t-h-d-a-y t-o y-o-u . . .?

Zuppa Inglese

Serves 8 to 12

This Italian cake is really a composite of two recipes plus a few extras of its own. The two recipes incorporated into this one are the Spongecake* and a rich custard sauce known as zabaglione. The zabaglione is quite superb by itself, served hot in balloon glasses or warm over fresh summer fruits.

1 Spongecake* cut into 3 equal layers	1 cup superfine sugar
½ to ¾ cup dark rum	1¾ cups Marsala wine
ZABAGLIONE CUSTARD SAUCE (for the easy way see Note)	GARNISH:
12 egg yolks	1 cup heavy cream, whipped

FOR THE ZABAGLIONE:

1. Using an electric mixer on medium speed, beat the egg yolks for 5 minutes, or until they are a pale lemon color.

2. Add the sugar and beat for 5 to 10 minutes more, or until the mixture is thick.

3. Continue to beat while very, very slowly adding the Marsala wine.

4. Pour the mixture into the top of a double boiler.

5. Fill the bottom of the double boiler with enough scalded water to come to within 1 inch of the top part. Place the top of the double boiler into the bottom and place it over a medium flame. (At no time let the water in the bottom part come to a boil, for this will curdle your eggs.)

6. Using a wire whisk, beat the egg mixture constantly until it thickens enough to form soft mounds (approximately 6 minutes).

7. Cool and thoroughly chill the zabaglione. (The fastest way to do this is to set the top part of the double boiler in a deep pan containing cold water and ice cubes; stir the zabaglione constantly until it cools.)

COMPOSING THE CAKE:

1. Place the first layer of the cake in the deep serving platter from which it is going to be served.

2. Spoon enough of the rum over the first layer to just soak it (not drown it).

3. Spread the rum-soaked layer with ½ of the zabaglione.

4. Add the second layer and spoon on enough rum to soak it. Spread with the remaining zabaglione and lay the third layer on top of this, soaking it with the remaining rum.

5. Cover the cake with plastic wrap or wax paper and refrigerate at least 24 hours.

Serving: Remove the wrapping from the cake and spread the top, center, and sides of the cake with the whipped cream. Garnish.

NOTE: When you order zabaglione in a fine Italian restaurant it is made in front of you from scartch with the maître d'hôtel whisking the egg yolks, sugar, and Marsala by hand until thick and custardy. This home version does almost the same thing, by beating the eggs with an electric mixer and then transferring them to a double boiler. We think the sauce tastes just as good . . . and my arm feels a lot better.

Traditional Passover Nut Cake

Makes 1 10-inch cake

10 eggs, separated, at room temperature
1¼ cups sugar
Juice of 1 large lemon
Juice of 1 large orange
1 tablespoon (or more) finely grated orange rind

1 teaspoon cinnamon
1¾ cups ground walnuts
¾ cup, plus 2 tablespoons, matzoh meal
2½ tablespoons matzoh cake flour

1. Preheat the oven to 350°.

2. Butter well and lightly flour (using potato starch) a 10-inch springform pan.

3. Using an electric beater on medium-high speed, beat the egg yolks for 4 minutes. Add the sugar a little at a time, and beat for 8 minutes after all the sugar has been absorbed (the mixture should be very thick, creamy, and a pale lemon color).

4. Add the lemon juice, orange juice, orange rind, and cinnamon and beat for 5 minutes more.

5. Add the walnuts, matzoh meal, and matzoh cake flour and beat *just* until these ingredients have been blended with the egg yolk mixture (approximately 45 seconds).

6. Using an electric mixer on high speed, beat the egg whites until stiff but not dry.

7. Stir one fourth of the egg whites into the batter (to lighten it), then fold in the remaining egg whites.

8. Spoon the batter into the spring-form pan and bake for 50 minutes, or until the top of the cake is a deep golden brown and springs back when lightly touched with the index finger.

9. Cool the cake in the pan.

Serving: When the cake is completely cooled, release the spring-form ring and lift it off the cake. Gently run a knife between the bottom of the cake and the bottom of the pan. Invert the cake on a doily-covered (optional) cake stand.

NOTE: If making this cake in advance, be sure to place it in a large airtight plastic bag to keep it moist, as it has a tendency to dry out if not completely covered.

Traditional Passover Spongecake

Makes 1 10-inch cake

9 eggs, separated, at room temperature
1½ cups sugar
¼ cup fresh lemon juice
1½ tablespoons finely grated lemon rind

6 tablespoons fresh orange juice
¾ cup matzoh cake flour
¾ cup potato starch

1. Preheat the oven to 350°.

2. Using an electric mixer on medium speed, beat the egg yolks for 4 minutes.

3. Add the sugar a little at a time and beat for 8 minutes after all the sugar has been absorbed (the mixture should be thick, creamy, and a pale lemon color).

4. Add the lemon juice, lemon rind, and orange juice and beat for 5 minutes more.

5. While the egg yolks are beating, sift together the matzoh cake flour and the potato starch. Add to the egg yolk mixture and beat *just* until it is blended (approximately 30 seconds).

6. Using an electric mixer on high speed, beat the egg whites until stiff but not dry.

7. Stir one fourth of the egg whites into the batter (to lighten it), then fold in the remaining egg whites.

8. Spoon the batter into an ungreased 10-inch tube spring-form pan.

9. Place the oven rack on the bottom rung and put the pan on the rack. Bake for 1 hour and 10 minutes, or until the top of the cake is a deep golden brown and springs back when lightly touched with the index finger.

10. The cake must be cooled thoroughly upside down. If your spring-form pan has legs, invert the pan and let it rest on them. If not, place the neck of a wine bottle in the tube and then invert the pan, letting it rest on the neck of the wine bottle.

Serving: When the cake is completely cooled (approximately 2 hours) stand it right side up. Run a sharp knife around the inside edge of the pan and around the tube and push the bottom of the pan up out of the "ring." Run a knife between the metal bottom and the cake. Gently lift the cake off the tube and place it on a doily-lined (optional) cake stand.

NOTE: If you are making this cake in advance, be sure to place in a large airtight plastic bag to keep it moist, as it has a tendency to dry out if not completely covered.

Basic Crêpes

Yields approximately 16 5-inch crêpes

For first courses, main courses, or desserts.

1 cup sifted unbleached flour
3 eggs, separated
1½ cups milk

½ cup Clarified Butter* at room temperature

1. Sift the flour twice.

2. Using an electric mixer on high speed, beat the egg whites until slight peaks begin to form.

3. Using an electric mixer on medium speed, beat the egg yolks until fluffy and a pale lemon color.

4. Combine the egg yolks, egg whites, and milk with the flour.

5. Lightly beat all the ingredients with a wire whisk just until all the lumps are out of the batter. *Do not overbeat.*

6. Refrigerate for at least 1 hour to permit the batter to thicken.

7. Put a little clarified butter in a 5-inch heavy skillet (which I use for nothing but crêpes) and melt it over a medium flame.

8. When the butter begins to sizzle (not sizzling), ladle a little of the batter into the pan. Lift the pan off the stove and tilt the pan so that the batter covers the entire bottom of the pan. Pour the excess batter back into the bowl. (The excess is poured out so as to obtain paper-thin crêpes.)

9. Brown the crêpes slightly, then flip it over and lightly brown it on the other side. Transfer the crêpe to a platter.

10. Repeat until all the batter is used up, adding a little butter to the skillet before making each crêpe.

NOTE: I generally quadruple this recipe and, working with 2 5-inch skillets, make approximately 64 crêpes. I then layer the crêpes between wax paper and make 8 separate packages (8 to a package) which I wrap totally in wax paper; then wrap in aluminum foil and place in an airtight plastic bag. The packages are placed in the freezer and whenever I am in need of crêpes I simply defrost as many packages as needed.

To defrost: Place the crêpes, unwrapped, on the kitchen counter for 1 hour or place them, unwrapped, in the refrigerator for 6 hours.

Dessert Crêpes

Serves 8

16 Basic Crêpes*
1 cup pure apricot preserves
1 cup blanched slivered almonds
½ cup unsweetened grated coconut

½ cup Clarified Butter,* melted
  (or ⅔ cup sweet butter)
½ cup blanched slivered almonds (optional)
⅓ cup apricot brandy (optional)

1. Preheat the oven to 325°.

2. Mix the apricot preserves with the 1 cup blanched slivered almonds.

3. Lay the crêpes on a flat surface. Place approximately 1½ tablespoons of the apricot mixture in the center of each crêpe. Fold one side over the mixture and then fold the other side on top of this.

4. Butter an attractive ovenproof baking dish, such as a copper au gratin dish, and lay the crêpes (flap side down) in the dish.

5. Drizzle the coconut over the crêpes and spoon some of the melted butter over them.

6. Sprinkle the ½ cup almonds over the crêpes and then spoon a little of the apricot brandy over them.

7. Bake for 20 minutes, or until piping hot.

Serving: Bring the baking dish to the table and serve the crépes on warm plates.

For a more dramatic presentation, bake the crêpes without the apricot brandy. When they are piping hot bring them to the table. Heat the apricot brandy in a brandy glass over a brandy warmer at the table (or heat the brandy in a saucepan in the kitchen and transfer it to a warmed brandy glass). Pour the brandy into the crêpe pan and ignite it with a match. Spoon the brandy over the crêpes until the flame goes out and serve at once on warm plates.

NOTE: You may make the dessert crêpes a day in advance and refrigerate them or you may make them well in advance and freeze them. Let them come to room temperature before baking.

Coconut Macaroons

Yield approximately
30 macaroons

4 egg whites	**2 cups unsweetened shredded**
1 teaspoon vanilla	**coconut (preferably fresh)**
1 cup confectioner's sugar	**½ cup unbleached flour, sifted**

1. Preheat the oven to 325°.

2. Heavily butter and lightly flour two cookie sheets and set aside.

3. Beat the egg whites, using an electric mixer on medium-high speed, until soft peaks form.

4. While continuing to beat, add the vanilla and gradually add the sugar. Continue to beat until the egg white mixture is stiff and glossy.

5. Fold in the coconut, then the flour. (Make sure the flour is well blended.)

6. Drop by teaspoonfuls onto the cookie sheets, 2½ inches apart.

7. Bake for approximately 25 minutes, or until the macaroons are a light golden brown.

8. Remove from the oven and let the macaroons cool for 10 minutes.

Serving: Place a paper doily on a silver, porcelain, or ceramic plate or tray and arrange the cooled macaroons in an interesting pattern. Leave them uncovered until completely cooled and then wrap tightly with plastic wrap. Remove when ready to serve.

Lace Cookies

Yields 4 dozen single lace cookies or 2 dozen chocolate-filled
lace "sandwich" cookies

They're easy and spectacular.

1 cup finely chopped walnuts
½ cup butter, at room tempera-
   ture
½ cup sugar
2 tablespoons unbleached flour
2 tablespoons milk

FILLING NO. 1:
6 ounces semi-sweet chocolate
   bits

1½ tablespoons sweet butter
1½ tablespoons milk

FILLING NO. 2:
2 squares unsweetened choco-
   late, grated
½ cup sugar
3 tablespoons sweet butter

1. Preheat the oven to 325°.
2. Line 4 cookie sheets with heavy-duty aluminum foil.
3. Heat the walnuts, butter, sugar, flour, and milk in a small heavy saucepan over a medium flame, stirring constantly until the butter is melted and the ingredients are totally blended.
4. Drip level ½ teaspoonfuls of the mixture onto the foil, 3 inches apart.
5. Bake for 12 to 15 minutes, or until the cookies are a light golden brown.
6. Cool thoroughly (approximately 15 minutes) on the foil, then peel the cookies off the foil. *These cookies are very delicate and must be suf-ficiently cooled to permit easy removal from the foil.*
7. Place the cookies on a tray and cool for at least another 10 minutes before filling, if desired.

FILLING NO. 1

1. Melt all ingredients in the top of a double boiler, with enough scalded water in the bottom part to come to within 1 inch of the top part, over a low-medium flame, stirring constantly until the filling is smooth.
2. Spread the filling lightly over the flat bottom of a cookie and lightly press the flat bottom of the second cookie to the filling, sandwich style.

FILLING NO. 2

Proceed as for Filling No. 1.

Serving: Since these are so splendid in appearance and taste, they deserve a special display. Take an attractive footed cake stand and line it with a doily. Place the cookies around the outer edge of the cake stand, each slightly overlapping the other, and then repeat with the next inner ring until the center is filled. Or take a rectangular silver tray lined with a doily and place your cookies slightly overlapping each other in rows.

Almond Cookies

Yields approximately
40 cookies

½ cup sweet butter	2 cups sifted flour
½ cup sugar	1 egg, lightly beaten
6 tablespoons heavy cream	¾ to 1 cup blanched almonds,
2 eggs	chopped medium fine

1. Using an electric mixer on low speed, beat the butter and sugar until thoroughly blended.

2. Beat in the cream and the 2 eggs.

3. Continuing to beat, add the flour a little at a time until it has been well blended with the other ingredients.

4. Roll the dough into a ball and cover tightly with wax paper. Refrigerate for 24 hours.

WHEN READY TO BAKE:

5. Preheat the oven to 375°.

6. Butter well and lightly flour 2 cookie sheets.

7. Flour a very cold pastry board and a very cold rolling pin (see method for making Pastry Crust*).

8. Roll out the dough ¼ inch thick and, using a pastry cutter (for a crimped edge) or a sharp knife (for a straight edge), cut the dough into 1-inch squares. Brush the tops of the squares with the lightly beaten egg and sprinkle with the almonds.

9. Place the squares on the cookie sheets and bake for 8 to 10 minutes, or until they are a light golden brown.

Serving: When the cookies are cold, transfer them to a china or wicker basket lined with a provincial printed fabric.

Apricot Bars

Yields 5 dozen bars

DOUGH:
1 cup sweet butter, at room temperature
2 cups brown sugar, firmly packed
3 eggs, at room temperature
1 teaspoon vanilla
1 tablespoon fresh lemon juice
4 cups unbleached flour, sifted
6 teaspoons salt-free baking powder

FILLING:
$^{1}/_{2}$ cup fresh orange juice
$^{1}/_{2}$ cup water
$1^{1}/_{2}$ cups dried apricots, ground
$^{3}/_{4}$ cup sugar
3 tablespoons unbleached flour
$^{1}/_{2}$ cup coarsely chopped walnuts
$2^{1}/_{2}$ tablespoons fresh orange juice

1. Using an electric mixer on low-medium speed, beat the butter and brown sugar until they are thoroughly blended.

2. Slowly add the eggs, vanilla, and lemon juice and beat well.

3. Combine flour and baking powder and beat in a little at a time, until all the ingredients are thoroughly blended. (Do not overbeat.)

4. Form the dough into a ball, wrap it in wax paper, and refrigerate at least 1 hour.

5. In the meantime, make the filling. Place the $^{1}/_{2}$ cup of orange juice and water in a heavy saucepan and bring to a boil over a medium flame. Add the apricots. Cover and boil for 5 minutes.

6. Mix the sugar and flour together until thoroughly blended and stir it into the apricot mixture. Cook over a low flame, stirring constantly, until the mixture is thick.

7. Stir in the nuts and $2^{1}/_{2}$ tablespoons of orange juice and blend well. Remove from the heat and cool for at least 35 minutes.

8. Preheat the oven to 375°.

9. Divide the chilled dough in half. Roll each half into a rectangle on a well-floured board. Cut into 3-inch-wide strips. Place the filling in the center of the strips (leaving $^{1}/_{4}$ of the dough on either end unfilled) and, using a wide spatula, fold the dough on either side of the filling toward the center, covering the filling in an envelope fashion. Pinch the open edges together.

10. Cut the strips into thirds and place them, seam side down, 2 inches apart on ungreased baking sheets.

11. Bake for 15 minutes, cool on wire racks, and cut into 2-inch bars.

Serving: Place the bars on a large serving tray or in a napkin-lined wicker basket.

NOTE: Prunes or figs may be substituted for the apricots.

Crescent Cookies

Yields approximately
48 crescents

This recipe is a joint effort of my daughter Patty and myself. It is one of our family's and friends' favorites. We hope you enjoy it.

¹/₂ pound sweet butter
5 tablespoons sugar
2 teaspoons vanilla
1 tablespoon ice water
2 cups sifted flour

2 cups pecans, chopped medium fine

GARNISH:
Confectioner's sugar

1. Preheat the oven to 325°.
2. Butter well and lightly flour two cookie sheets.
3. Place the butter in a large glass bowl and cream with a wire whisk. Still beating with the whisk, slowly add the sugar, vanilla, and water.
4. Stir in the sifted flour and mix well.
5. Add the pecans and blend thoroughly.
6. With your hands, roll the dough into 1-inch balls, then into rolls ¹/₂ by 2 inches.
7. Lay the rolls on the cookie sheets 1¹/₂ inches apart and shape into crescents.
8. Bake them for 20 minutes, or until they are a pale golden brown.
9. Remove the crescents to a tray and sprinkle them with confectioner's sugar.

Serving: Transfer the cookies to a doily-lined china or silver tray.

NOTE: To store these cookies, place one layer in a large tin lined with a double paper doily. Place another double paper doily on top of this layer and add another layer of cookies. Keep alternating between the doilies and the cookies, until all the cookies are in the tin. Cover tightly. They will stay fresh for weeks.

INDEX